The past few years has seen transformative changes UK, where GDPR and Brexit have created a host of new protection laws. In this book, Stewart and his team distil several decades of accumulated privacy, data protection and information governance experience and know-how into a guide that's essential reading for data protection newcomers and experienced practitioners alike.

**Toby Hayes FBCS CITP FIP CIPP/E CIPM**

An ideal resource and must read for new and seasoned privacy practitioners, *Data Protection and Compliance* provides a comprehensive overview of UK privacy requirements together with a practical focus on hot topics and emerging issues to watch out for. Uniquely, the book helps the reader understand how the breadth of the legal, policy and practical requirements all fit together with a contextual summary and tables, untangling the deluge of privacy data.

**Vivienne Artz OBE**, *NED, GLEIF, former CPO LSEG/Refinitiv/Thomson Reuters*

Stewart Room and his team apply their extensive knowledge of data protection law and practice to provide an invaluable resource on data protection that rightly goes beyond interpreting and understanding the law, and unpacks what this means on the ground for compliance leaders and their advisors. Full of practical insights on governance, risk and compliance in the data protection domain, every DPO should have this on their desk!

**Stephen Deadman**, *VP, DPO, Meta*

In a rapidly expanding digitised global economy, this book is a must-read and a go-to resource for legal and privacy professionals and all others interested in this field. Seeing data processing as a power for good, it contains a wealth of legal knowledge and practical insights into the key issues within the world of data protection. Highly recommended.

**Olivia Shirville CIPP/E CIPM**, *Lead Privacy Counsel (EMEA), Aon*

One of the biggest challenges to data protection law is how to effectively operationalise compliance and manage risk effectively within an evolving business structure. This book shows appreciation for this challenge and provides clear methods and concepts to address it. Operational landscape of data protection is summed up concisely and the concept of 'Technology Reference Architecture' linked to Privacy by Design, is incredibly insightful and relevant for businesses. I recommend this book for all data privacy practitioners, including in-house lawyers.

**Nargis Hassani**, *Solicitor*

*Data Protection and Compliance* tackles a rapidly evolving and complex regulatory landscape, in an easy to understand and practical manner. With data driving the digital evolution for most organisations, the ability to comprehend and apply an appropriate compliance framework, with respect to people, processes and systems, is increasingly challenging. For those organisations putting data at the heart of their business strategy, this is a comprehensive resource, which pulls together a wealth of subject matter expertise, tried and tested practical compliance approaches and useful insights into the rationale behind the legislation. Highly recommended.

**Janine McKelvey**, *BT General Counsel – Digital & Innovation, BT Group Data Protection and Ethics Officer*

There are many misconceptions about what is and isn't data protection, alongside the misinformation and scaremongering that arose in the early days of the GDPR. This book distils the considerable knowledge of its author and fellow contributors to deliver the key facts with clarity, supported with reference to landmark cases and regulatory texts. The chapter on Operational Data Protection is a timely reminder that data protection is people, paper (processes) and technology, and that all three are required to be effective.
**David Francis CIPP/E CIPT CIPM**, *Group Data Protection Officer, Canopius*

Stewart Room and his co-authors have certainly discovered the special sauce when seeking to create a book that will appeal to so many. *Data Protection and Compliance, 2nd edition*, is truly inimitable amongst a minefield of technical, legal, and business publications on data protection and privacy. Taking the reader on a journey through history to providing practical operational advice is not only educationally important but also invaluable to practitioners across the multidisciplinary spectrum, regardless of their sector or experience.
**Jane Wainwright, Director**, *Office of the Data Protection Officer, Meta*

The fourth industrial revolution is upon us. *Data Protection and Compliance* provides a timely and thorough orientation of the regulatory landscape but then importantly turns to the pragmatic steps that must be taken to operationalise data protection. While the explanations of the laws are comprehensive, the book embraces the notion of data protection as a foundation for accelerating innovation – seminal reading for all data practitioners.
**Jason du Preez**, *CEO, Privitar*

*Data Protection and Compliance* provides a clear and practical guide to the operationalisation of the GDPR. It outlines a structured and measured approach that doesn't focus on compliance for compliance sake, but encourages doing the right thing for the benefit of both the processing organisation and the data subject. It will serve as a useful reference manual on the bookshelf of any data protection professional.
**Lisa Townsend CIPP/E CIPP/US CIPM**, *DPO, Wella Company*

An invaluable source of astute guidance and pragmatic advice from one of the leading practitioners in this area as he leads you through the world of data protection and compliance in a way that demystifies the complexities of the subject matter. This book justifies a spot on the bookshelves of anyone practicing the law of data protection or just seeking to understand this area and how it impacts your day-to-day life.
**John Skelton**, *General Counsel (Shared Specialist Services) & Group DPO, Centrica plc*

*Data Protection and Compliance* is the book you need to bridge the gap between current legal developments and the practical steps companies can take to implement a successful data protection programme. The book offers something for everyone, whether you're starting out in data protection or an experienced practitioner looking to fine tune your data protection compliance programme.
**Andrea Chard LLM LLB BA**, *Group Data Protection Officer, easyJet*

This is your 'one-stop shop' resource for data protection guidance! This book effortlessly and coherently brings together the legislative and relevant case law on data protection into a well-structured and easy to follow book. This is a must have for any data protection professional looking to operationalise and embed data protection compliance within an organisation through a risk-based approach.

**Harrison Barrett CIPM CIPP/E**, *Deputy Data Protection Officer, Canopius*

Cuts nicely through the 'noise' of data protection regulation and developments, making this a uniquely comprehensive guide for any practitioner wanting to understand data protection practices better. The book provides detail where it needs to, and is succinct on more straightforward topics. The handy 'tables' are a useful ready-reckoner that moves the fingertips to the nub of the topic in an instant, a winner for the busy privacy team!

**Sonal Khimji FIP CIPM CIPP/E**, *Director and Founder, Omnigov Limited*

This revised edition of a venerable classic is a welcome addition to the reference library of data protection professionals navigating the landscape of data protection in the UK, post-Brexit.

**Daragh O Brien FICS IAPP FIP**, *Managing Director, Castlebridge*

*Data Protection and Compliance* is an excellent resource for anyone working in a data protection role. It's a rare text that balances theory, practical application and the social and political context in which the legal and regulatory framework is developing; key to designing and implementing an effective, risk-based approach to operationalising data protection. I'd highly recommend *Data Protection and Compliance* as a solid addition to anyone's data protection bookshelf.

**Naureen Hussain**, *Director of Data Estate, Virgin Media O2*

An indispensable book for data protection practitioners. The text includes exceptional detail, historical context, and relatable, pragmatic insights for this vast and complicated field. The style is approachable and delivers accessible, common-sense tables and summaries that will be the go-to resource for those advising businesses. A particularly useful reference for in-house privacy professionals as we face the 'regulatory bear market' and the need to push privacy into the very fabric of our electronically mediated lives. Well done, Stewart and team! You have re-forged a much-needed tool for our increasingly complex world with this edition.

**Eric Heath**, *Chief Privacy Officer and Deputy General Counsel, Ancestry*

An excellent guide to data protection and compliance. Takes the reader through an easy to follow journey to achieve and maintain regulatory compliance. Naturally focuses on GDPR but keeps relevant to other international laws. Illustrates the impact of Brexit, highlights issues of data sovereignty and discusses challenges with global data processing in an increasingly digital world. A great reference for ins and outs of data protection law and regulatory compliance, as well as for dealing with consequences of non-compliance and data breaches.

**Ashish Bhatt**, *Information and Data Management Officer, Queen's University Kingston, Ontario, Canada*

*Data Protection and Compliance: Second edition* is a must have companion for anyone involved in the data protection or compliance space. It begins with a useful introduction to data protection itself, the link into the General Data Protection Regulations (GDPR) and the Data Protection Act 2018 (DPA), providing an easy-to-read breakdown of the many complexities and challenges that organisations face when collecting, processing, and managing personal data. The book is full of useful guidance, advice, and good practice that all organisations should follow and is thoroughly recommended.

**Jim Fox CISM MBCS**, *Cyber & Information Security Risk Management Executive*

# DATA PROTECTION AND COMPLIANCE

## BCS, THE CHARTERED INSTITUTE FOR IT

BCS, The Chartered Institute for IT, is committed to making IT good for society. We use the power of our network to bring about positive, tangible change. We champion the global IT profession and the interests of individuals, engaged in that profession, for the benefit of all.

### Exchanging IT expertise and knowledge
The Institute fosters links between experts from industry, academia and business to promote new thinking, education and knowledge sharing.

### Supporting practitioners
Through continuing professional development and a series of respected IT qualifications, the Institute seeks to promote professional practice tuned to the demands of business. It provides practical support and information services to its members and volunteer communities around the world.

### Setting standards and frameworks
The Institute collaborates with government, industry and relevant bodies to establish good working practices, codes of conduct, skills frameworks and common standards. It also offers a range of consultancy services to employers to help them adopt best practice.

### Become a member
Over 70,000 people including students, teachers, professionals and practitioners enjoy the benefits of BCS membership. These include access to an international community, invitations to a roster of local and national events, career development tools and a quarterly thought-leadership magazine. Visit www.bcs.org/membership to find out more.

### Further information
BCS, The Chartered Institute for IT,
3 Newbridge Square,
Swindon, SN1 1BY, United Kingdom.
T +44 (0) 1793 417 417
(Monday to Friday, 09:00 to 17:00 UK time)
www.bcs.org/contact
http://shop.bcs.org/

# DATA PROTECTION AND COMPLIANCE
Second edition

**Edited by Stewart Room**

© BCS Learning and Development Ltd 2021

The right of Stewart Room to be identified as authors of this work has been asserted by them in accordance with sections 77 and 78 of the Copyright, Designs and Patents Act 1988.

All rights reserved. Apart from any fair dealing for the purposes of research or private study, or criticism or review, as permitted by the Copyright Designs and Patents Act 1988, no part of this publication may be reproduced, stored or transmitted in any form or by any means, except with the prior permission in writing of the publisher, or in the case of reprographic reproduction, in accordance with the terms of the licences issued by the Copyright Licensing Agency. Enquiries for permission to reproduce material outside those terms should be directed to the publisher.

All trade marks, registered names etc. acknowledged in this publication are the property of their respective owners. BCS and the BCS logo are the registered trade marks of the British Computer Society charity number 292786 (BCS).

Published by BCS Learning and Development Ltd, a wholly owned subsidiary of BCS, The Chartered Institute for IT, 3 Newbridge Square, Swindon, SN1 1BY, UK.
www.bcs.org

Paperback ISBN: 978-1-78017-5249
PDF ISBN: 978-1-78017-5256
ePUB ISBN: 978-1-78017-5263

British Cataloguing in Publication Data.
A CIP catalogue record for this book is available at the British Library.

Disclaimer:
The views expressed in this book are of the authors and do not necessarily reflect the views of the Institute or BCS Learning and Development Ltd except where explicitly stated as such. Although every care has been taken by the authors and BCS Learning and Development Ltd in the preparation of the publication, no warranty is given by the authors or BCS Learning and Development Ltd as publisher as to the accuracy or completeness of the information contained within it and neither the authors nor BCS Learning and Development Ltd shall be responsible or liable for any loss or damage whatsoever arising by virtue of such information or any instructions or advice contained within this publication or by any of the aforementioned.

All URLs were correct at the time of publication.

**Publisher's acknowledgements**
Reviewer: Toby Hayes
Publisher: Ian Borthwick
Commissioning editor: Rebecca Youé
Production manager: Florence Leroy
Project manager: Sunrise Setting Ltd
Copy-editor: Moira Eagling
Proofreader: Barbara Eastman
Indexer: Matthew Gale
Cover design: Alex Wright
Cover image: iStock © Zolga_F
Typeset by Lapiz Digital Services, Chennai, India
Printed and bound by Henry Ling Limited, at the Dorset Press, Dorchester DT1 1HD

# CONTENTS

|  |  |
|---|---|
| List of figures and tables | xx |
| Contributors | xxiii |
| Copyright notices | xxvi |
| Abbreviations | xxvii |
| Preface | xxx |

**PART I  THE BIG PICTURE** — 1

**1.  INTRODUCTION TO DATA PROTECTION** — 3

|  |  |
|---|---|
| What is data protection? | 3 |
| Does data protection mean privacy? | 4 |
|     What is privacy? | 5 |
|     Are there exceptions to the right to privacy? | 5 |
| What else should be protected? | 6 |
|     Protecting fundamental rights and freedoms ('human rights') | 7 |
|     Protecting the free movement of personal data (data flows, transfers and shares) | 9 |
| The protected activities | 9 |
|     Protecting processing | 10 |
|     Protecting personal data undergoing processing | 10 |
|     Special category data (or 'sensitive personal data') | 11 |
| Thematic priorities of data protection, trends and hot topics – supporting a risk-based approach | 12 |
|     AdTech and cookies | 12 |
|     Advanced technology and data processing techniques | 13 |
|     Advanced surveillance | 13 |
|     Artificial intelligence | 14 |
|     Automated facial recognition | 14 |
|     Connected vehicles | 14 |
|     Children | 14 |
|     Cybersecurity | 15 |
|     Data subject rights – timetable breaches | 15 |
|     Democracy | 15 |
|     HR problems | 16 |
|     International transfers | 16 |
|     Privacy and electronic communications ('ePrivacy') | 16 |
|     Profiling | 17 |
|     Virtual voice assistants | 17 |

| | | |
|---|---|---|
| | Core law | 18 |
| | The UK Data Protection Act and its relationship to the GDPR and other EU law | 18 |
| | The Data Protection Convention 1981 | 19 |
| | Regulatory guidance and decisions | 20 |
| | Court judgments | 20 |
| | Related law | 21 |
| | Data protection penalties and litigation | 23 |
| | The regulatory bear market | 24 |
| | Summary | 24 |
| **2.** | **INTRODUCTION TO THE GDPR** | **26** |
| | Brexit: the impacts for data protection and the impacts for this book | 26 |
| | The land mass in Europe to which the GDPR applies | 27 |
| | Recitals and articles of the GDPR | 27 |
| | Jurisdiction of the GDPR | 27 |
| | Nationality and location of people | 28 |
| | A.3.1 – processing in the context of EU establishments | 28 |
| | A.3.2 – targeting people in the EU | 29 |
| | Material scope of the GDPR | 32 |
| | The building blocks of the GDPR | 32 |
| | The actors | 33 |
| | Compliance framework – the standards of protection | 35 |
| | Data protection principles | 35 |
| | Lawful bases of processing | 36 |
| | Necessity | 38 |
| | Consent for processing | 39 |
| | Compliance framework – controls | 42 |
| | Appropriate technical and organisational measures | 42 |
| | Appropriate safeguards | 43 |
| | Prescribed controls | 43 |
| | Anonymisation and pseudonymisation | 44 |
| | Accountability | 44 |
| | Assessing appropriateness of controls | 44 |
| | Critical outcomes to be achieved | 45 |
| | Transparency | 45 |
| | Clarity of the lawful basis of processing | 46 |
| | Control | 47 |
| | Compensatory mechanisms to remedy non-compliance | 48 |
| | Regulator's enforcement powers | 48 |
| | Data subjects' enforcement powers | 49 |
| | Where the GDPR does not apply – exceptions and restrictions | 49 |
| | Domestic processing | 51 |
| | Restrictions and the UK DPA | 51 |
| | Brexit – the UK, Frozen and EU GDPR | 55 |
| | UK GDPR | 55 |
| | Frozen GDPR | 55 |
| | Brexit – international transfers of data | 56 |
| | Summary | 57 |

| | | |
|---|---|---|
| 3. | **INTRODUCTION TO EPRIVACY** | 58 |
| | Regulating the electronic communications sector | 58 |
| | The relationship between data protection and ePrivacy | 59 |
| | The actors and protected parties | 60 |
| | Confidentiality of communications | 60 |
| |     Exceptions to confidentiality | 61 |
| |     Consent for storing or accessing information in terminal equipment | 61 |
| |     Consent, transparency and the use of cookie notices and consent tools | 63 |
| |     Types of cookies | 63 |
| |     Cookies, behavioural advertising and real-time bidding | 64 |
| |     Cookies and legal risk | 65 |
| | Direct marketing | 65 |
| |     The position under PECR | 66 |
| |     Postal direct marketing | 66 |
| |     Opt-out, as a matter of law | 66 |
| |     Financial penalties for direct marketing contraventions | 67 |
| | Processing of traffic data, location data and value added services | 67 |
| | Security and personal data breach notification | 67 |
| |     Personal data breaches | 68 |
| |     Expanded rules for breach notifications | 69 |
| |     Interplay with the breach notification rules in the GDPR | 69 |
| | Calling line ID and directories of subscribers | 69 |
| | Law reform underway | 70 |
| | Summary | 71 |
| 4. | **INTRODUCTION TO OPERATIONAL DATA PROTECTION** | 72 |
| | Operational adequacy schemes – implementing data protection (operationalisation) | 72 |
| |     Focus on operational adequacy schemes | 72 |
| | The three layers of an organisation | 74 |
| | Implementing data protection in the people layer | 74 |
| |     Governance structures | 74 |
| |     Steering committee | 74 |
| |     Recruitment and onboarding | 74 |
| |     Education and training | 75 |
| |     Access rights and privileges | 75 |
| |     Monitoring | 75 |
| |     Worker discipline | 76 |
| |     Flowing requirements to data processors | 76 |
| | Implementing data protection in the paper layer | 76 |
| |     Data Protection by Design and Default (DPbDD, or PbD) | 76 |
| |     Governance structures | 76 |
| |     Records of processing activities | 77 |
| |     Risk registers and assessment tools and methodologies | 77 |
| |     Legitimate interests assessments | 77 |
| |     Transfer assessments | 77 |
| |     Transparency notices | 78 |
| |     Contracts and similar documents | 78 |
| |     Policies, procedures and controls frameworks | 79 |

| | | |
|---|---|---|
| | Records of significant events | 81 |
| | Programme and project plans | 82 |
| | Technology architecture | 83 |
| | Assurance records | 83 |
| | Other mechanisms for assurance | 84 |
| | Implementing data protection in the technology and data layer | 85 |
| | Privacy Enhancing Technologies | 86 |
| | Regulatory sandboxes | 87 |
| | 'The Journey to Code' | 88 |
| | Risk management – implementing measures to assess risks to rights and freedoms and the appropriateness of controls | 90 |
| | The adequacy test | 91 |
| | The impact of the 'consensus of professional opinion' – what are the risks and what should be done about them? | 91 |
| | Risk management – dealing with adverse scrutiny | 91 |
| | Globalisation – implementing data protection on an international stage | 93 |
| | International transfers – adequacy, appropriate safeguards and derogations | 93 |
| | Meaning of 'adequacy' for the purposes of international transfers | 93 |
| | Adequacy of the UK | 94 |
| | Appropriate safeguards | 94 |
| | Derogations | 94 |
| | Wider operational challenges of international activities | 95 |
| | Impacts for micro, small and medium-sized enterprises | 95 |
| | Size of enterprise and size of risk | 95 |
| | Financial resources, cost and risk | 96 |
| | Security and connection to wider legal and operational frameworks | 96 |
| | Summary | 98 |

## PART II  CORE LAW                                                              99

| | | |
|---|---|---|
| 5. | **THE PRINCIPLES OF DATA PROTECTION** | **101** |
| | A constant presence in data protection law | 101 |
| | The duty of compliance (accountability) | 101 |
| | Lawfulness, fairness and transparency – the first principle | 102 |
| | Lawfulness | 102 |
| | Fairness | 102 |
| | Transparency | 102 |
| | Purpose limitation – the second principle | 104 |
| | Expanded purposes – archiving in the public interest | 104 |
| | Expanded purposes – scientific and historical research | 104 |
| | Expanded purposes – statistics | 105 |
| | Compatibility | 105 |
| | Data minimisation – the third principle | 105 |
| | Accuracy – the fourth principle | 106 |
| | Storage limitation – the fifth principle | 107 |
| | Integrity and confidentiality (including security) – the sixth principle | 108 |
| | Accountability – the seventh principle | 108 |
| | Lawfulness of processing of personal data (Article 6) | 109 |

|  |  |  |
|---|---|---|
|  | Categorising the lawful bases of processing | 110 |
|  | Consent | 111 |
|  | Contract | 113 |
|  | Legal obligation | 114 |
|  | Vital interests | 114 |
|  | Public task | 115 |
|  | Legitimate interests | 115 |
|  | Lawfulness of processing – special category personal data and criminal convictions and offences | 116 |
|  | The ban on processing special category personal data – enhanced sensitivity, risks and legal requirement | 117 |
|  | Summary | 119 |
| 6. | **THE RIGHTS OF DATA SUBJECTS** | **120** |
|  | Informing and empowering the protected party | 120 |
|  | Transparency and information rights | 120 |
|  | General obligation of transparency – GDPR A.12 | 120 |
|  | Obtaining transparency – GDPR A.13 and 14 | 121 |
|  | The right of access to information – A.15 | 126 |
|  | Personal data breaches – Article 34 | 137 |
|  | Rights over data processing | 138 |
|  | Right to rectification – A.16 | 138 |
|  | Right to erasure, or 'the right to be forgotten' – A.17 | 140 |
|  | Right to restriction of processing – A.18 | 142 |
|  | Right to data portability – A.20 | 144 |
|  | Right to object – A.21 | 146 |
|  | Right not to be subject to automated decision making, including profiling – A.22 | 148 |
|  | Remedies and rights of redress | 150 |
|  | Summary | 153 |
| **PART III** | **OPERATING INTERNATIONALLY** | **155** |
| 7. | **NATIONAL SUPERVISION WITHIN AN INTERNATIONAL FRAMEWORK** | **157** |
|  | National regulatory systems and divergences | 157 |
|  | GDPR solution for international processing | 157 |
|  | Establishment of supervisory authorities | 158 |
|  | General conditions for members of supervisory authorities | 159 |
|  | Independence | 160 |
|  | Interference | 161 |
|  | Supervisory authority competence | 162 |
|  | Member competence | 163 |
|  | Tasks | 163 |
|  | Monitoring | 163 |
|  | Promotion and awareness | 164 |
|  | Advice and administration | 166 |
|  | Rights, complaints and enforcement | 168 |
|  | Powers | 169 |
|  | Lead supervisory authorities | 170 |
|  | Cross-border processing | 171 |

|   |   |   |
|---|---|---|
|   | Cooperation and mutual assistance | 172 |
|   | Choosing a lead supervisory authority | 173 |
|   | Appointing an EU Representative | 174 |
|   | Summary | 175 |
| 8. | **TRANSFERRING DATA BETWEEN THE GDPR LAND MASS AND THIRD COUNTRIES** | **176** |
|   | Why regulate international transfers? | 176 |
|   | What is a transfer? | 176 |
|   | General principles for transfers | 177 |
|   | Transfers on the basis of an adequacy decision | 179 |
|   | Elements considered in assessing adequacy | 179 |
|   | Adequacy decisions issued | 180 |
|   | UK adequacy | 181 |
|   | Partial adequacy decisions | 181 |
|   | Ongoing monitoring of adequacy decisions | 181 |
|   | Transfers subject to appropriate safeguards | 182 |
|   | Standard contractual clauses | 183 |
|   | Derogations for specific situations | 190 |
|   | Relying on the derogations in practice | 191 |
|   | Compelling legitimate interests | 192 |
|   | Litigation on international data transfers | 193 |
|   | *Schrems I* – Safe Harbor decision declared invalid | 193 |
|   | *Schrems II* – Privacy Shield declared invalid and SCCs declared valid subject to certain conditions | 194 |
|   | Navigating international data transfers | 195 |
|   | EDPB's six-step recommendations | 195 |
|   | Supplementary measures | 195 |
|   | A practical approach to international transfers | 199 |
|   | Getting to know your 'special characteristics' | 199 |
|   | Understanding the 'zone of precedent' | 201 |
|   | Knowing your 'adverse scrutineers' | 201 |
|   | Achieving operational adequacy | 201 |
|   | Upscaling protections | 202 |
|   | Considering options for deregulatory effects | 202 |
|   | Summary | 202 |
| 9. | **DATA PROTECTION BEYOND THE GDPR LAND MASS** | **203** |
|   | Multi-jurisdictional frameworks protecting rights and freedoms including data protection | 203 |
|   | The Universal Declaration of Human Rights | 203 |
|   | The OECD Guidelines on the Protection of Privacy and Transborder Flows of Personal Data | 204 |
|   | APEC Privacy Framework | 205 |
|   | National laws beyond the GDPR land mass | 205 |
|   | Notable new legislation | 206 |
|   | Comparative review between the GDPR and key international laws | 208 |
|   | United States | 208 |
|   | California | 209 |
|   | Virginia | 211 |

| | |
|---|---|
| Brazil | 212 |
| India | 214 |
| China | 216 |
| Data localisation | 217 |
|     Examples of localisation laws | 218 |
| Coping strategies for organisations operating globally | 220 |
|     Examples of coping mechanisms | 220 |
| Summary | 224 |

## PART IV DELIVERY — 225

### 10. MECHANISMS TO SUPPORT OPERATIONAL COMPLIANCE — 227

| | |
|---|---|
| Mechanisms within the GDPR | 227 |
| Technical and organisational measures | 228 |
|     Organisational measures | 228 |
|     Technical measures | 228 |
|     Codes of conduct and certification mechanisms | 228 |
|     Risk assessments | 228 |
| Data protection policies | 229 |
|     An overarching data protection policy | 229 |
|     Policies covering specific GDPR obligations | 229 |
|     Procedures | 229 |
|     Reflecting operational realities | 230 |
| Records of processing activities – a baseline for accountability | 231 |
|     Minimum content of ROPAs | 231 |
|     Wider benefits of ROPAs | 232 |
| Data Protection by Design and Default | 233 |
|     A formula for compliance | 233 |
|     Design | 234 |
|     Default | 234 |
| Data protection impact assessment | 235 |
|     Likely to result in a high risk | 235 |
|     Minimum features of a DPIA | 236 |
| Data protection officer | 237 |
|     Requirement to appoint a DPO | 237 |
|     Tasks of the DPO | 238 |
|     Position of the DPO | 239 |
| Contracts | 241 |
|     Article 28 processor contracts | 241 |
|     Joint controller contracts | 243 |
| Summary | 244 |

### 11. PROGRAMMATIC APPROACHES FOR DELIVERING DATA PROTECTION BY DESIGN AND DEFAULT — 245

| | |
|---|---|
| The origins of Data Protection by Design and Default | 245 |
| Data Protection by Design and Default in the GDPR | 245 |
|     The design element | 245 |
|     The default element | 246 |
| The need for DPbDD – compelling events that trigger data protection transformation | 246 |

| | |
|---|---|
| Embarking upon a transformation journey to achieve DPbDD | 248 |
|    A vision statement – laying the foundations for DPbDD | 249 |
|    Difference between data protection programmes and projects | 250 |
|    The beginning of work – building a business case | 250 |
|    The beginning of work – developing the brief | 251 |
|    Managing the work | 251 |
|    Initiating the work | 252 |
|    The workplans and workstreams | 253 |
| Governance frameworks required by DPbDD for accountability purposes | 254 |
|    Roles and responsibilities – who will do what? | 254 |
|    Management structures and reporting lines | 255 |
|    Setting a target operating model | 255 |
| Summary | 255 |

## 12. BEING ACCOUNTABLE FOR RECORDS OF PROCESSING, LEGITIMATE INTERESTS AND RISK MANAGEMENT — 257

| | |
|---|---|
| Accountability for our decisions, actions and behaviours | 257 |
| Accountability as a core principle of data protection | 257 |
| Demonstrating accountability – an ongoing obligation, not a moment-in-time issue | 258 |
| End-to-end accountability – from idea to reality | 258 |
| Accountability in practice | 259 |
|    Records of processing activities | 259 |
|    ROPAs – continuing obligations | 259 |
|    Understanding data | 260 |
|    Producing the ROPA on request | 261 |
|    Benefits of extended records of processing – going beyond A.30 | 261 |
|    Developing records of processing – discovery and analysis | 262 |
|    Technology-assisted data discovery | 264 |
|    ROPAs and Data Protection by Design and Default | 265 |
|    Gated development – upskilling | 266 |
|    Organisation type | 266 |
|    A combination of all the above | 267 |
|    Exemptions | 267 |
| Being accountable for legitimate interests | 267 |
|    Being accountable for the balancing exercise | 268 |
|    Considerations within legitimate interests | 269 |
|    Legitimate interests and the right to object to direct marketing | 269 |
|    Legitimate interests and data subject rights | 270 |
| Being accountable for risk management | 270 |
|    Being accountable for ATOM | 270 |
|    Risk of failure baked into design | 271 |
|    Being accountable for the 4-Ts | 272 |
|    Being accountable for embedding data protection risk management into change methodologies | 273 |
|    Being accountable for recognised controls | 274 |
|    Being accountable for assurance | 274 |
| Being accountable for adverse scrutiny | 276 |

|  |  | Being accountable for an accumulation of evidence | 276 |
|---|---|---|---|
|  |  | Production of evidence under pressure and scenario testing | 277 |
|  |  | Summary | 277 |
| 13. | **'THE JOURNEY TO CODE'** |  | **278** |
|  |  | The Journey to Code – working towards achieving compliance within technology and data themselves | 278 |
|  |  | The Journey has commenced | 278 |
|  |  | The nature of the problem | 279 |
|  |  | Email example | 279 |
|  |  | Malicious technology and code | 280 |
|  |  | A technology reference architecture for The Journey to Code | 281 |
|  |  | The Core Privacy Technology Value Chain | 282 |
|  |  | Privacy management technology | 282 |
|  |  | The rise of privacy management technologies | 283 |
|  |  | Arguments for the use of privacy management technology | 283 |
|  |  | Drawbacks associated with privacy management technology | 285 |
|  |  | Data intelligence technology | 286 |
|  |  | Native and third-party data intelligence technology | 286 |
|  |  | Third-party integrated data intelligence technology | 288 |
|  |  | Principles and rights technology | 290 |
|  |  | Producers of technology and data processing systems | 292 |
|  |  | A regulatory gap | 292 |
|  |  | Solutions to the regulatory gap | 292 |
|  |  | The risk of a litigation culture emerging | 293 |
|  |  | What comes next on The Journey to Code? | 293 |
|  |  | 'Your mission, should you choose to accept it' | 294 |
|  |  | Summary | 294 |
| **PART V** | **ADVERSE SCRUTINY** |  | **295** |
| 14. | **HOW TO PREPARE FOR THE RISKS OF CHALLENGE AND 'ADVERSE SCRUTINY'** |  | **297** |
|  |  | Challenge and scrutiny are inevitable | 297 |
|  |  | Challenge and scrutiny designed into regulatory law | 298 |
|  |  | Adverse scrutiny | 298 |
|  |  | The supervisory authority | 298 |
|  |  | The data subject | 299 |
|  |  | A legal duty to understand the risks of challenge and scrutiny | 299 |
|  |  | The continuum of challenge and scrutiny | 300 |
|  |  | Why a continuum? | 300 |
|  |  | Examples of internal challengers and scrutineers | 300 |
|  |  | Moral spectrum | 301 |
|  |  | Examples of external challengers and scrutineers | 301 |
|  |  | Modelling challenge and scrutiny risks | 302 |
|  |  | Situations in the GDPR calling for risk assessments | 303 |
|  |  | Risk scenarios and context-specific risk modelling | 304 |
|  |  | The special characteristics and how they relate to modelling | 304 |
|  |  | Modelling – challenge and scrutiny as reactive events | 308 |
|  |  | Tiers of visibility – catalysts of challenge and scrutiny | 309 |
|  |  | Modelling the domino effect of challenge and scrutiny | 311 |

| | | |
|---|---|---|
| | Other interests to be considered when modelling challenge and scrutiny risks | 312 |
| | The relative impacts of challengers and scrutineers | 313 |
| |     The impacts of data subject challenge and scrutiny | 313 |
| |     Privacy activists | 315 |
| |     The impacts of data protection regulators | 316 |
| | Outcomes versus structures and artefacts | 317 |
| |     Examples of structures and artefacts | 317 |
| |     Root cause analysis for operational failure | 318 |
| |     Confidence testing and sentiment analysis | 318 |
| | Summary | 319 |
| **15.** | **COMPLAINTS, RIGHTS REQUESTS, REGULATORY INVESTIGATIONS AND LITIGATION** | **320** |
| | Awareness levels driving scrutiny and challenge | 320 |
| | Accountability | 321 |
| |     Accounting for readiness to deal with challenge and scrutiny | 321 |
| | Dealing with complaints | 321 |
| |     Point of contact | 322 |
| |     Managing complaints and concerns received direct from data subjects | 322 |
| |     Managing complaints escalated to a supervisory authority | 323 |
| |     How to respond | 324 |
| | Dealing with regulatory investigations (investigatory powers) | 324 |
| |     Information Notices | 326 |
| |     Assessment Notices | 327 |
| |     Investigations and prosecutions of criminal offences | 328 |
| | Exercise of data subject rights | 330 |
| |     Escalation of problems – rights requests leading to adversity | 330 |
| |     Timing | 331 |
| |     Extensions | 332 |
| |     Manifestly unfounded or excessive requests | 332 |
| |     Compliance orders | 332 |
| | Litigation | 332 |
| |     Subject access and litigation | 333 |
| |     Data protection and litigation | 333 |
| |     Compensation and liability | 333 |
| |     Mass claims | 334 |
| | Summary | 335 |
| **16.** | **REGULATORY ACTION** | **336** |
| | The impacts of national laws and other contingencies on GDPR enforcement powers | 336 |
| | When can regulatory powers be used? | 337 |
| |     The investigatory phase of regulatory action | 337 |
| | Powers in Article 58 | 337 |
| |     Warnings of potential infringements – action to prevent things going wrong | 338 |
| |     Reprimands | 338 |
| |     Enforcement Notices | 338 |

|  |  |  |
|---|---|---|
| | Withdrawal of certification | 340 |
| | Financial penalties | 340 |
| | Determination of penalties | 341 |
| | Mitigating factors | 342 |
| | Reputational impact | 342 |
| | Appeals against regulatory action | 343 |
| | Preparing for the risk of regulatory action | 344 |
| | Preparation through understanding the true extent of regulator powers – privilege example | 345 |
| | Disposition – the stance and style to adopt when faced with regulatory action | 345 |
| | Summary | 346 |
| **17.** | **HANDLING PERSONAL DATA BREACHES** | **347** |
| | The legal obligation to be secure | 347 |
| | Relationship to ePrivacy | 347 |
| | Relationship to cybersecurity | 348 |
| | The protections to be achieved under GDPR A.5.1.f | 348 |
| | Protections to be achieved under GDPR A.32 | 348 |
| | Security of the full data processing environment | 349 |
| | Processing data for security purposes as a legitimate interest | 349 |
| | Accountability for security | 350 |
| | Operational security | 351 |
| | Expanded requirements for security found outside the GDPR | 351 |
| | The state of the art | 352 |
| | Costs of implementation | 354 |
| | The nature, scope, context and purpose of processing | 355 |
| | The risks of varying likelihood and severity | 355 |
| | Required outcomes | 356 |
| | Appropriateness – what risks will the law tolerate? | 358 |
| | Personal data breaches, breach notification and communications | 358 |
| | Philosophies within breach notification and communications – transparency and its effects | 359 |
| | Personal data breach definition | 360 |
| | Breach of security | 360 |
| | Incident detection and response | 361 |
| | Types of personal data breaches – risks to rights and freedoms | 361 |
| | Timetables for notification and communications | 362 |
| | Risks to rights and freedoms and the carve-out for encrypted data | 363 |
| | Interests of law enforcement | 366 |
| | A.34 communications and disproportionate effort | 366 |
| | Contents of notifications and communications | 369 |
| | Ordering A.34 communications | 369 |
| | Breach logs | 369 |
| | Summary | 370 |
| | Glossary | 371 |
| | Index | 377 |

# LIST OF FIGURES AND TABLES

| Figure 4.1 | The operational landscape for data protection | 73 |
| Figure 4.2 | The Journey to Code | 89 |
| Figure 5.1 | Categorisation of the lawful bases for processing | 110 |
| Figure 8.1 | Transfer roadmap | 178 |
| Figure 8.2 | Considerations for adequacy | 179 |
| Figure 8.3 | A *Schrems II* roadmap for compliance | 200 |
| Figure 12.1 | The accountability continuum | 258 |
| Figure 14.1 | The continuum of scrutiny | 300 |
| Figure 14.2 | Tiers of visibility | 309 |
| Figure 14.3 | Achieving outcomes with structures and artefacts | 317 |

| Table 1.1 | The right to privacy | 5 |
| Table 1.2 | Charter of fundamental rights of the EU | 7 |
| Table 1.3 | Elements within the concept of identifiability | 10 |
| Table 1.4 | Direct sources of data protection law – main legislation | 18 |
| Table 1.5 | Other legislation that impacts on data protection (examples) | 21 |
| Table 1.6 | Data protection financial impacts | 23 |
| Table 2.1 | The main building blocks of the GDPR | 32 |
| Table 2.2 | The actors identified by the GDPR | 33 |
| Table 2.3 | Lawful bases for processing | 37 |
| Table 2.4 | Conditions and quality of consent | 40 |
| Table 2.5 | Controls requirements (examples) | 42 |
| Table 2.6 | How the lawful basis of processing has operational impacts (examples) | 47 |
| Table 2.7 | Why 'control' is a GDPR priority | 47 |
| Table 2.8 | Regulatory enforcement powers within the UK DPA | 48 |
| Table 2.9 | Critical situations where the GDPR does not apply | 50 |
| Table 2.10 | Exemptions in the Data Protection Act 2018, cross-referenced to the GDPR | 52 |
| Table 2.11 | How the three types of GDPR apply in the UK | 55 |
| Table 4.1 | Types of data protection policies (examples) | 80 |
| Table 4.2 | Documents created as part of programme and project planning (examples) | 82 |
| Table 4.3 | Audits required by the GDPR (examples) | 84 |
| Table 4.4 | Alternatives to audit (examples) | 85 |
| Table 4.5 | GDPR requirements for technology risk management (examples) | 85 |

| | | |
|---|---|---|
| Table 4.6 | Benchmarks for risk assessments and for determining what is appropriate (examples) | 90 |
| Table 4.7 | Adverse scrutiny operational imperatives (examples) | 92 |
| Table 4.8 | Considerations within an international processing environment (examples) | 95 |
| Table 4.9 | Special treatment of micro, small and medium-sized enterprises | 96 |
| Table 4.10 | Situations within the GDPR where cost is a consideration within risk management | 97 |
| Table 4.11 | The two security regimes in the GDPR | 97 |
| Table 6.1 | Coping mechanisms for access requests | 134 |
| Table 6.2 | Data subjects' remedies and rights of redress | 151 |
| Table 7.1 | Rules on the establishment of the supervisory authority | 158 |
| Table 7.2 | Supervisory authority competences | 162 |
| Table 7.3 | Supervisory authority monitoring tasks | 164 |
| Table 7.4 | Promoting compliance and raising awareness | 165 |
| Table 7.5 | Administering good practice, including provision of advice | 167 |
| Table 7.6 | Rights, complaints and enforcement | 168 |
| Table 7.7 | Authorisation and advisory powers | 169 |
| Table 8.1 | Appropriate safeguards for international transfers | 182 |
| Table 8.2 | Information required as part of SCCs | 186 |
| Table 8.3 | Criteria for supervisory authority approval of BCRs | 189 |
| Table 8.4 | Derogations from the prohibition on transfers | 190 |
| Table 8.5 | Six-step recommendations for supplemental transfer tools | 196 |
| Table 8.6 | Prioritising focus areas for international transfers through a 'zone of precedent' test | 201 |
| Table 9.1 | Notable new data protection legislation | 206 |
| Table 9.2 | Examples of data localisation laws | 219 |
| Table 9.3 | Examples of coping mechanisms for global compliance | 221 |
| Table 10.1 | Minimum contents of ROPAs | 231 |
| Table 10.2 | Contractual obligations and requirements for processors | 242 |
| Table 11.1 | Compelling events that trigger data protection transformation | 247 |
| Table 12.1 | The benefits and drawbacks of manual data discovery | 263 |
| Table 12.2 | The benefits and drawbacks of technology-assisted data discovery | 264 |
| Table 12.3 | Risk trigger and treatment considerations | 272 |
| Table 13.1 | Technology segments within a technology reference architecture for DPbDD | 282 |
| Table 13.2 | How privacy management technology improves on traditional methodologies | 284 |
| Table 13.3 | Data intelligence functionality mapped to GDPR requirements | 288 |
| Table 13.4 | Example issues to consider when selecting data intelligence technology | 289 |
| Table 13.5 | Examples of principles and rights technology | 290 |
| Table 14.1 | Forms of challenge and scrutiny by the regulator | 298 |
| Table 14.2 | Types of internal challenger/scrutineer | 301 |
| Table 14.3 | Situations in the GDPR that require modelling of risk | 303 |
| Table 14.4 | Special characteristics of the controller and processor | 305 |

| | | |
|---|---|---|
| **Table 14.5** | Motives and motivations of challengers and scrutineers | 306 |
| **Table 14.6** | Adverse scrutiny as a reactive event | 308 |
| **Table 14.7** | Personal data breach – the domino effect of adverse scrutiny and tiers of visibility | 311 |
| **Table 14.8** | Differences between confidence testing/sentiment analysis and audit | 319 |
| **Table 15.1** | Factors in regulatory investigations | 325 |
| **Table 16.1** | GDPR fines | 341 |
| **Table 16.2** | Preparing for the risk of regulatory action | 344 |
| **Table 17.1** | Security outcomes defined by ICO and NSCS | 357 |

# CONTRIBUTORS

### Simon Davis

Simon is a barrister and associate in DWF's Data Protection and Cyber Security team. Prior to joining DWF in April 2021, he worked for a number of regulatory bodies and leading professional services organisations. Simon has significant experience of advising clients on regulatory and legal compliance issues, including the requirements of the GDPR and public law considerations. He has advised FTSE100 and equivalent clients on multi-jurisdictional contentious matters including large-scale data breach, incident response, regulatory enforcement and litigation. Simon has experience in presenting cases with a view to obtaining the best outcome for clients in high-pressure and sensitive situations.

### James Drury-Smith

James is a qualified solicitor and partner. He qualified in 2005 and has over 16 years' experience in technology, data protection and cybersecurity matters. He is the UK Data Protection and Cyber Security Leader at DWF. Prior to joining DWF, James was part of the leadership team for a Big 4 data protection practice. James has also worked in-house as a member of Barclays Bank data protection team. The legal directories recognise James for his expertise in data protection law. He has significant experience of working with international businesses in the UK, Europe and the US to build their data protection programmes, navigate global privacy requirements and develop operational responses to data protection and cybersecurity requirements.

### Richard Hall

Richard is a qualified solicitor specialising in data privacy, cybersecurity, regulatory investigations and engagement, cybercrime and litigation. He also holds certifications in cybersecurity (GIAC, GSEC) and has provided clients with representation as both an advocate and a litigant in a wide range of work. He has represented leaders in the technology, finance, insurance, telecoms, data broking and AdTech industries on a number of different matters, including both contentious and non-contentious legal business. As part of Richard's current role, he provides a wide range of services, including data protection gap analysis, privacy and breach risk impact assessments, policy and procedure review, legal drafting, data breach and compliance services (including investigations, risk advice, litigation and regulatory engagement) and strategy advice.

### Mark Hendry

Mark has been providing risk consultancy services to client organisations since 2006, with experience including a decade in a Big 4 risk consultancy and a prior background of consulting in leading technology and telecommunications companies. Mark's subject matter expertise spans cybersecurity, data protection, technology risk and strategic transformations. Mark leads DWF's Data Protection and Cyber Security consultancy services, working with leading organisations to deliver meaningful outcomes of change for information security and cybersecurity and data protection. Mark is also a highly experienced cyber and data incident responder, having assisted clients to contain, respond and recover from some of the most significant data breaches and security incidents of the past decade.

## Ben Johnson

Ben has two decades of experience as a litigation and regulatory practitioner and is a lead lawyer in DWF's Data Protection and Cyber Security team. Described in Legal 500 as providing 'clear advice and is practical and very responsive' and being 'quick to assimilate facts', Ben has acted in significant data breach cases since 2006 when he took a lead role acting for a payment processor in the world's largest card data breach. Since then Ben has developed a practice in data breach risk advice, litigation and management, acting in multiple investigations of data breach incidents, advising for banks in numerous multi-million-pound cyber litigation cases, and advising on one of the largest UK class actions derived from a data breach. He is a published author on cybersecurity.

## Michelle Maher

Michelle is a senior associate within the Dispute Resolution and Data Protection and Cyber Security teams at DWF, having trained and qualified at the firm. Michelle has vast experience acting for household brands defending a alleged breaches of data protection law and her work is at the cutting edge of data protection law. Recognised as a leading litigation lawyer, she was a member of the DWF legal team that successfully defended Morrisons in its appeal to the Supreme Court of the first-ever data protection group litigation to reach the English courts regarding the mass theft and disclosure of personal data.

## Shervin Nahid

Shervin is a data protection and cybersecurity solicitor and leads the data protection deals practice at DWF. He has over five years' experience working across all areas of data protection and cybersecurity. To date, he has been seconded to seven high-profile multinational clients across multiple industries. Shervin advises on complex technical data protection and cybersecurity issues, drafting and negotiating commercial agreements, advising on M&A, as well as providing management consultancy, strategy and risk advisory services on global privacy transformation projects.

## Niall O'Brien

Niall is an associate in the Dublin office of the Global Data Protection and Cyber Security team at DWF. He is qualified to practise in Ireland, and England and Wales. Niall is CIPP/E certified with extensive experience in International Commercial Court arbitration concerning SaaS agreements, encryption, related intellectual property rights and metadata. He also advises on non-contentious corporate and commercial matters such as corporate due diligence and large-scale records of processing reviews. He regularly advises on international data transfers in the clinical trial and pharmaceutical industries. Prior to joining DWF in Ireland Niall worked on cases such as the *Schrems II* Article 267 preliminary reference case to the Court of Justice of the European Union.

## Adam Panagiotopoulos

Adam is an EU qualified lawyer and CIPP/E certified professional experienced in data protection, privacy and information security. He is an Associate at the DWF Data Protection and Cyber Security team. Prior to that, he supported the design and compliance of digital solutions to the COVID-19 public health crisis. Over the past four years, he has provided DPO services to UK and international organisations and advised on their information governance compliance and complex business transformations. In addition to his legal positions, he has worked at highly ranked universities, supported policy making and conducted impact assessments in the area of emerging technologies. He has published a book on biobanks and data protection and contributed to papers on the interplay between new technologies and information governance.

## Stewart Room

Stewart is a dual-qualified barrister and solicitor, with over 30 years' experience. He is the Global Data Protection and Cyber Security Leader at DWF. Prior to that he held a similar role in a Big 4 professional services firm. Recognised by the legal directories as one of the UK's leading data protection lawyers, he has vast experience across all areas of data protection and cybersecurity, ranging from management consultancy, strategy and risk advisory services through to contentious and non-contentious legal business. As well as a long career as a published author, he is a past winner of the Financial Times Legal Innovator of the Year award, co-founder of the Cyber Security Challenge UK and President of the National Association of Data Protection Officers.

## Jamie Taylor

Jamie is a data protection and cybersecurity lawyer with over 20 years' experience of acting for clients within the insurance industry. He holds the CIPP/E and CIPM certifications and an MSc in cybercrime. Jamie has been a director at DWF for 10 years and has spent two decades within top 50 international law firms. Specialising in contentious data protection and cybersecurity law, and an experienced litigator, he is regularly instructed by clients to respond to data breaches and cybersecurity events, providing advice across a range of issues including incident response, regulatory reporting obligations and litigation.

## Tuğhan Thuraisingam

Tuğhan is a director and solicitor in DWF's Data Protection and Cyber Security team. He is the Financial Services Sector Leader of Data Protection and Cyber Security at DWF and is a member of the Data Protection Finance Group leadership team. He regularly advises clients on data protection strategy, legal and compliance issues. Prior to DWF, Tuğhan worked in the legal services business in a Big 4 professional services firm and spent over two years on secondment to one of the world's largest payments technology companies. He worked closely with innovation and technology teams to operationalise privacy outcomes into the client's business. Through his in-house experience, Tuğhan is able to provide unique insights and commercially focused solutions to the data protection issues faced by clients.

# COPYRIGHT NOTICES

### Information Commissioner's Office copyright

All extracts in this book that are taken from the guidance of the Information Commissioner's Office published at https://ico.org.uk are licensed under the Open Government Licence for public sector information, V3.0. The licence is available at www.nationalarchives.gov.uk/doc/open-government-licence/version/3/

### UK legislation copyright

All extracts in this book that are taken from UK legislation published at https://www.legislation.gov.uk are licensed under the Open Government Licence for public sector information.

### UK Court and Tribunal judgments

All extracts in this book that are taken from the judgments of the UK Judiciary published at https://www.judiciary.uk or at https://www.bailii.org are licensed under the Open Government Licence for public sector information.

### EU legislation copyright

All extracts in this book that are taken from EU legislation published at https://eur-lex.europa.eu/homepage.html are licensed under the terms of the Commission Decision 2011/833/EU on the reuse of documents from the EU institutions.

### European Data Protection Board's copyright

All extracts in this book that are taken from the guidance of the European Data Protection Board published at https://edpb.europa.eu/edpb_en are licensed in accordance with the EDPB's licence, which is available at https://edpb.europa.eu/about-edpb/legal-notices/copyright_en

# ABBREVIATIONS

| | |
|---|---|
| **AAIP** | Agencia de Acceso a la Información Pública, the Argentinian regulator |
| **AFR** | automated facial recognition |
| **AG** | Attorney General |
| **AI** | artificial intelligence |
| **ANDP** | National Data Protection Authority (Brazil) |
| **APEC** | Asia-Pacific Economic Cooperation |
| **APPI** | Act on the Protection of Personal Information (Japan) |
| **APT** | advanced persistent threat |
| **ATOM** | appropriate technical and organisational measures (GDPR A.5, 24, 25, 28, 32, 34) |
| **BCR** | binding corporate rules (GDPR A.47) |
| **BYOD** | bring your own device |
| **CCPA** | California Consumer Privacy Act (USA) |
| **CDPA** | [Virginia] Consumer Data Protection Act (USA) |
| **CERT** | computer emergency response team |
| **CJEU** | Court of Justice of the European Union |
| **COPPA** | Children's Online Privacy Protection Act (USA) |
| **CPR** | Civil Procedure Rules 1998 |
| **CRM** | customer relationship management |
| **CSIRT** | cyber security incident response team |
| **CSO** | civil society organisation |
| **DPA** | Data Protection Authority (India) |
| **DPbDD** | Data Protection by Design and Default (GDPR A.25) |
| **DORA** | Digital Operations Resilience Act (EU) |
| **DPIA** | data protection impact assessment (GDPR A.35) |
| **DPO** | data protection officer (GDPR A.37) |
| **DSAR** | data subject access request (GDPR A.15) |
| **EC** | European Community |
| **ECHR** | European Convention on Human Rights |

## ABBREVIATIONS

| | |
|---|---|
| ECtHR | European Court of Human Rights |
| EDPB | European Data Protection Board |
| EEA | European Economic Area |
| ENISA | EU Agency for Cyber Security |
| ERP | enterprise resource planning |
| Frozen GDPR | UK version of the GDPR that applied to data processed during the Brexit Implementation Period |
| GDPR | General Data Protection Regulation 2016 (EU) |
| GLBA | Gramm-Leach-Bliley Act (USA) |
| HIPAA | Health Insurance Portability and Accountability Act (USA) |
| ICO | Information Commissioner's Office |
| ICT | information and communication technology |
| IDTA | international data transfer agreement |
| IoT | Internet of Things |
| IP | internet protocol |
| IP Day | Implementation Period Day (Brexit) |
| IPA | Investigatory Powers Act 2016 (UK) |
| ISO | International Organization for Standardization |
| LED | Law Enforcement Directive (EU) |
| LGPD | General Personal Data Protection Law (Brazil) |
| LIA | legitimate interests assessment (GDPR A.6.1.f) |
| ML | machine learning |
| NCSC | National Cyber Security Centre (UK) |
| NDA | non-disclosure agreement |
| NIS | Directive Network and Information Security Directive |
| NIST | National Institute of Standards and Technology (USA) |
| OECD | Organisation for Economic Co-operation and Development |
| PbD | Privacy by Design (acronym for DPbDD) |
| PCI-DSS | Payment Card Industry Data Security Standard |
| PDPB | Personal Data Protection Bill (India) |
| PEC | Privacy and Electronic Communications Directive (EU) |
| PECR | Privacy and Electronic Communications Regulations (UK) |
| PET | Privacy Enhancing Technologies |
| PID | programme or project initiation document |
| PIPA | Personal Information Protection Act (South Korea) |
| PIPEDA | Personal Information Protection and Electronic Documents Act (Canada) |
| PIPL | Personal Information Protection Law (China) |
| PRC | People's Republic of China |

| | |
|---|---|
| **RACI** | Acronym for 'responsible', 'accountable', consult', 'inform', used in governance and risk management systems |
| **ROPA** | records of processing activities (GDPR A.30) |
| **SaaS** | software-as-a-service |
| **SAR** | subject access request (acronym for DSAR) (GDPR A.15) |
| **SCCs** | standard contractual clauses (GDPR A.46) |
| **STaaS** | storage-as-a-service |
| **TOM** | target operating model |
| **UDHR** | Universal Declaration of Human Rights |
| **UK DPA** | Data Protection Act 2018 |
| **UK GDPR** | UK version of the GDPR |
| **UN** | United Nations |
| **VVA** | Virtual Voice Assistant |

# PREFACE

I wrote the preface to the first edition of this book in May 2006. Back then Facebook wasn't publicly available; the iPhone wasn't on the market; the phrase cloud computing hadn't been coined; the UK hadn't adopted its first national cybersecurity strategy; phone hacking hadn't become a public scandal; Edward Snowden hadn't made his disclosures about mass surveillance; Max Schrems hadn't embarked upon his challenges to EU–USA data transfers; the AdTech industry was still in its infancy; the IAPP was of limited influence; AI was still a topic mainly for the science fiction books; there was no AFR or blockchain; DPOs were fringe roles in the public sector; there were no OneTrusts, BigIDs, Privitars or privacy tech unicorns; there was no compensation claims industry for personal data breaches; China hadn't become a global superpower; Russia wasn't using social media to disrupt Western democracies; Donald Trump's supporters hadn't stormed The Capitol; the UK was still in the EU; there was no Covid, contact tracing apps and vaccine passports; and, of course, there was no GDPR.

And I hadn't joined Fieldfisher, or PwC, or DWF.

Things will always change, for better or for worse, but to my eyes, at least, there have been two solid constants throughout the years since I last put pen to paper for this book.

Firstly, I still believe that the principles and rights of data protection remain essential beacons for civil liberties. As a young man at university, I watched with joy and relief as the Berlin Wall came crashing down, people freed from tyranny. As a middle-aged man, I am appalled and scared by the rise in populism, nationalism and demagogues that we have witnessed over recent years, including in the West and in my country. We need to protect and defend our rights. We need to stay invested in data protection.

Nevertheless, data protection should not be about a negative voice. Data processing is a power for good. It can improve lives and enrich societies in countless ways. If we get data protection right, the law is never going to stand in the way of advances using data. Despite what some people may claim, data protection has never acted as a barrier to innovation. Conversely, personal data is not the new oil. If you are saying that, move on and get some originality.

Secondly, you will always know who your friends and team are. I will come back to that shortly.

So what is this book about? In short, it provides the authors' insights into key issues within data protection and how to operationalise them. There are limitations on what we can do in print. Undoubtedly, we have missed out many things. However, the book builds on decades of real-world, multidisciplinary experiences helping clients to deliver meaningful and measurable operational change and reduction of risk, as well as fire-fighting problems during incident response, regulatory investigations and civil and criminal litigation, so you can be confident that the ideas expressed here for operationalisation are tried and tested.

Data protection means nothing if it is not operationalised. However, too many organisations are not doing enough to deliver meaningful outcomes. Part of the problem is that there are naked empires in parts of society and the economy, where cultures of conceit, flattery and concealment hide the reality of what is really going on within business operations. The emperors, who are not properly clothed, expose us, their colleagues and their organisations, to risks of considerable harm by not taking data protection seriously enough. This is going on in plain sight. It does not take a little boy at a parade to point out the obvious. Send a data subject access request and you might see some of the truth for yourself. To stress, this is not all organisations. I have worked with a countless number of excellent businesses over the years that are making a real effort and trying to do the right thing. However, if you want to take your organisation on a journey of good practice, I offer these suggestions, which are discussed in this book:

1. Focus on desired outcomes, not simply outputs such as structures and artefacts.
2. Remember that the whole point of data protection is operational adequacy, to minimise the risks to rights and freedoms of individuals.
3. To deliver operational adequacy, you should take account of your special characteristics and those of your data subjects, as well as the risks of adverse scrutiny that your organisation faces.
4. It is impossible to deliver operational adequacy without going on The Journey to Code. Meaningful and measurable outcomes for data protection must be achieved across all layers of your organisation, including in technology and data themselves.
5. Beware the Regulatory Bear Market. There are many challengers and scrutineers who have regulatory powers and effect. They can cause immense disruption and inflict real pain. You need to understand the motives and drivers of them all, not just the statutory regulator.
6. Recognise that a compensation-claims market has developed. Things are likely to get worse before they get better.
7. Data protection needs to be a matter of core business purpose, not an afterthought. The ESG agenda should help with that.
8. Build a risk to rights and freedoms calculator. You cannot understand the range of possible harms that can result from unmanaged data processing without this.
9. Never give up. Perhaps think about the people you love and the society you want to live in and do it for them. Read Orwell's *Nineteen Eighty-Four* if you need reminding why this is important stuff.
10. Don't be afraid of data processing. It is a power for good. An optimistic spirit is sometimes needed, but there is more to be positive about than you might imagine. Remain balanced at all times, however.

## PREFACE

In light of all that, I want to share some thoughts on the UK government's plans for data protection. These are contained in a consultation paper issued by the Department for Digital, Culture, Media and Sport dated September 2021, thus too late for discussion in this book. As an initial point, the proposals do not render this book irrelevant! HMG seems to be committed to retaining most of the GDPR.

I believe that we should approach the proposals with a balanced and open mind. The GDPR is not perfect by any stretch of the imagination. I do not see the proposals to do away with data protection impact assessments, compulsory data protection officers or records of processing activities as being unnecessarily retrograde, especially when the proposal to introduce a legal obligation to maintain data protection programmes is kept in mind, which I expect will deliver essentially the same outcomes, but with different labels. I also think that if we can move away from some of the bureaucracies that the GDPR involves, we might end up with better data protection outcomes in the end. I certainly do not see the proposals as constituting a let-off for business. In fact, it looks as if business will end up with a tougher enforcement environment to deal with if the proposals to increase PECR fines and introduce s.166 notices for breaches come to fruition.

My concerns with the proposals are about data subject rights, the independence of the Information Commissioner's Office and the risks associated with exponentially increasing the speed of innovative personal data use for economic growth reasons. I believe that government should tread carefully in these areas. Citizens should not be disenfranchised from their rights due to economic reasons; the regulator should never be beholden to the whims of government policy; and the use of personal data to drive growth needs to be properly thought through, on a case by case basis.

Furthermore, I am concerned about the wider context in which the proposals sit. The country has been through unprecedented upheavals with Brexit and the COVID-19 pandemic and we are not yet at the end of the line. I am concerned about the quality of policy creation in government; the apparent lack of an effective opposition; and the fact that we have endured an unprecedented circumvention of our civil liberties through lockdowns and social distancing. I believe that we need to pause for thought, before we experiment further with our rights on a mass scale.

Now that is out of the way, I turn to my second point. You will always know who your friends and team are. Therefore, I want to pay tribute to some of mine, who have been on the data protection journey with me over the past couple of decades, or who have inspired me. These are my former teammates and colleagues at Rowe Cohen, Fieldfisher and PwC, my teammates and colleagues at DWF, my friends and colleagues in the wider data protection and cybersecurity profession, and my clients. At Rowe Cohen, in particular I would like to thank Emily Chantzi. At Fieldfisher, Eduardo Ustaran, Mick Gorrill, Antonis Patrikios, Victoria Hordern, Sam Sayers, Brian Davidson, Olivia Shirville and Michelle Levin. At PwC, Jane Wainwright, Jay Cline, Jane Foord-Kelcey and Mick, Sam and Brian again. In the wider community, Mike Pritchard, Mark Saville, Ian Walden, Judy Baker, Sir Edmund Burton and Tim Pitt-Payne QC, my friends in the US, Ron Wills and Eric Heath, and my Nadpo and Cyber Security Challenge colleagues over the years and friends in the IAPP and the Data Protection World Forum. Client thanks go to Raj Roy and Stephen Deadman and, more recently, Caroline Withers, John Skelton, Phil Clancy, Kim Thomson, William Monelle and Andrew Howarth.

On the inspirational front, Professor Lawrence Lessig, Edward Snowden, Max Schrems and Ann Cavoukian stand out for me.

I would also like to thank my fellow authors, Jamie Taylor, Michelle Maher, Ben Johnson, Niall O'Brien and Adam Panagiotopoulus; Toby Hayes, for helping to steer the manuscript forward (you have made an enormous contribution) and Ian Borthwick and Rebecca Youé, my publishers at BCS (thanks for your patience).

Big thanks also to my clients and friends who offered to review the final draft: Jason Du Preez, Naureen Hussain, Andrea Chard, David Francis, Harrison Barrett, Vivienne Artz OBE, Nargis Hassani, Lisa Townsend, Janine McKelvey, William Malcolm, Martin Kostov, (and, again) Stephen Deadman, Jane Wainwright, John Skelton, Eric Heath, Phil Clancy and Olivia Shirville.

Most of all, I would like to thank James Drury-Smith, Tuğhan Thuraisingam, Mark Hendry, Richard Hall, Shervin Nahid and Simon Davis, the other co-authors of this book, who joined me at DWF from our former firm. I've helped to build market-leading practices before, but what we have done together, with our new colleagues at DWF, in 18 months, mostly in lockdown, is truly remarkable: we started a new practice, got it ranked in both Legal 500 and Chambers UK at the first time of asking and we've written this book. You have exceeded all of my expectations, by miles. You are the best of the best!

The final thanks go to my wife, Samantha, and our daughters, Annabel and Antonia. You put up with a heck of a lot (not just my guitar addiction).

People who know me well will remember this one: if Elvis were alive today, he would be a data protection professional. It is a great time to be doing what we are doing. Best wishes to everyone working in this space and keep up the good work.

Privacy Rock 'n' Roll!

Stewart Room
Hadley Wood, London
October 2021

# PART I
# THE BIG PICTURE

# 1 INTRODUCTION TO DATA PROTECTION

Stewart Room

This chapter acts as the foundation stone for all the issues discussed in this book. It introduces the core aims and objectives of data protection; explains how the topic relates to the right to privacy; provides illustrations of some of the critical priorities in this area; and identifies the main sources of law.

## WHAT IS DATA PROTECTION?

The idea of 'data protection' can be looked at in several ways. In an operational sense, it means achieving predefined outcomes during the collection, use and storage of personal data, which is called 'data processing'. In a legal sense, it means the regulatory framework that governs these activities. In a colloquial and limited sense, it is sometimes viewed as a synonym for the security of data, but this would not be representative of the established European view of things.

Taking the General Data Protection Regulation 2016 (GDPR) as a starting point, the title of this legislation clarifies that data protection means 'the protection of natural persons with regard to the processing of personal data and ... the free movement of such data'. Recital 6 of the GDPR summarises the issues perfectly.

### GDPR R.6 – Goals of data protection

Rapid technological developments and globalisation have brought new challenges for the protection of personal data. The scale of the collection and sharing of personal data has increased significantly. Technology allows both private companies and public authorities to make use of personal data on an unprecedented scale in order to pursue their activities. Natural persons increasingly make personal information available publicly and globally. Technology has transformed both the economy and social life, and should further facilitate the free flow of personal data within the Union and the transfer to third countries and international organisations, while ensuring a high level of the protection of personal data.

## DOES DATA PROTECTION MEANS PRIVACY?

To emphasise a point that is implicit within the title of the GDPR but not always obvious, the topic of data protection is not simply about the concept of privacy. In fact, many aspects of the law cut through the concept of privacy, such as the support that it gives to sharing of personal data in the public interest, that is, without the consent or permission of the person whose data are affected.

However, the modern concept of data protection does have its historical root in privacy law. This is demonstrated by the text in the Council of Europe Resolution (73) 22, explanatory report box, which is from the Council's 1973 Resolution on private sector[1] data banks. The 1973 Resolution was a landmark event in data protection, as it provided one of the first statements of the data protection principles: the principles are the foundation stone upon which all forms of data protection law are built. It was followed in 1974 by a companion resolution for the public sector.[2]

Perhaps the best way to look at how privacy relates to the topic of data protection is to see it as being a very significant part of the topic, but the topic is much bigger than privacy. Due to the significance of the topic of privacy within data protection, it is worth looking into it a little further at this stage.

**Council of Europe Resolution (73) 22, explanatory report**

1. It is generally recognised that the development of modern science and technology, which enable man to attain an advanced standard of living, brings in its wake certain dangers threatening the rights of individuals. This is the case, for instance, with the utilisation of new techniques for surveillance or observation of persons and for compiling and processing data pertaining to them,

2. A survey, conducted in 1968–70 by the Committee of Experts on Human Rights of the Council of Europe, on the legislation of the Member States with regard to human rights and modern scientific and technological developments has shown that the existing law does not provide sufficient protection for the citizen against intrusions on privacy by technical devices …

3. A particular new source of possible intrusion into privacy has been created by the rapid growth and popularisation of computer technology. The purposes which computers are increasingly serving in the public and private sectors are by themselves not basically different from those served by more traditional forms of data storage and processing.

---

[1] Resolution (73) 22 on the Protection of the Privacy of Individuals vis-à-vis Electronic Data Banks in the Private Sector.

[2] Resolution (74) 29 on the Protection of the Privacy of Individuals vis-à-vis Electronic Data Banks in the Public Sector.

## What is privacy?

There are many philosophical threads of ideas within the right to privacy, which cover concepts such as 'the right to be let alone',[3] through to the concept of personal data protection within the GDPR.

The right to privacy was crystallised within the European Convention on Human Rights (ECHR) in 1950 (see Article 8) and was restated by the EU Charter of Fundamental Rights in 2012 (see Article 7). In the UK the right to privacy has developed into a tort known as the tort of misuse of private information, a civil law right, breach of which is actionable in court and compensatable in damages. Table 1.1 sets out the wording of the right to privacy as it has crystallised within pan-European law.

**Table 1.1 The right to privacy**

| European Convention on Human Rights | Charter of Fundamental Rights of the European Union |
| --- | --- |
| Article 8:<br><br>Right to respect for private and family life<br><br>1. Everyone has the right to respect for his private and family life, his home and his correspondence.<br><br>2. There shall be no interference by a public authority with the exercise of this right except such as is in accordance with the law and is necessary in a democratic society in the interests of national security, public safety or the economic well-being of the country, for the prevention of disorder or crime, for the protection of health or morals, or for the protection of the rights and freedoms of others. | Article 7:<br><br>Respect for private and family life<br><br>Everyone has the right to respect for their private and family life, home and communications. |

## Are there exceptions to the right to privacy?

The right to privacy is not an absolute right. As shown by Article 8.2 of the ECHR, privacy can be interfered with, if the interference is authorised by law and is necessary and proportionate. This means that when questions about interferences with privacy come to be judged, a balancing act must be performed to understand both the legal justification for the interference and how the right to privacy compares with other competing rights in a relative sense.

### *Privacy versus freedom of expression*
A common situation where the balancing act needs to be performed is during press and media reporting of news stories, when the right to freedom of expression, crystallised

---

[3] 'The Right to Privacy', Samuel D. Warren; Louis. D. Brandeis, *Harvard Law Review*, Vol. 4, No. 5 (Dec. 15, 1890), pp 193–220.

by Article 10 of the ECHR, competes with the right to privacy. There have been countless court cases about this, often concerning celebrities,[4] sportspeople[5] and royalty,[6] and they will never end. The phone-hacking scandal, which led to the Leveson Inquiry and the closure of the *News of the World* newspaper, as well as the prosecution and imprisonment of various people in the newspaper industry, illustrates the damage that can be done when the exercise of the right of freedom of expression fails to have regard to the balancing act.

### Privacy versus security and law enforcement

Security and law and enforcement agencies override the right to privacy in the interests of national security, public safety, the prevention of disorder and crime and related public interests encapsulated by Article 8.2. Again, the balancing act must be performed and as with the case of freedom of expression, this has generated countless court cases and scandals. Examples of the subject matter that has been litigated over include automated facial recognition trials,[7] the DNA database[8] and long-term retention of criminal records.[9]

### Privacy versus public health

The COVID-19 pandemic that began in 2020 brings the balancing act between privacy and other interests right up to date. In the interests of public health, the right to a family life was curtailed by governments all around the world in the most unprecedented ways, through lockdowns and social distancing rules that prevented people from coming together in family groups except in limited bubbles. Contact tracing apps, which process infection information in the context of interactions between people as measured by Bluetooth signals from smartphones, and vaccine passports, which intend to distinguish between people deemed to be of good health and those who are potentially not, involve processing operations that engage with the very essence of privacy. The complexity of the balancing acts involved are enormous and, presumably, part of the long-term legacy of the pandemic will include court cases about these interferences with privacy.

## WHAT ELSE SHOULD BE PROTECTED?

So, if privacy is just a component of data protection, what else is covered? This is an essential question for controllers and processors, because it is impossible to achieve legal compliance without a clear understanding of the nature of the legal obligations that must be satisfied.

---

[4] For example, *Campbell v. Mirror Group Newspapers Ltd* (2004) UKHL 22, which concerned news reporting about Naomi Campbell's attendance at an addiction clinic.

[5] *Flitcroft v. Mirror Group Newspapers Ltd* (2002) EWCA Civ 337, which concerned reporting about a footballer's sex life.

[6] *HRH Duchess of Sussex v. Associated Newspapers Ltd* (2021) EWCH 273 (Ch), which concerned reporting about Meghan Markle's correspondence.

[7] *R (Bridges) v. Chief Constable of South Wales Police & Others* (2020) EWCA Civ 1058.

[8] *S. and Marper v. UK* (2008) ECHR 30567/00 and 30566.04.

[9] *M.M. v. UK* (2012) ECHR 24029/07.

## Protecting fundamental rights and freedoms ('human rights')

Amplifying the title of the legislation, Article 1.2 of the GDPR states that the focus of protection is the 'fundamental rights and freedoms of natural persons and in particular their right to the protection of personal data'. Collectively these rights and freedoms are commonly referred to as 'human rights'.

The protection of human rights has a historical lineage that traces back to the Universal Declaration of Human Rights, which was proclaimed by the United Nations General Assembly in 1948, following the horrors of the Second World War. The Universal Declaration was followed by the adoption of the European Convention on Human Rights in 1950.[10] The Charter of Fundamental Rights of the European Union provides the most recent statement of these rights and freedoms, which fall into six core categories, namely Dignity, Freedom, Equality, Solidarity, Citizens' Rights and Justice. The right to privacy is just one of these rights. Table 1.2 provides a full list of what is protected by the EU Charter. Data protection risk management needs to take account of risks to all these rights and freedoms.

**Table 1.2 Charter of fundamental rights of the EU**

| | | |
|---|---|---|
| Title I – Dignity | 1. | Human dignity |
| | 2. | Right to life |
| | 3. | Right to the integrity of the person |
| | 4. | Prohibition of torture and inhuman or degrading treatment or punishment |
| | 5. | Prohibition of slavery and forced labour |
| Title II – Freedom | 6. | Right to liberty and security |
| | 7. | Respect for private and family life |
| | 8. | Protection of personal data |
| | 9. | Right to marry and right to found a family |
| | 10. | Freedom of thought, conscience and religion |
| | 11. | Freedom of expression and information |
| | 12. | Freedom of assembly and of association |
| | 13. | Freedom of the arts and sciences |
| | 14. | Right to education |
| | 15. | Freedom to choose an occupation and right to engage in work |
| | 16. | Freedom to conduct a business |
| | 17. | Right to property |
| | 18. | Right to asylum |
| | 19. | Protection in the event of removal, expulsion or extradition |

*(Continued)*

---

10 The full title is 'The Convention for the Protection of Human Rights and Fundamental Freedoms'.

**Table 1.2 (Continued)**

| | |
|---|---|
| Title III – Equality | 20. Equality before the law |
| | 21. Non-discrimination |
| | 22. Cultural, religious and linguistic diversity |
| | 23. Equality between women and men |
| | 24. The rights of the child |
| | 25. The rights of the elderly |
| | 26. Integration of persons with disabilities |
| Title IV – Solidarity | 27. Workers' right to information and consultation within the undertaking |
| | 28. Right of collective bargaining and action |
| | 29. Right of access to placement services |
| | 30. Protection in the event of unjustified dismissal |
| | 31. Fair and just working conditions |
| | 32. Prohibition of child labour and protection of young people at work |
| | 33. Family and professional life |
| | 34. Social security and social assistance |
| | 35. Health care |
| | 36. Access to services of general economic interest |
| | 37. Environmental protection |
| | 38. Consumer protection |
| Title V – Citizens' Rights | 39. Right to vote and to stand as a candidate at elections to the European Parliament |
| | 40. Right to vote and to stand as a candidate at municipal elections |
| | 41. Right to good administration |
| | 42. Right of access to documents |
| | 43. European Ombudsman |
| | 44. Right to petition |
| | 45. Freedom of movement and of residence |
| | 46. Diplomatic and consular protection |

*(Continued)*

**Table 1.2 (Continued)**

| | |
|---|---|
| Title VI – Justice | 47. Right to an effective remedy and to a fair trial |
| | 48. Presumption of innocence and right of defence |
| | 49. Principles of legality and proportionality of criminal offences and penalties |
| | 50. Right not to be tried or punished twice in criminal proceedings for the same criminal offence |

It is worth spending a few moments with Table 1.2. It is only by recognising the vastness of human rights that the true significance of data protection can be understood. Thinking about this in an operational sense, the challenge that data protection presents to those who are regulated is truly awesome. Somehow, they must understand what all these rights mean and then give effect to them in practice. It is only when the extent of the challenge is recognised that the regulated party can begin to understand the real nature of the legal and operational risks that must be addressed.

## Protecting the free movement of personal data (data flows, transfers and shares)

The second aim of data protection is the maintenance of the free movement of personal data between people, organisations and countries, due to the societal and economic imperatives that are involved in data sharing. Data can flow in many ways, but it breaks down into three core categories:

- when information is obtained from people or returned to them;
- when information is transferred between data users;
- when information is transferred between these actors in different countries.

Human rights considerations will stand in the way of free movement if this is not done proportionately and in accordance with clear legal rules.

Therefore, to maintain confidence in data flows, transfers and shares, European data protection law sets a high bar for what must be achieved before and after these activities, so that personal data are protected at a high level wherever they may go. Through this approach, human rights concerns will not stand in the way of free movement that meets the law's standards.

All these situations are regulated by the GDPR.

## THE PROTECTED ACTIVITIES

As already mentioned, data protection is concerned with the processing of personal data.

## Protecting processing

The definition of processing is contained in A.4.2 of the GDPR (see GDPR A.4.2 – Definition of 'processing' box). As the definition shows, it covers a huge amount of ground, from the initial collection of personal data through to their ultimate destruction, deletion, or de-personalisation. In other words, processing means the entire data handling life cycle.

> **GDPR A.4.2 – Definition of 'processing'**
>
> 'Processing' means any operation or set of operations which is performed on personal data or on sets of personal data, whether or not by automated means, such as collection, recording, organisation, structuring, storage, adaptation or alteration, retrieval, consultation, use, disclosure by transmission, dissemination or otherwise making available, alignment or combination, restriction, erasure or destruction.

## Protecting personal data undergoing processing

> **GDPR A.4.2 – Definition of 'personal data'**
>
> 'Personal data' means any information relating to an identified or identifiable natural person ('data subject'); an identifiable natural person is one who can be identified, directly or indirectly, in particular by reference to an identifier such as a name, an identification number, location data, an online identifier or to one or more factors specific to the physical, physiological, genetic, mental, economic, cultural or social identity of that natural person.

The protected subject matter is personal data (see GDPR A.4.2 – Definition of 'personal data' box). Personal data means any information relating to an identified or identifiable natural person. Natural persons are living human beings, whom the law calls 'data subjects', not the deceased, nor companies, public authorities, or other organisations.

A person will be identifiable if they can be identified directly or indirectly from data. For example, if data include a person's name, they will be directly identifiable, but if data simply refer to an unnamed person's activities at a particular moment in time, they may be indirectly identifiable. Table 1.3 illustrates some of the ways in which a person can be identifiable.

**Table 1.3 Elements within the concept of identifiability**

| | |
|---|---|
| Directly identifiable | - Name |
| | - Address |
| | - Phone number |

*(Continued)*

**Table 1.3 (Continued)**

|  |  |
|---|---|
|  | • Email address |
|  | • Employment data |
|  | • Financial data |
|  | • Medical details |
|  | • Education details |
| Indirectly identifiable | • Car registration number |
|  | • Passport |
|  | • National Insurance number |
|  | • Biometric data, such as fingerprints |
| Online identifiers – these are the electronic footprints that are left when people engage in online activities | • Internet protocol (IP) addresses |
|  | • Cookie identifiers |
|  | • MAC addresses |
|  | • Advertising IDs |
|  | • Pixel tags |
|  | • Account handles |
|  | • Device fingerprints |

## Special category data (or 'sensitive personal data')

Special category data are types of personal data the processing of which poses heightened risks to the rights and freedoms of individuals, meaning that special care needs to be taken during their collection, handling and use. Sometimes referred to as 'sensitive personal data', they are defined in GDPR A.9.1 as:

- personal data revealing racial or ethnic origin;
- personal data revealing political opinions, religious or philosophical beliefs, or trade union membership;
- genetic data;
- biometric data, where they are processed for the purpose of uniquely identifying a natural person;
- data concerning health;
- data concerning a person's sex life or sexual orientation.

The GDPR's starting point is that the processing of special category data is prohibited. The ban will not apply, however, if one of the conditions in A.9.2 is satisfied. Those conditions are often referred to as 'the lawful bases of processing'. The data protection principles include a requirement that processing of personal data shall be lawful. One of the concepts within the idea of lawfulness is that processing should satisfy one of the lawful bases of processing, which means those set out in A.9.2 for special category data.[11]

Data relating to criminal convictions and offences are just as sensitive as special category data, but these fall within GDPR A.10 (and the Law Enforcement Directive, which is discussed below).

## THEMATIC PRIORITIES OF DATA PROTECTION, TRENDS AND HOT TOPICS – SUPPORTING A RISK-BASED APPROACH

The GDPR embraces a risk-based approach to processing activities, whereby controllers and processors have to consider risks both to themselves and to data subjects and take appropriate steps to mitigate those risks. The Information Commissioner, who is the UK data protection regulator, takes a similar approach to enforcement of the law.

Controllers and processors can be assisted with the development of a risk-based approach by taking account of the thematic priorities, trends and hot topics that are revealed within regulatory guidance and enforcement actions, court proceedings, compensation claims, news and media reports and the consensus of professional opinion. Illustrative examples are set out below.

### AdTech and cookies

AdTech, which includes the use of cookies, has been a persistent concern of data protection regulators and privacy activists, due to it involving problems with transparency, consent, sharing of data and international transfers. However, we are yet to see a concerted clampdown by the data protection regulators.

This does not mean that organisations can treat AdTech and cookies as risk-free endeavours. There has been very high-profile litigation about this subject, which includes the *Planet49* (2019)[12] case in the Court of Justice of the EU (CJEU) and *Vidal-Hall v. Google* (2015)[13] and *Lloyd v. Google* (2019)[14] in the UK. In late May 2021 the famous privacy activist organisation NOYB issued press statements heralding the launch of a campaign against non-compliance.

There is another story to be told of 'micro' compensation claims being made against businesses in increasing numbers by data subjects for non-compliant use of cookies. These claimants, who understand the impacts of 'nuisance claims' that cost more to defend that they do to settle, make demands for a relatively low sum of money, knowing that most website operators will not have the appetite to go to court. Due to the size of the problem and the size of the class of people affected, these claims are likely to increase in volume against organisations that fail to address non-compliance.

---

[11] See GDPR A.6 for the lawful bases for processing non-special category personal data.

[12] *Bundesverband der Verbraucherzentralen und Verbraucherverbände – Verbraucherzentrale Bundesverband e.V. v. Planet49 GmbH* (2019) C-673/17.

[13] *Vidal-Hall v. Google Inc.* (2015) EWCA Civ 311.

[14] *Lloyd v. Google* (2019) EWCA Civ 1599.

## Advanced technology and data processing techniques

While the GDPR recognises the importance of regulating paper files, most of the risks of data protection are found in the automated processing environment, so whenever significant leaps forward are made in technology and processing techniques, it can be expected that adverse scrutiny will not be long behind, by the regulators, privacy activists and civil society organisations.

The priority that the law places on regulatory supervision of technology is illustrated by the Information Commissioner's Technology Strategy 2018–2021.[15]

### Information Commissioner's Technology Strategy 2018–2021

Technology is driving changes to the societal, political, legal and business environment that the Information Commissioner's Office (ICO) needs to regulate. The most significant data protection risks to individuals are now driven by the use of new technologies. The risks are broad – from cyber-attacks to the growth of artificial intelligence and machine learning.

## Advanced surveillance

Worries about computer-powered surveillance techniques provided part of the original motivation for the development of the data protection principles in the late 1960s and early 1970s. Edward Snowden's disclosures in 2012 about mass surveillance by the intelligence agencies revealed the extent of the problem in modern times, triggering countless legal actions about privacy interference, including the *Schrems I* (2015)[16] and *Schrems II* (2020)[17] litigation in the CJEU about the EU–US international data transfers regime. Litigation about automated facial recognition provides another example of the nature of the concern.

Surveillance is not the preserve of intelligence agencies and law enforcement agencies, however; it is part and parcel of everyday life and ordinary business, including in the workplace. The world of AdTech is a surveillance system and this is used routinely by businesses, public authorities and other organisations within their online ecosystems. The Internet of Things (IoT) includes many examples of processing activities that fall under this umbrella, such as the connected vehicle and virtual voice assistant examples given below. The response to the COVID-19 pandemic has triggered concerns about surveillance, due to the use of contact tracing apps and proposals for vaccine certificates. It has been often said that we are 'sleepwalking into a surveillance society'. The adoption of surveillance activities in business has been termed 'surveillance capitalism'.[18]

---

[15] https://ico.org.uk/media/about-the-ico/documents/2258299/ico-technology-strategy-2018-2021.pdf

[16] *Maximilian Schrems v. Facebook Ireland Limited* (2015) C-498/16.

[17] *Data Protection Commissioner v. Facebook Ireland Limited and Maximillian Schrems* (2020) C-311/18.

[18] *The Age of Surveillance Capitalism. The Fight for a Human Future at the New Frontier of Power*, Shoshana Zuboff, Profile Books, 2019.

## Artificial intelligence

Progress in artificial intelligence (AI) and machine learning (ML) continues to leap forward. This has prompted the Information Commissioner's Office (ICO) to develop policy on auditing these systems and the EU to propose a new regulation on AI. Central to the reason for regulatory engagement is that AI provides unprecedented potential for automated decision making that impacts individuals, without the checks and balances of human intervention. GDPR A.22, which concerns the prohibition on automated decision making, engages directly with this area.

## Automated facial recognition

In the *Bridges* (2020)[19] case, the Court of Appeal held that an automated facial recognition (AFR) trial was unlawful, due to defects in the policy and risk assessment framework surrounding it. This teaches us the importance of taking care with these elements of compliance whenever the roll-out of new data protection technologies is contemplated.

Another concern about AFR is that the algorithms may have discriminatory effects due to disparities in false positives between people of different ethnic groups and gender. This reminds us that data protection is concerned about more than privacy, as equality issues fall within the scope of the human rights that the law is designed to protect.

## Connected vehicles

Connected vehicles are akin to smartphones on wheels, involving myriad data protection risks. Some of them are identified in guidance published by the European Data Protection Board (EDPB) in 2020.[20] They include potential for bodily harms, due to road safety risks; the processing of location data; information asymmetry, in the sense that the person who receives data protection transparency information, that is, the vehicle owner, may not be the driver; problems with managing consents, due to the highly complex and technical environment of the connected vehicle ecosystem, which includes many different actors; and problems with excessive data collection. In April 2021 the UK government announced that 'self-drive' cars would be allowed on UK roads before the end of the year and the pace of data protection concern is likely to accelerate proportionate to the speed of roll-out.

## Children

Children are afforded special protection within the law. The UN Convention on the Rights of the Child illustrates this point, as does the fact that there are Children's Commissioners in the UK. Not surprisingly, the GDPR and the UK Data Protection Act both make provision for the special interests of children. For example, the rules on legitimate interests processing in GDPR A.6.1.f specifically call out the need for controllers to pay attention to the rights and freedoms of children when they perform their balancing assessments. A.8 requires parental consent for the provision of information society services to children. The transparency rules in A.12 require that this information is suitable for children. A.57 requires the national regulators to pay specific attention to children's interests.

---

[19] *R (Bridges) v. Chief Constable of South Wales Police & Others* (2020) EWCA Civ 1058.

[20] https://edpb.europa.eu/sites/edpb/files/files/file1/edpb_guidelines_202001_connected_vehicles_v2.0_adopted_en.pdf

As far as the UK Data Protection Act is concerned, s.121 requires the Information Commissioner to publish an age-appropriate design code (see the box below) that 'contains such guidance as the Commissioner considers appropriate on standards of age-appropriate design of relevant information society services which are likely to be accessed by children'. This code[21] was published in September 2020 and came into effect in September 2021. It contains 15 standards that the controllers of online services targeted at children need to take account of. Failure to comply with the code can constitute evidence of non-compliance with the law.

> **Age-appropriate design code – executive summary**
>
> Children are being 'datafied' with companies and organisations recording many thousands of data points about them as they grow up. These can range from details about their mood and their friendships to what time they woke up and when they went to bed.

## Cybersecurity

In their 2017–2021 workplan, the Information Commissioner's Office described a goal to be 'an effective and knowledgeable regulator for cyber related data protection matters'. This reflected the general and rising concerns about cybersecurity in the economy. Unsurprisingly, the largest fines imposed by ICO since the introduction of the GDPR have been concerned with cyber-related personal data breaches (£20m and £18.4m respectively, in October 2020[22]). Cyber-related problems are also of great interest to the compensation claims industry (claims management companies, claimant law firms and litigation funders), due to providing an ideal focus for group litigation.

## Data subject rights – timetable breaches

Data subject rights provides a very fertile source for compensation claims, due to the prescriptive nature of the law's requirements and the very strict timetables for compliance. Data subject access requests (DSAR) need to be answered within one month, which is subject to a maximum extension of two months in complex cases. Once a deadline is breached, all the ingredients are in place to enable the data subject to claim distress, which is compensatable (these cases are already forming part of the 'micro' claim environment, discussed above).

## Democracy

Surveillance by governments and public authorities forms part the 'Big Brother' concern that has always existed at the heart of data protection law. Therefore, any use of data

---

21 Age Appropriate Design: a code of practice for online service, The Information Commissioner's Office. https://ico.org.uk/media/for-organisations/guide-to-data-protection/key-data-protection-themes/age-appropriate-design-a-code-of-practice-for-online-services-2-1.pdf

22 See ICO Monetary Penalty Notices imposed on British Airways plc and Marriott International Inc, respectively.

processing techniques to undermine democracy will always be treated very seriously by the law. This is illustrated by the Cambridge Analytica scandal, where millions of social media users' personal data were used for political advertising during the 2016 US presidential election. It was also suspected that the 2016 Brexit referendum was impacted, although this charge was later dismissed by the ICO. The ICO's investigation into 'Democracy Disrupted'[23] helps to illustrate how seriously negative impacts of data processing on democracy are viewed. The UK government's Online Harms Bill white paper, published in December 2020, provides more evidence of the degree of concern.

## HR problems

HR data protection problems often surface within a situation of adversity, such as when a person is being dismissed for misconduct or for redundancy, or where they perceive that they have been unfairly treated in breach of equality legislation or anti-victimisation legislation. These cases have significant potential to lead to problems of both regulatory enforcement and litigation. Factors that add to the risks include a unionised workplace and the presence of 'no win, no fee' legal services. In a landmark case in 2020, a German data protection regulator imposed a €35.3m fine[24] on a well-known international clothing retailer, for HR practices that infringed the GDPR's rules on transparency, retention and sharing. Data subject access requests are now regularly used in HR situations, as workers seek to obtain evidence to pursue grievances and legal remedies.

## International transfers

Following the judgment of the CJEU in the *Schrems II* (2020) case, which held that the Privacy Shield scheme for transferring personal data from the EU to the US was unlawful, many businesses received inquiries from privacy activists, compensation claimants and customers about their systems and operations governing the transfers of personal data to the US and other countries outside Europe. In tandem with this, the EDPB[25] and the European Commission issued new regulatory guidance and new standard contractual clauses. It is likely that these regulatory advances will provide new sources of challenge for multinationals and data exporters.

## Privacy and electronic communications ('ePrivacy')

The ePrivacy framework, which covers issues such as the security of publicly available communications services, the confidentiality of communications, the use of traffic and location data and direct marketing, involves many issues of utmost concern in the data protection field. The ePrivacy framework is contained in the Privacy and Electronic Communications Directive (PEC), which is given effect in the UK by the Privacy and Electronic Communications Regulations (PECR).

---

[23] https://ico.org.uk/media/action-weve-taken/2259369/democracy-disrupted-110718.pdf

[24] See details of H&M fine, on EDPB website: https://edpb.europa.eu/news/national-news/2020/hamburg-commissioner-fines-hm-353-million-euro-data-protection-violations_en

[25] https://edpb.europa.eu/sites/edpb/files/files/file1/edpb_recommendations_202002_europeanessentialguaranteessurveillance_en.pdf and
https://edpb.europa.eu/sites/edpb/files/consultation/edpb_recommendations_202001_supplementarymeasurestransferstools_en.pdf

Key points to note include:

- Direct marketing by telephone, email and SMS can be both highly intrusive and annoying, so these activities are a constant source of complaints from recipients, regularly triggering claims for compensation and regulatory investigations and inquiries. The AdTech issue has already been noted.
- The surveillance risks that the use of electronic communications networks and services involve are of the highest order of magnitude.
- The use of connected devices over these networks and services can enable a person to be geo-tracked and located anywhere in the world.
- The activities regulated by the ePrivacy framework are considerable contributors to profiling.

These are just some of the reasons why ePrivacy is considered to be one of the most sensitive issues in data protection.

## Profiling

Profiling is any form of automated processing of personal data that evaluates personal characteristics of people. Examples within the definition in GDPR A.4.4 are analysing and predicting aspects of a person's performance at work, their economic situation, health, personal preferences, interests, reliability, behaviour, location or movements. Profiling can be used to support automated decision making, in which case A.22 will apply if the decision produces legal effects for the person who is profiled, or similar significant effects.

Due to its intrusive nature, its increasingly common use in society and the role it can play in automated decisions, profiling is a topic of utmost concern in the field of data protection. Examples of profiles include credit files and targeted advertising based on online behaviours. Profiling has also been used for wholly unlawful purposes, such as happened in the Consulting Association[26] case that came to light in 2009, which concerned the use of profiles to 'blacklist' construction site workers. Otherwise legitimate activity, such as policing, can be rendered unlawful through the misuse of profiles, as happened in the Gangs Matrix case, where the Information Commissioner served an enforcement notice in 2018.

## Virtual voice assistants

The EDPB published guidance on virtual voice assistants (VVAs) in 2021.[27] Illustrative concerns noted by the guidance include the extent of their integration into IoT devices, ranging from smartphones to connected vehicles, smart TVs and smart speakers. The main beneficiaries of VVAs can include people with disabilities, whose rights need enhanced protection; they are used to process sensitive data, such as health data queries during the COVID-19 pandemic; they utilise AI and ML techniques; there is a wide array of actors involved in the execution chain; they may capture personal data by

---

[26] Firm 'sold workers' secret data', BBC News, 6 March 2009.

[27] https://edpb.europa.eu/sites/edpb/files/consultation/edpb_guidelines_022021_virtual_voice_assistants_adopted-public-consultation_en.pdf

The UK Data Protection Act 2018 continues to give effect to the UK's obligations under the Convention. Due to the overlap between the GDPR and the Convention (in effect, the rules in the Convention can be considered to be subsumed by the rules within the GDPR), the Act refers to the Convention only in the context of the Information Commissioner's functions as they concern international cooperation, such as where the Commissioner may need assistance from other regulators abroad to help UK data subjects who are affected by foreign data processing.

**Regulatory guidance and decisions**

Although it is a very detailed piece of legislation, the GDPR does not provide an exhaustive account of every single issue that arises in the field of data protection. Therefore, as well as leaving it to the Member States to fill in the gaps, this function is also performed by the European Data Protection Board and the national regulators such as the Information Commissioner, who issue regulatory guidance and perform supervisory roles.

The UK is no longer part of the EDPB or subject to its guidance, nor is it bound by any decisions of the national regulators in the EU, but the technical position in law is somewhat different to the position in practice, in the sense that the guidance and decisions of the EDPB and the EU national regulators currently do have significant influence in the UK. This is probably going to be the case for many years to come, or until such time that the UK's path diverges in a fundamental way so as to leave the EU position irrelevant. Therefore, we refer to EU regulatory guidance and decisions throughout this book, to help readers with their understanding of the topic.

**Court judgments**

Likewise, because of the need to fill the gaps in the legislation, judgments of the CJEU are likely to continue to be highly influential in the UK. Therefore, we refer to recent landmark judgments, such as those on international transfers of personal data (i.e. the *Schrems I* (2015) and *Schrems II* (2020) cases), the use of cookies (i.e. the *Planet49* (2019) case) and the use of social media plugs (i.e. the *Fashion ID* (2019)[30] case). Despite Brexit, CJEU court decisions made pre-IP Day still form part of UK law, although legal rules allow the UK to depart from them in various situations.

The provisions of the European Convention on Human Rights, which was adopted by the Council of Europe in 1950,[31] are justiciated by the European Court of Human Rights (ECtHR). The Human Rights Act 1998 gives effect to the ECHR in the UK and it requires our domestic courts to take account of any relevant judgment, decision, declaration, or advisory opinion of the ECtHR whenever a human rights issue arises in proceedings. The ECtHR has issued more than 100 judgments on data protection issues.[32]

Of course, judgments of the UK courts form a direct part of the law in this country.

---

[30] *Fashion ID GmbH & Co.KG v. Verbraucherzentrale NRW eV* (2019) C-40/17.

[31] The full title is 'The Convention for the Protection of Human Rights and Fundamental Freedoms'.

[32] Case Law of the European Court of Human Rights Concerning The Protection Of Personal Data, (2018) 15 June 2018.

**Related law**

There are many other pieces of legislation with direct and indirect impact on data protection. These include the Investigatory Powers Act 2016 (IPA) and the Digital Economy Act 2017. There is also the cybersecurity framework, represented by the Network and Information Security Directive (NIS) in the EU and the equivalent UK regulations. Table 1.5 provides examples of other legislation that can impact the operationalising or interpretation of data protection law.

**Table 1.5 Other legislation that impacts on data protection (examples)**

| | |
|---|---|
| Investigatory Powers Act 2016 | • This UK legislation provides a key part of the country's legal framework for surveillance. |
| | • The title of the Act describes its purpose: |
| | 'An Act to make provision about the interception of communications, equipment interference and the acquisition and retention of communications data, bulk personal datasets and other information; to make provision about the treatment of material held as a result of such interception, equipment interference or acquisition or retention; to establish the Investigatory Powers Commissioner and other Judicial Commissioners and make provision about them and other oversight arrangements; to make further provision about investigatory powers and national security; to amend sections 3 and 5 of the Intelligence Services Act 1994; and for connected purposes.' |
| | • Due to the fact it is a surveillance regime, the IPA was a material issue within the EU's assessment of the UK's adequacy under A.45 (international data transfers based on an adequacy decision). |
| Digital Economy Act 2017 | • Part 5 of this UK legislation is titled 'Digital Government' and it enables processing, including data sharing, to take place to improve public services; to reduce debt owed to public services; to reduce fraud against public services; and for research and statistics purposes. |
| | • Businesses working in gas, electricity, water and sewerage can be required to disclose information about their customers to public authorities. |
| | • The Information Commissioner's Office has used its audit powers to assess data processing and sharing under this Act. |
| NIS Directive and UK Regulations (Cyber Security) | • The Network and Information Security Directive and Regulations contain a framework for the development of national cybersecurity plans and implementing measures. |

*(Continued)*

## Table 1.5 (Continued)

|  |  |
|---|---|
|  | • They also place security and breach reporting obligations on operators of essential services (in the energy, transport, health and water sectors) and on providers of digital infrastructures (top level domain name registries and domain name service providers) and digital service providers (cloud, online marketplaces, online search engines). |
|  | • The EU and UK NIS regimes are currently under revision. |
| Draft EU AI Regulation | The focus of this draft regulation is summarised in this explanatory text: |
|  | 'This explanatory memorandum accompanies the proposal for a Regulation laying down harmonised rules on artificial intelligence (Artificial Intelligence Act). Artificial Intelligence (AI) is a fast-evolving family of technologies that can bring a wide array of economic and societal benefits across the entire spectrum of industries and social activities. By improving prediction, optimising operations and resource allocation, and personalising service delivery, the use of artificial intelligence can support socially and environmentally beneficial outcomes and provide key competitive advantages to companies and the European economy. Such action is especially needed in high-impact sectors, including climate change, environment and health, the public sector, finance, mobility, home affairs and agriculture. However, the same elements and techniques that power the socio-economic benefits of AI can also bring about new risks or negative consequences for individuals or the society. Considering the speed of technological change and possible challenges, the EU is committed to strive for a balanced approach. It is in the Union interest to preserve the EU's technological leadership and to ensure that Europeans can benefit from new technologies developed and functioning according to Union values, fundamental rights, and principles.' |
| Draft EU Digital Operations Resilience Act (DORA)[33] | This draft regulation proposes to introduce a new cybersecurity framework for financial services. The explanatory text sets out the objectives: |
|  | 'It is therefore necessary to put in place a detailed and comprehensive framework on digital operational resilience for EU financial entities. This framework will deepen the digital risk management dimension of the Single Rulebook. It will enhance and streamline the financial entities' conduct of ICT risk management, establish a thorough testing of ICT systems, increase supervisors' awareness of cyber risks and ICT-related incidents faced by financial entities, as well as introduce powers for financial |

*(Continued)*

---

[33] Proposal for a Regulation of the European Parliament and of the Council on digital operational resilience for the financial sector and amending Regulations (EC) No 1060/2009, (EU) No 648/2012. (EU) No 600/2014 and (EU) No 909/2014 COM/2020/595 final.

**Table 1.5 (Continued)**

| | |
|---|---|
| | supervisors to oversee risks stemming from financial entities' dependency on ICT third-party service providers. The proposal will create a consistent incident reporting mechanism that will help reduce administrative burdens for financial entities and strengthen supervisory effectiveness.' |

## DATA PROTECTION PENALTIES AND LITIGATION

The fact that data protection is required by law and the fact that it is designed to protect human rights and to advance wider societal and economic goals should be enough to make compliance a critical imperative for the holders and users of personal data, but the law recognises that sometimes it takes operational failure, punishment or reputation damage to trigger the correct actions. Table 1.6 illustrates some of the financial risks that controllers and processors are exposed to due to poor compliance.

**Table 1.6 Data protection financial impacts**

| | |
|---|---|
| Fines | • The data protection regulators have powers to impose fines on an 'undertaking' of up to 4% of their annual worldwide turnover in the previous year, or £17.5m/€20m, whichever is the higher. An undertaking is an entity engaged in economic activity, that is, a business. |
| | • If an entity is not an undertaking, for example, a public authority, the maximum fine is £17.5m/€20m. |
| Compensation in civil claims | • If an entity is sued for compensation in group litigation, the financial exposure could be very large. |
| | • For example, if group litigation following a personal data breach consisting of 10,000 claimants resulted in compensation of £500 per person, the total damages would be £5m. |
| | • Group litigation against an airline in the UK had 16,000 claimants (estimated). |
| | • Group litigation against a retailer in the UK had 9,000 claimants (estimated). |
| Largest GDPR fines | The GDPR came into effect in May 2018. Fines are increasing in size and frequency. The 10 largest fines are: |
| | 1. €50m – Search engine (France) |
| | 2. €35.3m – Clothes retailer (Germany) |
| | 3. €27.3m – Telecommunications company (Italy) |

*(Continued)*

**Table 1.6 (Continued)**

| | | |
|---|---|---|
| | 4. | £20m – Airline (UK) |
| | 5. | £18.4m – Hotel (UK) |
| | 6. | €18m – Post office (Austria) |
| | 7. | €17m – Telecommunications company (Italy) |
| | 8. | €10.4m – Electronics retailer (Germany) |
| | 9. | €10m – Dating site (Norway) |
| | 10. | €8m – Telecommunications company (Italy) |

## The regulatory bear market

A bear market, which is the opposite of a bull market, is a time of negative sentiment and loss of confidence that leads to negative outcomes. Most often spoken about in the context of the financial markets, its negative outcomes include a sustained loss of share prices.

A regulatory bear market displays the same features of negativity, but its special characteristics include the situation where all the data protection actors with regulatory or quasi-regulatory power feel increasingly negative about the prevailing situation of data protection both at large and within specific sectors and segments of data processing.

In the data protection field, the regulators consist of more than the supervisory authorities. There are many other actors with regulatory effect, particularly data subjects, who have rights to intervene in processing and pursue remedies, and civil society organisations, which are represented by 'privacy activists' and 'consumer champions'. Other actors in the regulatory bear market include members of the compensation claims industry, media commentators, and investors and shareholders.

A regulatory bear market for data protection has developed and it is now capable of inflicting real damage on controllers and processors that fail to deliver on the required outcomes. As time progresses, we are likely to see the quantum of regulatory fines continue to increase in value, more compensation claims and greater reputational damage for those organisations that fail to deliver on their duties and obligations. This will perpetuate negative sentiment about the state of data protection, encouraging ever-increasing amounts of regulatory interventions and financial consequences for errant controllers and processors.

## SUMMARY

In conclusion, this chapter gives readers a better understanding of:

- the breadth of data protection law and how it extends much further than the protection of privacy to cover all fundamental rights and freedoms (human rights) and how it aims to support the sharing of personal data between people, organisations and countries;

- the nature of the activities that the law regulates and protects, namely the processing of personal data relating to living individuals;
- the kinds of 'hot topics' that the law and regulation is concerned with and how these develop over time;
- the possible consequences of non-compliance with the law;
- where the core law is found and where to look for further research and understanding.

# 2  INTRODUCTION TO THE GDPR

**Stewart Room and Michelle Maher**

This chapter takes a closer look at the General Data Protection Regulation, expanding upon the introduction in Chapter 1 to lay more of the foundations for analysis and discussion in subsequent chapters. Issues covered in this chapter are the jurisdiction and territorial scope of the regulation, its material scope, the building blocks of the law, the critical outcomes to be achieved, and the impacts of Brexit.

**BREXIT: THE IMPACTS FOR DATA PROTECTION AND THE IMPACTS FOR THIS BOOK**

Brexit has had and will continue to have profound implications for the UK legal system. One of the central ideas of Brexit is that the UK is no longer subject to EU law, but in many respects it still has effect in the UK due to the agreements we have made with the EU, because of how international law operates, and because ideas and concepts within EU law are woven into the fabric of the UK legal system after 40 years of membership.

At the date of publication of this book, UK and EU data protection law remain virtually identical. The path has been prepared for future divergence, however, although we cannot be sure at this stage how the UK's data protection regime will develop in the years ahead relative to the EU's.

More of the technical detail and implications of Brexit are discussed at the end of this chapter (as well as in other chapters), but the following points help to explain the approach that the authors have taken in this book:

- Strictly speaking, there are three versions of the GDPR currently in existence, namely (1) the 'EU GDPR', (2) the 'UK GDPR', and (3) the 'Frozen GDPR' (these terms are explained later on), but to all intents and purposes their content is currently the same on the key issues addressed in this book.
- Therefore, references to 'the GDPR' mean the text of the original 2016 version (the EU GDPR), unless stated otherwise.
- In most situations, the 2016 version will suffice as the main reference point for UK readers, but they should monitor developments in the law.
- Similarly, although the UK is no longer bound by EU regulatory guidance or the judgments of the CJEU, these materials are likely to remain highly influential in the UK for many years to come. At least in the short to medium term, it can be

expected that UK controllers and processors of personal data will continue to have regard to these materials, particularly when they address the operational aspects of data protection. As noted in Chapter 1, CJEU judgments delivered before IP Day form part of UK law despite Brexit.

### The land mass in Europe to which the GDPR applies

When the GDPR was adopted, the UK was still one of the EU Member States. The UK GDPR removes all references to 'Member States', replacing them with references to the UK. References to 'Member States' in this book mean the land mass in Europe where the GDPR applies, that is, the remaining 27 EU Member States, the three European Economic Area (EEA) States,[1] Switzerland and the UK (unless stated otherwise). This approach is taken for convenience, to simplify the writing and editing process. Similarly, references to the 'EU' or 'Europe' mean the land mass in Europe where the GDPR applies (unless stated otherwise).

For example, GDPR A.45 allows personal data to be transferred to a 'third country' that has been declared 'adequate' for data protection purposes, judged by the GDPR's standards. In this book a third country will be anywhere other than the EU and EEA States, Switzerland and the UK.

## RECITALS AND ARTICLES OF THE GDPR

The GDPR is made up of recitals and articles. The articles are the operative provisions of the legislation, which set out the legal obligations and requirements. Recitals provide explanatory text, which set out the reasons for the operative provisions: they are not legally binding, but they should be considered when interpreting the articles.

The following abbreviations are used:

- recitals: Rec.; R.; r. (for example Rec. 6; R.6; r.6);
- articles: Art.; A.; a. (for example Art. 7; A.7; a.7).

## JURISDICTION OF THE GDPR

The GDPR applies in the land mass of Europe identified above, but it also has extra-territorial effect, in the sense that it has effects beyond that land mass. This is due to its rules on territorial scope, which are contained in Article 3.

These rules work by focusing on the 'establishments' of 'controllers' and 'processors'. Controllers and processors are the regulated parties under the law. They will be regulated in the following situations:

---

1  The GDPR applies in the European Economic Area, which consists of the EU Member States plus Iceland, Liechtenstein and Norway. The EEA forms the Single Market. Switzerland is also a member of the Single Market, but not the EEA.

- If they are established in the EU/UK and their processing activities take place in the context of their establishment (A.3.1).
- If they are not established in the EU/UK, they will still be regulated if they are offering goods or services to people in the EU/UK, or if they are monitoring the behaviours of people in the EU/UK (A.3.2).
- They will also be regulated if they are established in a place where the laws of an EU Member State or the UK apply by virtue of international law (A.3.3).

## Nationality and location of people

The GDPR's jurisdiction does not turn on the nationality of the protected party. The protected party is called the 'data subject'.

Non-EU/UK citizens will be protected if their data are processed in the ways envisaged by A.3.1, regardless of where they are physically situated. Those persons will also be protected in the ways envisaged by A.3.2, if they are located in the EU/UK.

For example, a controller based in the EU/UK could collect personal data via a website from people based in America, Asia or Africa. The GDPR will apply to the data that are collected, giving those people legal protections as data subjects. This is because of A.3.1. Similarly, if people from those areas move to the EU/UK and then use the same website, A.3.1 would apply. If while based in the EU/UK they use a different website, operated by controllers based in the countries from where they relocated, A.3.2 might apply.

### A.3.1 – processing in the context of EU establishments

The rules in A.3.1 are concerned with data processing activities that relate to controllers and processors with EU presence.

#### *Establishments*
The GDPR does not provide a definition of establishment, but R.22 explains that an establishment 'implies the effective and real exercise of activities through stable arrangements', then goes on to say that 'the legal form of such arrangements, whether through a branch or a subsidiary with a legal personality is not the determining factor in that respect'. The CJEU has confirmed that the phrase should be interpreted very broadly and has found that 'any real and effective activity, even a minimal one' via 'stable arrangements' in the EU or EEA may be sufficient to qualify as an establishment.

The threshold for a 'stable arrangement' is relatively low, especially in circumstances where the activities concerned are the provision of services online. The EDPB has confirmed[2] that a single employee or agent of a foreign entity present in the EU may be sufficient to constitute a stable arrangement, so that the application of the law must be considered 'in light of the specific nature of the economic activities and the provision of services concerned'. However, the EDPB draws a contrast between organisations where an employee is EU-based and the processing relates to a controller's activities based

---

[2] EDPB Guidelines 3/2018 on the territorial scope of the GDPR.

outside the EU. It has concluded that 'the mere presence of an employee in the EU is not ... sufficient to trigger the application of the GDPR' because to enable the processing to fall within the scope of the GDPR 'it must also be carried out in the context of the activities of the EU based employee'.

Once the analysis has confirmed whether a controller or processor is established in the EU/EEA, the next question is whether the processing is carried out in the context of the activities of the establishment.

### *Activities*

To satisfy the second limb of A.3.1, consideration needs to be given to whether the processing activities are carried out 'in the context of activities' of the controller's relevant establishment in the Union. The courts have taken a broad and purposive view of this issue, to link processing by a controller or processor outside the EEA to the activities of an establishment in the EEA. This is demonstrated in the *Google Spain* (2014)[3] case, about the right to be forgotten in the context of the 1995 Data Protection Directive, where it was held that Google Inc., a US business, was established in Spain due to having a local sales office there, which sold advertising space on the search engine. This is known as the 'inextricable link' test. This part of the judgment explains the position:

> In the light of that objective of Directive 95/46 and of the wording of Article 4(1)(a), it must be held that the processing of personal data for the purposes of the service of a search engine such as Google Search, which is operated by an undertaking that has its seat in a third State but has an establishment in a Member State, is carried out 'in the context of the activities' of that establishment if the latter is intended to promote and sell, in that Member State, advertising space offered by the search engine which serves to make the service offered by that engine profitable.

> In such circumstances, the activities of the operator of the search engine and those of its establishment situated in the Member State concerned are inextricably linked since the activities relating to the advertising space constitute the means of rendering the search engine at issue economically profitable and that engine is, at the same time, the means enabling those activities to be performed.

### *Location*

The final issue in A.3.1 is geographical location. It is irrelevant whether the actual processing activity occurs within the EU, provided that the controller or processor is established in the EU and the processing is carried out in the context of the establishment. Therefore, if an EU-based controller outsources data processing to a third country, such as India, that processing will be regulated by the GDPR.

### A.3.2 – targeting people in the EU

The rules in A.3.2 capture controllers and processors without EU establishments that are targeting people in the EU, either for goods or services, or to monitor them.

---

3  *Google Spain SL and Google Inc. v. Agencia Española de Protección de Datos (AEPD) and Mario Costeja González* (2014) CJEU Case C-131/12.

Before examining this in detail, it is important to briefly consider to which data subjects this applies. The EDPB guidance confirms that the data subject must be located in the EU at the time when the relevant 'trigger activity' takes place, which is 'at the moment of offering of goods or services or the moment when the behaviour is being monitored'. The guidance also clarifies that the provision is aimed at intentional targeting of individuals, not inadvertent or incidental targeting, so it excludes processing relating to a service offered exclusively to individuals outside the EU that is not withdrawn or discontinued when they enter the EU, for example when they visit on holiday. However, if the non-EU-based controller intentionally offers a service to people visiting the EU, this would fall within the scope of the GDPR, irrespective of the fact that the visitor's presence in the EU is temporary.

### Offering goods and services

The concept of targeting is wide, but it involves more than providing access to a website, email address or other contact details, or simply using the language generally used in the country in which the data subject is established. Consideration should be given to whether the controller or processor intends to offer goods or services to people in the EU.

**EDPB guidance on offering goods and services to people in the EU (Guidelines 3/2018)**

The EDPB guidance identifies the following factors for considering whether goods or services are offered to a data subject in the EU. It stresses that these elements taken alone do not necessarily amount to an explicit indication to offer goods or services to data subjects in the EU, but they can be considered together to determine whether the goods/services amount to an offer of goods/services directed at data subjects in the EU.

1. The EU or at least one Member State is designated by name referring to the good or service offered.
2. The data controller or processor pays a search engine operator for an internet referencing service to facilitate access to its site by consumers in the EU.
3. The data controller or processor has launched marketing and advertisement campaigns directed at EU data subjects as their audience.
4. The international nature of the activity.
5. The inclusion of a dedicated address or phone numbers to be reached from an EU country.
6. The use of a domain name in the country in which the controller or processor is established or neutral domain names such as '.eu'.
7. Travel instructions from one or more EU Member States to the place where the service is provided.
8. Reference to customers domiciled in various EU Member States.

9. Using a language or currency of one or more Member States.
10. Offering the delivery of goods in an EU Member State.

### *Monitoring of behaviour*
For the monitoring provision to be triggered, the behaviour being monitored must relate to a data subject within the EU and take place within the EU. An obvious example of monitoring is tracking a data subject on the internet and the use of data processing techniques that constitute profiling. The EDPB has confirmed that tracking through other types of networks or technology that involves personal data processing should be considered and provides wearable smart devices as an example.

Unlike the provision of goods or services, the controller or processor does not have to intend to target the data subject. Monitoring indicates that there is a specific purpose for the collection and reuse of the relevant data, however, so the EDPB's guidance is to consider the purpose to understand whether it involves subsequent behaviour analysis or profiling techniques.

**EDPB guidance on monitoring people in the EU (Guidelines 3/2018)**

The EDPB has provided a non-exhaustive list of what may be monitoring activities for the purposes of A.3.2:

- Behavioural advertising.
- Online tracking via cookies.
- CCTV.
- Marketing surveys.
- Personalised diet and health analytic services online.
- Monitoring or regular reporting on a data subject's health statistics.

### *Article 3.3 – application of international law*
As a reminder, A.3.3 confirms that the GDPR applies to the processing of personal data where the controller is not established in the Union, but in locations where Member State law applies by virtue of public international law.

Controllers and processors are within the scope of the GDPR where personal data are processed by EU Member States' embassies and consulates located outside the EU. A Member State's diplomatic post, for example, the French Consulate in Thailand, would be within the scope of the GDPR. So would a cruise ship registered to a Member State that is travelling in international waters, which is processing guests' personal data for the purpose of cruise services.

## MATERIAL SCOPE OF THE GDPR

Article 2 of the GDPR sets out the material scope of the law. It says that processing of personal data needs to be protected in two situations:

- where the processing is wholly or partly by automated means;
- where the processing does not involve automated means, but which does, or will, form part of a filing system.

Automated processing is commonly understood to mean computer-controller processing, which covers everything from PCs, smartphones, image and sound capture devices through to the scientific tools and equipment that capture and analyse information about the human body and mental state. A filing system is commonly understood to mean a structured paper file that makes personal data accessible, such as through an index.

Many processing activities fall outside the scope of the GDPR, however, such as domestic processing. These situations are discussed below, under 'Where the GDPR does not apply – exceptions and restrictions'.

## THE BUILDING BLOCKS OF THE GDPR

The GDPR's main building blocks fall within four core categories, which are shown in Table 2.1.

**Table 2.1 The main building blocks of the GDPR**

| | |
|---|---|
| Who are the main actors? | The GDPR identifies the beneficiaries of its protections, who is regulated and who the regulators are. |
| What should be protected? | The law protects personal data that are undergoing processing by controllers and processors. The core objectives of the law are:<br>• Controllers must identify and assess the risks to the rights and freedoms of individuals that data processing involves.<br>• Those risks must be appropriately addressed by technical and organisational measures. |
| Compliance framework | The main compliance goals are:<br>• Data processing should be conducted in a transparent manner, which applies to the full data processing life cycle, from initial collection of data through to end of life. |

*(Continued)*

**Table 2.1 (Continued)**

| | |
|---|---|
| | • Data processing must be appropriately controlled, to achieve the quality standards that the law prescribes. These standards are contained in the data protection principles. Appropriate technical and organisational measures need to be implemented for these purposes. |
| | • Controllers have to be accountable for their actions ('the accountability rule'). This involves them being able to prove that they have met the law's requirements. Various compliance structures are prescribed for these purposes, such as the maintenance of records of processing and achieving Data Protection by Design and Default. |
| Compensatory mechanisms to deter or address non-compliance | These include a variety of mechanisms that are intended to compensate for non-compliance by controllers and processors. Principally they are:<br>• The taking of appropriate regulatory action by the national supervisory authorities. |
| | • The taking of actions by data subjects themselves. This includes through the exercise of information and processing rights; through the right to bring complaints to the attention of the regulators; and through the right to pursue judicial remedies in court, including for compensation. Data subjects can appoint third parties to pursue these rights on their behalf. |

## THE ACTORS

The GDPR identifies more than just data subjects, controllers, processors and regulators. A full list of actors is shown in Table 2.2.

**Table 2.2 The actors identified by the GDPR**

| | |
|---|---|
| Data subjects | • These are the people who are identifiable from personal data that are undergoing processing. |
| | • Data subjects are the protected parties. |
| Controllers | • These are the persons or organisations/bodies that determine the purposes and means of data processing. |
| | • When two or more controllers are involved in these determinations, they will be treated as joint controllers. |
| | • This book uses the phases 'data controller' and 'controller' interchangeably. |

*(Continued)*

**Table 2.2 (Continued)**

| | |
|---|---|
| Processors | • These are persons or organisations/bodies that process personal data on behalf of controllers. |
| | • In contrast to controllers, processors do not determine the purposes and means of processing. |
| | • In the operational world of data protection, processors are sometimes referred to as suppliers or vendors of services. |
| Representatives | • These are persons or organisations/bodies based in the EU that represent non-EU-based controllers and processors. |
| | • The appointment of representatives is compulsory for organisations based outside the EU who are targeting people or personal data within the EU as part of their data processing activities. |
| | • The legislative purpose behind the requirement to appoint representatives is to provide a mechanism for the meaningful enforcement of the law against foreign organisations. |
| Recipients | • These are persons or organisations/bodies to whom personal data are disclosed. |
| | • Although a processor will be a recipient of data, as understood by the natural dictionary definition of the word, they are not recipients for the purposes of the legal meaning. |
| Third parties | • Any other person is referred to as third party. |
| Supervisory authorities | • These are the national data protection regulators. |
| | • Every EU Member State is required to appoint a supervisory authority. |
| | • The UK regulator is the Information Commissioner. |
| Lead supervisory authority | • Where a controller or processor is established in more than one EU Member State and they are involved in cross-border processing, the regulator in the country of their main establishment will be the lead supervisory authority for those cross-border activities. |
| | • This is known as the 'one-stop shop' idea, which is intended to simplify the supervisory system for cross-border processing, by putting one regulator in charge of those activities. |

*(Continued)*

**Table 2.2 (Continued)**

|   |   |
|---|---|
|   | • Cross-border processing covers two situations:<br>1. Where a controller or processor is established in more than one EU Member State, cross-border processing will occur if it concerns the activities of multiple establishments. An example is a shared IT system that is located in one country but is used in multiple countries.<br>2. Where a controller or processor is established in only one EU Member State, cross-border processing will occur if it substantially affects data subjects located in more than one Member State. |
| European Data Protection Board | The EDPB is an EU body that includes representatives of the EU supervisory authorities and the European Data Protection Supervisor. The EDPB's role is to ensure the consistent application of the GDPR. |
| Representatives of data subjects | • These are not-for-profit organisations that are properly constituted in accordance with the national laws in the countries where they operate, that have public interest objectives and that are active in the field of data protection.<br>• These organisations are sometimes called 'civil society organisations' (CSO).<br>• The GDPR gives data subjects the right to mandate CSOs to make complaints to regulators about controllers and processors and to pursue legal actions against them all. As part of their function, they can sue controllers and processors for compensation.<br>• The GDPR allows Member States to empower CSOs to make complaints and take legal action without the data subject's mandate, although this does not extend to enabling them to receive compensation. |
| Courts | The courts are the final arbiters of questions about compliance and remedies. |

## COMPLIANCE FRAMEWORK – THE STANDARDS OF PROTECTION

The standards of protection that need to be achieved for personal data undergoing processing consist of principles-based standards and controls-based standards.

### Data protection principles

The principles of data protection have over 50 years of history in Europe. Developed initially in the late 1960s, they were compiled into Resolutions by the Council of Europe in 1973 and 1974, which were followed by the Organisation for Economic Co-operation and Development (OECD) *Guidelines on the Protection of Privacy and Transborder*

*Flows of Personal Data* in 1980 (amended in 2013), then by the Council of Europe Data Protection Convention in 1981 (modernised in 2018). The European Community (EC) (the predecessor to the EU) legislated for them in 1995,[4] 1997,[5] 2002,[6] 2006[7] and 2009.[8]

The GDPR is just the latest iteration in a long legislative agenda. The principles are set out in Article 5 and they impose these standards for data processing:

- lawfulness, fairness and transparency;
- purpose limitation;
- data minimisation;
- accuracy;
- storage limitation;
- integrity and confidentiality.

**Lawful bases of processing**

The first data protection principle's requirement that the processing of personal data shall be lawful has two ideas within it.

First, processing shall conform to the laws of the land. This means, for example, that if processing is undertaken in furtherance of a crime, it will not be lawful.

Secondly, the processing must be lawful in the sense of it satisfying one of the grounds for lawful processing as set out in the GDPR.

These grounds are contained in Article 6 and Article 9 of the GDPR. The grounds in Article 6 apply to the processing of personal data. The grounds in Article 9 apply to special category data. Table 2.3 summarises the grounds that can be relied upon to render data processing lawful. Note that if special category data are processed, the controller must satisfy both articles. If the processing does not involve special category data, only A.6 will apply.

---

[4] Directive 95/46/EC of the European Parliament and of the Council of 24 October 1995 on the protection of individuals with regard to the processing of personal data and on the free movement of such data ('The Data Protection Directive').

[5] Directive 97/66/EC of the European Parliament and of the Council of 15 December 1997 concerning the processing of personal data and the protection of privacy in the telecommunications sector ('The Telecommunications Data Protection Directive').

[6] Directive 2002/58/EC of the European Parliament and of the Council of 12 July 2002 concerning the processing of personal data and the protection of privacy in the electronic communications sector (Directive on privacy and electronic communications) ('PEC Directive').

[7] Directive 2006/24/EC of the European Parliament and of the Council of 15 March 2006 on the retention of data generated or processed in connection with the provision of publicly available electronic communications services or of public communications networks and amending Directive 2002/58/EC ('Communications Data Retention Directive').

[8] Directive 2009/136/EC of the European Parliament and of the Council of 25 November 2009 amending Directive 2002/22/EC on universal service and users' rights relating to electronic communications networks and services, Directive 2002/58/EC concerning the processing of personal data and the protection of privacy in the electronic communications sector and Regulation (EC) No 2006/2004 on cooperation between national authorities responsible for the enforcement of consumer protection laws ('The Citizens Rights Directive').

**Table 2.3 Lawful bases for processing**

### Article 6 – Lawful bases for processing personal data

The data subject has consented.

The processing is necessary for the creation or performance of a contract with the data subject.

The processing is necessary for compliance with the controller's legal obligations.

The processing is necessary to protect the vital interests of the data subject or another person.

The processing is necessary in the public interest, or for the performance of an official task by the controller.

The processing is necessary for purposes of the legitimate interests of the controller or a third party unless those interests are overridden by the rights and freedoms of the data subject.

### Article 9 – Special category data

The GDPR's starting point is to prohibit (i.e. ban) the processing of special category data. The ban will not apply if one of the following conditions in A.9.2 is satisfied:

- The data subject has provided their explicit consent.
- The processing is necessary for carrying out obligations placed on controllers, or for exercising rights of controllers or data subjects, in the field of employment, social security and social protection law.
- The laws setting out these rights and obligations must include appropriate safeguards for the fundamental rights and interests of data subjects.
- The processing is necessary to protect the vital interests of the data subject or another person, where they are physically or legally incapable of giving consent.
- The processing is for the purposes of the legitimate activities of not-for-profit organisations that pursue political, philosophical, religious or trade union aims.
- The processing must be accompanied by appropriate safeguards; it must relate solely to members, or former members of the body, or to people having regular contact with it for those purposes; and the personal data must not be disclosed to others, without the data subject's consent.
- The processing relates to personal data that have been manifestly made public by the data subject.
- The processing is necessary for reasons of substantial public interests as set out in law, if it is proportionate, respects the essence of the right to data protection and provides suitable and specific measures to safeguard the fundamental rights and interests of the data subject.
- The processing is necessary for preventive or occupational medicine; or for assessing an employee's working capacity; or for medical diagnosis; or for providing health or social care and treatment; or for social care systems and services provided for by law; or pursuant to a contract with a health care professional who is subject to obligations of professional secrecy.

*(Continued)*

## Table 2.3 (Continued)

- The processing is necessary in the public interest in the area of public health (including protecting against serious cross-border health threats or ensuring quality and safety high standards for health care, medicinal products and medical devices) as prescribed by law, which shall provide for suitable measures to safeguard the rights and freedoms of data subjects and professional secrecy.
- The processing is necessary for archiving purposes in the public interest, or for scientific or historical research purposes, or for statistical purposes, as prescribed by law, if it is proportionate, respects the essence of the right to data protection and provides suitable and specific measures to safeguard the fundamental rights and interests of the data subject.

Other points to note about the lawful bases of processing:

- Where special category data are processed, the controller needs to satisfy a ground within both Article 9 and Article 6.
- Article 9 allows Member States to maintain, or introduce, further conditions and limitations for the processing of genetic data, biometric data, or data concerning health.
- Article 10 of the GDPR provides the lawful basis for the processing of criminal offences and conviction data, which is expanded on by the Law Enforcement Directive.

## Necessity

Many of the lawful bases of processing are qualified by a necessity test. The box below sets out the Information Commissioner's position on the meaning of necessity.[9]

### Meaning of necessity – Information Commissioner guidance

Many of the lawful bases for processing depend on the processing being 'necessary'. This does not mean that processing has to be absolutely essential. However, it must be more than just useful, and more than just standard practice. It must be a targeted and proportionate way of achieving a specific purpose. The lawful basis will not apply if you can reasonably achieve the purpose by some other less intrusive means, or by processing less data.

It is not enough to argue that processing is necessary because you have chosen to operate your business in a particular way. The question is whether the processing is objectively necessary for the stated purpose, not whether it is a necessary part of your chosen methods.

---

9  ICO Guide to the General Data Protection Regulation. https://ico.org.uk/for-organisations/guide-to-data-protection/guide-to-the-general-data-protection-regulation-gdpr/lawful-basis-for-processing/#when

## Consent for processing

The rules on consent are amplified by GDPR Articles 7 and 8, with the meaning of consent set out in A.4.11:

> 'consent' of the data subject means any freely given, specific, informed and unambiguous indication of the data subject's wishes by which he or she, by a statement or by a clear affirmative action, signifies agreement to the processing of personal data relating to him or her;

The concept of 'explicit consent' within GDPR Article 9 is not actually defined in the legislation, but it is obvious that it means consent of a higher quality. This is confirmed by the Information Commissioner's guidance on the GDPR,[10] which points to the idea of explicit consent being different to the idea of consent obtained through an affirmative action.

### Information Commissioner's guidance on meaning of explicit consent

Explicit consent is not defined in the UK GDPR, but it is not likely to be very different from the usual high standard of consent. All consent must involve a specific, informed, and unambiguous indication of the individual's wishes. The key difference is likely to be that 'explicit' consent must be affirmed in a clear statement (whether oral or written).

The definition of consent says the data subject can signify agreement either by a statement (which would count as explicit consent) or by a clear affirmative action (which would not). Consent that is inferred from someone's actions cannot be explicit consent, however obvious it might be that they consent. Explicit consent must be expressly confirmed in words.

Individuals do not have to write the consent statement in their own words; you can write it for them. However, you need to make sure that individuals can clearly indicate that they agree to the statement – for example by signing their name or ticking a box next to it.

If you need explicit consent, you should take extra care over the wording. Even in a written context, not all consent will be explicit. You should always use an express statement of consent.

There are many considerations within the idea of consent sprinkled around the GDPR. Table 2.4 brings them together in one place, to show what the essential elements are and what they require.

---

[10] https://ico.org.uk/for-organisations/guide-to-data-protection/guide-to-the-general-data-protection-regulation-gdpr/consent/what-is-valid-consent/#what5

**Table 2.4 Conditions and quality of consent**

| | |
|---|---|
| Definition, A.4.11 | • Consent must be freely given, specific, informed, and unambiguous.<br>• It needs to provide an indication of the data subject's wishes.<br>• Those wishes need to be contained in a statement from the data subject, or a clear affirmative action.<br>• The statement or action should signify the data subject's agreement to the processing of personal data relating to them. |
| Informed consent | R.42 says that for consent to be informed, the data subject should be aware of at least the identity of the controller and the intended processing purpose. |
| Proof of consent, A.7.1 | The controller carries the burden of proving that the data subject has consented. This rule forms part of the accountability rule. Note also that R.32 says:<br>• That due to consent requiring a statement from the data subject or clear affirmative action, silence, pre-ticked boxes, and inactivity do not constitute consent.<br>• If consent is requested by electronic means, the request must be clear, concise, and not unnecessarily disruptive to the provision of the service for which it is provided.<br>• Consent should cover all processing activities of the same purpose.<br>• If there are multiple processing purposes, consent is required for each of them. |
| Written declarations that concern other matters, A.7.2 | If the data subject's consent is given in the context of a written declaration that concerns other matters (e.g. within website terms of use):<br>• The request for consent should be presented in a manner that is clearly distinguishable from other matters.<br>• It shall be in an intelligible and easily accessible form.<br>• It shall use clear and plain language.<br><br>Any part of a written declaration that infringes these rules is invalid. |
| Withdrawal of consent, A.7.3 | • The data subject has the right to withdraw consent at any time.<br>• The withdrawal of consent does not affect the validity of processing up to that point.<br>• Before giving consent, the data subject shall be informed of their right of withdrawal.<br>• It shall be as easy to withdraw consent as it was to give consent. |

*(Continued)*

### Table 2.4 (Continued)

| | |
|---|---|
| Freely given consent, A.7.4 | • Controllers must take utmost account of whether consent is freely given. |
| | • Among other things they must take utmost account of whether the performance of a contract (including a service contract) is conditional on the provision of consent for data processing activities that are not necessary for the performance of the contract. R.43 says that there is a presumption that consent is not freely given in such circumstances. |
| | • R.43 also says that it is presumed that consent is not freely given if it does not allow separate consent to be given for different processing operations when that is otherwise appropriate. |
| | • R.43 also says that consent will not provide a valid basis for processing if there is a clear imbalance of power between the controller and data subject. This can arise where the controller is a public authority. |
| Parental consent, A.8 | The provision of 'information society services' (i.e. online services) to children requires parental consent. |

### *Parental consent*

Article 8 says that where the use of 'information society services' by children is consent-based, parental consent for children aged 16 and under is required, although the GDPR permits Member States to lower the age for parental consent to 13 (the UK has chosen to remain with the 16-year threshold). Information society services are online services, such as social media, and it does not matter whether these services are free or paid for.

Parental consent can only be given, or authorised, by the holder of parental responsibility for the child and when obtaining parental consent, the controller needs to make reasonable efforts to verify that it is provided by the holder of parental responsibility.

### *Cookie consent*

The Privacy and Electronic Communications framework (as represented by PEC and PECR) makes the use of cookies and similar technologies conditional on the giving of consent by the person whose equipment will be affected. This is sometimes called the 'Cookie Consent' rule, but what it is actually concerned with is the issue of confidentiality, due to the fact that cookies and similar technology can be stored on a person's devices, such as PCs, smartphones and the like (which the law calls 'terminal equipment'), or used to gain access to information stored within them. The way these technologies work means that the confidential nature of these devices is interfered with, hence why consent is needed. The quality of consent that is required for the use of cookies and so on is the GDPR's.

As with most aspects of data protection, there are exceptions to the rule. Cookies can be used without consent, where their use is strictly necessary to provide a service, or where the sole purpose of their use is enabling the transmission of a communication over an electronic communications network.

## COMPLIANCE FRAMEWORK – CONTROLS

When organisations are looking to put in place measures to achieve predefined outcomes, they often talk about implementing 'controls'. Controls can take a variety of forms, such as for governance, through the setting of roles and responsibilities; for the setting of rules, such as through policies and procedures; for managing relationships with third parties, such as through contracts; and through applying treatments to data themselves, such as encryption, anonymisation and pseudonymisation.

### Appropriate technical and organisational measures

The control standard is the taking of 'appropriate technical and organisational measures' for data protection (ATOM). These requirements are illustrated in Table 2.5.

**Table 2.5 Controls requirements (examples)**

| | |
|---|---|
| Storage limitation | • The storage limitation principle says that personal data should not be stored in a form that permits identification of data subjects for longer than is necessary to deliver on the processing purpose for which they were collected. This will need the controller/processor to adopt rules about what needs to happen to data when the processing purpose has been fulfilled. These rules will constitute organisational controls. |
| | • When the processing purpose has been achieved, the personal data should be destroyed or deleted, or rendered anonymous. This will require the implementational of both technical and organisational controls, which will include the use of technology that can apply the required treatments to the data. |
| | • However, as an exception to this rule, the GDPR permits personal data to be stored in an identifiable fashion for various public interest, research and statistical purposes. In that situation appropriate technical and organisational measures must be implemented to safeguard the rights and freedom of data subjects. Again, this will require a combination of technological and organisational controls, including a methodology for assessing when the public interest, research and statistical needs have crystallised and what is needed to satisfy them. |
| Integrity and confidentiality | • The integrity and confidentiality principle requires technical and organisational measures to be implemented to ensure an appropriate level of security for personal data. |
| | • The control framework that is developed for security will require many technology controls to be implemented, to protect systems and data from unauthorised and unlawful use. These technologies will include identity and access management; firewalls and perimeter protection; intrusion detection; anti-virus and malware protection; encryption; and backups. |

*(Continued)*

## Table 2.5 (Continued)

| | |
|---|---|
| Use of processors | • When engaging a data processor, the controller should ensure that the processor provides sufficient guarantees about implementing appropriate technical and organisational measures. |
| | • The controls that are adopted will need to deliver appropriate due diligence on the processor, such as through inspection of the processor's policies and procedures; review of their certifications and attestations; and conducting audits and penetration testing. If the processor satisfies the due diligence, the relationship with it will need to be governed by a contract, which should provide for ongoing due diligence and assurance over its lifetime. |

## Appropriate safeguards

The GDPR also sets requirements for the implementation of 'appropriate safeguards'. Examples of where this is found within the legislation include the following:

- A.9.2.b says that legal requirements for appropriate safeguards for the fundamental rights and the interests of the data subject need to be set by EU Member States when they adopt laws enabling special category data to be processed in an employment, social security and social protection context.
- A.9.2.d says that appropriate safeguards need to be implemented when special category data are processed by not-for-profit organisations.
- A.10 says that legal requirements for appropriate safeguards for the rights and freedoms of data subjects need to be set by EU Member States when they adopt laws permitting the processing of criminal convictions and offences data.

## Prescribed controls

Other examples of the prescribed controls within the GDPR include the following:

- Controllers are required to achieve Data Protection by Design and Default (DPbDD). This is often referred to as 'Privacy by Design' (or PbD). See Article 24.
- In some situations, controller and processors are required to appoint EU Representatives. See Article 27.
- Except in limited situations (which apply to organisations employing fewer than 250 persons), controllers and their representatives are required to create records of data processing. See Article 30.
- In some situations, controllers are required to notify personal data breaches to regulators and the people affected. See Articles 33 and 34.
- In some situations, controllers are required to perform data protection impact assessments (DPIA), then refer them to their regulators. See Articles 35 and 36.
- In some situations, controllers and processors are required to appoint data protection officers (DPOs). See Article 37.

## Anonymisation and pseudonymisation

Anonymisation is a process that renders data irretrievably de-identified, so that it is no longer personal data. If data are anonymised, this has a deregulatory effect, in the sense that it takes the information beyond the material scope of the GDPR (see Recital 26).

Pseudonymisation is different. Defined in A.4.5, it is a process that masks or obfuscates identifiers so they can no longer be attributed to a specific person without the use of additional data or techniques. To fall within the definition of pseudonymisation, the additional data that enable reidentification need to be kept separate from the pseudonymised data. The pseudonymised data should also be protected with controls that ensure that they are not attributed to an identified or identifiable person.

While it does not have deregulatory effect, pseudonymisation can substantially reduce risks to rights and freedoms. Thus, the GDPR promotes it as a control, in the sense that the legislation points to and actively promotes its use. For example, the use of pseudonymisation is a consideration within an assessment of whether it is lawful to use personal data for purposes other than that for which they were collected (see A.6.4.d). It is also treated as a measure for achieving data minimisation, as part of the rules on Data Protection by Design and Default (see A.25.1) and as a security control (see A.32.1.a).

## Accountability

The concept of accountability forms part of the data protection principles. It requires controllers to be able to demonstrate their compliance with the principles (see A.5.2). The practical implication of the accountability rule is that controllers need to be able to produce evidence proving that they have met the required standards of data protection, when required to do so by their regulators, or by data subjects during the exercise of their rights and powers, or by the courts.

The accountability principle is considered to be one of the GDPR's main innovations, as it was not written into its predecessor, the 1995 Data Protection Directive. The extent of its innovative effect is debatable, because as a matter of law it has always been the controller's duty to comply with the law, which by necessity has always involved the controller being able to demonstrate compliance, but, on the other hand, the inclusion of an express duty of accountability leaves controllers with no room for doubt about the extent of their duty.

## Assessing appropriateness of controls

Controllers and processors need to be confident that the controls they have adopted are appropriate. Key requirements within these assessments are set out in A.24 and 25. They require controllers and processors to understand and evaluate:

- the overall nature, scope, context and purposes of processing;
- the likelihood and severity of the risks to rights and freedoms;
- the state of the art as it pertains to controls for risk management;
- the cost of implementing controls.

## CRITICAL OUTCOMES TO BE ACHIEVED

The standards and controls of data protection are there to support the achievement of various critical outcomes by controllers and processors. Pivotal within them are:

- transparency;
- lawful processing;
- control over processing activities.

### Transparency

The idea of transparency provides a golden thread of protection that applies at the point that data processing starts and continues all the way through the processing life cycle, that is, to the end of data processing, when data are deleted, destroyed, or rendered anonymous. The duty of transparency also applies during operational failure, when a personal data breach is suffered.

The combined effect of the transparency rules is to shine an intense spotlight on the nature and quality of data processing operations. The rules are intended to help data subjects to make better decisions and informed choices about data processing risks and to help them and the regulators to take steps to reduce the risk of harms, including through further investigative procedures and legal action. Through their design, they narrow the opportunities for controllers to engage in harmful and abusive practices.

#### *Collection transparency (GDPR A.13 and 14)*
At the time of collection of personal data from a data subject, the controller must provide them with various pieces of transparency information, including:

- the controller's identity (i.e. the controller's identity cannot be concealed);
- the controller's contact details;
- identification of the processing purpose;
- identification of any recipients of the data;
- information about international transfers of data;
- information about the period of storage of the data;
- information about the data subject rights, such as the right of access;
- if the processing is based on consent, information about the data subject's right to withdraw consent;
- information about the data subject's right to lodge a complaint with the regulator;
- if the processing is necessary for performance of a contract or under statute, a statement to this effect;
- information about automated decision making, if that is happening;
- other information that is required to make the processing fair.

This information is usually provided within a 'privacy notice' (often referred to as a 'privacy policy'), which are often found on websites.

Similar rules apply to situations where the controller obtains information from a third party, rather than from the data subject. In those situations, the controller must provide the data subject with the transparency information after the information has been collected and within specified timeframes.

### Rights transparency (A.15 etc.)
Data subjects enjoy various rights that they can exercise against data controllers. Some of these rights form part of the GDPR's transparency framework, with the main example being the right of access to information (i.e. DSARs, or SARs as they are sometimes called). Much of the information that the data subject is entitled to under the right of access overlaps with the information they are entitled to under the rules on collection transparency.

Other rights that contain transparency requirements are:

- The right to restriction of processing entitles the data subject to be told if a restriction has been lifted. See A.18.3.
- The controller needs to tell the data subject of their right to object to direct marketing, which needs to be included in the first direct marketing message. See A.21.4.

### Breach transparency (A.33 and 34)
If a controller suffers a personal data breach that involves a risk to the rights and freedoms of individuals, they must notify their regulator of the breach without undue delay, which is subject to a 72-hour longstop (if feasible), commencing from the point of knowledge that a personal data breach has occurred (although controllers are allowed a reasonable period of time after detection of a suspected personal data breach to carry out investigations before the time period for reporting begins). If the breach is likely to result in a high risk to those rights and freedoms, they also must inform the affected data subjects, again without undue delay.

### Accountability and regulatory cooperation
The accountability rule is complemented by a rule on regulatory cooperation in A.31, which requires controllers, processors and their representatives to cooperate with their regulators during the performance of their tasks. In the UK, these rules are supplemented by the Information Commissioner's Information Notice and Assessment Notice powers within the Data Protection Act, which the regulator can use to obtain information and other evidence about data processing from persons and organisations under investigation.

## Clarity of the lawful basis of processing

Controllers need to have absolute clarity of the lawful basis that they rely upon to justify processing, because the lawful basis has a direct impact on the nature of the controller's compliance duties and what they need to operationalise for compliance. Some of these impacts are set out in Table 2.6.

### Table 2.6 How the lawful basis of processing has operational impacts (examples)

| | |
|---|---|
| Accountability | • The accountability rule requires the controller to be able to identify their choice of lawful basis and, if need be, justify their selections. |
| | • By implication, this means that controllers will need to document their positions and their thinking on their choice of legal basis. |
| Transparency | The lawful basis needs to be explained in the transparency information that must be provided to data subjects at the point of collection of their data, or shortly afterwards. |
| Rights | The application of some of the data subject rights is conditional on the lawful basis of proceeding that applies. See the right to erasure, for example (A.17.1.b). |
| Assessments | • The need to perform a legitimate interests assessment (LIA) is conditional on the controller relying upon the legitimate interest grounds for processing. |
| | • See also the rules on data protection impact assessments. |

## Control

When the GDPR was going through the EU legislative process from 2012 to 2016, one of the stated objectives of the European Commission was to give people more control over their data.

Control works in a variety of ways, including through the transparency mechanisms discussed above. Other elements are shown in Table 2.7.

### Table 2.7 Why 'control' is a GDPR priority

| | |
|---|---|
| Data controller | • The main target of regulation is the data controller. This nomenclature shows the significance of the concept of control within data protection. |
| Controls framework | • The controls framework within the GDPR places the idea of control at the heart of the rules that apply to data processing in supply chains and globalisation. |
| | • For example, the rules on the appointment of processors seek to extend the controller's control over data that are disclosed, using contracts, audits and other techniques. |
| | • The rules on international transfers seek to achieve the same outcomes, through the binding corporate rules and standard contractual clauses mechanisms. |
| Personal data breaches | • A loss of control over data, caused by a personal data breach, is the operative event that requires controllers to notify these incidents to their regulators and the people affected. |

*(Continued)*

**Table 2.7 (Continued)**

| | |
|---|---|
| Data sharing | • Section 121 of the UK Data Protection Act requires the Information Commissioner to publish a code of practice on data sharing. |
| | • In a data sharing situation, control over data is passed from one actor to another and the presence of a statutory obligation for a code of practice helps to illustrate the significance that Parliament attaches to the issue of control. |

The focus on control also helps to illustrate perhaps the most significant design feature of data protection law, which is that the GDPR is not focused on matters of data ownership. By focusing on control rather than ownership, the law transcends property rights issues, thereby maximising the law's scope and potential. This also preserves the data subject's interest in their data, from which they are not alienated, which would happen in an ownership-based regime.

## COMPENSATORY MECHANISMS TO REMEDY NON-COMPLIANCE

The GDPR contains a series of mechanisms that are intended to compensate for weak data protection by controllers and processors. The personal data breach notification rules, which operate to require transparency in breach situations that present risks to rights and freedoms, compensate for the controller's, or processor's, failure to prevent security breaches by giving regulators and people affected the opportunity to take steps to mitigate harms. The accountability and regulatory cooperation rules operate in the same way.

### Regulator's enforcement powers

In addition, the GDPR empowers the regulators to reshape data processing activities, using enforcement powers and through the deterrent effect of fines. Table 2.8 summarises the enforcement powers of the Information Commissioner.

**Table 2.8 Regulatory enforcement powers within the UK DPA**

| | |
|---|---|
| Information Notices (s.142) | • This power enables the Information Commissioner to request information from a controller or processor that is reasonably required to enable the Commissioner to carry out their functions. |
| | • The information obtained through these notices can be used to support the taking of corrective action or the imposition of penalties. |
| Assessment Notices (s.146) | • This power enables the Commissioner to enter premises and inspect information, documents and equipment. |
| | • This is usually done by way of audit. |
| | • The insights that are obtained through these notices can also be used to support the taking of corrective action or the imposition of penalties. |

*(Continued)*

## Table 2.8 (Continued)

| | |
|---|---|
| Enforcement Notices (s.149) | • This power enables the Commissioner to order controllers and processors (and other persons) to take corrective action to remedy non-compliance, either by ordering the recipient of the notice to take steps or to refrain from taking steps. |
| Penalty Notices (s.155) | • The Commissioner can impose fines of up to 4% of the annual worldwide turnover of an undertaking, or £17.5m, for breaches of the GDPR or for failure to comply with one of the above notices. |

### Data subjects' enforcement powers

Data subjects can seek to enforce the law through the courts and in appropriate cases the courts can award them compensation, to be paid by the controller, for material and non-material damage they have suffered. Material damage includes financial loss, while non-material damage includes distress. The *Vidal-Hall* (2015) case, brought under the UK Data Protection Act 1998 (which has been repealed and replaced by the 2018 Act), established that compensation for distress caused by breaches of data protection is compensatable, without requiring any additional material damages to be suffered. The UK Supreme Court heard an appeal against this judgment in April 2021.

Data subjects can also enforce their rights by making complaints to the regulators.

It is common now for data subjects to use their enforcement powers in combination and sometimes concurrently, for example, by making a data subject access request to obtain information from a controller, then after the reply has been received, referring the matter to the Information Commissioner – sometimes alongside engaging lawyers to progress a claim for compensation. Employment disputes are commonly prefaced with a DSAR by the employee, or lawyers acting on their behalf, to obtain copies of relevant personal data that can be used as evidence in the dispute.

The claims management industry, which includes claims management companies, claimant law firms and litigation funders, proactively seeks out data subjects and encourages them to use their rights as part of a compensation claim process. Following large-scale personal data breaches, members of the claims management industry will set up websites, social media groups and pursue internet, radio and TV advertising campaigns to encourage data subjects to come forward for the purposes of bringing claims.

## WHERE THE GDPR DOES NOT APPLY – EXCEPTIONS AND RESTRICTIONS

The GDPR does not apply to all situations of personal data processing. Some areas automatically fall outside the scope of the law. In other situations, the EU and Member States can adopt restrictions, which will limit the application of the law. These areas are summarised in Table 2.9.

**Table 2.9 Critical situations where the GDPR does not apply**

| | |
|---|---|
| Personal or household processing | • The law does not apply to processing that is conducted during a purely personal or household activity.<br>• The use of dashcams on public highways and home CCTV cameras that make video recordings of members of the public do not fall within this exemption.[11] |
| Foreign and security policy | • The GDPR does not apply to matters that fall within the EU's Common Foreign and Security Policy.<br>• The UK GDPR removes this language and by virtue of Part 4 of the Data Protection Act 2018, the law applies to the UK intelligence services, in a modified form. |
| Policing and law enforcement | • This is covered by the Law Enforcement Directive.<br>• The LED has been implemented in the UK by Part 3 of the Data Protection Act. |
| Restrictions that are necessary and proportionate in a democratic society | • A.23 enables the EU and Member States to restrict the requirements of A.5 (the data protection principles), A.12–22 (transparency and data subject rights) and A.34 (communication of personal data breaches) in a variety of public interest situations, where that is necessary and proportionate in a democratic situation. These situations include:<br>• National security.<br>• Defence.<br>• Public security.<br>• Law enforcement and preventing threats to public security.<br>• Important objectives of general public interest, for example, the economy and public finance.<br>• Judicial independence and judicial proceedings.<br>• Performance of regulatory functions and official functions.<br>• Protecting the data subject and the rights and freedoms of others.<br>• Enforcement of civil law claims. |
| Restrictions for freedom of expression | • A.85 requires Member States to adopt restrictions for freedom of expression purposes, covering journalistic, academic, artistic and literary purposes.<br>• The scope of the required restrictions is broad, covering virtually all areas of the GDPR. |

*(Continued)*

---

11 See EDPB Guidelines 3/2019 on processing of personal data through video devices.

## Table 2.9 (Continued)

| | |
|---|---|
| Restrictions for archiving, research and statistical purposes | • A.89 also allows the EU and Member States to adopt various restrictions from the data subject rights, where processing is performed for scientific or historical research purposes, or for statistical purposes, or for archiving purposes in the public interest. |

### Domestic processing

The exemption for personal and household processing does not capture everything that a person may do for personal reasons or in their home. Given the use of social networking sites and communications platforms for user-generated content, it is easy to publish information about family, friends and colleagues and be caught by the GDPR.

Recital 18 provides a non-exhaustive list of purely personal or household activities that are within the scope of this exemption. Examples include personal correspondence, the holding of addresses (e.g. an address book) and 'social networking and online activity undertaken within the context of such personal or household activity'. The recital reflects the European Court of Justice's decision in the *Lindqvist* (2003)[12] case, where it was held that the act of identifying a natural person on an internet site by name, or other personal identifiers, constituted 'processing' of personal data within the meaning of the Data Protection Directive 1995. In that case Mrs Lindqvist posted information about fellow members of her church, which fell outside the scope of the domestic purposes exemption.

Another case is the CJEU decision in *Tietosuojavaltuutettu* (2018),[13] where the CJEU held that Jehovah's Witness members, when visiting households and collecting individuals' details as part of their door-to-door activities, are data controllers with their activities falling outside the domestic purposes exemption. The reasoning for this decision was:

- It is the supposed controller's activity that needs to be personal or domestic.
- It cannot be domestic or purely personal purposes if the data are made available to an unrestricted class of people.
- Attending non-Jehovah's Witnesses' doors is activity that is directed outwards from the personal space of the members themselves and they are therefore data controllers.

### Restrictions and the UK DPA

As illustrated in Table 2.9, Member States can adopt various restrictions under GDPR A.23, 85 and 89. In the UK these restrictions are contained in the 2018 Act. The legislative language and structure of the exemptions is sometimes very complex and the relationship of the restrictions to the GDPR can be hard to understand. Table 2.10 summarises those restrictions and relationships.

---

[12] Case C-101-01 (2003) 1.

[13] Case C-25/17.

## Table 2.10 Exemptions in the Data Protection Act 2018, cross-referenced to the GDPR

**Schedule 2, Part 1 – Crime, immigration and legal proceedings**

| GDPR articles affected: | Root of exemptions: |
|---|---|
| A.5 (data protection principles) | A.6(3) |
| A.13–21 (transparency and rights) | A.23(1) |

Topics covered by the exemptions:

- Crime and taxation
- Immigration control
- Legal proceedings

**Schedule 2, Part 2 – Protecting the public and public functions**

GDPR articles affected:  Root of exemptions:

- A.13–21 (transparency and rights)   A.23(1)
- A.34 (personal data breach communications)

Topics covered by exemptions:

Functions designed to protect the public, covering topics such as:

- Malpractice in financial services
- Bankruptcy
- Charities
- Health and safety at work
- Maladminstration in public services
- Competition in the markets
- Government audit
- Bank of England
- Regulation of legal services, health services and children protection
- Regulators such as ICO, Pensions Ombudsman, Consumer Protection enforcers
- Parliamentary privilege
- Judiciary
- Crown honours, dignities and appointments

**Schedule 2, Part 3 – Protecting the rights of others**

GDPR articles affected:  Root of exemptions:

- A.15 (right of access)
- A.23(1)

Topics covered by exemptions:

- Third-party information
- Health, social and education work

**Schedule 2, Part 4 – The right of access to information (transparency and DSARs)**

GDPR articles affected:  Root of exemptions:

- A.13–15 (transparency and right of access)
- A.23(1)

*(Continued)*

**Table 2.10 (Continued)**

Topics covered by exemptions:

| | |
|---|---|
| • Legal professional privilege | • Negotiations |
| • Self incrimination | • Confidential references |
| • Corporate finance | • Exam scripts and marks |
| • Management forecasts | |

Schedule 2, Part 5 – The special purposes

| GDPR articles affected: | Root of exemptions: |
|---|---|
| A.5 (data protection principles) | A.85(2) |
| A.6 (lawful basis of processing) | |
| A.13–21 (transparency and rights) | |
| A.34 (personal data breach communications) | |
| A.36 (DPIAs) | |
| A.44 (international transfers) | |

Topics covered by exemptions:

- Journalistic, academic, artistic and literary purposes (known as 'the special purposes')

Schedule 2, Part 6 – Research, statistics and archiving

| GDPR articles affected: | Root of exemptions: |
|---|---|
| A.15 (right of access) | A.89 |
| A.16 (right to rectification) | |
| A.18 (right of restriction) | |
| A.20 (right to portability) | |
| A.21 (right to object) | |

Topics covered by exemptions:

| | |
|---|---|
| • Research and statistics | • Archiving in the public interest |

Schedule 3, Part 2 – Health data

| GDPR articles affected: | Root of exemptions: |
|---|---|
| A.5 (data protection principles) | A.23 |
| A.13–21 (transparency and rights, except A.19) | |

Topics covered by exemptions:

Health data including where:

| | |
|---|---|
| • Processed by courts | • Data could cause serious harm |
| • Related to data subject's expectations and wishes | • Prior opinion of health professional |

*(Continued)*

## Table 2.10 (Continued)

| | |
|---|---|
| **Schedule 3, Part 3 – Social work data** | |
| GDPR articles affected: | Root of exemptions: |
| A.5 (data protection principles) | A.23 |
| A.13–21 (transparency and rights, except A.19) | |
| Topics covered by exemptions: | |
| • Social work | • Child protection |
| • Social services | • Court proceedings related to above |
| **Schedule 3, Part 4 – Educational records** | |
| GDPR articles affected: | Root of exemptions: |
| A.5 (data protection principles) | A.23 |
| A.13–21 (transparency and rights, except A.19) | |
| Topics covered by exemptions: | |
| • Educational records processed by schools and academies | • Educational records processed by local authorities and educational authorities |
| **Schedule 3, Part 5 – Child abuse data** | |
| GDPR articles affected: | Root of exemptions: |
| A.15 (right of access) | A.23 |
| Topics covered by exemptions: | |
| • Access requests for child abuse data held by a legally authorised body, where the request is made by a person with parental authority or someone with a power of attorney | |
| **Schedule 4 – Disclosures prohibited by law** | |
| GDPR articles affected: | Root of exemptions: |
| A.5 (data protection principles) | A.23 |
| A.15 (right of access) | |
| Topics covered by exemptions: | |
| • Human fertilisation and embryology | • Statements of educational needs |
| • Adoption records and report | • Parental order records and reports |
| | • Court hearings relating to children |

## BREXIT – THE UK, FROZEN AND EU GDPR

The UK left the EU on 31 January 2020, after which the country entered the 'Implementation Period'. The Implementation Period expired at 11 p.m. on 31 December 2021 (this is known as IP Day). During the Implementation Period the GDPR remained in force in the UK, through provisions within the European Union (Withdrawal) Act 2018 ('Withdrawal Act').

## UK GDPR

On IP Day the Data Protection, Privacy and Electronic Communications (Amendments etc.) (EU Exit) Regulations 2020 came into effect (known as the DP Exit Regulations). The DP Exit Regulations created the 'UK GDPR'. The UK GDPR consists of the original version of the GDPR adopted in 2016 (i.e. the 'EU GDPR'), merged with the 'Applied GDPR',[14] plus amendments to remove otiose language, such as references to 'Member States'. The DP Exit Regulations also made necessary amendments to the PEC Regulations and the Data Protection Act 2018 to ensure continuity of the law.

## Frozen GDPR

Article 71 of the Withdrawal Agreement[15] (which is implemented in UK law by the Withdrawal Act) continued to apply the EU GDPR to processing by UK-based controllers and processors of personal data during the Implementation Period.

At the end of the Implementation Period the EU GDPR was preserved, or frozen in place, as the governing law for processing by UK-based controllers and processors of personal data relating to people living outside the UK that were collected before the end of the Implementation Period. That preserved version of the GDPR is now referred to as the 'Frozen GDPR'.

Data collected after 1 January 2021 are regulated by the UK GDPR, regardless of where the data subject is resident. Table 2.11 shows how the GDPR has been modified because of Brexit.

**Table 2.11 How the three types of GDPR apply in the UK**

| | |
|---|---|
| Pre-Brexit | Before 31 January 2020<br>• Brexit happened on 31 January 2020 ('Exit Day').<br>• Personal data processed by UK-based controllers and processors up to the point of Exit Day were regulated by the 2016 version of the GDPR (i.e. the EU GDPR) |
| During the Implementation Period | Between 31 January and 31 December 2020<br>• Brexit was followed immediately by the Implementation Period.<br>• During the Implementation Period, the processing of personal data by UK-based controllers and processors continued to be governed by the EU GDPR. |

*(Continued)*

---

[14] As shown in Table 2.9, the GDPR does not apply to matters covered by foreign and security policy. Section 21 of the UK DPA applied the GDPR to this area and also to unstructured files held by public authorities that are subject to the Freedom of Information Act 2000.

[15] Agreement on the withdrawal of the United Kingdom of Great Britain and Northern Ireland from the European Union and the European Atomic Energy Community (2019/C 384 I/01).

**Table 2.11 (Continued)**

|  |  |
|---|---|
|  | • At the end of the Implementation Period the EU GDPR was preserved, or frozen in place, for the processing of personal data relating to non-UK residents by UK-based controllers and processors that was collected before the expiry of the Implementation Period. |
|  | • Processing of those legacy data are therefore still governed by the Frozen GDPR. |
|  | • If the EU subsequently changes its version of the GDPR, that will not impact the application of the Frozen GDPR to those legacy data. |
| At the end of the Implementation Period | From 11 p.m. on 31 December 2020<br>• The processing of personal data collected by UK-based controllers and processors after the end of the transition period is governed by the UK GDPR.<br>• This applies to personal data relating to people living in the UK and people outside the UK. |

## Brexit – international transfers of data

During the Implementation Period the UK was treated as if it was still a member of the EU for the purposes of international data transfers. That meant that UK-based controllers and processors did not need to rely upon standard contractual clauses, binding corporate rules (BCR), or any of the derogations that overcome the ban on data flows from the EU to non-adequate third countries to keep data flowing.

After the end of the Implementation Period and as part of the trade deal, UK-based controllers and processors benefitted from an additional grace period of four months, known as 'the Bridge', which was extended by two months, and was put in place to allow data transfers between the UK and EU to continue uninterrupted while the adequacy decision process continued. The Bridge period was due to end on 30 June 2021, but on 28 June the European Commission adopted two adequacy decisions in respect of the UK: one for the GDPR and the other for the LED. Personal data can now flow unencumbered from the EU/EEA to the UK under these decisions, which are both subject to four-year sunset clauses.

### *Adequacy decisions – transfers of data from the UK to the EU and elsewhere*
The UK GDPR operates in the same way as the EU GDPR concerning international transfers of data to third countries. Regarding transfers from the UK to the EU, the government is treating the EU as adequate, so data can flow uninterrupted.

Regarding transfers to other countries, the government recognises the EU standard contractual clauses and the adequacy decisions made by the EU so far, so they can still be used and relied upon by UK-based controllers and processors intending to transfer data from the UK to countries outside Europe. The BCR regime does not currently benefit from a mutual recognition process, however, but BCRs approved before the end of the Implementation Period can be confirmed in the UK.

The UK also has the power to make its own adequacy regulations.

## SUMMARY

In conclusion, this chapter gives readers a better understanding of:

- the geographical scope of the GDPR and core activities that it regulates, namely the processing of personal data wholly or partly by automated means and personal data that form part of non-automated filing systems;
- the main building blocks of the GDPR and the compliance objectives that it requires controllers and processors to achieve;
- the requirement for data processing to be conducted in accordance with the GDPR's principles of data protection, which includes requirements for transparency and a clear lawful basis;
- the nature of the 'controls' framework required by the GDPR, which requires appropriate technical and organisational measures to be adopted and for controllers to be accountable for them;
- the mechanisms that can be used to enforce the GDPR and remediate non-compliance and any harms that result;
- the situations where the GDPR will not apply, due to exceptions and restrictions;
- the impacts of Brexit and how the UK's version of the GDPR relates to the EU's.

# 3 INTRODUCTION TO EPRIVACY

## Stewart Room, Niall O'Brien and Adam Panagiotopoulos

This chapter explores the key components of the legal framework for privacy and electronic communications, which is contained in the EU Privacy and Electronic Communications Directive 2002 (as amended)[1] and its UK equivalent, the Privacy and Electronic Communications Regulations 2003 (as amended). This area of the law is commonly referred to as 'ePrivacy'.

### REGULATING THE ELECTRONIC COMMUNICATIONS SECTOR

The legal framework for ePrivacy sits alongside the data protection regime and provides for privacy rights in relation to electronic communications. This regulatory framework also includes rules about the confidentiality and security of communications, marketing messages, and the tracking and monitoring of users and subscribers of public electronic communications services. In light of the advancement of technologies, the aim of this framework was also to introduce 'technology-neutral' provisions so that individuals are provided with the same level of protection regardless of the technology used.

Due to its focus on safeguarding the confidentiality and security of private information in the electronic communications sector, it also plays a crucial role in keeping personal data protected, safe and secure, where personal data are processed. In particular, this legal framework underpins the provision of telecommunications and internet services, over the top of which sits the World Wide Web, the Internet of Things, the cloud and the app ecosystem that we use through our smartphones and similar devices.[2]

---

1 Directive 2002/58/EC of the European Parliament and of the Council of 12 July 2002 concerning the processing of personal data and the protection of privacy in the electronic communications sector, as amended by Directive 2009/136/EC of the European Parliament and of the Council of 25 November 2009.

2 See, for example, EDPB, Guidelines 1/2020 on processing personal data in the context of connected vehicles and mobility related applications, adopted on 28 January 2020 and EDPB, Guidelines 04/2020 on the use of location data and contact tracing tools in the context of the COVID-19 outbreak, adopted on 21 April 2020.

> **Article 1(1) PEC**
>
> Scope and aim of ePrivacy
>
> This Directive harmonises the provisions of the Member States required *to ensure an equivalent level of protection of fundamental rights and freedoms, and in particular the right to privacy*, with respect to the processing of personal data in the electronic communication sector and *to ensure the free movement of such data and of electronic communication equipment and services in the Community* (emphasis added).

## THE RELATIONSHIP BETWEEN DATA PROTECTION AND EPRIVACY

As explained in Chapter 1, there is a clear overlap between data protection and privacy. The same applies to ePrivacy (see the box above), which can be considered as a subset of privacy rules and rights in the digital economy, covered under Article 7 of the Charter of Fundamental Rights of the European Union. Indeed, ePrivacy applies regardless of whether personal data, as defined under data protection law, is processed. In addition, ePrivacy also protects the rights of legal persons as opposed to the main focus of data protection law, which is intended to protect natural persons ('data subjects').

Where both data protection and ePrivacy regimes apply simultaneously, this relationship is regulated under Article 95 GDPR. Article 95 explains that where PEC deals with a matter covered by the GDPR, PEC shall apply and take precedence over the more general provisions of the GDPR. This does not exclude the simultaneous application of both frameworks. Indeed, the CJEU has confirmed that processing can fall within both regimes at the same time. In the *Wirtschaftsakademie* (2018)[3] case, the CJEU applied the Data Protection Directive 1995, notwithstanding that the underlying processing operations fell within the material scope of PEC. The *Fashion ID* (2019)[4] case is another example of this point, concerning social media plug-ins and cookies. See also the *Digital Rights Ireland* (2014)[5] and *Tele2* (2016)[6] cases.

Although recitals are not legally binding, Recital 173 GDPR is useful in delineating the relationship of these two frameworks and drawing the line between the application scope of ePrivacy and data protection law.

---

3   CJEU, C-210/16, 5 June 2018, C-210/16, ECLI:EU:C:2018:388.

4   *Fashion ID GmbH & Co.KG v. Verbraucherzentrale NRW eV* (2019) C-40/17.

5   *Digital Rights Ireland Ltd v. Minister for Communications, Marine and Natural Resources* and *Kärntner Landesregierung, Seitlinger and Others*, Joined Cases C-293/12 and C-594/12, 8 April 2014.

6   *Tele2 Sverige AB v. Post-och telestyrelsen* and *Secretary of State for the Home Department v. Tom Watson and Others*, Joined Cases C-203/15 and C-698/15, 21 December 2016.

> **Recital 173 GDPR**
>
> This Regulation should apply to all matters concerning the protection of fundamental rights and freedoms vis-à-vis the processing of personal data which are not subject to specific obligations with the same objective set out in Directive 2002/58/EC of the European Parliament and of the Council (18), including the obligations on the controller and the rights of natural persons.
>
> In order to clarify the relationship between this Regulation and Directive 2002/58/EC, that Directive should be amended accordingly.
>
> Once this Regulation is adopted, Directive 2002/58/EC should be reviewed in particular in order to ensure consistency with this Regulation.

Indeed, Article 95 and Recital 173 GDPR are critical in ensuring legal clarity, otherwise the responsible parties would be burdened with additional obligations for the same objective under PEC and GDPR (see the section below on data breaches). Article 95 should be read together with Article 1(2) PEC, which states that PEC particularises and complements the data protection framework. This means that PEC constitutes specific and sectoral legislation in relation to data protection law. Recital 10 PEC clarifies that the data protection framework applies in particular to all matters concerning the protection of fundamental rights and freedoms, which are not specifically covered by PEC.

## THE ACTORS AND PROTECTED PARTIES

The key actors to whom ePrivacy requirements apply are service providers and network providers. ePrivacy regulates the providers of publicly available electronic communications networks and services, which are telecommunications companies and internet access providers (sometimes the term 'internet service provider' is used) and any person that makes use of these networks and services to send direct marketing communications, or to set cookies and similar technologies.

The protected parties are the subscribers and users of these services. In particular, ePrivacy sets out rights and safeguards for subscribers to publicly available electronic communications services, who are the people and organisations that enter into service contracts with telecommunications companies and internet access providers. ePrivacy also protects the users of these services who are not themselves subscribers (for example, in a domestic situation a subscriber is likely to make their subscription available to other household members to use).

## CONFIDENTIALITY OF COMMUNICATIONS

Article 5 of PEC contains two key provisions relating to the confidentiality of communications:

- First, it requires the Member States to ensure the confidentiality of communications and traffic data that are conveyed by publicly available networks and services. This is to prevent surreptitious and non-consensual surveillance, such as by way of listening, tapping, storage or other kinds of interception or surveillance.
- Secondly, it prohibits the use of electronic communications networks to store information in, or to gain access to information stored in the terminal equipment of subscribers and users without their consent. Commonly referred to as the 'cookie rule' (although it applies to more technologies than cookies, such as web beacons and pixels), it protects the equipment that subscribers and users use for making and receiving electronic communications, such as smartphones, personal computers, smartwatches and similar devices. The Ireland Data Protection Commissioner has pointed out that 'even a toy or a voice-activated assistant which uses cookies or other tracking technologies can be considered "terminal equipment" for the purposes of the Regulations'. [7]

## Exceptions to confidentiality

The rules on confidentiality are not absolute in nature. Article 15 of PEC allows Member States to restrict the protections provided by A.5, where those restrictions are necessary and proportionate in a democratic society for the following purposes:

- to safeguard national security, or for defence, or for public security;
- to prevent, investigate, detect and prosecute criminal offences;
- to prevent, investigate, detect and prosecute the unauthorised use of the electronic communications system.

In the UK the Investigatory Powers Act 2016 is the primary piece of legislation governing communications surveillance and interception. Pre-Brexit, the UK relied upon Article 15 of PEC to justify the IPA, as an exception to the confidentiality provisions in A.5.

The rule against accessing and storing information in terminal equipment without consent is subject to two carve-outs for:

- where there is 'technical storage or access for the sole purpose of carrying out the transmission of a communication over an electronic communications network';
- where technical storage or access is 'strictly necessary in order to provide an information society service explicitly requested by the subscriber or user'.

## Consent for storing or accessing information in terminal equipment

The requirement for consent for storage of, or access to, information within terminal equipment, which is found in PEC A.5.3, was introduced into the law as an amendment in 2009, by the Citizens Rights Directive. Up until that point, these activities were permitted until the subscriber or user opted out, provided that they were given prior information

---

[7] Data Protection Commission of Ireland, Guidance Note: Cookies and other tracking technologies, April 2020.

about them. Since the introduction of the GDPR, the quality of consent that is needed to satisfy PEC A.5.3 is that required by the GDPR, as defined in GDPR A.4.11. According to Article 2(f), 'consent by a user or subscriber corresponds to the data subject's consent in Directive 95/46/EC'. Article 94(2) GDPR states that references to the Data Protection Directive shall be construed as references to the GDPR. This means that the concept of consent under PEC should be understood as set out in Article 4(11) GDPR. 'Therefore, the GDPR conditions for obtaining valid consent are applicable in situations falling within the scope of the e-Privacy Directive.'[8] The CJEU recently clarified that the requirement for consent applies regardless of whether personal data are processed or not. Even where no personal data are involved and only PEC applies, the GDPR threshold of consent applies.[9]

The Citizens Rights Directive explains that consent can be obtained through browser settings (see Recital 66), and this has been incorporated into the laws of some of the Member States (including France, Ireland, Luxembourg, Greece, Poland, Slovakia, Slovenia, Spain) and the UK. However, an opinion of the predecessor to the EDPB, the Article 29 Working Party, says that because browsers do not normally block cookies by default and because the average internet user is not always familiar with browser settings or the implications of them, they cannot be deemed to have consented simply because they are using a browser that allows cookies.[10] The opinion further adds that browsers and other applications will only be able to obtain valid consent if they reject cookies by default and then require users to engage in affirmative actions to accept the use of cookies, details about which have to be fully specified.

Similar to this, cookie walls raise concerns about compliance with ePrivacy and data protection law. According to the ICO, cookie walls (also known as 'tracking walls'), require 'users to "agree" or "accept" the setting of cookies before they can access an online service's content'[11] (see EDPB guidance on cookie walls box). The ICO advises that cookie tracking is not necessarily inappropriate, intrusive or high risk and the specific conditions under data protection law and ePrivacy should be considered to assess the legality of this practice.[12]

> **EDPB guidance on cookie walls**
>
> A website provider puts into place a script that will block content from being visible except for a request to accept cookies and the information about which cookies are being set and for what purposes data will be processed. There is no possibility to access the content without clicking on the 'Accept cookies' button. Since the data subject is not presented with a genuine choice, its consent is not freely given.

---

[8] EDPB, Guidelines 05/2020 on consent under Regulation 2016/679, 2020, p. 6.

[9] *Planet49*.

[10] Article 29 Working Party, WP 171 'Opinion 2/2010 in online behavioural advertising', adopted 22 June 2010, p. 13.

[11] https://ico.org.uk/for-organisations/guide-to-pecr/guidance-on-the-use-of-cookies-and-similar-technologies/how-do-we-comply-with-the-cookie-rules/

[12] Ibid.

This does not constitute valid consent, as the provision of the service relies on the data subject clicking the 'Accept cookies' button. It is not presented with a genuine choice.[13]

**Consent, transparency and the use of cookie notices and consent tools**

One of the techniques that is deployed to help obtain consent for cookies is the publication of a cookie notice, which is a prominent website notice that seeks to give information about the types of cookies that will be set, to enable the website user to make informed choices. The purpose of these notices is to fulfil the essential transparency requirements with the GDPR meaning of consent.

The use of these notices is controversial, because often they are displayed after cookies have been set and, often, they do not provide sufficient information about the cookies, who is in charge of them and what will happen after they are set. The notices often therefore fall short of the meaning of consent within GDPR A.4.11.

Cookie consent tools are also common on websites, consisting of consoles that enable website users to accept or reject cookies by category and type. If the default settings are set to accept cookies, that will be a problem for everything but 'strictly necessary' cookies. Best practice requires an opt-in process, so that the website administrator can evidence an affirmative action on the part of the user, which is one of the key ingredients within the GDPR definition of consent. However, it should be noted that consent management tools by themselves do not alleviate website operators from complying with PEC.

**Types of cookies**

Cookies that are 'strictly necessary' to provide information society services[14] can be set without consent. The ICO clarifies that this type of cookies is restricted 'to what is essential to provide the service requested by the user' and 'what is "strictly necessary" should be assessed from the point of view of the user or subscriber'.[15] Examples would include cookies that support an online shopping cart, or ones that enable a user to log into a secure part of a website.

---

13 EDPB, Guidelines 05/2020 on consent under Regulation 2016/679, adopted on 4 May 2020, p. 12.

14 In brief, information society services are services delivered over the internet, such as websites and applications. For the purposes of the ePrivacy framework, Recital 17 of the Directive on electronic commerce (Directive 2000/31/EC) defines information society services as 'any service normally provided for remuneration, at a distance, by means of electronic equipment for the processing (including digital compression) and storage of data, and at the individual request of a recipient of a service'. In the UK, the concept of 'information society services' adopted by PECR is defined under Regulation 2(1) of the Electronic Commerce (EC Directive) Regulations 2002 in a similar manner.

15 ICO, What are the rules on cookies and similar technologies? https://ico.org.uk/for-organisations/guide-to-pecr/guidance-on-the-use-of-cookies-and-similar-technologies/what-are-the-rules-on-cookies-and-similar-technologies/

Although 'strictly necessary' cookies are the only type with a clear legislative root, other categories have emerged over time, reflecting industry usage and parlance:

- Performance cookies. These collect information about how visitors use websites, such as information about the pages they visit. They are most often used (or justified) to help website administrators improve their services.
- Functionality cookies. These allow a website to remember choices that visitors make, such as username and language, and provide enhanced, personalised results.
- Tracking and advertising cookies. These are used to deliver targeted adverts based on the website visitors' interests. Often they track people across websites and so are considered to be highly privacy-intrusive.

Tracking and advertising cookies themselves break down into various types. Two prominent categories are 'first-party' and 'third-party' cookies. First-party cookies are set by the website publisher, through its own web server or web scripts. Third-party cookies are set on a publisher's website by a third-party server or third-party web script, often by AdTech vendors.

## Cookies, behavioural advertising and real-time bidding

Behavioural advertising involves people being profiled, to support targeted advertising. Profile building is a highly intrusive activity that the GDPR treats with utmost seriousness, due to the risks that people can be singled out and be subjected to discriminatory treatment. In the field of advertising, it might be argued that profiling is less risky than in other walks of life (such as in the fields of insurance or medical treatment, or in the workplace), because it may not always produce legal or similar effects (see GDPR A.22), but this does not avoid the need for profiling for advertising purposes to be conducted fully in accordance with the law. The complexity of behavioural advertising is heightened by the fact that it engages both the GDPR framework and the ePrivacy framework if cookies are used to build the profile itself or to support the targeting of the advertisements. Other elements that add to the complexity of the situation, in both a legal and an operational sense, include the fact that there can be multiple actors involved in the profile building and the resulting advertising activities, challenges with transparency issues because it is so hard for the average consumer to understand the complexity of AdTech networks, and for the same reason, challenges with upholding information rights.

Real-time bidding, which permits online advertisers to bid for advertising space on websites and apps in fractions of a second so that advertisers can choose to whom they wish to serve their adverts and what they wish to pay to do so, is another area of concern. This is a highly privacy-intrusive industry, because the value of the bids is connected to the depth of understanding that the bidder has about the target audience. The richer the data, the more precise the advertising can be, with greater sales and conversion rates at the end of the process. The ICO is, at the time of writing, currently conducting a high-profile investigation into this industry, examining issues such as transparency, consent and data supply. The ICO's concerns include the fact that special category data, such as health data, are often shared within the bidding process, without explicit consent and without proper consideration of the wider risks involved, which include security risks.

## Cookies and legal risk

Despite the introduction of the cookie rule in 2009 and the GDPR in 2018, the rule has been under-enforced.

This seems to be changing. There has been a series of high-profile legal actions in recent years involving their use. For example, in the UK the well-known cases of *Vidal-Hall* (2015) and *Lloyd v. Google* (2019) are both concerned with the misuse of cookies. In 2019 the CJEU gave judgment in the *Planet49* (2019) case, confirming that GDPR consent applies to the use of cookies and that pre-ticked boxes will not suffice for these purposes. In late 2020 the French regulator, CNIL, fined Google Inc. and Google Ireland a total of €100m for cookie consent and transparency failings and Amazon €35m. In summer 2021 Max Schrems, the privacy activist behind the Safe Harbor and Privacy Shield international transfers cases, filed mass complaints about cookie malpractice across Europe through NOYB, the civil society organisation that he founded.

Members of the public are also adding their own momentum. In the UK many organisations have received compensation claims from lone individuals who scour the web to find contraventions, after which they lodge a demand for money.

The momentum for legal claims and regulatory action is only going to increase.

## DIRECT MARKETING

As has been seen, cookies play a pivotal role in the online advertising ecosystem, but PEC's concerns about direct marketing are much broader than cookies, covering email, SMS, fax, automated calling machines and telephone calls. There are different rules for different types of communication – for example, stricter rules apply for marketing to individuals (business-to-consumer marketing) than for marketing to companies (business-to-business). The rules, set out in A.13 PEC, are as follows:

- Email, facsimile machines (fax), automated calling machines. The use of these to send directing marketing communications to individuals needs the individual's prior consent, that is, an 'opt-in'. Note that email for these purposes includes SMS.

- Email where contact details have been obtained from an individual in the context of a sale of a product or services. As an exception to the previous rule, emails can be used to market similar products and services on an 'opt-out' basis (this is sometimes called a 'soft opt-in'). In other words, these can be sent without prior consent, provided that:
    - The marketing communication is sent by the same person or company who received the contact details of the recipient during the original sale.
    - The marketing relates to the sender's own products and service, not a third party's.

- The recipient is given clear information about their right to opt out and a free-of-charge means to do so. The information about the right to opt out has to be provided at the point when the contact details are originally obtained from the recipient and within each marketing communication thereafter.
- Telephone calls. PEC gives Member States the option to allow these on either an opt-in or opt-out basis.
- Legal persons (e.g. companies). PEC gives Member States the option to extend the protection of these rules to companies.

## The position under PECR

The equivalent rules to A.13 for the UK are contained in Regulations 19–26 of PECR. Key points are:

- Telephone calls to individuals and companies can be made on an opt-out basis, without prior consent, but the caller must screen the calls against the Telephone Preference Service register of numbers that do not want to receive cold calls. Exceptions to this rule apply under PECR, for example when the call relates to claims management services or where the recipient of the call has previously objected to receiving marketing calls. Specific rules apply to automated calls.
- The rules for sending emails and SMS messages to individuals are the same as in PEC, as detailed above. Emails and SMS can be sent to companies on an opt-out basis, without prior consent.
- The rules for sending marketing faxes to individuals are the same as in PEC, requiring prior consent. They can be sent to companies on an opt-out basis, without prior consent, provided that the sender screens against the Fax Preference Service register.
- Sole traders and some partnerships are treated the same as individual subscribers and users, not as companies.

## Postal direct marketing

Direct marketing by post is not covered by PEC or PECR. This is regulated by the GDPR to the extent that processing of personal data is included, and they can be sent on an opt-out basis.

## Opt-out, as a matter of law

An opt-out is a colloquialism for the 'legitimate interests' basis of lawful processing, which is contained GDPR A.6.1.f. Where PEC and PECR recognise the validity of opt-out processing, it is because the underlying law recognises the business legitimacy of the processing activities. Due to the recognition of the legitimacy of these activities in law, organisations would not be expected to perform legitimate interests assessments for routine direct marketing activities.

### Financial penalties for direct marketing contraventions

UK law permits the Information Commissioner to impose fines of up to £500,000 for contraventions of direct marketing law in PECR. This is considerably lower than the maximum amounts under the GDPR. However, the ICO can also impose penalties of up this amount on the directors of companies that contravene the PECR marketing rules, which gives the law added teeth. Currently, the ICO's strategy is to seek the disqualification of company directors if their companies fail to pay their fines.

## PROCESSING OF TRAFFIC DATA, LOCATION DATA AND VALUE ADDED SERVICES

Traffic data are any data that are 'processed for the purpose of the conveyance of a communication on an electronic communications network or for the billing thereof'. Article 6 of PEC says that traffic data must be erased or made anonymous when they are no longer required for communication or billing purposes, except if the subscriber has given their prior consent for another use. These other uses can be the marketing of electronic communications services or the provision of 'value added services'.

Location data are 'any data processed in an electronic communications network, indicating the geographic position of the terminal equipment of a user of a publicly available electronic communications service'. Location data can only be processed when they are made anonymous, or if not made anonymous then only with the consent of the subscriber or user concerned for the provision of a value added service, as set out in Regulation 14 PECR.

A value added service is 'any service which requires the processing of traffic data or location data beyond that which is necessary for the transmission of a communication or the billing in respect of that communication'. For example, this may include an email content-filtering service offered by an internet service provider, which monitors traffic data to scan incoming emails.

## SECURITY AND PERSONAL DATA BREACH NOTIFICATION

Article 4 places an obligation on the providers of publicly available communications services to take appropriate technical and organisational measures to safeguard the security of their services, if necessary in conjunction with the network provider who will be responsible for network security. These measures shall include ones that ensure that personal data can be accessed only by authorised personnel for legally authorised purposes and that protect personal data against accidental or unlawful destruction, loss, alteration, storage, access or disclosure. A.4 requires the service provider to adopt a risk-based approach to its obligations, saying that having regard to the state of the art and the cost of implementation, the measures taken shall be appropriate to the risk presented. These obligations are very similar to the ones in Article 32 GDPR.

Unlike the GDPR, there is also an express requirement for transparency about the risks of security breaches. Where there is a particular risk of a breach of the security of the network, which is beyond the capacity of the service provider to remedy, it must inform the subscribers of those risks and any possible remedies, including an indication of the likely costs involved.

## Personal data breaches

A.4.3 PEC also imposes personal data breach notification obligations on service providers. These are defined as 'a breach of security leading to the accidental or unlawful destruction, loss, alteration, unauthorised disclosure of, or access to, personal data transmitted, stored or otherwise processed in connection with the provision of a publicly available electronic communications service in the Community' under PEC.

There are two notification obligations with this rule. First, if a personal data breach occurs, the service provider should notify the regulator within 24 hours of detection of the incident, where feasible (this timeframe was introduced by the EU Notification Regulation[16] with direct effect in EU Member States in 2013, which modified the original requirement on service providers to give notice 'without undue delay'). Secondly, if the breach is 'likely to adversely affect the personal data or the privacy of a subscriber or individual', they also have to notify those persons without undue delay. Other key points to note include:

- The duty to notify impacted subscribers and individuals does not apply if the service provider can demonstrate to the regulator's satisfaction that it has 'implemented appropriate technological protection measures to the data concerned by the security breach'. This means the application of encryption, as A.4.3 continues by saying 'such technological protection measures shall render the data unintelligible to any person who is not authorised to access it'.

- When notifying impacted subscribers and individuals, the service provider must provide this information at a minimum: a description of the nature of the breach; contact points where more information can be obtained; recommended measures to mitigate the possible adverse effects of the breach.

- When notifying the regulators, in addition to the information the service provider is required to supply to impacted subscribers and individuals, it should describe the consequences of the breach and the measures proposed or taken to address the breach.

- The regulators can order service providers to notify impacted subscribers and individuals, if they have not already done so.

- Service providers must keep inventories of breaches, their effects and remedial actions taken, to enable the regulators to verify compliance with the rules.

- Technical implementing measures can be adopted by the European Commission covering the format and procedures for giving notifications.

---

[16] Commission Regulation (EU) No 611/2013 of 24 June 2013 on the measures applicable to the notification of personal data breaches under Directive 2002/58/EC of the European Parliament and of the Council on privacy and electronic communications.

- The regulators are permitted to issue guidelines and instructions on when notifications should be made and the format and manner of them.

**Expanded rules for breach notifications**

The rules in PEC A.4 are expanded by the above-mentioned EU Notification Regulation adopted in 2013, which:

- modified the timeframe for giving notification to the regulator;
- clarified the position on when data are rendered unintelligible through the use of encryption (so as to avoid the duty to notify impacted subscribers and individuals);
- provided tests for measuring adverse effects on individuals;
- provided further details on the contents of notifications.

Regarding the tests for adverse effects, they include:

- The nature and content of the personal data that are breached. Financial information, special categories of data, location data, internet log files, web browsing histories, email data and itemised call lists are identified as types of data to be considered.
- The likely consequences of the personal data breach for the subscriber or individual concerned. Issues to consider include whether the breach could result in identity theft, fraud, physical harm, distress, humiliation or reputational damage.
- The circumstances of the breach. Factors to consider include whether the data have been stolen or have come into the possession of an unauthorised third party.

**Interplay with the breach notification rules in the GDPR**

Service providers potentially fall under the GDPR breach notification regime (see GDPR A.33 and 34), as well as PEC's equivalent. However, due to GDPR A.95, service providers only have to comply with the PEC breach notification regime. This has been confirmed by the EDPB in guidelines published in 2019.[17]

## CALLING LINE ID AND DIRECTORIES OF SUBSCRIBERS

PEC also provides that subscribers should be given the opportunity not to have their telephone numbers disclosed when they make a call, although this can be overridden to trace malicious or nuisance calls. In the UK, the law requires that all outgoing marketing calls must display a valid calling line ID.

PEC also says that subscribers must be informed of any intention to include their data in a publicly available directory of subscribers.

---

[17] Opinion 5/2019 on the interplay between the ePrivacy Directive and the GDPR, in particular regarding the competence, tasks and powers of data protection authorities, adopted on 12 March 2019.

## LAW REFORM UNDERWAY

This area of the law is, at the time of writing, currently undergoing a process of reform, with a draft ePrivacy Regulation working its way through the EU's legislative process. The European Commission has opted in favour of the legal instrument of 'Regulation', similar to the GDPR, to ensure direct application and legal certainty across the EU. The proposal aims at introducing targeted measures for the effective protection of the right to privacy and communications. It covers electronic communications as well as the integrity of the information on one's device, regardless of whether it is personal or non-personal data. Individuals' rights and choices over their information and devices are enhanced and new technologies are also covered in the proposal. At the same time, the proposal aims to strike a fair balance between the level of protection of natural and legal persons and the free flow of electronic communications. For example, the aim of the proposal is to support traditional telecommunications services and enable them to process metadata to provide additional services and develop their business, where they comply with the rules set out in the proposal.

The proposed regulation[18] will make a number of significant improvements to the current legal framework in the EU, including:

- New actors to be regulated. The proposed regulation will apply to 'over the top' electronic communications services, which are those that use the underlying communications system provided by telecommunications companies and internet access providers. Examples include WhatsApp, Facebook Messenger and Skype. The proposed reforms will ensure that these popular services guarantee the same level of confidentiality of communications as traditional providers of communications networks and services.

- Stronger legislation. All people and businesses in the EU will enjoy the same level of protection for their electronic communications in the Member States. It is also hoped that regulated businesses will benefit from having to comply with a single piece of EU legislation, rather than multiple national implementations as is currently the case.

- Enhanced commercial opportunities. In contrast to the current framework, the proposed regulation will broaden the commercial possibilities for providers of electronic communications services to use communications metadata (information about other information, which includes, for example, information on location, duration and recipient of communications).

- Simpler cookies legislation. The current legal framework for cookies within PEC, which has resulted in an overload of consent requests for web users, will be streamlined. The proposed regulation is intended to be more user-friendly, as browser settings will provide for an easy way to accept or refuse tracking cookies and other identifiers. The proposed regulation also clarifies that consent will not be needed for non-privacy-intrusive cookies that improve internet experience, or which count the number of visitors to a website.

---

[18] Regulation of the European Parliament and of the Council concerning the respect for private life and the protection of personal data in electronic communications.

- High fines. The proposal reflects the GDPR fining system and includes high fines. In particular, infringements of ePrivacy rules are subject to administrative fines up to EUR 10m, or in the case of an undertaking, up to 2 per cent of the total worldwide annual turnover of the preceding financial year, whichever is higher.

Due to Brexit, the UK will not be subject to the regulation when it is adopted. The UK might mimic the EU's approach at that point, or the laws of the two jurisdictions might part ways. The UK may also consider aligning its ePrivacy regime with the EU Regulation, when adopted, if this would support the renewal and continuous effect of the UK GDPR adequacy decision.

## SUMMARY

In conclusion, this chapter gives readers a better understanding of:

- the scope of ePrivacy law and how it relates to the GDPR;
- the range of priorities addressed by the law;
- the key issues within the cookies and direct marketing rules;
- how personal data breach notifications apply to electronic communications;
- the current trajectory of law reform.

# 4 INTRODUCTION TO OPERATIONAL DATA PROTECTION

## Stewart Room

This chapter introduces the topic of operational data protection, to identify the major implementation priorities that controllers and processors of personal data need to deliver on, in order to achieve compliance with the law and to be able to demonstrate that they have done so, in accordance with the requirements of the accountability principle.

## OPERATIONAL ADEQUACY SCHEMES – IMPLEMENTING DATA PROTECTION (OPERATIONALISATION)

The requirements of data protection law need to be operationalised. Controllers and processors must develop schemes to deliver operationally adequate systems and operations for data protection before they begin their data processing activities. Where necessary, they also need to retrofit controls into any legacy data processing environments that do not meet required current standards.

### Focus on operational adequacy schemes

The focus on operational adequacy for data protection is now increasing, but this is a recent development. For decades most of the effort made to operationalise the requirements of data protection did not get past the 'paper layer' of the organisation, in the sense that while policies, procedures, notices, contracts and similar artefacts were commonly found in organisations involved in data processing, the required outcomes rarely made their way through to the technology and data themselves. The GDPR has given the momentum for change and in the landmark case about the Privacy Shield, the CJEU identified the real significance of operational adequacy schemes: organisations cannot export personal data to countries outside the GDPR land mass without paying proper attention to the need to deliver real operational protections for personal data in the receiving country, which, if necessary, means protections against government snooping. Relying on contracts and other paperwork simply is not enough. The CJEU's approach to international transfers must apply to every other facet of data protection.

Compliance must be achieved throughout three layers of the organisation, that is, the people layer, the paper layer and the technology and data layer.[1] Once that is done, compliance has to be sustained and enduring. Figure 4.1 illustrates the nature of the operational aspects of data protection compliance that need to be achieved.

---

1 The physical environment must also be considered, for security and business continuity protections, in order to keep data and processing equipment physically safe from threats and harms, which cover everything from burglaries through to natural disasters.

**Figure 4.1 The operational landscape for data protection**

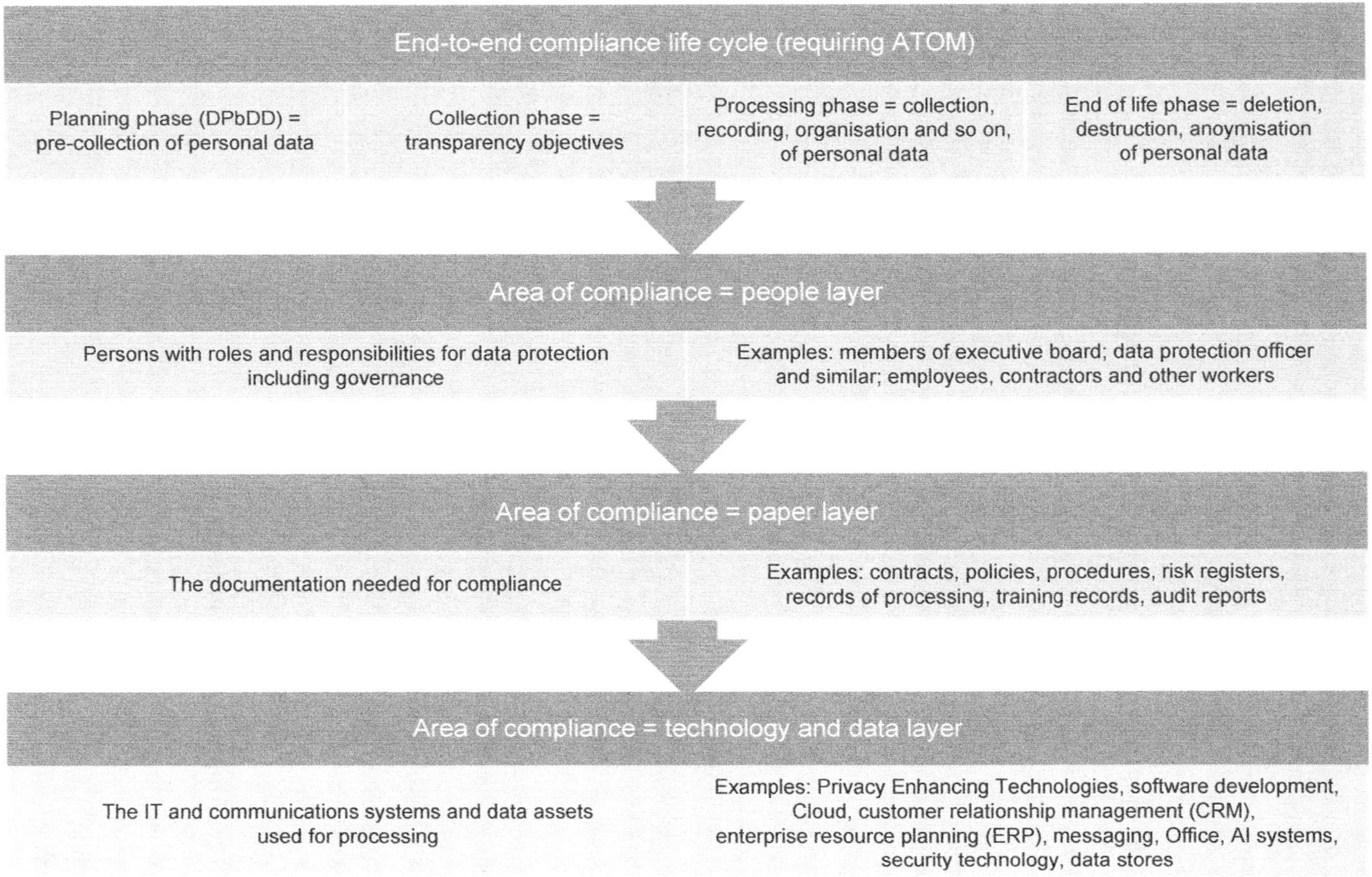

**End-to-end compliance life cycle (requiring ATOM)**

- Planning phase (DPbDD) = pre-collection of personal data
- Collection phase = transparency objectives
- Processing phase = collection, recording, organisation and so on, of personal data
- End of life phase = deletion, destruction, anonymisation of personal data

**Area of compliance = people layer**

Persons with roles and responsibilities for data protection including governance

Examples: members of executive board; data protection officer and similar; employees, contractors and other workers

**Area of compliance = paper layer**

The documentation needed for compliance

Examples: contracts, policies, procedures, risk registers, records of processing, training records, audit reports

**Area of compliance = technology and data layer**

The IT and communications systems and data assets used for processing

Examples: Privacy Enhancing Technologies, software development, Cloud, customer relationship management (CRM), enterprise resource planning (ERP), messaging, Office, AI systems, security technology, data stores

## THE THREE LAYERS OF AN ORGANISATION

The process of operationalising data protection can be akin to a business transformation exercise. This is most obviously the case when data protection is retrofitted into legacy processing environments where Data Protection by Design and Default ideas have been overlooked, or when a new law is adopted that requires significant changes to be made to business operations (as happened when the GDPR was adopted in 2016). When the operationalisation of data protection is viewed in this way, the three layers of the organisation, identified above, come into view.

## IMPLEMENTING DATA PROTECTION IN THE PEOPLE LAYER

Although most of the data protection risks reside in technology and data themselves, operationalising data protection and achieving compliance with the law is impossible without paying attention to the roles that people play in delivering these outcomes. For example, the actions of people can present the gravest risks to the rights and freedoms of individuals, such as where they misuse access rights and privileges with malign intent to cause harms to their employers and their colleagues, as happened in the *Morrisons* (2020)[2] case. In that case the Supreme Court dismissed the claim that the controller should be held vicariously liable for the actions of a rogue insider, but the outcome could be different in other cases.

Elements of the people layer that should be addressed within a data protection compliance programme or project are summarised below.

### Governance structures

People provide the overall governance functions for data processing activities, so critical roles and responsibilities that need to be fulfilled should be identified and appointments made, following which people should be empowered to do their jobs properly, including through training and access to appropriate tools and resources. The executive board or other controlling mind of the organisation should carry overall responsibility for good governance, with chains of command that lead directly to them. Where required, data protection officers should be appointed.

### Steering committee

Large-scale data protection programmes and significant new projects are likely to require a steering committee to oversee the work. This naturally forms part of the overall governance structure of the organisation and is an integral element of Data Protection by Design and Default.

### Recruitment and onboarding

Due to the critical role that people play within data processing and the risks that their wrongful behaviours present to rights and freedoms of data subjects, great care needs to be taken with the procedures for onboarding employees and workers. This begins with the recruitment process, which should consider the candidate's suitability to perform any data processing activities that their role requires and the need for background checks,

---

[2] *WM Morrison Supermarkets Plc v. Various Claimants* (2020) UKSC 2018/0213.

with appropriate induction procedures when they arrive. Sandwiched between these two requirements is the contractual process, which forms part of the paper layer.

## Education and training

The employee/worker induction process should involve education and training on data protection matters. These are ongoing requirements and ideally the content of education and training should be role-specific and relevant to the data processing activities that the person will be involved with. There are no hard-and-fast rules about the form that education and training should take, but it is clear from the ICO's regulatory practices that the production of training records is commonly sought in regulatory investigations and inquiries, in compliance with the accountability and regulatory cooperation rules. For example, when the ICO performs an audit utilising the Assessment Notice power in the Data Protection Act, they will normally request these records. The records themselves form part of the paper layer of the business.

## Access rights and privileges

Employees and workers should not have general access rights to data processing systems and personal data, because that would infringe the data minimisation principle and would risk infringements of the integrity and confidentiality principle. Instead, controllers should aim for role-based access, that is, access necessary for the performance of the employee/worker's job. For example, while a HR professional would legitimately have access to some HR systems, not all of them would need access to payroll systems and it would be hard to justify access to CRM systems containing personal data that have nothing to do with their role. Controllers and processors should be careful to ensure that access rights are kept under review and properly terminated at the end of employment or suspended as appropriate during serious investigations into disciplinary matters.

## Monitoring

There are circumstances when the monitoring of employee/worker behaviour will be legitimate, such as part of an appropriate set of security controls, but due to the rights and freedoms that employees and workers enjoy in the workplace, controllers and processors need to be careful to establish clear boundary lines for monitoring and then only do what is necessary for the fulfilment of a legitimate purpose or other legal obligations.

Overstepping the boundary into infringement of employee rights frequently leads to legal problems. The Consulting Association scandal, which concerned blacklisting of construction workers, points to a deeply problematic issue within the overall spectrum of monitoring, that is, profile building. Other famous cases include *Halford* (1997),[3] about the monitoring of telephone calls, and *Copland* (2007),[4] about the monitoring of web and email activities. The *Bărbulescu* (2017)[5] case highlights the importance of transparency about workplace monitoring, which is achieved through appropriate employee handbooks, notices and other awareness-raising mechanisms.

---

3   *Halford v. UK* (1997) ECtHR 20605/92.

4   *Copland v. UK* (2007) ECtHR 62617/00.

5   *Bărbulescu v. Romania* (2017) ECtHR 61496/08.

Emphasising the significance of workplace monitoring in the mind of the regulator, in 2011 the ICO published the Employment Practice Code, a code of practice that set out the ICO's expectations in this area. Although the code was published pursuant to the ICO's powers under the Data Protection Act 1998, which has been repealed and replaced by the 2018 Act, the ICO has recently confirmed that the underlying principles of the code still apply. The ICO has also confirmed that the code is being redrafted to bring it up to date for the GDPR.

## Worker discipline

Contraventions of data protection rules by employees and workers need to be properly dealt with, which involves appropriate investigations and, if needed, the imposition of corrective measures to cure the non-compliance. In serious situations, breaches of data protection can result in dismissals. Of course, employees and workers need to be treated fairly during disciplinary processes, which involves an understanding of employment and equality law issues, which fall outside the scope of this book.

## Flowing requirements to data processors

If a controller engages a data processor, the GDPR requires the controller to take steps to ensure that the processor acts in accordance with the requirements of the regulation (see A.28). The mechanisms that the controller puts in place to achieve this need to result in the processor's employees and workers operating consistently with the GDPR. An express legislative requirement, which needs to be stated in the contract or other legal instrument that appoints the processor, is that the processor shall ensure that persons whom it authorises to process the data are committed to confidentiality or are under a statutory obligation of confidentiality. This is intended to limit the risks of misuse of personal data by the processor's employees and workers.

## IMPLEMENTING DATA PROTECTION IN THE PAPER LAYER

The are many items of paperwork that need to be put in place to properly operationalise the law, although these documents can be in electronic form rather than having to be in hard copy.

## Data Protection by Design and Default (DPbDD, or PbD)

The idea of Data Protection by Design and Default includes expectations about the creation of compliance paperwork, because an undocumented design is unlikely to provide sufficient assurance about compliance, putting the controller in breach of the accountability principle (because such proof cannot be achieved simply through oral testimony). Therefore, documentary evidence is essential to deliver accountability.

Many of the documentary elements discussed below are features of a DPbDD framework. These requirements arise both expressly and impliedly in the law.

## Governance structures

Corresponding to the need to establish appropriate governance structures for data processing, controllers and processors will want to consider how this is documented.

Organisational charts, hierarchies, reporting lines and operating models are illustrations of the kinds of document that can be considered.

## Records of processing activities

Controllers and their representatives are required to maintain records of processing activities under their responsibility. Sometimes these records are called ROPAs or 'data maps' (albeit this language does not appear in the legislation). These are foundational documents within a system for compliance, because the insights that they provide support the performance of risk assessments. Without a comprehensive record, the controller is effectively operating blind. Controllers undergoing regulatory investigation can expect the regulator to request disclosure of their ROPAs.

As previously mentioned, the requirement for ROPAs generally does not apply to enterprises and organisations employing fewer than 250 people (see A.30.5).

## Risk registers and assessment tools and methodologies

The obligations placed on controllers and processors to implement appropriate technical and organisational measures for the management of risks to rights and freedoms naturally requires them to create and retain documentation that records those risks and enables the performance of risk assessments.

The requirement for data protection impact assessments provides a clear example of when a documented risk assessment is required, due to the obligation placed on the controller to consult with the regulator in high-risk situations. The consultation requirement includes an inherent requirement to share the risk assessment with the regulator (see Articles 35 and 36).

## Legitimate interests assessments

Processing for the purposes of the controller's legitimate interests provides one of the lawful bases for data processing, but the GDPR requires the controller to perform an assessment of whether these interests are overridden by the interests or fundamental rights and freedoms of the data subject, with particular care being needed in the case of children's data (see A.6.1.f).

Again, the accountability rule applies, so if there is a regulatory investigation or litigation about data processing based on the legitimate interests rule, the controller may need to prove that they have performed the necessary assessment. This will require not only the production of proof that the assessment was performed, but also proof of the underlying assessment methodology that was used.

## Transfer assessments

One of the results of the decision of the CJEU in the Privacy Shield case is a need for data exporters to assess the legal environment of countries outside Europe that receive personal data, to establish whether the third country provides guarantees for data protection that are essentially equivalent to those within Europe.

The regulatory guidance issued by the EDPB identifies four guarantees that need to be assessed:[6]

- processing in the third country should be based on clear, precise and accessible rules;
- necessity and proportionality regarding the legitimate objectives pursued need to be demonstrated;
- an independent oversight mechanism is needed;
- effective remedies need to be available to the individual.

## Transparency notices

The transparency rules cover: (1) the information that needs to be provided to the data subject at the point of collection of data from them (or, if the data are collected from a third party, within a reasonable period, but not exceeding one month); (2) the information that needs to be supplied after the exercise of the right of access and the right of objection to automated decision making; and (3) the information that needs to be communicated to data subjects after a personal data breach.

The transparency rules need documentation to be created for compliance. The rules confirm that this information 'shall be provided in writing', or by other means, including where appropriate by electronic means. They also describe the required characteristics of this information:

- the information provided should be concise, transparent and intelligible;
- it should be provided in an easily accessible form;
- it should use clear and plain language;
- the language shall be suitable for children if they are the target reader.

These rules are contained in Article 12. Common examples of transparency notices include website privacy notices and cookie policies.

In some situations, the interactions between the data subject and the controller will be conducted orally, such as when a person phones a contact centre or uses a digital assistant or other IoT device. In those cases, there will still be underlying documentation, which provides the script for the words used and a record of what was said.

## Contracts and similar documents

Contracts and other legally binding mechanisms are used in a variety of circumstances to regulate data processing, such as in the employment context, but within the GDPR itself we see several examples of the significance of contractual paperwork:

- as an option for providing the lawful basis of processing (see GDPR A.6.1.b);

---

[6] See EDPB Recommendations 02/2020 on the European Essential Guarantees for surveillance measures. https://edpb.europa.eu/sites/edpb/files/files/file1/edpb_recommendations_202002_europeanessentialguaranteessurveillance_en.pdf

- for establishing and regulating the relationship between controllers and processors (see GDPR A.28.1);
- as safeguards to enable the transfer of personal data to countries outside Europe that have not benefitted from an 'adequacy decision' (see GDPR A.46.2.a, b, c, d), or as a derogation from those rules (see GDPR A.49.1.b).

Another form of contractual document that is commonly used in a data protection context is a non-disclosure agreement (NDA). NDAs are often used alongside employment contracts, alongside data processor contracts and as part of data sharing agreements.

Data sharing agreements form part of the UK's legislative framework within the Data Protection Act 2018. Section 121 of the Act requires the Information Commissioner to publish a code of practice for data sharing, adherence to which acts as evidence of compliance with the law. The code of practice is available on the ICO's website and it is meant to be used in situations where two or more controllers operate as joint controllers, due to rules in the GDPR requiring them to determine their respective responsibilities for compliance in a transparent fashion (see A.26.1).

There are situations where the use of contracts can put the controller into breach of the law, however, if they are misused. If performance of a contract is conditional upon the data subject giving their consent to processing activities that are unnecessary for performance, that will undermine the lawfulness of the processing, due to the consent not being freely given (see GDPR A.7.4).

## Policies, procedures and controls frameworks

For an issue as significant as policies within the activities that controllers and processors need to perform to operationalise the law, references to them within the GDPR are surprisingly sparse, but the basic rule is established in A.24.2, which says that controllers shall implement appropriate policies as part of the appropriate technical and organisational measures that they deploy for compliance, albeit this is subject to a proportionality test. The issue of policies is also picked up within the rules on the tasks of the data protection officer, who is required to monitor compliance by the controller or processor, which includes compliance with their policies (see A.39.1.b).

It is also noteworthy that the definition of binding corporate rules says that they are policies that are adhered to by controllers and processors for the purposes of international transfers (see A.4.20).

The UK Data Protection Act contains more reference to policies than the GDPR, however. Some of these arise in relation to the rules on law enforcement processing, which give effect to the Law Enforcement Directive, emphasising the importance of policies in the policing context (an issue that was a contributing factor in the decision of the Court of Appeal in the *Bridges* (2020) case). The Act mandates the use of policies when special category personal data are processed for the purposes of policing.

### *Policy examples*
Subject to the application of the proportionality rule and the situations within the Data Protection Act where policies are mandated, controllers and processors have a free reign over the policy framework that they adopt. Table 4.1 provides some examples of

the policies that controllers and processors may adopt. This list is illustrative and non-exhaustive. Ultimately, controllers and processors have a choice over the policies they adopt, subject to specific requirements in the Act.

It is possible to wrap everything up within a single, overarching document, which might suitably be called a 'Data Protection Policy'.

**Table 4.1 Types of data protection policies (examples)**

| | |
|---|---|
| Employment policies and handbooks | These will describe the expectations placed on employees and should include clear rules about monitoring and discipline. |
| Retention policies | These will set out retention periods and standards, as well as deletion rules. Anonymisation and pseudonymisation rules might be found in these policies, or standalone documents. |
| Cookie policies | These are created for the purposes of compliance with the Privacy and Electronic Communications rules. Often these documents are found alongside, or within, wider website privacy policies. |
| Security policies | These are often conformed to a wide spectrum of requirements contained within international standards. Incident response and breach notification might appear in these policies, or in standalone documents. |
| Subject rights policies | These cover the rules within Chapter III of the GDPR. The handling of complaints and compensation claims might also be part of these policies. |
| Marketing and advertising policies | These will deal with consent and permissions requirements, including the use of preference centres through which data subjects may set and change their preferences for the receipt of direct marketing communications. |
| Data Protection by Design and Default policies | These might include rules on risk assessments and controls frameworks. |
| Data sharing and transfer policies | These might cover issues relating to matters such as joint controllership, engagement of processors and exports to countries outside Europe. |

*Procedures*
Policies are often supplemented by written procedures, which provide more detail on the actual steps that need to be followed to operationalise the law. These might include process flowcharts, which set out in a linear and sequential fashion the operational steps and activities that need to be followed in defined situations, such as those that arise after receipt of a data subject rights request, or a request to suppress processing,

to ensure that the required outcomes are achieved by the required date. These might identify the business functions and persons involved in these processes.

## *Playbooks*
Another variant within this area is the 'playbook', which can be a hybrid document that contains policy information, procedures, methodologies, tools and narratives about the use cases and scenarios involved. These are most often used for incident response following a personal data breach or a cybersecurity event, where the controller or processor will benefit from clear rules and guidance due to these matters often being high-impact, highly stressful and urgent, with strict requirements about notifying regulators and data subjects and risks of adverse publicity.

## *Controls frameworks*
Controllers and processors should consider how they record their controls frameworks that are adopted for the purposes of ensuring compliance with the rules on the taking of appropriate technical and organisational measures for compliance. Again, there are no hard-and-fast rules on the form and detail that these records should take, but the need to produce records of controls frameworks can extend much further than simply producing policies and procedures in serious cases, such as regulatory investigations into high-profile cybersecurity incidents affecting personal data.

## Records of significant events

There are situations in the GDPR that require controllers and processors to maintain records of significant events.

### *Personal data breaches*
The operation of the breach notification rules is contingent on the breach involving risks to the rights and freedoms of individuals. If those risks do not exist, or if another exemption applies, the controller will avoid these transparency requirements. This contains scope for abuse, but the law caters for this by requiring controllers to document all personal data breaches, with the functions of these records being to provide the regulator with an evidential basis for assessing compliance with the transparency rules (see GDPR A.33.5). Similar obligations are placed implicitly on data processors, due to how A.28 is written. This is another example of the accountability rule.

### *Rights requests, complaints and claims*
Due to the strict timetables that apply and the risks of escalation, the receipt of rights requests from data subjects should be documented, as should the outcome and the action taken. This arises implicitly from the language of the GDPR, as part of the accountability rule, but it is also a defence mechanism for controllers and processors. Similar logic applies to the receipt of complaints and compensation claims.

In appropriate circumstances, the keeping of records of rights requests, complaints and claims can be justified as being necessary for compliance with legal obligations and as a legitimate business activity (see GDPR A.5.1.c, f). Controllers and processors should also keep in mind that procedural rules that apply to litigation may require the retention of records, albeit this issue falls outside the scope of this book.

Controllers, their officers and employees should also note section 173 of the Data Protection Act 2018, which makes it a criminal offence to delete or tamper with records to avoid complying with data subject access requests and data portability requests. This underscores the importance of good records keeping.

## Marketing and other suppressions

Data subjects have powers to request the cessation of direct marketing activities; cessation of processing that is based on a public interest or official power; and cessation of automated decision making. They also have rights to request the erasure of data. Controllers will have to judge how they address the exercise of these rights, but in some circumstances this may lead them to conclude that they should create processing suppression mechanisms. These matters should be properly documented.

## Programme and project plans

Following the adoption of the GDPR in May 2016, vast numbers of controllers and processors pursued business transformation programmes, in readiness for the law coming into effect in May 2018. In theory at least, these programmes would address compliance across all three layers of the organisation and to do so they would generate documentation necessary for the effective running and management of them. Examples are shown in Table 4.2.

**Table 4.2 Documents created as part of programme and project planning (examples)**

| | |
|---|---|
| The 'business case' | Although compliance with the law is mandatory, making this happen in business often needs a documented business case to be developed, which forms the basis of approvals for expenditure and use of other resources. |
| Programme Office | Business transformations do not run themselves, so a function is needed to manage the day-to-day operations. That function might consist of a 'Programme Office', with personnel involved including:<br>• Programme sponsor (a person who will have managerial accountability for ensuring that the programme delivers on its objectives).<br>• Programme director (who will be in charge of the running of the programme).<br>• Project manager (who will assist the director).<br>• Business analysts (who will liaise with the people outside the Programme Office who are responsible for achieving the delivery objectives of the programme). |
| Workplans | This document divides the programme into various workstreams, identifying the required deliverables and the timeline for delivery, as well as dependencies between deliverables. The workplans are used by the Programme Office, to track and report on progress made. |

*(Continued)*

**Table 4.2 (Continued)**

| | |
|---|---|
| RACIs | This document shows the specific roles and responsibilities for the achievement of specific work items, identifying:<br>• The person who is responsible (R) for doing the work.<br>• The person who has accountability (A) for ensuring that the work is done properly.<br>• Persons who need to be consulted (C) during the delivery of the work, for the purpose of eliciting opinions (such as subject matter experts).<br>• Persons who need to be informed (I) about progress and kept up to date. |

Programme documentation of this kind can be described in several different ways for the purposes of data protection compliance. It might be treated as forming part of the objectives and deliverables required for Data Protection by Design and Default. It might be described as forming part of the appropriate technical and organisational measures required for the purposes of the data protection control framework. It might be described as forming part of the accountability documentation.

## Technology architecture

Organisations that have experienced either complex ICO investigations following personal data breaches caused by cybersecurity events or related large-scale litigation will be able to confirm that documentation about the technology estate forms part of the focus of accountability within these processes of adverse scrutiny. System descriptions, network and systems diagrams and IT asset registers are part of a panoply of documents that need to be considered within the controller's and processor's approach to operationalising the law.

## Assurance records

As shown in Figure 4.1, rather than being a moment-in-time issue, compliance is an ongoing obligation that covers the full life cycle of data processing, from before personal data are obtained (i.e. the design stage), through the initial collecting of personal data (e.g. the transparency objectives), through the actual processing activities themselves and through to the end-of-life stage (deletion, destruction and anonymisation). The multidimensional nature of operational compliance means that controllers and processors must plan for how they will gain assurance that operations are going to plan over time.

### *Audits*
Audit is one of the conventional processes of assurance, when an evidential review is performed of data processing activities, to identify the control objectives that have been put in place and their effectiveness. While an audit conventionally takes a moment-in-time approach, it can be repeated periodically, building up a picture of compliance over

time. Unsurprisingly, audit records are of interest to the ICO during their investigations, as well as disclosable documentation in litigation. Part of the attraction of audit reports in these processes of scrutiny is that they may constitute 'smoking gun' evidence, in the sense of them identifying gaps in controls and their effectiveness that may act as evidence of non-compliance.

The GDPR recognises the significance of audits in several ways, as illustrated in Table 4.3.

**Table 4.3 Audits required by the GDPR (examples)**

| | |
|---|---|
| Processors | When controllers engage processors, the contract (or other legal instrument that appoints them) needs to contain provisions about audits, which commit the processor to engaging in audits conducted by or on behalf of the controller (see A.28.3.h). |
| Data protection officer | The tasks of the DPO include monitoring their organisation's compliance with their audit policies (see A.39.1.b). |
| Binding corporate rules | Where organisations choose to rely on BCR to legitimise international data transfers, they must include audits within their mechanisms for verification of compliance (see A.47.2.j). |
| Regulator powers | The GDPR requires that data protection regulators must be able to carry out audits as part of their investigative powers (see A.58.1.b). |

## *Assessment Notices*

The UK Data Protection Act has dealt with the regulatory audit power through the Assessment Notice procedure. The ICO's current approach to audits prefers a 'consensual' approach, whereby controllers and processors agree to be audited, rather than a 'coercive approach' that follows the imposition of an Assessment Notice. It is a moot point whether there can ever be such a thing as a consensual audit when the regulator carries the threat of coercive powers (there are certainly several important legal questions that arise about the legal rights and protections that an organisation has when they agree to a consensual audit), but for further information about how ICO audits work in practice, see their Audit Guide.[7]

## Other mechanisms for assurance

If the idea of assurance is viewed as a means for gaining documentary evidence that desired outcomes have been achieved, then there are a wide range of other techniques that controllers and processors can use for these purposes when operationalising data protection. Other examples are shown in Table 4.4.

---

7   https://ico.org.uk/for-organisations/audits/

### Table 4.4 Alternatives to audit (examples)

| | |
|---|---|
| Attestations | Controllers might seek written attestations from their employees and workers, or from processors (and processors from their sub-processors) about behaviours and outcomes. |
| Certifications | The GDPR encourages the establishment of data protection certification mechanisms, seals and Kitemarks, for the purposes of demonstrating compliance (see A.42). Standards boards, such as the British Standards Institution, issue standards and certifications on a range of matters that fall within the overall envelope of operational data protection, such as BS 10012 on Personal Information Management. |
| IT controls | Incident prevention and detection technologies should provide an 'audit trail' of evidence (e.g. IP logs and reports) about the performance and use of systems (see, for example, GDPR Recital 87). |
| Training records | These are perceived by data protection regulators and data protection and security professionals as critical evidence within the overall process of assurance. |

## IMPLEMENTING DATA PROTECTION IN THE TECHNOLOGY AND DATA LAYER

For the reasons discussed earlier, the technology and data layer of the organisation constitutes the epicentre of concern for data protection. Therefore, the GDPR places two core obligations on controllers and processors concerning the use of technology:

- Technology risk: They are required to understand the risks to rights and freedoms that are caused by their use of technology. For example, the use of new technologies is one of the factors to be considered when assessing whether to perform a data protection impact assessment.
- Technology controls: They are required to understand the nature of the technology controls that need to be adopted to reduce and mitigate risks to rights and freedoms. These will include physical controls, for example to keep computer equipment physically safe.

Table 4.5 provides some examples of situations within the GDPR where the use of technology is considered from a risk management perspective.

### Table 4.5 GDPR requirements for technology risk management (examples)

| | |
|---|---|
| Identifiability of people, R.26 | • For the purpose of assessing whether information constitutes personal data, account should be taken of all the means reasonably likely to be used to identify a person.<br>• Within the objective factors to be considered is 'available technology' at the time of processing and technological development. |

*(Continued)*

**Table 4.5 (Continued)**

| | |
|---|---|
| Right to be forgotten, R.66; A.17.2 | • When a controller receives an erasure request relating to personal data that they have made public, they must take reasonable steps to inform other controllers who are processing the data of the request.<br><br>• These steps include 'technical measures', taking into account 'available technology'. |
| DPIAs, R.84, 91, 94; A.35, 36. | • The use of new technology on a large scale is provided as an example of processing that could result in a high risk to rights and freedoms, thereby requiring a DPIA.<br><br>• An inability to use available technology to mitigate risk is a factor within an assessment of whether the DPIA needs to be to be referred to the regulator for their review. |
| Children data and consent, A.8.2 | • Where there is a requirement on controllers to obtain parental consent for the provision of 'information society services' to children (i.e. online services) they must make reasonable efforts to verify that the consent is provided by a person with parental responsibility over the child in question.<br><br>• These efforts should take account of available technology. Identity verification technology would form part of these considerations. |
| DPbDD and security, A.25.1, 32.1 | • The obligations placed on controllers to implement appropriate technical and organisational measures for Data Protection by Design and Default and for security, which encompass technology, include a state-of-the-art requirement.<br><br>• This means that controllers must keep abreast of the state of technological development. |
| Incident detection, R.87 | • To give full effect to the personal data breach notification and communication requirements in A.33 and 34, controllers need to implement appropriate technological protection measures (in addition to organisational measures) so that they can establish immediately whether a personal data breach has taken place.<br><br>• These incident detection measures would likely include intrusion detection technologies, for example. |

## Privacy Enhancing Technologies

The requirements for technology controls mean that the use of Privacy Enhancing Technologies (PET) needs to be considered during the design phase of operational data protection. PETs have a long history within operational data protection, as illustrated by the EU PETs Communication in 2007.[8]

---

[8] Communication from the Commission to the European Parliament and the Council on Promoting Data Protection by Privacy Enhancing Technologies (PETs) COM/2007/0228 final.

**Communication on PETs, 2007**

For instance, according to the EC-funded PISA project, PET stands for a coherent system of ICT measures that protects privacy by eliminating or reducing personal data or by preventing unnecessary and/or undesired processing of personal data, all without losing the functionality of the information system. The use of PETs can help to design information and communication systems and services in a way that minimises the collection and use of personal data and facilitate compliance with data protection rules ...

There are many types of PETs available on the market, covering a diverse range of topics such as:

- consent and preference management tools, which aim to give people additional control over how their data are used for analytical purposes, often in the context of marketing-related processing activities;
- cookie-cutters, which help people to manage website tracking technologies;
- differential privacy technologies, which reduce reidentification risks when databases are processed (including publicly shared) for analytics purposes using pseudonymisation techniques.

**Regulatory sandboxes**

A regulatory sandbox provides an environment for regulated entities and their regulators to liaise and interact about innovations and inventions, with the spectre of enforcement risk removed from the conversation. In return for giving the regulator access to information about new products and services that might involve unforeseen or novel risks, the regulated entity gets access to the advice and guidance from the regulator and, if things go well, opportunities to leverage that assistance in a brand-enhancing way.

### *ICO sandbox and children's data*

The UK Information Commissioner's Office launched its sandbox initiative in late 2018 and while it has not been limited to PETs, they have been a key part of its focus. The 2020–21 priority[9] for the sandbox is children's data, due to the introduction of the Age Appropriate Design Code. Issues within this priority zone include: connected toys transparency challenges (including how to deliver relevant information); in-game communications risks (e.g. grooming by predators); and geolocation processing (e.g. how to reduce tracking risks).

### *AI sandbox*

The role that regulatory sandboxes will play in the PET field is only set to increase, as illustrated by the EU's draft AI Regulation, which was published in April 2021.[10]

---

9   https://ico.org.uk/media/for-organisations/documents/2618112/our-key-areas-of-focus-for-regulatory-sandbox.pdf

10  https://digital-strategy.ec.europa.eu/en/library/proposal-regulation-european-approach-artificial-intelligence

> **EU's AI Sandbox, explanatory text**
>
> [The EU] ... encourages national competent authorities to set up regulatory sandboxes and sets a basic framework in terms of governance, supervision and liability. AI regulatory sandboxes establish a controlled environment to test innovative technologies for a limited time on the basis of a testing plan agreed with the competent authorities ...

## 'The Journey to Code'

In his seminal work, *Code and Other Laws of Cyberspace*, published in 1999, Professor Lawrence Lessig argued that in a cyber environment, which is constructed of technology and data, computer code performs the functions of law, in the sense that it regulates and controls the behaviour of technology and data. Therefore, whoever controls the computer code effectively has law-making powers akin to those that were once the sole preserve of the state in the pre-cyber/digital era.

Natural consequences of this situation include that the controllers of code can usurp the law-making functions of the state, or they can work alongside the state to help it to deliver on its public policy objectives within cyberspace and the wider digital environment. The relationship between the state, the traditional lawmaker, and the controllers of code, the new lawmakers, is therefore a complex one, which consists of potential for cooperation, rivalry and tension. Cryptocurrency provides a current example of these dynamics, as the design of Bitcoin and the like are intended to provide an alternative to the state-controlled financial system. In contrast, during the COVID-19 pandemic an alliance was formed between Google and Apple that worked alongside the activities of the state, to develop a decentralised system for contact tracing apps.

The trajectory of data protection law is one where the traditional lawmakers of the state will have ever-increasing concern about the technology and data layer and, ultimately, how data protection is operationalised through the computer code that controls technology and data. As such, it seems obvious that data protection law requires data controllers and processors to go on 'The Journey to Code' and it can be anticipated that the quality of computer code and its performance will increasingly form part of the scrutiny that is applied to data processing, particularly in adverse situations such as regulatory enforcement actions and in legal proceedings.

Figure 4.2 is a high-level technology reference architecture document that provides an illustration of some of the elements of technology that support data processing and where compliance objectives reside.

## Figure 4.2 The Journey to Code

The Journey to Code: a technology reference architecture for Privacy by Design, inc. GDPR

In recent years there has been an explosion of interest and awareness in data protection matters (sometimes called 'data privacy'), due to a combination of factors, including high-profile data-handing scandals and abuses, the persistence of civil society organisations in their defence of privacy rights, the engagement of mainstream news reporting and major legal changes, such as GDPR in Europe and the California Consumer Privacy Act in the United States.

These factors are driving business and organisational change, but the evidence provided by many sources, including the regulatory system itself, shows that the mechanisms used to deliver the requirements of data protection are still sub-optimal in many situations. The requirements include the principles and rights of data protection, such as transparency about processing activities, minimisation of processing activities, the right of access to personal data and the right to be forgotten.

The performance of organisations on data protection might be improved by the development of a technology reference architecture (TRA) that can address both the needs of 'privacy management' and the need to deliver functional outcomes in technology and data themselves. A TRA would also support 'The Journey to Code', a point in time when the requirements of data protection are actually coded in to technology and data. These ideas would form part of a Privacy by Design (PbD) framework.

A legal case for a TRA can be made. For example, GDPR Article 24 requires controllers of personal data to 'implement appropriate technical and organisational measures' for data protection, while A. 25 imposes a 'state-of-the-art' test for those measures. Collectively, these articles can be interpreted to require a TRA as that in turn will help the process of identifying relevant state-of-the-art technologies that should be considered for deployment.

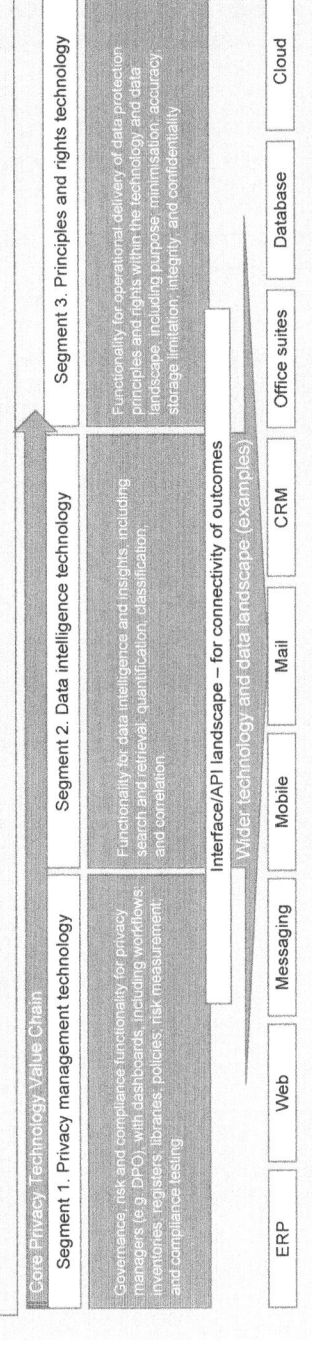

**Core Privacy Technology: Value Chain**

| Segment 1. Privacy management technology | Segment 2. Data intelligence technology | Segment 3. Principles and rights technology |
|---|---|---|
| Governance, risk and compliance functionality for privacy managers (e.g. DPO), with dashboards, including workflows; inventories, registers, libraries, policies, risk measurement; and compliance testing | Functionality for data intelligence and insights, including search and retrieval; quantification, classification; and correlation. | Functionality for operational delivery of data protection principles and rights within the technology and data landscape, including purpose, minimisation; accuracy; storage limitation; integrity; and confidentiality |

Interface/API landscape – for connectivity of outcomes

Wider technology and data landscape (examples)

| ERP | Web | Messaging | Mobile | Mail | CRM | Office suites | Database | Cloud |

Legal-functionality map. The functionality within each segment of the Core Privacy Technology Value Chain should be mapped to the legal requirements for data protection in which the TRA will be used. In Segment 1., for example, a dashboard would map to GDPR A.5.2 (accountability principle) and A.39 (tasks of the data protection officer). The functionality in Segment 2. would map to A.24, etc. Segment 3 would map to GDPR Chapter III, for example. The mapping would also cover case law, regulatory guidance and enforcement cases, etc.

## RISK MANAGEMENT – IMPLEMENTING MEASURES TO ASSESS RISKS TO RIGHTS AND FREEDOMS AND THE APPROPRIATENESS OF CONTROLS

A risk-based approach to operational data protection requires that the largest risks or most immediate risks need to be prioritised above lesser risks. Therefore, the risk assessment methodology that is deployed needs to be able to assess the likelihood, size and impacts of risk and the nature and appropriateness of the controls that should be applied in mitigation. This cannot be done without the use of reliable benchmarks against which these issues can be compared, contrasted and judged. Table 4.6 illustrates the types of benchmark that might be considered within developing risk assessment methodologies.

**Table 4.6 Benchmarks for risk assessments and for determining what is appropriate (examples)**

| | |
|---|---|
| Identifying the rights and freedoms covered by data protection law | The EU Charter of Fundamental Rights is the most comprehensive statement of rights currently available. It helpfully reminds us that data protection is about much more than the right to privacy. |
| Data protection regulatory enforcement action | The EDPB, the ICO and other national regulators publish information on their websites about the action they have taken. This can guide controllers and processors on the causes of operational failure, the impacts of failure and the level of seriousness that attaches. |
| Data protection regulatory guidance | This provides information about priorities, desired outcomes and good and bad practice. |
| Judicial decisions | Case law operates in the same way as regulatory enforcement actions, but with a higher authoritative value, due to the superiority of the courts in the legal system. Outcomes in criminal cases can have higher authoritative value than civil cases due to the enhanced rigour of the criminal law process. |
| Standards for best practice | Technical standards published by bodies such as the International Organization for Standardization (ISO), the National Institute of Standards and Technology (NIST) and the EU Agency for Cyber Security (ENISA) can provide very granular assistance with risk management. |
| Sectoral requirements | Many sectors of the economy have their own regulators. Their sector-specific requirements should be considered within risk management. |
| Professional requirements | Similarly, many parts of the economy have professional requirements, which should also be considered. |
| Alerts and advisories | From time-to-time bodies such as the National Cyber Security Centre in the UK (NCSC), anti-fraud organisations and law enforcement agencies will issue alerts and advisories about prevailing data protection threats and corresponding safeguards. Technology companies and professional services firms are other good sources of current awareness. |

*(Continued)*

## Table 4.6 (Continued)

| | |
|---|---|
| Stakeholder viewpoints and evidence | Civil society organisations such as Liberty, Privacy International and Big Brother Watch regularly publish viewpoints and evidence on matters of high concern. Parliament regularly receives expert evidence on these issues. |
| Threat and vulnerability assessments | Analysis of the threat landscape can be tailored specifically for named organisations. |
| Dark Web and rogue fora | The Dark Web and rogue fora on the Surface Web provide marketplaces for stolen personal data and services and tools that are used to commit data protection crimes. This provides compelling insights into the real nature of harms that result from data misuse. |

### The adequacy test

The validity and utility of the kind of benchmarks described in Table 4.6 is supported by the adequacy test for international transfers that is contained in A.45.2. This identifies a range of factors that need to be assessed when judging the adequacy of data protection in countries that are not subject to the GDPR. These include sectoral rules, professional rules and security measures in place in those countries.

### The impact of the 'consensus of professional opinion' – what are the risks and what should be done about them?

Information that supports risk management that is found outside the express requirements of the GDPR (i.e. everything within Table 4.6) can be compiled under a single heading, namely 'the consensus of professional opinion', which is sometimes referred to as 'the consensus of expert opinion'. The consensus of these opinions on matters of technical expertise provides a basis recognised in law for forming judgments and making decisions on matters of risk management. Risk management for data protection is a matter of technical expertise (as the phrase 'appropriate technical and organisation measures' demonstrates). Thus, the answers to the questions 'what are the risks?' and 'what should be done about them?' are always found within the consensus of professional, expert opinion.

### Risk management – dealing with adverse scrutiny

Despite data processing benefitting humankind in ways that are simply too numerous to list, controllers and processors must be prepared for the risks of criticism and challenges, even in situations that they feel are clear-cut. For example, in the fight against COVID-19, it might be hard to argue against contact tracing apps and vaccine passports from a public health perspective, but when looked at through the lens of data protection, the risks they involve are perceived to be huge, so they cannot simply be 'waved through'.

Instead, they must be robustly challenged as part of a system of necessary checks and balances, which needs the application of 'adverse scrutiny'. This means testing the data processing system against the benchmark of the strongest criticism and challenge that might be encountered when the system is live. Failure to do so may result in legal and operational flaws in the system being overlooked. The *Bridges* (2020) case on AFR shows what can happen if adverse scrutiny is not applied during planning of the system. Other examples include:

- During the 'War on Terror', increased surveillance through data processing was part of the response, but this led to the creation of the mass surveillance system that was exposed by Edward Snowden, who applied the adverse scrutiny of a whistle-blower. Thereafter, there were numerous court cases, and the system did not survive this process of adverse scrutiny completely intact.
- Proponents of the free web argue that direct marketing to its users is a fair quid pro quo. The GDPR imposes many conditions around this, and civil society organisations have shown themselves ready to use litigation against the underlying the AdTech. The *Vidal-Hall* (2015) and *Lloyd v. Google* (2019) cases are illustrations of the kind of adverse scrutiny that may arise.
- If a personal data breach is communicated to data subjects under GDPR A.34, compensation claims must be expected. These can put the defendant's systems and controls for data security under intense scrutiny.

Table 4.7 illustrates some of the considerations when planning for and dealing with adverse scrutiny.

**Table 4.7 Adverse scrutiny operational imperatives (examples)**

| | |
|---|---|
| Data Protection by Design and Default | • During the planning phase of data protection, the risk assessment methodology should identify the situations where challenge and scrutiny may arise, the form this might take and the impacts involved. |
| | • Scenario planning might include 'war-gaming', 'rehearsals' and 'dry-runs' of challenging events. |
| Detection and categorisation | • In a security sense, adverse scrutiny may take the form of a cybercrime or malware attack and an absence of appropriate detection capabilities will constitute a breach of the integrity and confidentiality principle if personal data are at risk. |
| | • A DSAR does not need to be labelled as such, or even contained in writing, so their receipt might be overlooked, putting the controller at peril of breaching the strict timetable that applies for responses. |
| | • Failing to deal with problems properly in a customer contact centre is often the reason for why initially minor and seemingly solvable problems escalate into larger intractable ones. |
| Crisis management | • Effective crisis management is associated with good planning, which can involve scenario testing in appropriate cases and the development of playbooks. |
| | • Want of planning can easily lead to a crisis being mishandled. |

*(Continued)*

**Table 4.7 (Continued)**

| | |
|---|---|
| Legal professional privilege and circles of confidence | • Knowing when and how legal professional privilege can be used to help protect communications from third-party inspection can be a critical operational objective. |
| | • This includes understanding the interplay between the maintenance of confidentiality in communications and the protection of privilege. |
| Style and posture | • The style and posture of the response to criticism and challenge will differ across situations. |
| | • For example, in a ransomware negotiation where the controller is dealing with criminals to secure decryptors or avoid publication of the event on the Dark Web, the controller has no leverage other than money. |
| | • In a litigation situation a controller has significant leverage, even in seemingly losing situations. |
| | • An aggressive and confrontational style in a regulatory investigation will always be counterproductive. However, a firm, strong and challenging style may be unavoidable if the regulator is embarking upon a questionable legal pathway. |

## GLOBALISATION – IMPLEMENTING DATA PROTECTION ON AN INTERNATIONAL STAGE

Controllers and processors that operate on the international stage have the added operational challenge of dealing with differences in national laws.

### International transfers – adequacy, appropriate safeguards and derogations

The basic rule is that personal data cannot be transferred to a 'third country', which means a country outside the land mass in Europe where the GDPR applies, if that country does not provide an adequate system of data protection, as judged by the GDPR's standards (A.44 and 45). However, the prohibition can be overcome if the transfer takes place pursuant to appropriate safeguards (A.46), or if a derogation to the rule applies (A.49).

### Meaning of 'adequacy' for the purposes of international transfers

The meaning of adequacy is set out in A.45 and it was explored by the CJEU in the *Schrems I* (2015) and *Schrems II* (2020) cases. A third country's data protection system will be adequate if it is essentially equivalent to the GDPR's. Guidance issued by the EDPB after the *Schrems II* judgment explains more about what this involves (see 'Transfer assessments', above).

The European Commission takes charge of the determination of adequacy of third countries. Once satisfied that a country is adequate the Commission will adopt an adequacy decision. There is an equivalent system in the UK GDPR, which allows adequacy regulations to be adopted.

The current list of countries that have been deemed adequate by the EU are Andorra, Argentina, Canada (commercial organisations), Faroe Islands, Guernsey, Israel, Isle of Man, Japan, Jersey, New Zealand, South Korea, Switzerland, Uruguay and the UK.

## Adequacy of the UK

The European Commission adopted two adequacy decisions in respect of the UK on 28 June 2021, one in respect of the GDPR and the other in respect of the LED. Data can now flow freely from the EU to the UK, but the decisions are subject to ongoing monitoring and four-year 'sunset clauses' (i.e. the adequacy decisions will have to be reviewed and extended before the end of the four-year periods, otherwise they will expire).

## Appropriate safeguards

Appropriate safeguards for personal data that are transferred to third countries can be provided through these mechanisms:

- legally binding instruments between public authorities/bodies;
- standard data protection clauses adopted by the European Commission, or by the UK Secretary of State;
- standard data protection clauses adopted by national regulators (in the case of those adopted by the regulators in the 27 EU Member States, these need to be approved by the European Commission, but an equivalent process of approval is not required under the UK GDPR);
- the use of approved schemes issues under the Code of Conduct and Certification rules in A. 40 and 42;
- the use of binding corporate rules (A.47);
- ad hoc mechanisms approved by the national regulators.

Standard data protection clauses have been approved by the European Commission. After the *Schrems II* (2020) judgment, the EDPB issued guidance[11] on how their use can be supplemental with additional guarantees. This was done to address some of the operational challenges of using contractual mechanisms to achieve essentially equivalent outcomes in third countries.

## Derogations

The derogations against the ban on transfers to non-adequate third countries include:

- the explicit consent of the data subject;

---

[11] EDPB Recommendations 01/2020 on measures that supplement transfer tools to ensure compliance with the EU level of protection of personal data.

- performance of contracts with, or for the benefit of, the data subject, where the transfer is necessary to achieve that;
- for important reasons of public interest, where the transfer is necessary for that purpose;
- for the establishment, exercise and defence of legal claims, where the transfer is necessary for that purpose.

**Wider operational challenges of international activities**

Leaving aside the Brexit issues, those related to international data transfers and the aftermath of the CJEU judgment in the *Schrems II* (2020) case, key issues are illustrated in Table 4.8.

**Table 4.8 Considerations within an international processing environment (examples)**

| | |
|---|---|
| One size model | • Should organisations build to a single, common global standard (i.e. a one size fits all approach), or should its approach reflect the actual realities of data protection in the countries within which it operates? |
| | • The operational advantages of a unified approach include having certainty of aims and objectives, which in theory should make planning easier. |
| | • Disadvantages include the risk of creating heightened expectations and perhaps even heightened legal obligations in countries where the mandatory requirements of data protection are lower than those set by the unified standard. |
| | • A unified approach might also involve problems associated with perceptions about 'cultural imperialism', where the ideals of one part of the world are being imposed on others. |
| Divergences | • Adopting a unified approach will not by itself absolve the multinational from a requirement to understand, track and deal with developments in the countries where it operates. |

## IMPACTS FOR MICRO, SMALL AND MEDIUM-SIZED ENTERPRISES

The legal and operational needs of data protection do not make many allowances for smaller organisations, nor do risks to rights and freedoms. The places in the GDPR where these organisations get special treatment are set out in Table 4.9.

### Size of enterprise and size of risk

The fact that an enterprise is micro, small, or medium-sized does not automatically mean that their risks are micro, small, or medium-sized when compared to larger organisations. The size of risk is determined by the overall nature, scope, context and purposes of processing (see A.25.1). Size of the organisation is a factor within the overall context, and risk levels might be enhanced by an enterprise's smaller size, if the size constrains the resources for risk management. A small organisation that plays a pivotal role in, say, ecommerce fulfilment might be a much riskier proposition than a very large 'bricks and mortar' business, where data processing is a minor element of their business, rather than a goal.

**Table 4.9 Special treatment of micro, small and medium-sized enterprises**

| | |
|---|---|
| Records of processing activities, A.30.3 | The requirement to maintain ROPAs is relaxed for an enterprise or organisation employing fewer than 250 persons, unless:<br>• Its processing is likely to result in a risk to rights and freedoms, or<br>• The processing is not occasional, or<br>• The processing involves special category data or criminal convictions and offences. |
| Codes of conduct, A.40 | • The GDPR requires Member States, the national regulators, the EDPB and the European Commission to encourage the drawing up of codes of conduct for the proper application of the law (i.e. for operationalisation of the law).<br>• The need for these to take account of micro, small and medium-sized enterprises is specifically called out. |
| Certification, A.42 | • Similar requirements are provided for certification mechanisms, seals and marks. |

### Financial resources, cost and risk

The GDPR refers to the issue of cost of implementing data protection controls in several situations, with the rule being that cost can be taken account of during risk management, but an organisation's inability to afford appropriate data protection controls does not operate as a 'get-out-of-jail-free' card. If an organisation cannot afford to address risks to an appropriate level, the law's solution is for it to cease, or not commence, data processing. Table 4.10 illustrates how cost can be a factor within risk management.

## SECURITY AND CONNECTION TO WIDER LEGAL AND OPERATIONAL FRAMEWORKS

Most of the expectations for security are not described in the GDPR. Instead, the GDPR borrows from the wider consensus of professional opinion, due to setting the obligation for security as the taking of appropriate technical and organisational measures.

### Table 4.10 Situations within the GDPR where cost is a consideration within risk management

| | |
|---|---|
| Identifiability, R.26 | • If data cannot identify a person, those data are not personal data and so are not regulated by the GDPR. |
| | • To determine whether data are identifiable, a list of illustrative factors are included in R.26, one of which is the cost. |
| Security, R.83 and A.32.1 | These provisions explain that cost is a factor in determining the appropriateness of security controls. |
| Data protection impact assessments, R.84, 94 | • If a DPIA concludes that processing is high risk, the matter should be referred to the regulator if the risks cannot be mitigated. |
| | • When determining whether a risk can be mitigated, cost is a factor. |
| Right to be forgotten, A.17.2 | • The exercise of the right to be forgotten may require the controller to take reasonable steps to inform other controllers of the need for erasure. |
| | • One of the factors to consider when assessing the reasonableness of these steps is the cost of implementing technology for this purpose. |
| Data Protection by Design and Default, A.25.1 | Cost is a factor within the assessment of the appropriateness of the controls that are needed to operationalise the data protection principles. |

That being said, there are two security regimes in the GDPR, which are both distinct and interrelated, both of which have to be operationalised. These are summarised in Table 4.11.

### Table 4.11 The two security regimes in the GDPR

| | |
|---|---|
| Preventative and restorative security | • These are the rules contained within A.5.1.f and 32, which require controllers to implement appropriate technical and organisation measures to ensure that personal data are protected against unauthorised or unlawful processing and accidental loss, destruction, or damage. |
| | • The rules are preventative, in the sense that they are aimed at preventing personal data breaches from happening. |
| | • They are also restorative, in the sense that they require controllers to remedy security breaches. |

*(Continued)*

**Table 4.11 (Continued)**

| | |
|---|---|
| Personal data breach notification and communication | • These transparency rules are contained in A.33 and 34. |
| | • The requirement for incident detection technology, which is mentioned in R.87, provides the operational glue that binds the two frameworks together. |
| | • It is important to note that the definition of a personal data breach, contained in A.4.12, does not require a security control to be circumvented for the personal data breach notification and communications rules to apply. |

## SUMMARY

In conclusion, this chapter gives readers a better understanding of:

- the law's requirements for operational data protection;
- the layers of the organisation in which the legal requirements need to be operationalised;
- the range of issues that need to be addressed when operationalising data protection;
- the need for operational risk management;
- the issues that arise for international organisations and small and micro organisations.

# PART II
# CORE LAW

# 5 THE PRINCIPLES OF DATA PROTECTION

## Shervin Nahid

This chapter provides an overview of the data protection principles, which are the compliance backbone of not just the GDPR, but similar legal instruments the world over. This chapter also provides an overview of the lawful bases for the processing of personal data, which form part of the first data protection principle.

### A CONSTANT PRESENCE IN DATA PROTECTION LAW

The focus of the data protection principles embodied in the GDPR has remained remarkably constant over the 50-year history of the law and while being a European invention, they have been internationalised, with notable examples including the OECD Guidelines on the Protection of Privacy and Transborder Flows of Personal Data, adopted in 1980, and the APEC Privacy Framework, adopted in 2005. Recent legislative developments in the USA, Brazil and India also take similar, principles-based approaches to data protection.

Such is the success of the principles, they can be regarded as having transcended the strict confines of legislative and regulatory law, into standards for operational best practice that trustworthy and responsible holders and users of personal data will choose to adhere to when processing personal data, regardless of the state of the law on the ground in the countries where they operate. The internationalisation of the principles should not be confused with the idea of perfect harmonisation of laws or operational practices, however. Despite their widespread popularity, the principles have not caused a worldwide consensus to be achieved on all aspects of data protection.

### THE DUTY OF COMPLIANCE (ACCOUNTABILITY)

The principles are set out in Article 5.1 of the GDPR, together with the duty of compliance: Article 5.2 says that 'the controller shall be responsible for, and be able to demonstrate compliance with', the principles. This duty of demonstrable compliance is called accountability and it is backed up with regulatory enforcement powers, which include the risk of fines. Article 83.5a states that infringements of the principles may be subject to the maximum administrative fine under the GDPR, which demonstrates their significance and the incentive for controllers to comply with them.

## LAWFULNESS, FAIRNESS AND TRANSPARENCY – THE FIRST PRINCIPLE

The first principle at Article 5.1.a says that personal data shall be 'processed lawfully, fairly and in a transparent manner in relation to the data subject'. Collectively, the ideas of 'lawful', 'fair' and 'transparent' processing cover a lot of ground.

### Lawfulness

To meet the requirement of lawful processing, organisations must identify a specific lawful basis for processing personal data. The options are contained in A.6. Additionally, where special categories of personal data are being processed, a condition in A.9 must be satisfied. If a controller is unable to identify a lawful basis, the processing will be automatically unlawful. In addition, carrying out any processing activity that does not comply with the wider provisions of the GDPR would also be considered unlawful. In other words, processing will not be lawful if the controller is unable to satisfy all of its legal obligations as set out in the legislation.

However, the concept of lawfulness means much more than compliance with the GDPR itself. It also means that processing should be lawful as judged by reference to the totality of the laws that may apply to the situation of processing.

This idea is brought to life when the situation of automated facial recognition is considered. Concerns have been raised about the quality of the algorithms that support AFR, in that evidence has been found about differing accuracy levels across ethnic and gender groups, which might produce discriminatory 'false positive' effects, including risks of false arrests in a policing situation. Therefore, if discrimination law is breached through the use of AFR technology, the first principle would hold the processing to be unlawful for data protection law purposes.

### Fairness

To meet the requirement of fair processing, it is important that personal data are processed in accordance with an individual's reasonable expectations and in a way that does not have an unjustified adverse effect on them. It is typically at the point of data collection where an individual's expectations are set. Therefore, where an individual is coerced into accepting an organisation's processing due to an imbalance of bargaining power between them and the organisation, such conduct is unlikely to be regarded as 'fair'. Processing is also unlikely to be fair when it deceives or misleads individuals.[1] It is therefore important that the concept of fairness is embedded into an organisation's measures for transparency.

### Transparency

The transparency requirement relates to individuals being informed of how and for what purposes their personal data will be processed and any associated consequences of that processing.[2] It also includes informing individuals about profiling and whether

---

[1] ICO Guidance, For organisations, Guide to Data Protection, Guide to the General Data Protection Regulation (GDPR), Principles, Principle (a): Lawfulness, fairness and transparency.

their data have been involved in high-risk data breaches. In its guidance on the concept of transparency, the EDPB states that transparency 'is about engendering trust in the processes which affect the citizen by enabling them to understand, and if necessary, challenge those processes'.[3]

The details of how transparency should work are set out Article 12 and it identifies the situations where a duty of transparency arises and how the duty is fulfilled. These situations cover:

- during the collection of data phase of processing, when data are first obtained from a data subject, or from a third party. See A.13 and 14;
- during the exercise of the data subject rights. See A.15 to 22;
- after a personal data breach. See A.34.

The transparency information that is provided to an individual should make them aware of the risks, rules, safeguards and rights relating to the processing and how to exercise their rights.[4] The provision of information must be in compliance with the following rules:

- Transparency information must be 'concise, transparent, intelligible and easily accessible'.[5] This refers to information being presented 'efficiently and succinctly in order to avoid information fatigue'.[6] The information should be separated from non-privacy related information and understandable to an average member of the intended audience. Also, the individual should not have to seek out the information. Instead, it should be immediately apparent to them where and how to access it. This can be achieved, for example, by an online link to a layered privacy statement.[7] A layered approach means providing a short piece of key information (the first layer) with links to expanded sections (i.e. to additional layers) that provide more detailed information.
- Clear, plain and the native language of the intended audience must be used. This idea ties closely to the intelligibility requirement and requires the information to be conveyed in as simple a manner as possible using concrete and definitive language, avoiding complex sentence and language structures.[8] When processing children's personal data, particular care must be taken to ensure communications are appropriately adapted considering the vocabulary used, tone and style.
- The information must be provided in writing or by other means, including, where appropriate, electronically. As well as privacy statements, electronic means of presenting information may include pop-up notices, three-dimensional (3D) touch

---

2   Recitals 39 and 60 GDPR.
3   Page 4, Art. 29 WP Guidelines on Transparency under Regulation 2016/679, WP260 rev.01.
4   Recital 39.
5   Article 12(1) GDPR.
6   Page 7, Art. 29 WP Guidelines on Transparency under Regulation 2016/679, WP260 rev.01.
7   Page 8, ibid.
8   Ibid.

or hover-over notices and privacy dashboards (sometimes called, or forming part, of 'preference centres').[9] Where requested by the individual (and their identity has been verified), the information may be provided orally.[10] The specific context of the processing can help organisations in deciding which is the most appropriate communication tool.

- The information generally must be provided free of charge.[11] This also means that information cannot be made conditional upon financial transactions, for example payment for a service.[12]

## PURPOSE LIMITATION – THE SECOND PRINCIPLE

The purpose limitation principle states that personal data should be 'collected for specified, explicit and legitimate purposes and not further processed in a manner that is incompatible with those purposes'. The aims of this principle include avoiding confusion and ambiguity about the processing purpose and the occurrence of 'purpose creep' (sometimes called 'function creep'), when processing for an initial purpose leads to processing for other, unrelated purposes.

The principle requires organisations to clearly identify a specific processing purpose and convey that purpose in a clear and transparent way to individuals. Once a lawful purpose is identified by the controller, it should be documented appropriately, for example within the organisation's records of processing activities that needs to be created for compliance with A.30. Periodic reviews of the ROPA will assist the organisation in confirming that all processing is compatible with the original documented purpose and that no purpose creep has occurred.

Due to how the principle is stated, expanding the existing processing of personal data to pursue a new purpose is likely to be problematic in most cases. However, Article 5.1.b highlights three specific purposes that may reconcile this issue and enable an organisation to continue its data processing beyond its original purpose, for a new purpose.

### Expanded purposes – archiving in the public interest

Whilst unlikely to be available to most controllers, some public authorities will seek to rely on this purpose when carrying out their legal obligation to 'provide access to records of enduring value for general public interest'.[13] This would cover records such as court files, for example.

### Expanded purposes – scientific and historical research

This can cover any raw microdata that requires preservation for these expanded purposes. Historical research purposes might cover significant research that may relate

---

[9] Page 12, ibid.

[10] Article 12.1 GDPR.

[11] Article 12.5 GDPR.

[12] Page 13, Art. 29 WP Guidelines on Transparency under Regulation 2016/679, WP260 rev.01.

[13] Recital 158 GDPR.

to family history or historical figures (whilst noting that the GDPR does not apply to deceased persons).[14] In relation to scientific purposes, due to the possible sensitivity of the personal data, Recital 159 says that 'special conditions ... in particular as regards the publication or otherwise disclosure of personal data' should attach to those data.

### Expanded purposes – statistics

Statistical purposes means 'any operation of collection and the processing of personal data necessary for statistical surveys or for the production of statistical results'.[15] For example, the use of travel data for surveys and the production of statistics relating to travelling habits can fall within this expanded purpose. Statistical purposes do not provide grounds for processing personal data if the same outcomes could be achieved with anonymised personal data, however.

### Compatibility

The expanded purposes are permissible because the GDPR deems that they remain compatible with the original purpose for which the data were processed.[16] Moving past those expanded purposes, a new purpose is likely to be compatible with the original purpose when the following requirements are satisfied:

- a link exists between the old and new purposes;
- the data subject would reasonably expect their data to be processed for a new purpose;
- the personal data are not particularly sensitive;
- the new purpose causes no, or minimal, potential consequences for the data subject;
- appropriate safeguards are put in place, such as encryption or pseudonymisation.[17]

If these requirements cannot be satisfied, the controller will need to rely upon a new legal basis to process the data for a new purpose (and then follow all of the compliance rules that apply, including repeating all necessary transparency requirements), which might include obtaining specific consent for the new purpose. Seeking consent is likely to be the most common course of action for a controller in this situation, given the relatively limited set of circumstances where the original processing purpose will be compatible with the new purpose.

## DATA MINIMISATION – THE THIRD PRINCIPLE

To satisfy the data minimisation principle, personal data processing must be 'adequate, relevant and limited to what is necessary in relation to the purposes for which they are

---

14 Recital 160 GDPR.

15 Recital 162 GDPR.

16 Recital 50 GDPR.

17 ICO Guidance, For organisations, Guide to Data Protection, Guide to the General Data Protection Regulation (GDPR), Principles, Principle (b): Purpose limitation.

processed'.[18] This principle seeks to stop organisations from hoarding data beyond what is necessary to fulfil their data processing purpose. A controller should understand what its minimum viable product is in terms of the amount of data processing required.

The GDPR breaks down data minimisation into the following three components:

- ensuring the data processed are adequate, that is, sufficient to properly fulfil the controller's stated purpose, but no more;
- the personal data are relevant, that is, they have a reasonably foreseeable link to that purpose;
- the data are limited to what is necessary, that is, no more are used than are needed for that purpose.

The data subject rights assist controllers with their data minimisation obligations. For example, where incomplete data are inadequate to fulfil a controller's purposes, an individual may be able to exercise their right to rectification to correct or complete them. Where excessive data are being processed, an individual may be able to exercise their right to erasure.

## ACCURACY – THE FOURTH PRINCIPLE

Article 5.1.d says that personal data shall be 'accurate and, where necessary, kept up to date; every reasonable step must be taken to ensure that personal data that are inaccurate, having regard to the purposes for which they are processed, are erased or rectified without delay'.

Accuracy is not defined by the GDPR, but section 205 of the UK DPA defines inaccurate personal data as 'incorrect or misleading as to any matter of fact'. To lessen the chances of data being perceived to be inaccurate, controllers should be clear about what they intend their record of processing to show. For example, where an employer holds a current address for one of its employees and the employee moves to a new address, the old address is only inaccurate if it is still labelled as being the employee's current address. However, if the old address is recorded as no longer being the current address, it is not inaccurate personal data.

Two nuanced circumstances may arise when considering the accuracy principle. The first is the keeping of records of processing mistakes. It may be necessary to keep a record of a mistake made, provided that it is clearly labelled as a mistake and the correction is clear (e.g. a retailer overcharging for a product and later refunding the difference in price whilst keeping a copy of the receipts). The second circumstance is the accuracy of opinions. An individual may disagree with an opinion, but that does not make an opinion inaccurate, even where the opinion is later proved to be wrong. An opinion is a statement that is not conclusive, as opposed to facts, which are true statements.

How an organisation should keep personal data up to date will depend on the specifics of the processing. For example, in some cases it can be reasonable to rely on the data

---

[18] Article 5.1c GDPR.

subject to inform the controller about changes of fact, such as changes of address. In other cases, a controller should proactively update its records, such as when updating employee payroll records to record when pay rises occur.

## STORAGE LIMITATION – THE FIFTH PRINCIPLE

To comply with the storage limitation principle, organisations must ensure personal data are 'kept in a form which permits identification of data subjects for no longer than is necessary for the purposes for which the personal data are processed'.[19]

The importance of the storage limitation principle stems from the risk that personal data eventually become irrelevant, excessive, inaccurate or out of date. Storing personal data unnecessarily is likely to be unlawful and inefficient: unlawful because once the purpose of the processing has been satisfied, there will be no further need for processing and so the data should be erased or anonymised; inefficient because secure storage for the excess personal data is likely to incur additional unnecessary costs.

The GDPR does not set specific data storage limits, but other laws may dictate minimum or maximum retention periods (for example, tax laws, statutes of limitation, or rules on 'litigation hold' that mandate data retention when court proceedings are contemplated). For many processing activities, no specific data retention legislation exists, so controllers will need to make a justifiable judgment as to the appropriate retention period and document the logic behind it.[20]

Most organisations will need to establish standard retention periods for their processing activities, which should be documented in a retention policy or schedule. Data retention policies assist an organisation by maintaining governance and regulatory compliance. Regular reviews of retention periods should be undertaken at appropriate intervals. Using automated systems to flag records for review or to automatically erase personal data after a predetermined period are particularly helpful as they minimise the risk of human error. Implementing such technology aligns with the concept of 'The Journey to Code', explored elsewhere in this book.

Permanently deleting personal data from a system is not always straightforward, for example if copies exist in multiple backups that cannot be modified without corrupting the archive. However, the ICO has recognised this and stated that deletion requirements would be satisfied by 'putting information "beyond use"', if not actually deleted.[21] The ICO provides four safeguards that must be satisfied by organisations to meet its requirements of deletion. The organisation:

- is not able, or will not attempt, to use the personal data to inform any decision in respect of any individual or in a manner that affects the individual in any way;
- does not give any other organisation access to the personal data;

---

[19] Article 5.1e GDPR.

[20] Page 10, Data Retention Guidance, Data Protection Network, 4 June 2020.

[21] Page 5, Deleting Personal Data, ICO Guidance, 26 February 2014.

- surrounds the personal data with appropriate technical and organisational security; and
- commits to permanent deletion of the information if, or when, this becomes possible.[22]

As with the purpose limitation principle, processing for archiving purposes in the public interest, scientific or historical research or statistical purposes are permissible for indefinite periods so long as these are lawfully available to the controller.

## INTEGRITY AND CONFIDENTIALITY (INCLUDING SECURITY) – THE SIXTH PRINCIPLE

To satisfy the integrity and confidentiality principle (the 'security principle'), personal data must be 'processed in a manner that ensures appropriate security of the personal data, including protection against unauthorised or unlawful processing and against accidental loss, destruction or damage, using appropriate technical or organisational measures'.[23]

Security is required to protect personal data against internal and external threats. Controllers have a responsibility to protect personal data from accidental and deliberate compromise. The duty of security covers organisational security measures, physical measures and technological measures.

The security principle is supported by A.32, which is titled 'Security of processing'. A.32 does not define the security measures required by organisations, but instead demands that the level of security must be appropriate to the risks presented to the data and the impacts that insecurity will have on the people affected, which clearly will vary from organisation to organisation. A.32 does not pose a static requirement, but, instead, it requires controllers and processors to continuously consider new and evolving security measures by 'taking into account the state of the art'.[24]

Technical and organisational measures considered from a data security perspective are a vast subject area and one that extends beyond the remit of this book. The reader may consider other useful resources such as the NIST Privacy Framework,[25] which sets out specific activities and outcomes relevant to managing privacy risk that will assist in implementing such measures.

## ACCOUNTABILITY – THE SEVENTH PRINCIPLE

The accountability principle in A.5.2 states that 'the controller shall be responsible for, and be able to demonstrate compliance with, paragraph 1', with paragraph 1 being

---

**22** Ibid.

**23** Article 5.1f GDPR.

**24** Article 32.1 GDPR.

**25** NIST Privacy Framework: A tool for improving privacy through enterprise risk management, January 2020.

the preceding principles discussed above. The duty of demonstrable compliance that it imposes means that the controller will need to be able to show a regulator and potentially the courts that it has achieved the outcomes required by the principles in its systems and operations.

Due to the expansive nature of data protection compliance, things will go wrong from time to time, even in the best run organisation, but if the controller can actively demonstrate its consideration of risks and safeguards, it is far more likely to avoid serious regulatory enforcement action and litigation than one with a more cavalier attitude.

Accountability documentation should include data maps, legitimate interests assessments, risk assessments (e.g. DPIAs), records of processing and events (e.g. ROPAs and breach logs), assurance activities and third-party contracting paperwork. However, organisations should be cognisant of the fact that the mere creation of paper-based documentation will not suffice to evidence accountability, which requires the paper-policy to be operationalised across the organisation. To be responsible for and demonstrate compliance with the GDPR, an effective data protection management framework that covers all key data processing areas of the organisation is essential.

## LAWFULNESS OF PROCESSING OF PERSONAL DATA (ARTICLE 6)

Data protection law places a duty on controllers to identify an appropriate 'lawful basis' for their processing activities. Article 6 sets out the six lawful bases, which are:

1. Consent, where a data subject has given their consent to the processing of their personal data for a specific purpose.
2. Contract, where the processing is necessary for a contract to which the individual is subject, or because that individual has asked the organisation to take specific steps before entering into a contract, for example by providing a quotation.
3. Legal obligation, where the processing is necessary for an organisation to comply with the law (not including contractual obligations).
4. Vital interest, where the processing is necessary to protect someone's life.
5. Public task, where the processing is necessary for an organisation to perform a task in the public interest, or as part of its official functions, and the task or function has a clear basis in law. This lawful basis is rarely available to controllers that are not public authorities. Section 8 of the UK DPA provides clarity on this lawful basis application in the UK by providing an exhaustive list of processing activities included (set out below).
6. Legitimate interests where the processing is necessary for the legitimate interests of the organisation or the legitimate interests of a third party, unless there is a good reason to protect the individual's personal data that overrides those legitimate interests. Legitimate interests will typically not apply as a lawful basis for public authorities, as most of their functions and processing purposes are set out in primary legislation. Therefore, public authorities carrying out their public functions are not acting in their own interests, but as prescribed by law. For example, the ICO's functions are set out in Part 5 of the UK DPA.

If an organisation has not identified a lawful basis for its processing, it will be in breach of the first data protection principle (to process data **lawfully**, fairly and in a transparent manner). As mentioned above, the accountability principle requires controllers to demonstrate that they are complying with the GDPR, which clearly extends to them demonstrating that they have considered which lawful basis, or bases, apply to each of their processing activities. A record should be kept that matches up all processing purposes with a respective lawful basis or bases (in a ROPA), which can be extracted and displayed to data subjects in a privacy notice.

No lawful basis takes priority over any others and adopting a broad-brush approach to identifying a lawful basis can be problematic. The ICO has confirmed this by stating that 'No single basis is "better" or more important than the others', meaning it does not consider a hierarchy to exist.[26]

## Categorising the lawful bases of processing

In practice, organisations may bundle their processing activities together into three categories to ensure consistency in application of a lawful basis. The categories are same-interest processing, compulsion processing and controller's interest (see Figure 5.1).

**Figure 5.1 Categorisation of the lawful bases for processing**

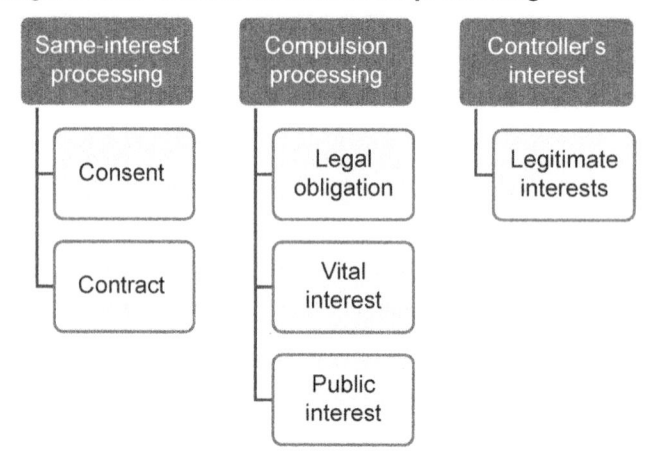

- Same-interest processing
  - Consent
  - Contract
- Compulsion processing
  - Legal obligation
  - Vital interest
  - Public interest
- Controller's interest
  - Legitimate interests

Same-interest processing represents situations where an individual optionally chooses to engage with the organisation, for example to purchase a mobile phone contract. The controller needs to process the individual's personal data to complete the details of the contract between the parties. Another example is where a supermarket asks its customer whether they wish to receive tailored offers based upon their shopping habits. It is entirely up to the individual whether to consent to this benefit with the

---

[26] Lawful basis of processing/Guide to the General Data Protection Regulation (GDPR)/Guide to Data Protection/For organisations, ICO guidance.

associated profiling activities included. Compulsion processing covers situations where a legal or moral obligation is placed on organisations that necessitate personal data processing. Controller's interest, that is, legitimate interests covers the self-interests of the organisation, so far as they are not overridden by the individual's fundamental rights and freedoms.

Organisations may have more than one applicable lawful basis depending on the processing purpose. For example, where a business contracts with an individual for the provision of its services, both the legitimate interest and contractual necessity lawful bases may be applicable. In such instances, subject to the information conveyed to the individual, the organisation may take a practical decision, paying particular attention to what individual rights attach to different lawful bases. This is because not all individual rights are attached to every lawful basis. In the example above, should the business opt for contractual necessity as the lawful basis for processing, the individual would be unable to apply their right to object (unless in respect of direct marketing).

In some instances, switching lawful bases is not possible once the processing has commenced. For example, consent cannot usually be swapped for another basis. Therefore, undertaking a clear assessment that considers all practical implications in advance of data processing will enable the organisation to have more confidence in its selected lawful basis.[27]

### Consent

Consent in a data protection context is defined in Article 4.12 as meaning 'any freely given, specific, informed and unambiguous indication of the data subject's wishes by which he or she, by a statement or by a clear affirmative action, signifies agreement to the processing of personal data relating to him or her'. Recital 32 further explains that 'silence, pre-ticked boxes or inactivity should not therefore constitute consent'.

Consent is distinct from the other lawful bases as it is the only basis that does not require necessity. Where an organisation clearly articulates its processing intentions, an individual can ultimately sign up to even the most intrusive data processing, albeit they cannot sign away their fundamental rights and other legal protections. However, Article 7 GDPR sets out further conditions that must be satisfied by organisations seeking to rely upon consent.

- In line with the accountability principle, organisations should keep records of their consent statements so that they can evidence to what the data subject consented at the time.
- Requests for consent should have clarity and be prominently displayed.
- A clear right to withdraw consent at any time and without penalty should be present.[28]

---

[27] Ibid.

[28] This is not to say that consent cannot be incentivised. A retailer, for example, may use a loyalty scheme with money-off vouchers to obtain consent to process individuals' personal data.

- I t should be ensured that performance of a contract is not dependent on consent if the consent is not necessary for performance.

### Freely given consent

This element of consent relates to real choice and control for individuals. Factors such as (1) forced consent, (2) bundled consents that are non-negotiable, (3) an inability to withdraw consent without detriment, and (4) a power imbalance between the individual and the organisation, all indicate instances where consent is unlikely to be valid.[29]

For example, where an employer seeks to gain consent from its employee, the employee may be unable to deny consent for fear of detrimental effects as a result of a refusal.[30] Where an employer requires the bank details of its employees for salary payments to fulfil the employment contract obligations, it may be more appropriate to rely upon the 'necessity for the performance of a contract' lawful basis, rather than consent.

### Specific consent

Specific consent means that a granular description of the consent request is offered, which specifies the purpose or purposes of processing, and that separates consent language from other privacy information.[31] Specific consent reduces the risk of blurring processing purposes and causing unanticipated use of personal data and a loss of control to the individual.

A practical example of this is where Company A sells some of its assets, including its marketing lists, to Company B as part of an asset sale. If consent for marketing has been originally collected by Company A for its marketing activities, the marketing list cannot be readily used by Company B regardless of it having acquired the list within the assets purchased. The specific consents collected by Company A will be invalid for Company B and its respective marketing activities. This is because the initial consents collected are specific to Company A's marketing activities only and the individuals concerned will be unaware of a new company processing their information (and may not want this to happen).

### Informed consent

Providing information to individuals prior to data collection is essential to help them make informed decisions and understand what they are agreeing to. Tied to the transparency principle, the requirements to meet the 'informed' element of consent include at a minimum:

(i) the controller's identity;

(ii) the purpose of each of the processing operations for which consent is sought;

(iii) what (type of) data will be collected and used;

(iv) the existence of the right to withdraw consent;

---

[29] Page 7, EDPB Guidelines 05/2020 on consent under Regulation 2016/679.

[30] Page 9, ibid.

[31] Page 14, ibid

(v) information about the use of the data for automated decision making in accordance with Article 22(2)(c) where relevant; and

(vi) on the possible risks of data transfers due to absence of an adequacy decision and of appropriate safeguards as described in Article 46 GDPR.[32]

### *Unambiguous consent*

Consent can be collected by written or (a recorded) oral statement.[33] In an ideal world, asking the individual to articulate what they are consenting to achieves a clear and affirmative act, but this is not always practical in reality. Therefore, when consent mechanisms are designed, organisations should develop processes that suit their operations that contain the physical motions required (e.g. using 'just-in-time' privacy notices,[34] active 'opt-in' tick-boxes and privacy dashboards with radio buttons). Pre-ticked boxes or radio buttons set to a default consent setting are not valid consent mechanisms under the GDPR.

Organisations should be aware that the same tick-box cannot be used for agreeing a contract or accepting terms and conditions as for obtaining consent. Additionally, obtaining consent should not be designed to be unnecessarily disruptive to the use of the service, and 'click fatigue' should be considered to avoid an overload of text. Overall, organisations should ensure that information is catered to the respective audience, particularly when communicating with children.

### Contract

The contractual lawful basis covers both a contract to which the individual is a party, and an 'invitation to treat' ahead of entering into the contract (e.g. by providing a quote). Distinct from consent, the contractual basis requires objective necessity for it to apply. It is not enough to satisfy the necessity requirement by simply including terms within a contract. Processing under this lawful basis must 'reflect the objectives of data protection law' and therefore involve consideration of the fundamental right to privacy and protection of personal data.[35] As such, a fact-based assessment of the processing is required to ascertain whether a less intrusive, alternate processing basis is available.

The EDPB guidance on the applicability of the contract basis in an online context highlights the importance of organisations being transparent about which lawful basis is being relied on.[36] For example, there may be circumstances where an individual mistakenly assumes that by consenting to the terms of service that they are in fact consenting under the definition of Article 6.1, where in fact the processing in question may rely on a distinct lawful basis.

---

[32] Pages 15–16, ibid.

[33] Recital 32 GDPR and page 16, ibid.

[34] A just-in-time notice appears at the point of data collection where a brief message is presented (usually by pop-up) that explains how the individual's data will be used.

[35] Page 8, EDPB Guidelines 2/2019 on the processing of personal data under Article 6(1)(b) GDPR in the context of the provision of online services to data subjects, 8 October 2019.

[36] Page 7, ibid.

To assist organisations in an online context, the EDPB provides specific examples where it is unlikely be appropriate to use a contract as the lawful basis of processing.

- Service improvement. Data gathered on user engagement and improvements to be made do not meet the necessity criteria as the service could still operate without the provision of such engagements and improvements.[37]
- Fraud prevention. Previous guidance by the Art. 29 Working Party (the predecessor to the EDPB) has stated that fraud prevention is likely to cover monitoring and profiling activities. This extends beyond objective necessity in the eyes of the EDPB and may therefore be more suited to the legitimate interest lawful basis.[38]
- Online behavioural advertising. Advertising of this nature is a relatively new introduction into modern day business, and as such, the associated data processing is unlikely to be contingent on the new service offering, given other forms of advertising have previously existed.
- Personalisation of content. Much like service improvement, this is an ancillary addition to the core service offering and therefore in many instances may not be appropriate for the contractual lawful basis.

## Legal obligation

The legal obligation lawful basis relates to circumstances where an organisation is obliged to process the personal data of an individual in order to comply with the law. 'The law' is limited in the GDPR to Union law or laws of the relevant Member States.[39] Recital 41 confirms that the legal obligation does not need to be an explicit statutory obligation. It is sufficient that the law is foreseeable to individuals, and as such, covers clear common law obligations, which the ICO has confirmed in its guidance.[40] The ICO guidance also states that organisations should be able to reference the legal obligation they are relying upon, either directly or by reference to a government website or industry guidance (for example, an employer complying with its legal obligation by disclosing its employees' salary details to HMRC).

## Vital interests

The vital interests basis operates in a very limited set of circumstances and covers processing that is 'essential for the life of the [individual]'.[41] Whilst not a legal obligation, vital interests includes a moral obligation on the organisation processing personal data to protect the life of another, for example in the provision of emergency medical care, or where the data subject has lost mental faculty. However, where an individual is capable

---

[37] Page 14, ibid.

[38] Ibid and page 17, Art. 29 WP Opinion 06/2014 on the notion of legitimate interests of the data controller under Article 7 of Directive 95/46/EC (WP217).

[39] Article 6(3) GDPR.

[40] Legal Obligation/Lawful basis of processing/Guide to the General Data Protection Regulation (GDPR)/Guide to Data Protection/For organisations, ICO guidance.

[41] Recital 46 GDPR.

of giving consent (even if they refuse to), vital interests cannot be used (for example, in the provision of medical care that is planned in advance).

## Public task

The public task lawful basis relates to performance of tasks carried out in the public interest or in the exercise of official authority. The ICO explains that the relevant task or authority does not need to be explicitly laid out in law and that, in fact, even statutory guidance may be covered.[42] The UK DPA provides helpful clarity for the UK on which tasks are covered by tasks in the public interest or exercising of official authority:

a) the administration of justice,

b) the exercise of a function of either House of Parliament,

c) the exercise of a function conferred on a person by an enactment or rule of law,

d) the exercise of a function of the Crown, a Minister of the Crown or a government department, or

e) an activity that supports or promotes democratic engagement.[43]

The ICO states the list above is non-exhaustive and that the key requirement is that the underlying task or function be clear and foreseeable.[44] For example, private water companies (not covered by the public authority definition in the UK DPA) are still likely to be able to rely upon the public task lawful basis given their public function, despite most private companies not being able to rely upon the lawful basis.

## Legitimate interests

The sixth lawful basis is legitimate interests, which covers controllers' (or third parties') pursued interests in processing an individual's personal data. The list of such processing activities is infinite, but they must be for a reasonable purpose, which arguably makes legitimate interests the most flexible of all lawful bases. Examples of possible legitimate interest purposes include fraud prevention; network and information security; and acting on possible criminal acts or threats to public security. Recital 47 GDPR uses direct marketing as an example of processing that can rely upon legitimate interests.

The *ASNEF* (2011) and *FECEMD* (2011) judgments confirmed that Member States cannot add additional components that limit the flexibility of application of the legitimate interests lawful basis.[45] The Spanish case, which was referred to the CJEU, concerned the localisation of the Data Protection Directive 1995 by the Spanish authorities by Royal Decree (1720/2007) that sought to limit the legitimate interest principle by only enabling its use where such data appeared in 'public sources', which the CJEU refused to accept.[46]

---

[42] ICO Guide to the General Data Protection Regulation (version 01 January 2021 – 1.1.106), p. 77.

[43] Section 8 Data Protection Act 2018.

[44] Ibid.

[45] *ASNEF* and *FECEMD*, C-468/10 and C-469/10, EU:C:2011:777.

[46] Ibid, paragraphs 29–32.

However, whilst the underlying basis is flexible, an organisation is still required to prove that it has balanced its own interests against the rights and freedoms of the individuals whose personal data it is processing, taking into account the particular circumstances that arise in the context of the processing activity. This assessment is called a legitimate interests assessment and has three distinct parts: the purpose test, the necessity test and the balancing test. A record of all LIAs completed by an organisation should be kept (and periodically updated) to assist it with demonstrating its compliance with the accountability principle.

- Purpose test. Is the organisation pursuing a legitimate interest? This test seeks to understand the 'what and the 'why' of the purpose for processing.
- Necessity test. Is the processing necessary for that purpose? It is important to note that if another reasonable and less intrusive way of processing an individual's personal data is available, legitimate interests cannot be relied upon.
- Balancing test. Do individuals' rights override the organisations' legitimate interest? If an individual would not reasonably expect an organisation to use their personal data in the intended way, or if the use would cause unwarranted harm, the individual's interest is likely to override the organisation's interest.

### *The balancing test*

The fact that processing might have a negative impact on an individual does not automatically mean that their interests override the controller's. It depends on the severity of the impact and whether it is warranted in light of the controller's purpose. Such interest must be more compelling than the impact on the individual, but if a serious mismatch in interests exists, the individual's interest is likely to take precedence. For example, the ICO has set out some criteria that should be considered, as the outcome will depend on the circumstances of the overall processing.[47]

- [the individual] would not reasonably expect the processing;
- they would be likely to object to the processing;
- the processing would have a significant impact on them;
- the processing would prevent them exercising their rights; or
- the data you are processing is particularly sensitive, for example special category data, criminal offence data, or children's data.[48]

## LAWFULNESS OF PROCESSING – SPECIAL CATEGORY PERSONAL DATA AND CRIMINAL CONVICTIONS AND OFFENCES

Special category personal data are more sensitive than personal data, so additional requirements have to be satisfied in order to process them.

---

[47] ICO Guide to the General Data Protection Regulation: What is the 'legitimate interests' basis?
[48] ICO Guide to the General Data Protection Regulation.

## The ban on processing special category personal data – enhanced sensitivity, risks and legal requirement

The starting point is that the processing of special category data is prohibited, that is, banned, unless a condition in A.9 of the GDPR is satisfied. This is in addition to having to satisfy one of the lawful bases for processing required under A.6. However, a linkage between the A.6 lawful base and the A.9 condition is not required.

Another example of the enhanced legal requirements for special category data is that a DPIA under A.35 is often likely to be required before they can be processed, given their sensitivity. Furthermore, the UK DPA prescribes specific circumstances where an 'appropriate policy document' must be put in place as part of the overall framework of conditions that need to be satisfied to render the processing of special category data lawful.

### *Types of special category data*
A.9.1 GDPR defines special category data (or sensitive data, as they are commonly known) as:

- Personal data revealing racial or ethnic origin.
- Personal data revealing political opinions, religious or philosophical beliefs, or trade union membership.
- Genetic data. The GDPR at A.4.13 defines genetic data as meaning 'personal data relating to the inherited or acquired genetic characteristics of a natural person which give unique information about the physiology or the health of that natural person and which result, in particular, from an analysis of a biological sample from the natural person in question'.
- Biometric data, where they are processed for the purpose of uniquely identifying a natural person. A.4.14 defines biometric data as meaning 'personal data resulting from specific technical processing relating to the physical, physiological or behavioural characteristics of a natural person, which allow or confirm the unique identification of that natural person, such as facial images or dactyloscopic data'.
- Data concerning health. A.4.15 defines data concerning health as meaning 'personal data related to the physical or mental health of a natural person, including the provision of health care services, which reveal information about his or her health status'.
- Data concerning a person's sex life or sexual orientation.

### *Grounds for overcoming the ban on processing*
A.9.2 GDPR sets out the different conditions available to enable processing of special category data, as otherwise prohibited by A.9.1. The conditions are as follows:

(a) Explicit consent.
(b) Necessary for employment, social security and social protection law as authorised under law.*[49]

---
[49] Additional requirements under Part 1 of Schedule 1 to the UK DPA must be satisfied.

(c) Vital interests.
(d) Legitimate activities of not-for-profit bodies, so far as such data are not disclosed outside that body without data subject consent.
(e) Made public by the data subject.
(f) Necessary for the establishment, exercise or defence of legal claims or judicial acts.
(g) Necessary for reasons of substantial public interest under a basis in law (i.e. meet one of the 23 specific substantial public interest conditions set out in Part 2 of Schedule 1 to the UK DPA).
(h) Necessary for health or social care.
(i) Necessary for public health.
(j) Necessary for archiving in the public interest, scientific or historical research, and statistics.

### *Criminal convictions and offences data*

Personal data demanding some of the highest levels of protection are criminal convictions and offences data. Criminal convictions and offences data cover a broad remit of information:

- criminal activity;
- allegations of criminal behaviour (including unproven allegations);
- investigations;
- proceedings;
- information relating to the absence of convictions;
- personal data of victims and witnesses of crime;
- personal data about penalties imposed;
- conditions or restrictions placed on an individual as part of the criminal justice process;
- civil measures, which may lead to a criminal penalty if not adhered to.

Processing such data requires the same protections for special category processing (e.g. a DPIA and an appropriate policy document) but with extra requirements, namely:

- Processing being under the control of an official authority. For example, a comprehensive database of criminal convictions (e.g. the Police National Computer) can only be used by competent authorities authorised by a separate law enforcement regime.
- Authorised by domestic law, that is, meeting one of the conditions in Schedule 1 to the UK DPA.

Tasks given to public or private bodies to process criminal offence data may constitute 'official authority' if prescribed by law. This official authority may derive from either common law or statute. Part 3 of the Data Protection Act 2018 brought the EU Law Enforcement Directive[50] into UK law. This body of law seeks to complement the UK GDPR and sets out requirements for processing personal data for criminal law enforcement purposes.

## SUMMARY

In conclusion, this chapter gives readers a better understanding of:

- the range and scope of the principles of data protection;
- the duty of accountability and the need for controllers to be able to prove their operational compliance with the law;
- the lawful bases for processing of personal data and when they can be relied on;
- the nature of special category personal data;
- the conditions that need to be satisfied in order to overcome the prohibition against the processing of special category data.

---

[50] EU 2016/680.

# 6    THE RIGHTS OF DATA SUBJECTS

Stewart Room

This chapter examines the data subject's rights of transparency, their rights over processing, and their remedies and rights of redress for infringements of the GDPR.

## INFORMING AND EMPOWERING THE PROTECTED PARTY

As the protected party under data protection law, the data subject enjoys a series of legal rights that are designed to inform and empower them and, where possible to put them in control over data processing. These rights fall into three categories:

- transparency and information rights;
- rights over data processing;
- remedies and rights of redress.

## TRANSPARENCY AND INFORMATION RIGHTS

The transparency and information rights are contained in Articles 12–15 and 34 of the GDPR and they build upon the first data protection principle in A.5.1.a, which says that personal data shall be 'processed lawfully, fairly and in a transparent manner in relation to the data subject'. Other key points to note are as follows.

### General obligation of transparency – GDPR A.12

Article 12.1 applies a general obligation of transparency to all the rights within Articles 13 to 22 and 34, saying that 'the controller shall take appropriate measures to provide any information ... and any communication [referred to in those Articles] ... in a concise, transparent, intelligible and easily accessible form, using clear and plain language ...'

### Modalities for providing information, the identity of the requester, time limits and exceptions

Other elements within the general obligation of transparency are:

- Special care with the provision of information should be taken in the case of children.
- Information shall be provided in writing, or by other means, which can include electronic means, where appropriate.

- The controller shall 'facilitate' the exercise of the rights in A.15 to 22, unless it can demonstrate that it is not able to identify the data subject. If the controller has reasonable doubts about the identity of the person making a rights request, it can ask the requester to provide information about their identity.

- Information required by A.15 to 22 shall be provided within one calendar month, although the time can be extended by two months if reasons are supplied. The data subject should be informed of a controller's refusal or inability to action a rights request without undue delay, again with reasons, which is subject to a one-month longstop.

- The default position is that information and communications required by A.13 to 22 and 34 shall be provided free of charge. However, where a rights request is manifestly unfounded or excessive, the controller can either choose to charge a reasonable fee, based on its administrative costs, or it can refuse to act on the request.

## Obtaining transparency – GDPR A.13 and 14

Articles 13 and 14 are concerned with transparency at the point of obtaining of personal data, or shortly afterwards. Article 13 applies to the situation where personal data are obtained direct from the data subject. Article 14 applies where the controller obtains personal data from a third party, that is, otherwise than direct from the data subject.

### *Obtaining of personal data from the data subject – A.13*

The information that needs to be supplied to the data subject under A.13 breaks down into two categories. The first category, in A.13.1, is simply a list of required information. The second category, in A.13.2, is another list of required information, but it is prefaced as being 'necessary to ensure fair and transparent process'. The reason for the distinction between the two categories is unclear, but the full list of required information is as follows.

### *Information required under A.13.1*

- The identity and contact details of the controller, or, where applicable, its representative (see A.27).
- The contact details of the data protection officer, where applicable (see A.37).
- The intended purposes of processing and the legal basis for processing (see the second data protection principle and A.6, respectively).
- If the processing is based on the controller's legitimate interests under A.6.1.f, a statement of those interests.
- The recipients, or categories, of recipients of the data, if there are any.
- Information about international transfers of personal data to third countries. The existence of absence of adequacy decisions relating to those transfers should be included in the information, as should information about safeguards.

### *Information required under A.13.2*

- the period for which the data will be stored, or information about the criteria used for determining that period;

data will have on them. The more significant the effect, the less likely you will be able to rely on this exception.

This is an exception to the general obligation of transparency, and should be treated as the exception, not the rule. You should not use it to routinely escape your obligations to inform individuals about your use of their data. If you want to rely on disproportionate effort, you need to be confident you can justify why contacting individuals is genuinely disproportionate in the particular circumstances.

The ICO's guidance identifies the essence of the test of proportionality that applies in these situations: is the gain or benefit to the data subject worth the effort invested by the controller in delivering the information required by A.14? This gain/effort test is supported by a decision of the Court of Appeal in the *Dawson-Damer* (2017)[1] case, which concerned the data subject's right of access to personal data within the Data Protection Act 1998 (which was repealed by the Data Protection Act 2018, to give effect to the GDPR). Under the old rules, disproportionate effort operated as an exception to the right of access. The Court of Appeal held in that case:

In my judgment, the word 'supply' is used so that what is weighed up in the proportionality exercise is the end object of the search, namely the potential benefit that the supply of the information might bring to the data subject, as against the means by which that information is obtained. It will be a question for evaluation in each particular case whether disproportionate effort will be involved in finding and supplying the information as against the benefits it might bring to the data subject.

As far as other safeguards are concerned, the ICO's guidance draws attention to the need to make the A.14 information publicly available and it also asserts that a data protection impact assessment should be performed:

If you determine that providing privacy information to individuals does involve a disproportionate effort, you must still publish the privacy information (e.g. on your website), and you should carry out a DPIA.

The EU regulators' transparency guidance[2] provides further insight into the use of the disproportionate effort exception, which points out that it should not be routinely relied upon outside archiving, research and statistics:

Recital 62 also references these objectives as cases where the provision of information to the data subject would involve a disproportionate effort and states that in this regard, the number of data subjects, the age of the data and any appropriate safeguards adopted should be taken into consideration. Given the emphasis in Recital 62 and Article 14.5(b) on archiving, research and statistical purposes with regard to the application of this exemption, WP29's position is that this exception should not be routinely relied upon by data controllers who are not processing personal data for the purposes of archiving in the public interest, for scientific or historical research purposes or statistical purposes.

---

1   *Dawson-Damer & Ors v. Taylor Wessing LLP* (2017) EWCA Civ 74.

2   Guidelines on transparency under Regulation 2016/679, adopted on 29 November 2017, as last Revised and Adopted on 11 April 2018, WP260 rev.01.

***Techniques for providing the information required by A.13 and 14***
***Website privacy notices***   A.13 and A.14 both talk about providing the data subject with the required information. This seems to suggest that the information needs to be supplied directly to the data subject, which contrasts with the idea of simply making information publicly available. This distinction also helps to make sense of the rule in A.14.5.b to make information publicly available when provision of it to the data subject would constitute disproportionate effort.

Posting a 'privacy notice' on a website is a common way of making information publicly available, but is this enough to satisfy the obligation to provide information to the data subject? The EU data protection regulators suggest that it is. Their transparency guidance puts it in these terms:

> However, the GDPR also allows for other, unspecified 'means' including electronic means to be used. WP29's position with regard to written electronic means is that where a data controller maintains (or operates, in part or in full, through) a website, WP29 recommends the use of layered privacy statements/notices, which allow website visitors to navigate to particular aspects of the relevant privacy statement/notice that are of most interest to them ...

The guidance also says:

> Every organisation that maintains a website should publish a privacy statement/notice on the website. A direct link to this privacy statement/notice should be clearly visible on each page of this website under a commonly used term (such as 'Privacy', 'Privacy Policy' or 'Data Protection Notice'). Positioning or colour schemes that make a text or link less noticeable, or hard to find on a webpage, are not considered easily accessible.

An alternative view is that if the information is not deliberately and demonstrably put before the data subject as they browse their way through the website, they will not have been provided with the information in the manner required by A.13 and 14. However, for the time being at least, website privacy notices will be enough to satisfy the data protection regulators about compliance with the transparency rules in these environments.

***Oral transparency information***   A.12.1 says that transparency information can be provided orally, where that is requested by the data subject and their identify can be 'proven by other means'. However, the EU transparency guidance clarifies that the need to prove the data subject's identify does not apply to A.13 and 14, only to the data subject rights in A.15 to 22 and 34. Therefore, A.12.1 would permit, for example, a digital assistant such as Alexa or Siri providing oral transparency information if the user asks for it. The guidance says:

> Article 12.1 specifically contemplates that information may be provided orally to a data subject on request, provided that their identity is proven by other means. In other words, the means employed should be more than reliance on a mere assertion by the individual that they are a specific named person and the means should enable the controller to verify a data subject's identity with sufficient assurance. The requirement to verify the identity of the data subject before providing information

orally only applies to information relating to the exercise by a specific data subject of their rights under Articles 15 to 22 and 34. This precondition to the provision of oral information cannot apply to the provision of general privacy information as outlined in Articles 13 and 14, since information required under Articles 13 and 14 must also be made accessible to future users/customers (whose identity a data controller would not be in a position to verify). Hence, information to be provided under Articles 13 and 14 may be provided by oral means without the controller requiring a data subject's identity to be proven.

***Icons***   Article 12.7 allows the A.13 and 14 information to be provided 'in combination with standardised icons in order to give in an easily visible, intelligible and clearly legible manner a meaningful overview of the intended processing'. Icons have not been adopted as a mainstream compliance mechanism, but that might change over time.

***Transparency, Data Protection by Design and Default and accountability***   Controllers should still take care with the design of their transparency systems, keeping in mind the rules about Data Protection by Design and Default and the accountability principle, which places a duty on them to prove their compliance with the GDPR. Current best practice guidance from the ICO points to these techniques for providing the transparency information:

- A layered approach – short notices containing key privacy information that have additional layers of more detailed information.
- Dashboards – preference management tools that inform people how you use their data and allow them to manage what happens with it.
- Just-in-time notices – relevant and focused privacy information delivered at the time you collect individual pieces of information about people.
- Icons – small, meaningful, symbols that indicate the existence of a particular type of data processing.
- Mobile and smart device functionalities – including pop-ups, voice alerts and mobile device gestures.[3]

The EU's transparency guidance provides other best practice recommendations.

## The right of access to information – A.15

The right of access to information that is guaranteed by A.15 is one of the most impactful of the data subject rights, in terms of the platform that it provides data subjects to intervene in data processing, to bring complaints and to pursue remedies.

### *The weaponised right*
Many controllers now regard data subject access requests (DSARs or SARs) as 'weaponised', in the sense that they can be used by individuals to pursue agendas beyond data protection, such as to support the bringing of litigation and compensation claims in employment law disputes. In fact, a point has been reached where controllers

---

[3] https://ico.org.uk/for-organisations/guide-to-data-protection/guide-to-the-general-data-protection-regulation-gdpr/individual-rights/right-to-be-informed/#exceptions

should treat the receipt of DSARs as a likely part of the disciplinary or exit process in messy employment situations.

The weaponising effect of DSARs derives from the fact that the right of access to information is a transparency mechanism, which brings into focus the adage 'knowledge is power'. Due to the expansive meaning of 'personal data' (see A.4.1), which covers 'any information' relating to an identified or identifiable living individual, the right of access means that the data subject can gain access not only to factual matters relating to them, but also untruths and mere opinions. Thus, in the workplace, where people may not always be mindful of the perils and risks of access requests, DSARs can be used to uncover very toxic information, the nature of which may justify the bringing of complaints about victimisation, discrimination, defamation and other kinds of unlawful activities.

The motive of the data subject when making an access request has been examined in several court cases under the provisions of the Data Protection Act 1998. Although now repealed, decisions under that Act are still helpful on the question of legitimacy of an access request where it serves a collateral purpose beyond data protection, particularly where it is used to obtain disclosure of evidence to support court cases (for example, see the *Dawson-Damer* (2017) case). The current position of the law is that a data subject's collateral purpose, such as a wish to gain evidence to be used in litigation, will not invalidate their right of access under A.15.

### The data subject's entitlements under the right of access
The right of access provides the data subject with various entitlements.

***First entitlement – confirmation of processing*** The right of access consists of three parts. First, the data subject has a right to be told whether the controller is processing personal data 'concerning' them. In other words, the controller must tell the data subject whether it is processing their personal data.

***Second entitlement – provision of information about processing*** Secondly, if the controller is processing the data subject's personal data, then it must supply the data subject with various pieces of information about the processing activities. This information corresponds closely with the types of information that need to be provided by A.13 and 14. In summary, the categories of information to be supplied are:

- The purposes of processing.
- Categories of personal data.
- Recipients, or categories of recipients, to whom the data have been, or will be disclosed.[4] This must include information about recipients in third countries (i.e. those beyond the EU and EEA).
- The storage period, if possible, or the criteria for determining that period.
- The existence of the rights of rectification, erasure and restriction.

---

[4] In February 2021 the Austrian Supreme Court referred a case to the CJEU for a preliminary ruling on whether A.15 requires an actual list of recipients to be provided, rather than just categories.

- The right to lodge a complaint before the supervisory authority.
- Information about the controller's source, if the data were not obtained from the data subject.
- The existence of automated decision making, including profiling, and the logic involved.
- Where personal data are transferred to a third country, or to an international organisation, outside the EU/EEA, they should be told about the appropriate safeguards that have been put in place.

***Third entitlement – provision of a copy of the personal data being processed (not copies of documents)***   Thirdly, if the controller is processing the data subject's personal data, they also must be supplied with a copy of the data. The copy must be supplied in a 'commonly used electronic form', if the data subject makes the request by electronic means and does not request an alternative format, such as orally (see A.12.3).

It is important to understand that the data subject's entitlement does not extend to receiving copies of documents. The right concerns copies of information and the point of distinction to keep in mind is that a document is a container for information, rather than information itself. Therefore, it is open to the controller to transpose information from one document to another, then to supply the new document. For example, if information is contained in a Word file, the controller could legitimately copy information from it, then paste it into a new Word file, then edit the new file before disclosing it. The ICO's guidance[5] puts it in this way:

> The right of access enables individuals to obtain their personal data rather than giving them a right to see copies of documents containing their personal data. You may therefore provide the information in the form of transcripts of relevant documents (or of sections of documents that contain the personal data), or by providing a print-out of the relevant information from your computer systems. While it is reasonable to supply a transcript if it exists, we do not expect controllers to create new information to respond to a SAR. Although the easiest way to provide the relevant information is often to supply copies of original documents, you are not obliged to do so.

### *Formalities of access requests*

The GDPR does not prescribe any formats for the making of access requests. They do not have to be labelled as such. They do not have to be sent to a designated point of contact (such as the DPO).

***No prescribed formats – oral requests suffice***   Nor do they have to be made in writing; oral requests will suffice. Therefore, it would be open to the data subject to make an access request when speaking to a person in a contact centre, or by sending it through social media to the controller's account. Due to the flexibility that the right affords the data subject, controllers need to devise processes to be able to quickly identify the receipt of an access request across all the communications channels that it uses. Failure to quickly identify access requests erodes the time that the controller

---

[5]   https://ico.org.uk/for-organisations/guide-to-data-protection/guide-to-the-general-data-protection-regulation-gdpr/right-of-access/how-should-we-supply-information-to-the-requester/

has to deal with them. If they are completely overlooked, the controller will be guilty of serious non-compliance.

**Fees** The default position is that the controller cannot levy a charge for dealing with access requests. The position changes in these circumstances:

- Where the request is manifestly unfounded or excessive, which can arise when a request is repetitive in nature. In that case, the controller can charge a reasonable fee that reflects its administrative costs of providing the information. Alternatively, the controller can refuse to act on the request. However, in all cases the controller carries the burden of demonstrating that the request is manifestly unfounded or excessive. See A.12.5.
- If the data subject requests further copies of the information that has been provided, the controller can charge a reasonable fee based on its administrative costs. See A.15.3.

**Manifestly unfounded or excessive requests** The GDPR does not define what is meant by manifestly unfounded or excessive, but the ICO guidance provides some insights into the regulator's mindset. Regarding manifestly unfounded requests, the guidance points to situations where the data subject has no intention to exercise their right of access, which would be evidenced by making a request and then offering to withdraw it in return for a benefit, such as a monetary payment. The guidance also refers to requests that are malicious, harassing and intended only to cause disruption. Examples of the kinds of behaviours that ICO cites as being capable of falling into these categories of behaviours are:

- the data subject explicitly states that they intend to cause disruption;
- the data subject makes unsubstantiated allegations that are obviously malicious;
- they target a person, due to a grudge;
- they are part of a systematic campaign to cause disruption.

Regarding manifestly excessive requests, the ICO guidance says that they must be clearly or obviously unreasonable and that the proportionality of the issue should be judged against the burden and costs of dealing with it. Factors that the ICO identifies as being potentially relevant to the assessment include whether the request overlaps with other requests or is repetitive in nature. The impacts on the individual should also be considered.

Bearing in mind that the controller bears the burden of proof on these matters and the use of the word 'manifestly', it seems clear that the law sets a very high bar for the controller to overcome if it chooses to rely on these exceptions.

### The response
As indicated earlier, A.12.1 says that the information required by A.15 (and the other data subject rights) should be provided in writing 'or by other means, including, where appropriate, by electronic means'. A.12.1 goes on to say that the data subject can request the information to be provided orally. A.12.3 continues by saying that where the data subject makes the request by electronic form, the information should be provided by electronic means where possible, unless the data subject requests otherwise.

***Format of the response*** Breaking this down, the options for the response are as follows:

- If the data subject makes a 'hard copy' request in writing, such as by a letter sent by post, the response should be provided in the same format.
- If the data subject makes a request using electronic means, such as by email, the response should be provided by electronic means, if that is possible. If it is not possible to provide the information by electronic means, the only other options are in hard copy, or orally.
- Oral responses are only allowed where the data subject requests this, provided that the controller is satisfied of the data subject's identity (but proof of identity cannot be provided orally).

There is nothing in the GDPR that prevents the controller from providing options to the data subject for the format of the response, or that prevents the controller from stating its preference. Provided that the data subject is not coerced, cajoled, or otherwise unfairly treated, controllers can legitimately 'funnel' data subjects through a predesigned access response pathway, to aid efficiencies.

***Identification*** In most cases the identity of the data subject will not be in issue, but there have been many examples of 'data thieves' seeking to unlawfully obtain personal data by masquerading as someone else. There is also an inherent risk that from time to time a person's information will be accidentally mixed-up with another person's. Data can easily be misdirected in transmission, such as by putting the wrong information into an envelope, or by sending information to an incorrect email address. Article 15.4 warns controllers that the right of access 'shall not adversely affect the rights and freedoms of others'.

Therefore, from time to time a controller might have doubts about the requester's identity. To cater for this, A.12.6 provides that 'where the controller has reasonable doubts concerning the identity of the natural person making the request referred to in Articles 15 to 22, the controller may request the provision of additional information necessary to confirm the identity of the data subject'.

Where it is necessary for the controller to request proof of identity, the timeframe for complying with the access request is suspended and does not restart until the proof of identity is provided. A.12.2 says that the controller can refuse to act on an access request (and other rights requests) if it 'demonstrates that it is not in a position to identify the data subject'.

***Timeframe*** As indicated earlier, access requests (and the other rights requests) must be complied with 'without undue delay', which is subject to a one calendar month longstop. However, in cases of complexity, which can include situations where the controller is facing multiple requests all at the same time, the timeframe can be extended by up to two months, but the controller must inform the data subject of the need for an extension before the expiry of the initial one calendar month period, providing reasons. If the data subject believes that the controller does not need the additional time and is only stalling, they can take a complaint to the regulator, or seek to enforce their rights in court, but the reality of the situation is such that these are likely to result in pyrrhic victories at best, due to the length of time that the regulatory and court processes take to deal with these matters.

***Third-party information*** It would amount to a breach of a person's data protection rights if their information were to be disclosed to another person during an access request, if that disclosure adversely affected their rights and freedoms, hence the rule in A.15.4, mentioned above.

To operationalise the requirements of A.15.4, controllers must:

- Implement appropriate technical and organisational measures to identify and deal with situations where a third party's personal data are involved in a data subject's access request.
- Once they have identified these situations, the measures need to support an assessment of whether the disclosure of the third party's data could adversely affect their rights and freedoms.
- If there could be adverse effects, the measures need to include mechanisms to weed-out the third-party data, to prevent unlawful disclosures, if that is necessary. Those mechanisms might result in deletion of the third party's data, or anonymisation or pseudonymisation of it.

A.15.4 is concerned with the protection of a third party's data where its disclosure would adversely their rights and freedoms. The UK Data Protection Act, Schedule 2 Part 3 takes matters a little further, saying that the right of access does 'not oblige a controller to disclose information to the data subject to the extent that doing so would involve disclosing information relating to another individual who can be identified from the information'. This presents a lower threshold to the embargo against disclosure of third-party data than A.15.4. However, the Act goes on to say that this rule does not remove the controller's obligation to comply with an access request if (a) the third party has consented to the disclosure of their information to the data subject, or (b) it is reasonable to disclose the third-party information to the data subject without the consent of the other individual. The Act then goes on to say that 'in determining whether it is reasonable to disclose the [third party] information without consent, the controller must have regard to all the relevant circumstances, including (a) the type of information that would be disclosed, (b) any duty of confidentiality owed to the other individual, (c) any steps taken by the controller with a view to seeking the consent of the other individual, (d) whether the other individual is capable of giving consent, and (e) any express refusal of consent by the other individual'.

The ICO has summarised these provisions of the Act within a three-step test:[6]

1. Does the request require the disclosure of information that identifies another individual?
2. Has the other individual given their consent to the disclosure of their information?
3. Is it reasonable to disclose the information without consent?

---

[6] https://ico.org.uk/for-organisations/guide-to-data-protection/guide-to-the-general-data-protection-regulation-gdpr/right-of-access/information-about-other-individuals/

## Criminal offences

Section 173(3) of the Data Protection Act makes it a criminal offence for a controller or person working for or directed by a controller to take various steps to defeat a valid access request:

> It is an offence for a person listed in subsection (4) to alter, deface, block, erase, destroy or conceal information with the intention of preventing disclosure of all or part of the information that the person making the request would have been entitled to receive.

Defences are contained in section 173(5):

> It is a defence for a person charged with an offence under subsection (3) to prove that:
>
> (a) the alteration, defacing, blocking, erasure, destruction or concealment of the information would have occurred in the absence of a request made in exercise of a data subject access right, or
>
> (b) the person acted in the reasonable belief that the person making the request was not entitled to receive the information in response to the request.

## Restrictions

In addition to the exception in A.12.5 for manifestly unfounded and excessive requests, A.23 of the GDPR allows Member States to adopt various restrictions from the rights in A.15 to 22 and 34, on serious national and public interest grounds, that is:

- national security;
- defence;
- public security;
- the prevention and detection of crime;
- other important objectives of public interest, such as economic matters, public health and social security;
- protection of judicial independence and proceedings;
- prevention and detection of breaches of ethics in the regulated professions;
- regulatory and official functions;
- the protection of the data subject and the rights of others;
- the enforcement of civil law claims.

A.85 also permits Member States to adopt restrictions for the purposes of freedom of expression (such as for journalistic, academic, artistic and literary purpose) and A.89 permits the same for the purpose of archiving in the public interest, scientific or historical research purposes or for statistical purposes.

The UK restrictions are contained in Schedules 2 and 3 of the Data Protection Act. Table 2.10 in Chapter 2 provides a fuller overview, but in summary, these are the areas covered by the restrictions:

- Sch 2 Pt 1 – Crime, immigration and legal proceedings;
- Sch 2 Pt 2 – Protecting the public and public functions;
- Sch 2 Pt 3 – Protecting the rights of others;
- Sch 2 Pt 4 – The right of access to information;
- Sch 2 Pt 5 – The special purposes;
- Sch 2 Pt 6 – Research, statistics and archiving;
- Sch 3 Pt 2 – Health data;
- Sch 3 Pt 3 – Social work data;
- Sch 3 Pt 4 – Educational records;
- Sch 3 Pt 5 – Child abuse data;
- Sch 3 Pt 4 – Disclosures prohibited by law.

**Restrictions in Schedule 2 Part 4 of the Data Protection Act 2018**   The schedules should be consulted on a case-by-case basis when considering the application of the restrictions, but in most access request situations, it is those falling with Sch 2 Pt 3 and 4 that have the greatest application. The restrictions to protect the rights of others are discussed above. The restrictions falling within Pt 4 cover:

- legal professional privilege;
- self-incrimination;
- corporate finance;
- management forecasts;
- negotiations with the data subject;
- confidential references;
- exam scripts and marks.

The corporate finance, management forecasts and negotiations restrictions are all subject to prejudice tests, in the sense the access request does not need to be complied with if it would prejudice the achievement of the objectives covered by the restrictions. In the employment context, where access requests feature heavily, it is the negotiations and confidential references restrictions that are likely to have the most impact. The negotiations restriction would prevent the data subject gaining access to information about exit negotiations. The confidential references restriction would prevent them gaining access to any that are given, or received, by the controller.

**Informing the data subject of reliance on restrictions**   A.12.4 says that if the controller does not act on the request of a data subject, which applies to all the rights in A.15 to 22, then it shall inform the data subject without delay (which is subject to a one-month longstop, starting from the receipt of the request), providing reasons. Therefore, if the controller relies upon any of the restrictions, it should explain this when rejecting the access request. However, the GDPR does not include an obligation to be specific about which restrictions have been relied upon, but controllers should judge on case-by-case basis whether they want to be more specific. As the rejection must also inform the data subject of their right to lodge a complaint with the regulator, the controller might have to give an account of their reasons to the regulator if they decide to investigate.

### Coping mechanisms

The rules on Data Protection by Design and Default and the accountability principle apply to the data subject rights regime and due to the potential that access requests have for deep adverse scrutiny and challenge of the controller, often a lot of planning needs to go into the design and operation of the systems for coping with them. Table 6.1 identifies some of the issues that controllers should consider. Many of these points apply generally to the rights regime within A.15 to A.22.

**Table 6.1 Coping mechanisms for access requests**

| | |
|---|---|
| Data Protection by Design and Default and accountability | • It is implicit within these rules that controllers need to take care to implement appropriate technical and organisational measures to comply with access requests. |
| | • The accountability principle will require controllers to document their design and to log the receipt of access requests and decisions and actions taken on them. |
| Processors | • Controllers might need the support of their processors to fulfil access requests. |
| | • A.28 requires controllers to flow compliance obligations through to their processors. Therefore, they should be appropriately 'inducted' into the controller's procedures, systems and operations for compliance. |
| Compliance across the three layers of the organisation, at speed | • People need to be appointed and trained to deal with access requests. This covers recognising when they have been received, through to the actual handling of them in a substantive sense. |
| | • Paper – policies, procedures and process flows that set out the controller's rules for handling access requests should be created. Step-by-step guides can be useful. Detailed rules on handling the exceptions and restrictions could be very helpful. |

*(Continued)*

## Table 6.1 (Continued)

| | |
|---|---|
| | • Technology and data – the substantive steps within the response to the access request will need to flow into the technology and data landscape of the controller. This will include search and retrieval capabilities to locate data for review; potentially technologies to aid the weeding out of irrelevant or out-of-scope data (such as redaction technology to delete third-party information or identifiers); and technologies to deliver information in a commonly used electronic format. |
| Detection of access requests | • Mechanisms need to be put in place to identify the receipt of access requests across all communications channels used by the controller. |
| | • Special care needs to be taken to detect oral access requests, so the controller needs to think about where oral interactions with data subjects are likely to be received, such as in contact centres. |
| | • The processes that are adopted for dealing with access requests need to ensure speedy progression of them from the point of receipt to their substantive handling. |
| Timetables | • The criticality of timetables needs to be understood and catered for within the technical and organisational measures adopted for compliance. |
| Specialist advice | • The controller needs to bake-in the need that often arises for taking external specialist advice and support. |
| | • For example, computer forensics support might be needed to search for and retrieve personal data. 'eDiscovery' capability might be needed to review, de-duplify, annotate and delete electronic data. |
| | • Legal support might be needed, to help with the application of exceptions and restrictions. |
| | • If external support is needed, it needs to be sought early in the one-month timetable for responding. Seeking support in the last days of this timeframe can be a risk flag to professional services providers, who may decline to provide support, considering that the controller is in disarray and could be a problematic client to deal with. |
| Handling the data subject | • Taking account of the risks of escalation, for example by the making of complaints to the regulator or through the court process, the controller needs to ensure that it creates a good impression in the record that is generated following receipt of the access request. For example, the controller will want to demonstrate to the regulator and potentially to the courts that it is proactive, aware of its obligations and committed to acting appropriately and reasonably. |

*(Continued)*

DATA PROTECTION AND COMPLIANCE

**Table 6.1 (Continued)**

|  |  |
|---|---|
|  | • Therefore, speedy and polite acknowledgment of receipt of the access request is essential. |
|  | • If there is a need for an extension of time, it should be requested as soon as possible within the (initial) one month timeframe, with reasons provided. |
|  | • If there is a need to request identification information, or to seek clarifications about the scope of the access request, again this should be done as soon as possible within the (initial) one month timeframe. |
| Funnelling the data subject | • The GDPR does not prevent the controller from seeking to funnel the data subject through a process flow to gain efficiencies in the handling of the response, nor does it prevent the controller from seeking to narrow the scope of an access request. |
|  | • The design of a funnelling approach needs careful consideration, plus the controller needs to avoid giving the impression that the data subject is being coerced or cajoled. |
|  | • The creation of funnels does not oblige the data subject to follow the controller's set process, nor does it absolve the controller from the need to be able to identify the receipt of access requests, including oral ones, across all its communications channels. |
|  | • Examples of funnels, include the creation of website forms with options provided, preference centres and dialling systems in contact centres. |
| Third-party information | • Great care needs to be taken to avoid unlawful disclosures of third-party information in the response to the access request. |
|  | • Having appropriate technical and organisational measures to verify the requester's identity form part of the mitigations against the risk of unlawful disclosures. |
|  | • Additionally, the controller needs to consider putting in place systems that enable it to seek third-party consent for disclosure of their information, as well as rules for assessing whether it is appropriate to make disclosure without consent. |
|  | • Care needs to be taken to understand the meaning of 'identifiability' within the definition of personal data, because simply stripping out a third party's name might not be enough to prevent them from being identified, particularly in circumstances where the third party is already known to the data subject, such as in employment situations. |

*(Continued)*

**Table 6.1 (Continued)**

|  |  |
|---|---|
|  | • Where physical redaction techniques are used to mask third-party identifiers, such as the use of black marker pens, care should be taken to examine whether the attempted redaction is complete. Sometimes, it is still possible to see what is hidden using black marker pens, such as by viewing a document in different light sources. |
| Use of exceptions and restrictions | • The controller needs to develop a thorough understanding of the exceptions and restrictions, or gain access to support that can provide these insights. |
|  | • Inappropriate or overuse of exceptions and restrictions can tip the controller into non-compliance, thereby exposing it to additional regulatory and litigation risk. |
|  | • Conversely, some restrictions should not be ignored. For example, waiver of legal professional privilege in an access request response might undermine the controller in substantive legal proceedings. Similarly, disclosing sensitive health records might cause the data subject long-lasting harm. |
| Escalations | • Strategies for dealing with escalations of access requests, such as complaints to the regulator and litigation, would be advantageous, especially where the controller is faced with large volumes of access requests, such as after a personal data breach. |
| Records keeping | • For accountability purposes, controllers should keep a record of the receipt of access requests and the action taken in response. |
|  | • The record itself needs to be held in a compliant manner, with set retention periods, and secure. |
| Consistency in transparency | • There are significant overlaps between the transparency regimes in A.13, 14, 15 and 34. |
|  | • The responses given in answer to an access request can provide the potential for disparities between the controller's positions across these transparency requirements to be revealed. |
|  | • Controllers need to ensure that their positions across these requirements are consistent and properly conformed. |

## Personal data breaches – Article 34

Article 34 of the GDPR requires controllers to communicate information about personal data breaches to impacted individuals without undue delay, where those breaches are likely to result in a high risk to their rights and freedoms. This transparency mechanism sits alongside a parallel obligation to notify the regulators of these breaches, under A.33.

The information required by A.34 overlaps with the information required by A.13, 14 and 15. As with A.15, it provides data subjects with insights about data processing that can trigger further processes of adverse scrutiny and challenge, such as the making of complaints to regulators, the bringing of compensation claims and litigation. Again, A.12 applies to A.34.

A.34 is discussed in more depth in Chapter 17.

## RIGHTS OVER DATA PROCESSING

The data subject's rights over data processing are contained in section 3 of the GDPR, which is titled 'Rectification and erasure' and section 4, which is titled 'Right to object and automated decision-making'. These rights enable the data subject to intervene in the controller's processing activities and shape how they are performed.

As already indicated, A.12 applies to the rights, as do the exceptions and the restrictions that have been adopted under A.23, 85 and 89. The above discussion of these matters applies equally here.

### Right to rectification – A.16

The right of rectification has two elements within in it. First, the data subject is entitled to inaccurate personal data concerning them to be rectified. That is to enable inaccuracies to be cured. Secondly and taking account of the purpose of the processing, if personal data are incomplete the data subject has the right to have them completed, which can include having a supplementary statement added to the data set.

#### *Connection to the fourth data protection principle*
The right to rectification sits alongside the fourth data protection principle in A.5.1.d, which says that personal data shall be:

> accurate and, where necessary, kept up to date; every reasonable step must be taken to ensure that personal data that are inaccurate, having regard to the purposes for which they are processed, are erased or rectified without delay ('accuracy').

#### *Meaning of accuracy*
The GDPR does not provide a definition of accuracy, but under the Data Protection Act 1998, which has been repealed and replaced by the 2018 Act, data was deemed inaccurate if it was incorrect or misleading on any matters of fact. Thus, the old law was concerned only with issues of fact, which creates a distinction between those matters (such as a person's age) and personal data concerning matters of opinion.

***Accuracy of opinions*** Opinion information is essentially subjective, even where it is based on underlying factual matters. Examples include medical reports. Data subjects often want to challenge opinion information, particularly if they are aggrieved, but it is doubtful that A.16 extends that far. The ICO guidance[7] seems to support this point of view:

---

[7] https://ico.org.uk/for-organisations/guide-to-data-protection/guide-to-the-general-data-protection-regulation-gdpr/individual-rights/right-to-rectification/

It is also complex if the data in question records an opinion. Opinions are, by their very nature, subjective, and it can be difficult to conclude that the record of an opinion is inaccurate. As long as the record shows clearly that the information is an opinion and, where appropriate, whose opinion it is, it may be difficult to say that it is inaccurate and needs to be rectified.

Under the old law, the issue of accuracy often turned on whether the information was accurately recorded, rather than whether it was factually correct. For example, a controller might be given inaccurate information by the data subject in error, which inaccuracies are accurately recorded. Under the current law, the fact that data are substantially inaccurate provides grounds for the exercise of the right of rectification, so it would seem to provide the controller with no defence to say that the data were accurately recorded. Instead, the controller will have to cure the inaccuracy (subject to the application of the exceptions and restrictions), but it would be legitimate for the controller in these cases to create a record to say that the data were accurately recorded in the first place. The ICO guidance touches upon these points:

> Determining whether personal data is inaccurate can be more complex if the data refers to a mistake that has subsequently been resolved. It may be possible to argue that the record of the mistake is, in itself, accurate and should be kept. In such circumstances the fact that a mistake was made and the correct information should also be included in the individuals data.

### Restriction of processing pending determination of accuracy
Resolving challenges about accuracy can often be complex, time-consuming and contentious exercises. On the other hand, processing inaccurate data can cause harm to the impacted individual. Therefore, while things are being sorted out, the controller faces a choice: should it continue processing the disputed data, or not? That choice will be taken away from the controller, however, if the data subject also exercises their right to restriction under A.18.

***Relationship to A.18 and the right of restriction***  Article 18 of the GDPR says that the data subject can request the restriction of processing of contested data while the controller is verifying its accuracy. Regardless of whether the data subject makes a request for restriction, this is an option that is always open to the controller and when considering its choices, the controller should reflect upon the impacts to the rights and freedoms of the individual of continuing to process potentially inaccurate information. The ICO guidance suggests voluntary restriction as a matter of good practice pending the resolution of the issues:

> Under Article 18 an individual has the right to request restriction of the processing of their personal data where they contest its accuracy and you are checking it. As a matter of good practice, you should restrict the processing of the personal data in question whilst you are verifying its accuracy, whether or not the individual has exercised their right to restriction.

### Notifying others of rectification of data – impact of A.19
If a controller rectifies personal data following receipt a request, A.19 requires it to communicate the fact of rectification and what has been done to each recipient to whom the personal data have been disclosed, unless that would be impossible or involve

disproportionate effort. If the data subject requests information about those recipients, the controller should provide that information.

### *Other compliance issues*
Article 16 says that the data subject is entitled to rectification without undue delay. Again, this is subject to the one-month longstop in A.12, which can be extended by up to two months in complex cases or where the controller is dealing with many requests. As a reminder, the other compliance issues in A.12 apply, namely:

- Communications with the data subject shall be concise, transparent, intelligible, easily accessible, and use clear and plain language.
- An inability to properly identify the data subject provides grounds for the controller to refuse to comply with the request. The controller can also request identification information, which stops the clock on compliance.
- If the controller refuses to act, it should inform the data subject of this without undue delay and within the one-month longstop period, providing reasons.
- Exceptions apply for manifestly unfounded and excessive requests.

### Right to erasure, or 'the right to be forgotten' – A.17

The right to erasure, or 'the right to be forgotten', received widespread attention in 2014, when the CJEU gave judgment in the *Google Spain* (2014)[8] case. In that case it was held that Google Inc., the controller of the Google search engine, is obliged to remove links to freely available website reports where the data in those reports are 'inadequate, irrelevant or no longer relevant, or excessive'. In a subsequent case in 2017,[9] the CJEU held that it was permissible for Google to apply a geo-fenced approach to the right to be forgotten, so that offending links are only to be removed within the local versions of the search engine accessible in the EU Member States. The Google cases involve complex issues of law relating to the balancing act between the right of data protection and the right to freedom of expression, as well as complexities surrounding the meaning of controller, but for current purposes they help to illustrate the expansive nature of the right to be forgotten.

### *When the right to be forgotten applies*
Under A.17.1 the data subject is entitled to obtain the erasure of their data in these circumstances:

- The personal data are no longer necessary in relation to the purposes for which they were collected or otherwise processed.
- The data subject withdraws their consent for processing and there is no other legal ground to justify the continuation of processing.
- The data subject objects to the processing pursuant to A.21(1) and there are no overriding legitimate grounds for the processing. This concerns the processing of

---

8  *Google Spain SL, Google Inc. v. Agencia Española de Protección de Datos, Mario Costeja González*, C-131/12.

9  *Google LLC, venant aux droits de Google Inc. v. Commission nationale de l'informatique et des libertés (CNIL)*, C-507/17.

personal data where the lawful basis for processing is the performance of task carried out in the public interest or the exercise of official authority (see A.6.1.e) and processing that is carried out in the controller's legitimate interests (see A.6.1.f).

- The data subject objects to the processing pursuant to A.21(2). This concerns processing for direct marketing purposes.
- The personal data have been unlawfully processed.
- The personal data must be erased to comply with a legal obligation.
- The personal data have been collected in relation to the offer of information society services referred to in A.8.1.

The above list of circumstances requiring erasure point to several interesting situations. First, there are substantial connections to the data protection principles with GDPR A.5 and the lawful bases of processing. The first circumstance relates to the second data protection principle, that is, purpose limitation. The reference to unlawful processing relates to the first data protection principle. The references to consent, A.21 and A.8.1 concern the lawful bases of processing in A.6. This shows how the right to be forgotten and the ability to deal with it properly is anchored to the controller having a thorough understanding of these core building blocks of data protection. The references to the right to object show some of the linkages between the data subject rights, in a similar fashion to how the right to rectification in A.16 cross-refers to the right of restriction in A.18.

### *Exceptions to the right to be forgotten*
Article 17.3 sets out the exceptions to the right to be forgotten, saying that erasure is not required where the processing is necessary for the following purposes:

- For exercising the right of freedom of expression and information.
- For compliance with a legal obligation, or for the performance of a task carried out in the public interest or in the exercise of official authority vested in the controller.
- For reasons of public interest in the area of public health in accordance A.9.2.h and i and for the purposes of A.9.3. These relate to the processing of special category data, particularly data relating to health.
- For archiving purposes in the public interest, scientific or historical research purposes or statistical purposes in accordance with A.89(1) in so far as the right to erasure would be likely to render impossible or seriously impair the achievement of the objectives of that processing.
- For the establishment, exercise or defence of legal claims.

These exceptions are additional to the right of controllers to avoid compliance with rights requests that are manifestly unfounded or excessive.

***Restrictions*** Referring again to the UK restrictions within Schedules 2 and 3 of the Data Protection Act, as set out in Table 2.10, these parts apply to A.17:

- Sch 2 Pt 1 – Crime, immigration and legal proceedings;
- Sch 2 Pt 2 – Protecting the public and public functions;

- Sch 2 Pt 5 – The special purposes;
- Sch 3 Pt 2 – Health data;
- Sch 3 Pt 3 – Social work data;
- Sch 3 Pt 4 – Educational records.

### *Informing others of erasure requests*
A.17.2 places an obligation on the controller to take reasonable steps, including technical measures, to notify others that are processing personal data of valid erasure requests received. This obligation applies where the controller has made the personal data public and the data subject has requested that the other controllers should also erase any links to, or copies or replications of those data. This covers the situations discussed in the Google cases mentioned above.

In determining what is reasonable, the controller should take account of available technology and the costs of implementation.

### *Notifying others of erasures – impact of A.19*
A.19, which is discussed above, also applies to erasures of data.

### *Other compliance issues*
See the discussion under A.16 for the other compliance issues that apply.

### Right to restriction of processing – A.18

The right to restriction of processing enables the data subject to put an end to data processing, save for residual storage of the data and other limited processing operations.

### *When the right to restriction applies*
The right to restriction applies in these situations:

- The accuracy of the personal data is contested by the data subject. In this situation the data must be restricted while the controller verifies the accuracy of the personal data. If the data are inaccurate, they will have to be rectified in accordance with A.16. If the controller considers that the data are accurate it must notify the data subject of its position, as required by A.12, at which point the restriction period will end, although the data subject will be able to challenge the controller's decision if they wish to, through a complaint to the regulator, or the commencement of legal action.

- The processing is unlawful and the data subject opposes the erasure of the personal data and requests restriction instead. A data subject might prefer restriction over erasure to ensure that an evidence trail is maintained for other purposes.

- The controller no longer needs the personal data for the purposes of the processing, but they are required by the data subject for the establishment, exercise or defence of legal claims. This is to prevent the controller from destroying important evidence that is needed by the data subject to advance their legal rights.

- The data subject has objected to processing pursuant to A.21(1). The restriction will then operate pending verification of whether the legitimate grounds of the controller override those of the data subject.

### Methods by which processing can be restricted
Recital 67 provides examples of the methods that might be used to restrict data:

> Methods by which to restrict the processing of personal data could include, inter alia, temporarily moving the selected data to another processing system, making the selected personal data unavailable to users, or temporarily removing published data from a website. In automated filing systems, the restriction of processing should in principle be ensured by technical means in such a manner that the personal data are not subject to further processing operations and cannot be changed. The fact that the processing of personal data is restricted should be clearly indicated in the system.

### Processing during the period of restriction
During the period of restriction the processing activities that can be performed by the controller are limited to mere storage, unless one of the grounds in A.18.2 apply that permit additional forms of processing:

- the data subject consents to the additional forms of processing;
- the additional processing is required for the establishment, exercise or defence of legal claims;
- the additional processing is needed for the protection of the rights of another natural or legal person or for reasons of important public interest.

### Informing the data subject of the lifting of the restriction
If the controller is required to restrict processing, it will not be allowed to lift the restriction before informing the data subject (see A.18.3). This will give the data subject the option to request further restriction, or possibly erasure of data, or they can pursue their remedies before the regulator or the courts.

### Notifying others of restrictions
A.19, discussed above, also applies to restrictions of data.

### Exceptions
The exceptions for manifestly unfounded or excessive requests in A.12.5 applies to A.19.

**Restrictions under the Data Protection Act**   Referring again to the UK restrictions within Schedules 2 and 3 of the Data Protection Act, these parts apply to A.17:

- Sch 2 Pt 1 – Crime, immigration and legal proceedings;
- Sch 2 Pt 2 – Protecting the public and public functions;
- Sch 2 Pt 5 – The special purposes;
- Sch 2 Pt 6 – Research, statistics and archiving;
- Sch 3 Pt 2 – Health data;
- Sch 3 Pt 3 – Social work data;
- Sch 3 Pt 4 – Educational records.

## Other compliance issues
See the discussion under A.16 for the other compliance issues that apply.

## Right to data portability – A.20

The right to data portability is a new data subject right, introduced by the GDPR. While still in its infancy in terms of usage, arguably it is the epitome of putting the data subject in control of their personal data, as it enables them to receive their personal data from the controller and transmit it to another controller. The right to portability can be exercised in conjunction with the right of erasure in A.17, meaning that as well as receiving their data from the controller the data subject can put an end to continuing processing by the controller. The right to portability also helps to illustrate a point made elsewhere in this book, which is that the controller does not own the personal data that they process, in the sense of them having property rights in the data, but, rather, the law simply gives them a licence to use the data, providing that they operate fully in accordance with the requirements of the GDPR. By exercising the right to portability in conjunction with the right of erasure, the data subject effectively terminates that licence.

## When the right to portability applies
For the right to portability to apply, the following conditions must be satisfied:

- The data subject must have provided the data to the controller. The right will not apply if the controller obtained the data from a third party.
- The processing must be based on consent, per the requirements of A.6.1.a or A.9.2.a, or based on contract, per A.6.1.b. This demonstrates once again how the lawful basis of processing impacts the operation of data subject rights.

**Meaning of information 'provided' to the controller**   A data subject can actively provide their information to a controller, for example by submitting it through an online form. However, the idea of providing information to the controller is perceived to be wider, in the sense that the regulators see it as covering information that the controller obtains through observing the data subject. In other words the idea of the data subject providing information encompasses the situation where the controller obtains information from the data subject otherwise than through their active provision of it. This does not cover information obtained through surreptitious surveillance, however, since the right applies only where the processing is based on consent or contract, which presumes that the data subject permits the obtaining of their information.

ICO guidance[10] puts it in this way:

> Sometimes the personal data an individual has provided to you will be easy to identify (for example, their mailing address, username, age). However, the meaning of data 'provided to' you is not limited to this. It is also personal data resulting from observation of an individual's activities (for example, where using a device or service).

---

10  https://ico.org.uk/for-organisations/guide-to-data-protection/guide-to-the-general-data-protection-regulation-gdpr/individual-rights/right-to-data-portability/#ib4

This may include:

- history of website usage or search activities;
- traffic and location data; or
- 'raw' data processed by connected objects such as smart meters and wearable devices.

Controllers regularly obtain personal data from data subjects, which they combine with other data, or otherwise deal with, to create new data sets. The regulators consider that the right does not apply to those new data sets, with the ICO guidance[11] putting it as follows:

> ... does not include any additional data that you have created based on the data an individual has provided to you. For example, if you use the data they have provided to create a user profile then this data would not be in scope of data portability.
>
> You should however note that if this 'inferred' or 'derived' data is personal data, you still need to provide it to an individual if they make a subject access request. Bearing this in mind, if it is clear that the individual is seeking access to the inferred/derived data, as part of a wider portability request, it would be good practice to include this data in your response.

### Porting the data

The controller is required to port the data to the data subject 'in a structured, commonly used and machine-readable format'. Once they have received the data, the data subject can transmit the data to a new controller. In this situation, there is no direct controller-to-controller transmission. However, A.20.2 provides for direct controller-to-controller transmission, saying that the data subject is entitled to have this happen 'where technically feasible'. According to Recital 68, this does not require controllers 'to adopt or maintain processing systems which are technically compatible' with those of other organisations. These is some ambiguity in this language, but ICO guidance suggests 'you should take a reasonable approach, and this should not generally create a barrier to transmission'.

Regarding the other elements of the duty, the ICO guidance points to the *Open Data Handbook*,[12] and these definitions:

- Structured data. 'Data where the structural relation between elements is explicit in the way the data is stored on a computer disk.'
- Machine-readable. 'Data in a data format that can be automatically read and processed by a computer.'

Regarding formats, the ICO guidance says:

---

[11] https://ico.org.uk/for-organisations/guide-to-data-protection/guide-to-the-general-data-protection-regulation-gdpr/individual-rights/right-to-data-portability/#ib4

[12] http://opendatahandbook.org/

Where no specific format is in common use within your industry or sector, you should provide personal data using open formats such as CSV, XML and JSON. You may also find that these formats are the easiest for you to use when answering data portability requests.

***Without hindrance*** An integral part of the controller's duty is to ensure data portability 'without hindrance'. This suggests that the controller cannot put arbitrary barriers in the way of portability, such as creating unnecessary complications or unjustified delay. Due to the accountability principle, if the data subject encounters complications or delay, the onus will be on the controller to explain and justify them.

### *Exceptions*

A.20.4 contains an exception to the right of portability for information that relates to other people. It says that the right 'shall not adversely affect the rights and freedoms of others'. This replicates the exception in A.15.4, for subject access rights, and the discussion above applies equally here.

The exceptions for manifestly unfounded or excessive requests in A.12.5 applies to A.19.

***Restrictions under the Data Protection Act*** Referring again to the UK restrictions within Schedules 2 and 3 of the Data Protection Act, these parts apply to A.20:

- Sch 2 Pt 1 – Crime, immigration and legal proceedings;
- Sch 2 Pt 2 – Protecting the public and public functions;
- Sch 2 Pt 5 – The special purposes;
- Sch 2 Pt 6 – Research, statistics and archiving;
- Sch 3 Pt 2 – Health data;
- Sch 3 Pt 3 – Social work data;
- Sch 3 Pt 4 – Educational records.

### *Other compliance issues*

See the discussion under A.16 for the other compliance issues that apply.

### Right to object – A.21

Where the right to object applies, the controller shall no longer process the data. Giving this requirement its ordinary meaning and due to the expansive meaning of processing within A.4.2, it means that the controller must erase the data in all cases. The ICO regulatory guidance[13] points to a different conclusion, however, suggesting that data can be processed after the right to object, although in a very limited sense, such as to manage marketing suppression lists:

- Where you have received an objection to the processing of personal data and you have no grounds to refuse, you need to stop or not begin processing the data.

---

[13] https://ico.org.uk/for-organisations/guide-to-data-protection/guide-to-the-general-data-protection-regulation-gdpr/individual-rights/right-to-object/#ib6

- This may mean that you need to erase personal data, as the definition of processing under the UK GDPR is broad, and includes storing data. However, as noted above, this will not always be the most appropriate action to take.

- Erasure may not be appropriate if you process the data for other purposes as you need to retain the data for those purposes. For example, when an individual objects to the processing of their data for direct marketing, you can place their details onto a suppression list to ensure that you continue to comply with their objection. However, you need to ensure that the data are clearly marked so that they are not processed for purposes the individual has objected to.

### *When the right to object applies*
The right to object to processing applies in four situations:

- Where the processing is based on A.6.1.e, that is, for a task carried out in the public interest or in the exercise of official authority vested in the controller. In these situations, the processing must cease, unless the controller can demonstrate compelling legitimate grounds to continue processing that override the interests, rights and freedoms of the data subject, or unless the processing is for the establishment, exercise or defence of legal claims. See A.21.1.

- Where the processing is based on A.6.1.f, that is, it is carried out for the purposes of the controller's legitimate interests. The qualifiers that apply to A.6.1.e apply equally here. See A.21.1.

- Where the processing is for the purposes of direct marketing, in which case the processing for these purposes shall cease. See A.21.2.

- Where the processing is for scientific or historical research purposes, or for statistical purposes. In this situation, the processing must cease unless it is necessary for the performance of a task carried out for reasons of public interest. See A.21.6.

### *Information society services*
These are online services. In these cases the data subject may exercise the right to object by automated means using technical specifications.

### *Informing the data subject of the right to object*
At the very latest, the controller must inform the data subject of the right to object at the time of the first communication with them, by 'explicitly' bringing it to their attention. This is additional to the obligation to provide the information required by A.13 and 14. When providing this information, it must be 'presented clearly and separately from any other information' (see A.21.4).

### *Exceptions*
The exceptions for manifestly unfounded or excessive requests in A.12.5 applies to A.21.

**Restrictions under the Data Protection Act** Referring again to the UK restrictions within Schedules 2 and 3 of the Data Protection Act, these parts apply to A.21:

- Sch 2 Pt 1 – Crime, immigration and legal proceedings;
- Sch 2 Pt 2 – Protecting the public and public functions;
- Sch 2 Pt 5 – The special purposes;
- Sch 2 Pt 6 – Research, statistics and archiving;
- Sch 3 Pt 2 – Health data;
- Sch 3 Pt 3 – Social work data;
- Sch 3 Pt 4 – Educational records.

*Other compliance issues*
See the discussion under A.16 for the other compliance issues that apply.

### Right not to be subject to automated decision making, including profiling – A.22

Decision making based solely on automated processing carries significant potential for highly invasive activities to be conducted rapidly, at huge volumes and without human checks and balances. These potentials increase as technology develops, costs of adoption decrease and ubiquity increases. Moreover, if errors, vulnerabilities and biases are built in to automated processing systems, the risks to the rights and freedoms of individuals will increase exponentially and, potentially, become industrialised. The huge leaps and bounds that have been made in AI over recent years and the adoption of technologies such as automated facial recognition present a fear that society could be on the cusp of enabling huge civil liberties harms through automated decision making. For example, in the field of AFR, concerns have been expressed about the potential for computer code to result in gender biases and ethnicity biases, leading to increased risks of false positives in surveillance and identity systems. Obviously, if this becomes a problem in the field of law enforcement, there could be wrongful arrests and possibly even threats to life.

On the other hand, wholly automated processing has the potential to enhance countless aspects of life, society and the economy. If human errors can be removed from the road and be replaced with failsafe automated vehicles, road accidents and fatalities might reduce, but traffic speed may increase leading to shortened journey times. AI-enabled processing of big data sets in health and pharmaceuticals could have the potential to find cures to hideous diseases. Urban life in smart cities could become cleaner and safer. Productivity gains in industry could be great, freeing up human time for more strategic business pursuits and leisure.

The right to object to within A.22 is the GDPR's attempt to insert some checks and balances into these areas, by enabling human oversight and control over a computer-controlled world.

*When the right not to be subject to automated decisions applies*
The right in A.22 applies in these situations:

- a decision affecting the data subject is based solely on automated processing, including profiling;
- that decision needs to produce legal effects concerning the data subject, or similarly significant effects.

### Decisions solely based on automated processing

The requirement that the decision needs to be based solely on automated processing means that where the decision is only partly based on automated processing, that is, where the decision involves human intervention, the right in A.22 will not apply. This is because the decision involves the necessary human element that A.22 is seeking to achieve through the insertion of the checks and balances provided by the right. As the ICO guidance[14] puts it, 'for something to be solely automated there must be no human involvement in the decision-making process'.

### Profiling

Profiling is defined in A.4.4 in these terms:

> ... any form of automated processing of personal data consisting of the use of personal data to evaluate certain personal aspects relating to a natural person, in particular to analyse or predict aspects concerning that natural person's performance at work, economic situation, health, personal preferences, interests, reliability, behaviour, location or movements.

As the definition shows, the concept of profiling is highly invasive, not simply due to the areas of the human personality that analysis through profiling can involve, but also because it can involve predictive analysis, that is, determining human behaviours before they happen. This echoes the dystopian systems in literature such as *Nineteen Eighty-Four* and *Minority Report*. If profiling could have significant legal or similar effects on the individual based on predictive analysis, the consequences for rights and freedoms could be chilling in the absence of necessary checks and balances.

In a more mundane sense, profiling is already part and parcel of ordinary business. The ICO points out that it happens in health care, education, financial services and marketing, for example, and the sources of data that can be used in profiling including 'Internet searches, buying habits, lifestyle and behaviour data gathered from mobile phones, social networks, video surveillance systems and the Internet of Things'. Profiling is embedded into the AdTech industry, to drive personalised marketing based on behavioural analytics.

### Legal and similarly significant effects

A legal effect is something that impacts on a person's legal rights, which covers a very broad range of considerations, from a depriving a person of the opportunity to enter a contract, through to depriving them of their liberty. Terminating a person's contract of employment would fall within this category. The meaning of 'similarly significant effects' is not defined in the GDPR, but it brings the controller back to the idea of rights and freedoms and the broad ground they cover as set out in the EU Charter of Fundamental Rights and the Human Rights Act. On a case-by-case basis, the controller needs to

---

[14] https://ico.org.uk/for-organisations/guide-to-data-protection/guide-to-the-general-data-protection-regulation-gdpr/individual-rights/rights-related-to-automated-decision-making-including-profiling/

understand the range of impacts that arise from profiling then make a determination of whether they are significant, having regard to the overall context, including the special characteristics of the individual concerned. The ICO guidance points to the fact that 'significant effects are more difficult to define', but it provides as examples the automatic refusal of an online credit application and e-recruiting practices without human intervention.

### *When the right does not apply*
The right in A.22 does not apply in these circumstances:

- the decision is necessary for entering, or performance of, a contract between the data subject and a data controller;
- the decision is authorised by law, if the law lays down suitable measures to safeguard the data subject's rights and freedoms or legitimate interests;
- the decision is based on the data subject's explicit consent.

In the first and third situations, the controller is required to implement suitable measures to safeguard the data subject's rights and freedoms and legitimate interests. This includes giving the data subject the right to:

- obtain human intervention;
- express their point of view;
- contest the decision.

**Special category data**   In the above situations, decisions cannot be based on the processing of special category data (as listed in A.9.1) unless:

- A.9.2.a applies, that is, the data subject's explicit consent is obtained; or
- A.9.2.g applies, that is, the processing is necessary for reasons of substantial public interests; and
- suitable measures are put in place to safeguard the data subject's rights and freedoms and legitimate interests.

### *Exceptions*
The exceptions for manifestly unfounded or excessive requests in A.12.5 applies to A.22.

### *Other compliance issues*
See the discussion under A.16 for the other compliance issues that apply.

## REMEDIES AND RIGHTS OF REDRESS

Data subjects benefit from various remedies and rights of redress, which are contained in GDPR Chapter VIII. These rights are summarised in Table 6.2 and, as alluded to above, they enable the data subject to take action against controllers and processors through the bringing of complaints to the regulators and through direct action in court, which they can conduct in conjunction with civil society organisations. The GDPR also permits Member States to allow CSOs to bring representative actions without needing the mandate or approval of the data subjects whom they say they represent. This is already the position in the UK, through the rules on representative actions that apply in the English and Welsh courts.

Regulators themselves are not immune from complaint and legal proceedings. If the regulators fail to do their jobs properly, data subjects can bring court action against them, as can CSOs. At the moment this is not a common occurrence, but the privacy activist Max Schrems has shown what can be done when a data subject brings a complaint against a regulator alleging a failure to fulfil their duties: by taking action against the Ireland Data Protection Commissioner ('judicial review' proceedings) relating to Facebook and international data transfers, he triggered a chain of events that led to the Safe Harbor and Privacy Shield transfer arrangements both being declared unlawful by the CJEU in 2015 and 2020 respectively.

In many countries we are seeing the emergence of a compensation culture for data protection infringements. Compensation claims are increasingly common after personal data breaches, particularly large-scale ones that can impact many people. Non-compliant use of cookies is also a common trigger to compensation claims.

**Table 6.2 Data subjects' remedies and rights of redress**

| | |
|---|---|
| Right to lodge a complaint with a supervisory authority – A.77 | • Data subjects are entitled to lodge complaints with the regulators if they consider that the processing of personal data relating to them infringes the requirements of the GDPR. |
| | • They can lodge their complaints before the regulator in the country of their habitual residence, or the regulator for their place of work, or the regulator where the infringement occurred, if different. |
| | • The regulator must keep the data subject informed of the progress of their complaint and the outcome. |
| | • The regulator also must inform the data subject of the possibility for them to seek a judicial remedy against the regulator, under A.78. |
| Right to an effective judicial remedy against a supervisory authority – A.78 | • Data subjects have the right to an effective judicial remedy against a legally binding decision of the regulator concerning them. |
| | • The right to a judicial remedy against the regulator, including where they act as the lead supervisory authority under the 'one-stop shop', arises where they do not deal with a complaint properly, or do not inform the data subject of the progress or outcome of the complaint. |
| | • The data subject must commence these proceedings in the courts of the country where the regulator is established. |

*(Continued)*

**Table 6.2 (Continued)**

| | |
|---|---|
| Right to an effective judicial remedy against a controller or processor – A.79 | • Data subjects have the right to an effective judicial remedy against controllers and processors for non-compliance.<br><br>• Unless the controller/processor is a public authority, the data subject has the choice of suing in the courts of the controller/processor, or in the courts of their country of habitual residence. If the controller/processor is a public authority, they must be sued in their courts.<br><br>• Data subjects can bring legal proceedings for any infringement of the GDPR that affects them, not just breaches of the rights in A.12 to 22 and 34. |
| Right to representation – A.80 | • Data subjects have the right to mandate not-for-profit organisations to represent their interests during the pursuit of their remedies listed in this table.<br><br>• These not-for-profit bodies must be properly constituted in accordance with the laws of the Member States where they operate; they must have public interest statutory objectives; and they must be active in the field of data protection.<br><br>• Member States may permit these organisations to exercise data subject powers under the articles set out above (i.e. excluding A.82) with the data subject's mandate.<br><br>• These powers are enabling increased activism by civil society organisations. Max Schrem's organisation NYOB is utilising these powers to advance a range of data protection concerns relating to access requests and the use of cookies. In the UK, the *Lloyd v. Google* (2019) case is a leading example of the significant impact that representative actions can have. |
| Right to compensation – A.82 | • Any person who has suffered material or non-material damage because of an infringement of the GDPR is entitled to receive compensation from the controller or processor responsible.<br><br>• Material damage means damage such as financial loss and bodily harm (such as a recognised psychological harm). Non-material damage means distress.<br><br>• Controllers and processors will be exempt from liability if they prove that they are not in any way responsible for the event giving rise to the damage.<br><br>• Where more than one party is responsible for the damage caused, each of them shall be held fully liable for the entire damage. This is to ensure effective compensation for the data subject. |

*(Continued)*

**Table 6.2 (Continued)**

- Where a controller or processor is held liable and they have paid the compensation in full, they are entitled to seek contributions from other liable parties.
- The rules on the jurisdiction of the courts are same as in A.79.

## SUMMARY

In conclusion, this chapter gives readers a better understanding of:

- the purpose and significance of the data subject rights;
- the range and scope of them;
- when the rights apply;
- the rules for dealing with the exercise of them;
- the exceptions and restrictions that apply, which limit the application of the rights.

# PART III
# OPERATING INTERNATIONALLY

# 7 NATIONAL SUPERVISION WITHIN AN INTERNATIONAL FRAMEWORK

## Richard Hall

This chapter provides an overview of the role and powers of the EU and UK data protection supervisory authorities, who are the national regulatory bodies that are responsible for the monitoring and enforcement of the law in the land mass of the GDPR, as well as the requirements for identifying and selecting a lead supervisory authority and appointing European representative.

### NATIONAL REGULATORY SYSTEMS AND DIVERGENCES

As with any piece of legislation, the GDPR needs a body, or bodies, to have the responsibility and powers to monitor and enforce compliance, without which there would be no real motivation (outside morality and reputational reasons) for compliance, especially where doing so may be seen as complex, creating cost or potentially impacting on financial or other gains.

Therefore, the establishment and appointment of supervisory authorities across each Member State and the fulfilment of their roles is fundamental to the proper and expected operation of the GDPR, without which the expected outcomes of the GDPR could not be achieved.

This is not to say that the operation of multiple supervisory authorities across different territories is not without issue. Challenges arise due to the different approaches to interpretation and enforcement of the law that the supervisory authorities may take.

Different approaches by the supervisory authorities, coupled with varying national legislation in related areas such as employment or distance selling, create a distinct issue for international organisations and organisations operating across more than one Member State. For example, they may encounter difficulties in assessing or implementing controls around the expected requirements, especially where contradicting guidance is issued by different supervisory authorities, or where different approaches to enforcement are taken. In turn, this poses difficulties for organisations when assessing their regulatory risk and the 'correct' approach to compliance.

### GDPR SOLUTION FOR INTERNATIONAL PROCESSING

These problems were not overlooked by the GDPR. Measures are included in the legislation that attempt to remove, or at least reduce, the risks and impacts of differing approaches.

They include rules and requirements for the supervisory authorities themselves. These are designed not just to specify the supervisory authority powers and where they may be used, but also to create consistency and engagement between them. This is further complemented by the introduction of the concept of lead supervisory authorities, also referred to as the 'one-stop shop', and the requirement for controllers and processors based outside the EU to appoint European representatives where their processing activities are governed by the GDPR. The effect of these rules is to give controllers and processors one key supervisory authority to which they are primarily expected to answer, even where they act in multiple territories under the supervision of different supervisory authorities.

## ESTABLISHMENT OF SUPERVISORY AUTHORITIES

As previously noted, without the establishment of appropriate bodies to monitor and enforce compliance at a national level, the GDPR would be ineffective. This was recognised by legislators when drafting the GDPR and, as such, the law creates a specific requirement on Member States to establish/appoint a supervisory authority (or multiple authorities if it chooses to do so),[1] whose purpose is to carry out the tasks of a supervisory authority set out in the GDPR (see 'Tasks' later in this chapter for further information).

Where a Member State chooses to establish or appoint more than one supervisory authority, it is required to designate one of them to represent the Member State on the EDPB (referred to in this chapter as the 'Board').

A.54 of the GDPR requires that each Member State create legislation that covers certain requirements for the establishment of supervisory authorities. Table 7.1 lists the relevant parts of A.54 relating to these requirements, but is not reflective of A.54 in its entirety. Some parts have also been amended for readability. As such, for any direct citations or references readers should consult the regulation directly.

**Table 7.1 Rules on the establishment of the supervisory authority**

| Source | Requirement |
| --- | --- |
| A.54(1)(a) | To establish each supervisory authority under the laws of the Member State. |
| A.54(1)(b) | To establish the qualifications and eligibility conditions required to be appointed as a member of each supervisory authority. |
| A.54(1)(c) | To establish the rules and procedures for the appointment of the member(s) of each supervisory authority. |
| A.54(1)(d) | To establish the duration of the term of the member(s) of each supervisory authority, which shall be no less than four years. |

*(Continued)*

---

[1] GDPR, A.51.

Table 7.1 (Continued)

| Source | Requirement |
|---|---|
| A.54(1)(e) | To establish whether members are able to be reappointed and, if so, for how many terms. |
| A.54(1)(f) | To establish the conditions governing the obligations of the member(s) or members and staff of each supervisory authority, prohibitions on actions, occupations and benefits incompatible therewith during and after the term of office and rules governing the cessation of employment. |
| A.54(2) | To ensure member(s) and the staff of each supervisory authority shall, in accordance with Union or Member State law, be subject to a duty of professional secrecy both during and after their term of office, with regard to any confidential information that has come to their knowledge in the course of the performance of their tasks or exercise of their powers. |
| | During their term of office, that duty of professional secrecy shall in particular apply to reporting by natural persons of infringements of the GDPR. |

In establishing and maintaining a supervisory authority, Member States must also have regard for the requirements for independence, competence and other general conditions laid out in the GDPR.

**General conditions for members of supervisory authorities**

The general conditions for members of the supervisory authorities are contained in A.53 of the GDPR, which requires that:

- Member States shall provide for each member of their supervisory authorities to be appointed by means of a transparent procedure.[2]
- Each member shall have the qualifications, experience and skills, in particular in the area of the protection of personal data, required to perform their duties and exercise their powers.[3]
- The duties of a member shall end in the event of the expiry of the term of office, resignation or compulsory retirement, in accordance with the law of the Member State concerned.[4]
- A member shall be dismissed only in cases of serious misconduct or if the member no longer fulfils the conditions required for the performance of the duties.[5]

---

2  GDPR, A.53(1).
3  GDPR, A.53(1).
4  GDPR, A.53(3).
5  GDPR, A.53(4).

When assessing member conditions, one must also assess the legislation enacted by each Member State pursuant to A.54 of the GDPR. The conditions are not specified within the GDPR and are left to each Member State to decide through enactment of their own legislation. This is just one example of where inconsistencies between supervisory authorities start to arise.

## INDEPENDENCE

Supervisory authority independence and independence of its members is of vital importance to the proper governance of the GDPR and performance of the supervisory authorities' tasks.

Without sufficient independence, supervisory authorities may become subject to, or more easily subject to, political or other interference and perhaps even corruption. Undue control, interference and/or corruption, involving regulatory and judicial bodies, can be evidenced through time and across jurisdictions worldwide, and is often linked to political or personal gain, or self-protection of individuals within or linked to those entities.

Given the reason why the GDPR exists (i.e. for the protection of fundamental data protection rights of individuals), the potential benefits that organisations can obtain through avoiding the GDPR regime, and the potential detriment that can be caused to individuals and organisations alike through the misuse of enforcement powers, it is not hard to see why supervisory authority independence is of such importance.

This is recognised by the GDPR in A.52, which sets out that:

- Each supervisory authority shall act with complete independence in performing its tasks and exercising its powers in accordance with the GDPR.[6]
- The member(s) of each supervisory authority shall, in the performance of their tasks and exercise of their powers in accordance with the GDPR, remain free from external influence, whether direct or indirect, and shall neither seek nor take instructions from anybody.[7]
- The member(s) of each supervisory authority shall refrain from any action incompatible with their duties and shall not, during their term of office, engage in any incompatible occupation, whether gainful or not. [8]
- Each Member State shall ensure that each supervisory authority chooses and has its own staff which shall be subject to the exclusive direction of the member or members of the supervisory authority concerned.[9]

---

[6] GDPR, A.52(1).
[7] GDPR, A.52(2).
[8] GDPR, A.52(3).
[9] GDPR, A.52(5).

In order to ensure that supervisory authorities maintain independence, A.52 also sets out that each Member State must ensure that it is provided with the human, technical and financial resources, premises and infrastructure necessary for the effective performance of its tasks and exercise of its powers,[10] and that supervisory authorities have separate public annual budgets.

## Interference

Despite these controls, the presence of political interferences and lack of human, technical and financial resources for supervisory authorities, in particular, have played some part in the perceived failures of the GDPR to date.

Media and privacy activist publications suggest that some Member States in the EU have become 'safe havens' for businesses who benefit from the use of data, such as the so-called 'big tech' companies. Those same reports include inferences, and in some instances, direct statements, that supervisory authorities have been overwhelmed and unduly influenced by political goals and related economic pressures, or have not been appropriately supported (because data regulation is not in some Member States' interests), which in turn have impacted on supervisory authorities enforcement regimes. However, these reports stop short of direct allegations of 'interference', due to the seriousness of such allegations.

It is common knowledge that it is not in the interests of any of the Member States to drive away business due to the economic harm that this can cause. As such, it would be naïve to think that these pressures at a national level do not filter through to public bodies, including supervisory authorities. Whether it is addressed as 'interference' or 'influence' is immaterial, as both potentially impact on supervisory authority independence.

Despite there being very real risks to independence of supervisory authorities, it is highly unlikely that without hard and irrefutable evidence, any action or inquiries will ever be brought in respect of supervisory authority independence, unless such action is taken by those who feel they have been caused harm by such interference (e.g. by organisations which feel that they have been subject to a decision due to political or other pressure, or data subjects who feel the supervisory authorities have failed to act where required due to the same pressures).

However, bringing a regulator's or other public office's independence into disrepute is no small thing, and, depending on the type of independence issue raised, in some territories may also amount to a serious criminal complaint (e.g. misconduct in public office, corruption). As such, such allegations cannot be made at a whim and should always be based on clear demonstrable evidence or, at the very least, on honest and thought-out belief.

Due to the serious nature of making allegations in this regard, unless independence issues are at the very heart of challenging a supervisory authority decision or a failure to act, either by way of complaint, appeal or judicial review, organisations and individuals

---

[10] GDPR, A.52(4).

alike would be better suited in the first instance to assess whether their complaints are better grounded on the basis of 'competence'.

## SUPERVISORY AUTHORITY COMPETENCE

Competence, much like independence, is a fundamental requirement for the effective monitoring and enforcement of the GDPR.

Within the GDPR supervisory authority competence is specifically dealt with through two distinct articles, A.55 and 56, summarised in Table 7.2.

**Table 7.2 Supervisory authority competences**

| Article | Overview |
| --- | --- |
| A.55 | Article 55 provides that all supervisory authorities must be competent to perform their tasks and excise their powers in accordance with the GDPR. |
| A.56 | Article 56 expands on the general competence requirement contained in Article 55 and provides that a supervisory authority of the main establishment or of the single establishment of a controller or processor must also be competent to act as lead supervisory authority for the cross-border processing carried out by that controller or processor. |

Supervisory authority and member competence can be judged in a number of different ways, but generally relates to their ability to perform their tasks under the GDPR. This on first glance may seem a simple and straightforward enough concept, but given the wide application of the GDPR to a range of activities, which include highly complex subject matters (AdTech, cybersecurity, automated processing, machine learning, etc.), the requirement for competence is wide-reaching and not as straightforward as may initially be thought.

For a supervisory authority to be 'competent' it will require the right individuals, with the necessary breadth and depth, or specialist knowledge, to understand the requirements of the legislation as well as the data processing operations that it governs. Added to this, supervisory authorities require appropriate financial backing to deploy their resources and people effectively.

When reflecting on what it means to be 'competent', it is not necessary to look far to start finding issues in respect of each and every supervisory authority. Competence in a completely holistic sense is frankly unachievable for supervisory authorities, at least as things stand. This is due to the fact that, generally, supervisory authorities are underfunded and unable to employ the right number of people, or retain staff with the requisite specialist knowledge across the breadth and depth of the processing operations subject to the requirements of the GDPR.

Therefore, supervisory authorities need to have regard to their ability to enforce or provide guidance on specialist subjects, which should be reserved to subject matter experts. Failures to do so may lead to harm being caused to those they regulate (i.e. through incorrect or baseless enforcement decisions). For this reason, supervisory authorities tend to set out key areas for monitoring and enforcement, which align to their abilities and the most pressing needs in their jurisdictions (led through complaint volumes, potential harms and public interests). Through little fault of their own, this approach contributes to the inconsistency we see today across the GDPR land mass in respect of supervisory authority priorities, which, in turn, creates inequalities between organisations regulated across different jurisdictions within the GDPR land mass and for the data subjects who are provided different treatment for the same or similar complaints, or who are offered differing levels of protection by their supervisory authorities.

### Member competence

The conditions and requirements for competence of the supervisory authority member(s) will be reflective of the conditions set out by the laws of each Member State pursuant to the requirements of A.54 of the GDPR (see 'Establishment of supervisory authorities'). This, on the face of it, is a strange decision to leave solely at the discretion of each Member State, especially due to the fact that such requirements could have been set out in principle within the GDPR with little effort. However, as currently implemented, this unfortunately creates cause for further inconsistencies in implementation and effect across the GDPR land mass insofar as local laws differ on implementation.

## TASKS

The tasks of the supervisory authorities and their members are set out in A.57 of the GDPR, which contains 23 separate tasks. These tasks can generally be placed into the following categories:

- monitoring;
- promotion and awareness;
- advice and administration;
- rights, complaints and enforcement.

### Monitoring

Supervisory authority monitoring requirements are split into two distinct categories, as shown by the Articles summarised in Table 7.3.

To conduct monitoring and enforcement under A.57(1)(a) is a burdensome task for all of the supervisory authorities, due to each supervisory authority being responsible for monitoring and enforcement of the legislation in respect of all controllers, processors and individuals within their respective territories. Thus, supervisory authorities are led by strategic areas for review and the complaints they receive, rather than through

**Table 7.3 Supervisory authority monitoring tasks**

| Source | Task |
| --- | --- |
| A.57(1)(a) | To monitor and enforce the application of the GDPR within its jurisdiction. |
| A.57(1)(i) | To monitor relevant developments, insofar as they have an impact on the protection of personal data, in particular the development of information and communication technologies and commercial practices. |

proactive and total monitoring and enforcement. This leads to further non-static divergences in approach between the supervisory authorities in each territory.

A.57(1)(i) is intended to cure some issues formed through divergence, by seeking to ensure that supervisory authorities stay abreast of recent developments impacting the protection of personal data, which would include other supervisory authority approaches to new technologies, the enforcement they undertake and of any court decisions affecting the application/interpretation of the legislation (as well as creating a general requirement to monitor for new technologies and processing activities).

However, supervisory authority independence means that it is possible for some of these divergences to remain *in situ* and become engrained in guidance in one territory, completely in conflict with that of another. One clear example, although not one that relates primarily to the GDPR, can be found in the application of consent in respect of cookies and similar technologies throughout the EU. For example, in France the CNIL guidance states that some first-party analytic cookies and similar technologies may be set without consent, but in the UK (pre-Brexit) and in other Member States clear guidance has been issued stating that all non-essential cookies, including analytic cookies, require a GDPR-level consent (informed, active and freely given) before such cookies can be set or information can be read from them. Each supervisory authority has formed their own independent views through their interpretation of the CJEU judgment in the *Planet49* (2019) case, which in this instance are in direct conflict with each other. Moreover, through their requirements to monitor developments, each must be distinctly aware of the others' conflicting guidance, however they have failed to align their positions on the use of these technologies, which they could do by conferring with one another or, alternatively, seeking clarification from the EDPB.

**Promotion and awareness**

Of the supervisory authority tasks, the promotion and creation of awareness of the GDPR is among the most important. Bearing in mind the difficulties in completing monitoring on a large scale, as noted above, promotion and awareness become vitally important. The primary tasks for the promotion and creation of awareness of the GDPR are split into three main areas and are set out in Table 7.4.

**Table 7.4 Promoting compliance and raising awareness**

| Source | Task |
| --- | --- |
| A.57(1)(b) | To promote public awareness and understanding of the risks, rules, safeguards and rights in relation to processing. Activities addressed specifically to children shall receive specific attention. |
| A.57(1)(c) | To advise, in accordance with Member State law, the national parliament, the government, and other institutions and bodies on legislative and administrative measures relating to the protection of natural persons' rights and freedoms with regard to processing. |
| A.57(1)(d) | To promote the awareness to controllers and processors of their obligations under the GDPR. |

Promotion of public awareness and understanding in relation to A.57(1)(b) and (d) can be achieved in a number of different ways. These include:

- the creation of guidelines;
- the publishing of blogs and/or other online content, and through advertisements;
- through direct discussions and advice to organisations (e.g. under the prior consultation mechanism for high-risk processing activities, further to A.35 and 36);
- advice to national parliament, government, and other institutions and bodies on legislative and administrative measures under A.57(1)(c);
- advising data subjects of their rights through the complaints and advice processes;
- through carrying out and publishing enforcement decisions.

Arguably, the publishing of enforcement decisions is likely to draw the most interest from organisations and individuals alike, since these matters are ones that attract the most publicity, especially where particularly large financial penalties are issued, making such information more easily accessible to the public.

### *Issues caused through promotion and awareness activities*
Promotion of the GDPR and creation of awareness of it is of great importance to building compliance and protecting the rights of individuals. However, for new pieces of legislation that have been largely untested, especially principle-based legislation like the GDPR where matters of interpretation and application are key, there are also issues that arise through active promotion and awareness.

There are multiple examples of cases where supervisory authorities have actively promoted their interpretation of the legislation through multiple channels (as they are required to do), including through official guidance, which has later turned out to be incorrect. It is the active promotion of these misinterpretations that has contributed to the creation of a system of disinformation and/or confusion in relation to the requirements of the GDPR. Once published, this disinformation is extremely difficult to remove from public access and creates the need for supervisory authorities to create further awareness activities to correct the previous mistake. Ultimately however, it is usually those subject to the GDPR that pay the price for ingesting materially incorrect guidance and advice, through no fault of their own.

Where organisations have properly utilised supervisory guidance that is later changed or corrected by the courts, or by the supervisory authority without prompt, this in turn creates a dilemma for supervisory authorities in respect of how enforcement is carried out and for those subject to the legislation. Through experience, most supervisory authorities will allow an unofficial grace period for correcting activities that were incorrectly promoted. This is not a universal solution, however, and there is no compensation for organisations who expend financial resources on compliance activities that were based, or reliant on, advice and guidance issued by supervisory authorities that later turns out to be incorrect. Nor does it provide a complete defence to litigation from potential claimants who are impacted by actions carried out otherwise than in accordance with the legislation (even where such actions were originally carried out pursuant to advice and guidance issued by the relevant supervisory authority).

Therefore, complete reliance on the materials and/or information and opinions promoted by supervisory authorities and their members can be risky. These materials should not always be treated as absolute fact, but instead should be used as an indication of how a certain supervisory authority will approach its monitoring and/or enforcement of the GDPR. Taking this approach will allow an organisation to make informed risk decisions, especially where guidance does not appear to reflect judicial interpretation of the legislation, or where an alternate approach to the guidance is taken (i.e. because an organisation does not accept the supervisory authority interpretation of the law).

## Advice and administration

The supervisory authorities have multiple tasks relating to distinct elements of the GDPR, including requirements for the administration and provision of advice in respect of:

- the mechanisms for transfers of personal data to third countries, including the adoption and authorisation of standard contractual clauses and binding corporate rules;
- the management of data protection impact assessments, including the prior consultation processes and advice provided in connection with the same;
- encouragement, support and guidance in the drawing up of codes of conduct and certification mechanisms;
- setting out the requirements for accreditation, and accrediting bodies responsible for certification and creating codes of conduct;
- record keeping in relation to requirements for data protection impact assessments, infringements of the GDPR and of enforcement action taken;
- the contribution to activities of the Board.

These tasks are outlined in Table 7.5, along with the associated GDPR articles.

**Table 7.5 Administering good practice, including provision of advice**

| Source | Task |
|---|---|
| A.57(1)(j) | To adopt standard contractual clauses referred to in Article 28(8) and in point (d) of Article 46(2) (i.e. for transfers of personal data to third countries). |
| A.57(1)(r) | To authorise contractual clauses and provisions referred to in Article 46(3). |
| A.57(1)(k) | To establish and maintain a list in relation to the requirement for data protection impact assessment pursuant to Article 35(4) (i.e. for processing operations that are likely to result in a high risk to the rights and freedoms). |
| A.57(1)(s) | To approve binding corporate rules pursuant to Article 47. |
| A.57(1)(t) | To contribute to the activities of the Board. |
| A.57(1)(u) | To keep internal records of infringements of the GDPR and of measures taken in accordance with Article 58(2) (i.e. enforcement). |
| A.57(1)(l) | To give advice on the processing operations referred to in Article 36(2) (i.e. processing that may infringe on the GDPR). |
| A.57(1)(m) | To encourage the drawing up of codes of conduct pursuant to Article 40(1) and provide an opinion and approve such codes of conduct that provide sufficient safeguards, pursuant to Article 40(5). |
| A.57(1)(n) | To encourage the establishment of data protection certification mechanisms and of data protection seals and marks pursuant to Article 42(1), and approve the criteria of certification pursuant to Article 42(5). |
| A.57(1)(o) | To, where applicable, carry out a periodic review of certifications issued in accordance with Article 42(7). |
| A.57(1)(p) | To draft and publish the requirements for accreditation of a body for monitoring codes of conduct pursuant to Article 41 and of a certification body pursuant to Article 43. |
| A.57(1)(q) | To conduct the accreditation of a body for monitoring codes of conduct pursuant to Article 41 and of a certification body pursuant to Article 43. |

The supervisory authorities are at varying levels of compliance in these tasks. Generally they have either been achieved to a large extent or are being completed on an ongoing basis (e.g. records keeping). However, there is one area in particular where there has been very little progress made by most supervisory authorities, namely, the accreditation of certification bodies and the appointment of bodies responsible for providing codes of conduct. Movement has been unexpectedly slow here, especially given the potential benefits that the creation of codes of conduct and certification mechanisms can bring.

Certification mechanisms would, in theory, offer benefits to supervisory authorities, organisations and individuals alike, including providing:

- the supervisory authorities with visibility of those organisations who have met a predetermined standard for certification;
- assistance to supervisory authorities in the potential identification of targets for investigation (through absence of certification) or to inform measures already in place when conducting investigations;
- added promotion and awareness of the GDPR;
- individuals with indication of those organisations that are more likely to treat data responsibly;
- encouragement of compliance with the GDPR through data subject expectations for certifications, seals and quality marks;
- organisations with a mechanism to increase data subject trust;
- decreased enforcement risks for certified organisations.

## Rights, complaints and enforcement

The remaining tasks can be grouped together in respect of rights, complaints and enforcement of the GDPR. These tasks are self-explanatory and are summarised in Table 7.6.

**Table 7.6 Rights, complaints and enforcement**

| Source | Task |
| --- | --- |
| A.57(1)(e) | To, upon request, provide information to any data subject concerning the exercise of their rights under the GDPR and, if appropriate, cooperate with the supervisory authorities in other Member States to that end. |
| A.57(1)(f) | To handle complaints lodged by a data subject, or by a body, organisation or association in accordance with Article 80, and investigate, to the extent appropriate, the subject matter of the complaint and inform the complainant of the progress and the outcome of the investigation within a reasonable period, in particular if further investigation or coordination with another supervisory authority is necessary. |
| A.57(1)(h) | To conduct investigations into the application of the regulation, including on the basis of information received from another supervisory authority or other public authority. |
| A.57(1)(v) | To fulfil tasks related to the protection of personal data. |
| A.57(2) | To facilitate the submission of complaints lodged by data subjects, or by a body, organisation or association, by introducing measures such as a complaint submission form that can also be completed electronically, without excluding other means of communication. |

It is worth noting A.57(1)(v) in particular. Although this article will primarily be cited for the purposes of carrying out enforcement tasks, it also provides a 'catch-all' to enable supervisory authorities to carry out other tasks (of their choosing and as they deem fit) for the purpose of protecting personal data. This essentially allows the supervisory authorities to move beyond those tasks specifically highlighted in the GDPR, as long as such tasks are completed for the purpose of protecting personal data and they are carried out in accordance with the limitation of their powers (see the next section).

## Powers

The powers afforded to supervisory authorities under the GDPR are set out in A.58. These powers are designed to allow the supervisory authorities to fulfil their tasks under A.57, by providing:

- authorisation powers;[11]
- advisory powers;[12]
- enforcement powers.[13]

The supervisory authority authorisation and advisory powers, along with the corresponding tasks to which they relate, are set out in Table 7.7. The table is not reflective of A.58 in its entirety. Some parts have also been amended for readability. As such, for any direct citations or references, readers should consult the regulation directly.

**Table 7.7 Authorisation and advisory powers**

| Source | Power | Corresponding task(s) |
|---|---|---|
| A.58(3)(a) | To provide advice as part of the prior consultation mechanism for high-risk processing activities, further to Articles 35 and 36. | A.57(1)(d), A.57(1)(l) and A.57(1)(v) |
| A.58(3)(b) | To issue opinions to the national parliament, the Member State government or, in accordance with Member State law, to other institutions and bodies as well as to the public on any issue related to the protection of personal data. | A.57(1)(c) |

*(Continued)*

---

[11] For example, power to accredit certification providers under A.58(3)(e).

[12] For example, powers to provide advice on compliance through prior consultation mechanisms under A.58(3)(a).

[13] For example, investigatory, corrective and punitive powers provided under A.58(1) and (2).

**Table 7.7 (Continued)**

| Source | Power | Corresponding task(s) |
|---|---|---|
| A.58(3)(c) | To authorise processing referred to in Article 36(5), if the law of the Member State requires such prior authorisation (i.e. high-risk processing activities carried out by the controller in performance of a task in the public interest, including processing in relation to social protection and public health). | Member State legislation dependent. |
| A.58(3)(d) | To issue opinions and approve draft codes of conduct pursuant to Article 40(5). | A.57(1)(m) and A.57(1)(q) |
| A.58(3)(e) | To accredit certification bodies pursuant to Article 43. | A.57(1)(n) and A.57(1)(p) |
| A.58(3)(f) | To issue certifications and approve criteria of certification in accordance with Article 42(5). | A.57(1)(n) and A.57(1)(o) |
| A.58(3)(g) | To adopt standard data protection clauses referred to in Article 28(8) and Article 46(2)(d). | A.57(1)(j) |
| A.58(3)(h) | To authorise contractual clauses referred to Article 46(3)(a). | A.57(1)(r) |
| A.58(3)(i) | To authorise administrative arrangements referred to Article 46(3)(b). | A.57(1)(r) |
| A.58(3)(j) | To approve binding corporate rules pursuant to Article 47. | A.57(1)(s) |

## LEAD SUPERVISORY AUTHORITIES

Where organisations operate in more than one Member State and inconsistencies are created due to the reasons previously stated within this chapter, this creates compliance complexity. For example, a controller or processor may implement controls, policies and procedures to comply with guidance issued by one supervisory authority, only for a different supervisory authority to take a different or competing approach. This causes significant difficulties in assessing and choosing the appropriate compliance controls, policies and procedures and/or potentially creates the requirement for conflicting controls, policies or procedures across different Member States. It is both costly and in some instances completely infeasible to set out controls in one jurisdiction that conflict with another.

The very nature of the EU Single Market and the purpose of EU legislation with direct effect (across all EU jurisdictions) is to remove barriers, legal disparities and other issues that will disrupt organisations operating efficiently throughout the EU. This is no different with the GDPR. In order to remove these potential frictions, the 'one-stop shop' mechanism was created in the GDPR, through the designation of lead supervisory authorities. The purpose of this mechanism is to provide controllers and processors with a primary regulator under the GDPR, to whom they are answerable. Due to Brexit, the UK is no longer part of the 'one-stop shop'.

The lead supervisory authority's duty is to cooperate with other concerned authorities and act as a primary decision maker, in respect of complaints or issues that arise under the GDPR (in respect of entities for whom it is the lead supervisory authority), including those complaints and issues that arise in other supervisory authorities' jurisdictions.

Essentially, in assessing their regulatory risk, controllers and processors can have a primary focus on their lead supervisory authority's interpretation and application of the GDPR, which can be found in the guidance published and enforcement decisions taken by that authority. Where conflicts arise between different supervisory authorities' guidance and enforcement decisions, those regulated by the GDPR should always take heed of decisions of courts within their local jurisdictions, the CJEU and of the EDPB in the first instance (as these will always take precedence). However, where these do not exist, they should look to the guidance of their lead supervisory authority's position as a starting point, as it will be that supervisory authority with primary responsibility for running enforcement.

This mechanism is intended to provide a level of protection for those subject to the GDPR, against inconsistent regulation of the GDPR across Member States by providing a primary point of guidance on the interpretation and application of the GDPR. However, it was not intended to act as a blocker to enforcement action being undertaken that is in the interests of other supervisory authorities (i.e. because the infringements impact on data or data subjects within their jurisdiction).

## Cross-border processing

The lead supervisory authority's role applies in the context of cross-border processing of personal data. Cross-border processing happens in two situations, as defined in A.4(23):

- Where a controller or processor is established in more than one Member State and a processing activity takes place in the context of more than one establishment. In this situation, multiple countries are impacted, which means that multiple regulator's interests are engaged. To simplify the situation, the lead supervisory authority has competence under A.56 to lead the supervision and enforcement of the law as it relates to the cross-border processing activities.
- Where a controller or processor is established in only one Member State, but the processing activity affects data subjects in more than one Member State. Again, there are multiple regulators' interests engaged. A.56 applies in this situation too.

A.56 usurps the usual role of regulatory supervision contained in A.55, that is, the regulator in the Member State where a data processing activity has an effect is competent to enforce the law as it pertains to the effects in this country. Instead, A.56 puts the lead supervisory authority in charge, meaning that other regulators are effectively inferior to the lead supervisory authority on these matters of cross-border processing.

Naturally, these rules can create tension and hostility between the regulators. Therefore, a cooperation and consistency mechanism is required, which is found in A.60–63.

There are exceptions to the lead supervisory authority rule for cross-border processing. For example, if the processing activity relates only to an establishment in another Member State, or if it substantially affects data subjects only in that Member State, the regulator for that Member State can lead on the matter, rather than the lead supervisory authority.

Furthermore, in exceptional cases of urgency any regulator can act, rather than leaving things to the lead supervisory authority (see A.60(11)), as was confirmed by the CJEU judgment in *Facebook v. Gegevensbeschermingsautoriteit* (2021).[14]

## Cooperation and mutual assistance

A lead supervisory authority does not have a remit to enforce its own decisions and ignore the views of other supervisory authorities. The GDPR, by virtue of A.60–63 in particular, requires that supervisory authorities provide each other with cooperation[15] and mutual assistance,[16] and in doing so maintain consistency of the application of the GDPR throughout the EU.[17]

In respect of enforcement in particular, the lead supervisory authority should reach consensus with the other supervisory authorities concerned and each supervisory authority, including the lead supervisory authority, are required to exchange all relevant information with each other to assist in making such decisions.[18] In turn, the lead supervisory authority may request other supervisory authorities to provide mutual assistance at any time, and where appropriate may conduct joint operations pursuant to A.62, in particular for carrying out investigations or for monitoring the implementation of a measure concerning an entity established in another Member State.[19]

Importantly, the lead supervisory authority is required to submit any draft decisions to other concerned supervisory authorities without delay and must take due account of their views in respect of the same, especially that of the supervisory authority where any complaint is lodged, following the rules set out in A.60 in relation to any objections to a decision or part of a decision that are lodged.

Where disputes are raised in relation to which entity should be the appropriate lead supervisory authority, or, where disputes are raised in relation to a lead supervisory authority's conduct under A.60, including in respect of objections raised but not accepted, the EDPB may be engaged for the purposes of dispute resolution pursuant to A.65, whose decision will be binding in relation to such disputes.

---

[14] C2021:483, 15 June 2021.

[15] GDPR, A.60.

[16] GDPR, A.61.

[17] GDPR, A.63.

[18] GDPR, A.60(1).

[19] GDPR, A.60(2).

In theory, these controls should prevent or reduce the potential for the protection or preferential regulation of entities in certain jurisdictions under the GDPR and create the ability for supervisory authorities, where they are not the lead supervisory authority, to raise enforcement through the lead supervisory authority where an entity has contravened the GDPR, or affects data subjects, within their jurisdiction. Any inconsistencies in interpretation of the legislation (where these are at fault) can then also be remedied between the supervisory authorities. However, there is evidence of lead supervisory authorities acting in ways that frustrate enforcement and the interests of other supervisory authorities, such as by prolonging investigations and delaying enforcement action, leading to disputes between the regulators and loss of trust. Even if a direct dispute does not arise between supervisory authorities, the lead supervisory authority's conduct of an investigation is likely to significantly impact the enforcement decisions made (i.e. through coordination, direction and information gathering). As such, there are significant benefits for controllers that can be gained through strategic selection of a lead supervisory authority that is less inclined to take enforcement or that adopts an interpretation of the law that benefits certain types of entities or processing activities.

### Choosing a lead supervisory authority

Technically speaking, those who are regulated under the GDPR in more than one Member State do not 'choose' or 'select' their lead supervisory authority. A supervisory authority will become a lead supervisory authority for an entity by virtue of being the responsible supervisory authority in the Member State where the entity has its 'main establishment'. However, those entities do have some power over deciding on which Member State they will place their 'main establishment'.

Due to the impact the lead supervisory authority has on how controllers and processors will be regulated under the GDPR throughout the entirety of the EU, controllers and processors being able to strategically place their main establishment in a jurisdiction where the supervisory authority is less inclined to issue enforcement or has interpreted the legislation in a way that suits their business can be of great benefit and importance, especially for those organisations who process large amounts of data or for those whose primary business is in data. In an attempt to avoid this issue of organisations simply picking a jurisdiction and stating 'this is our main establishment', the GDPR sets out the criteria for how a main establishment will be identified (see Recital 36 of the GDPR), which, in summary, provides that the main establishment of an organisation shall be 'the place of its central administration in the [EU], unless the decisions on the purposes and means of the processing of personal data are taken in another establishment of the controller in the [EU], in which case that other establishment should be considered to be the main establishment'.[20]

Although the second determining factor under Recital 36 (i.e. the establishment that decides the purposes and means for processing of personal data) is easier to engineer through the establishment of those processes in the chosen jurisdiction, the strategic 'selection' of a lead supervisory authority is realistically only available to controllers

---

[20] GDPR, Recital 36.

and processors that can afford to move such processes and/or alter the structure or locations of their businesses, whilst maintaining the tangible benefit of doing so.

## APPOINTING AN EU REPRESENTATIVE

Controllers and processors that are not established in the EU, can still be subject to the GDPR, where:

- they offer goods or services, irrespective of whether a payment of the data subject is required, to such data subjects in the EU; or
- they engage in the monitoring of data subject's behaviour, as far as their behaviour takes place within the EU.[21]

By virtue of the extraterritorial effect of the GDPR, the legislators responsible for creating the GDPR needed to account for how this would be managed in practice, especially where controllers and processors were not already based in any one Member State or answerable to a designated supervisory authority. A.27 of the GDPR deals specifically with this issue and creates the requirement for controllers and/or processors based outside the EU, but subject to its requirements, to designate a representative in the EU in one of the Member States where the data subjects, whose data are being processed, are located. These are known as 'EU Representatives', who will be subject to the supervisory authority with responsibility for the jurisdiction where the EU Representative resides.

A controller or processor not established in the EU, but subject to the GDPR, who fails to designate an EU Representative would therefore be in breach of the GDPR.

Technically, an entity's appointment of an EU Representative in a Member State will lead to the supervisory authority for that Member State de facto becoming the main supervisory authority within the EU for that entity. However, this will not work in the same way as an official designation of a lead supervisory authority for entities established in the EU, because an EU Representative may be addressed by any supervisory authority.[22] The appointment of an EU Representative also does not prevent action being taken against the controller or the processor directly.[23]

Despite the above, the appointment of an EU Representative involves significant implications for both the entity appointing the representative and the representative itself, because A.27 requires that:

> The [EU Representative] shall be mandated by the controller or processor to be addressed in addition to or instead of the controller or the processor by, in particular, supervisory authorities and data subjects, on all issues related to processing, for the purposes of ensuring compliance with [the GDPR].

---

[21] GDPR, A.3(2).

[22] GDPR, Recital 80.

[23] GDRP, A.27(5).

In summary, this means that the EU Representative must be explicitly designated by mandate of the entity to act on its behalf with regard to its obligations under the GDPR.[24] Acting with such mandate can also create liability for the designating entity, by virtue of responsibility for actions taken by the EU Representative under its mandate. Therefore, selection of an EU Representative requires careful consideration by the designating entity and should be appropriately protected through contractual means, which provide clear direction for the representative on how they should fulfill their role.

Equally, the entity being appointed as the EU Representative should be aware that they do not just pick up responsibility for acting on the mandate of the designating entity under the GDPR. They may also be subject to direct enforcement proceedings in the event of non-compliance by the designating entity.

Now that the UK is no longer part of the EU, controllers based in the UK that are engaging with people in the EU will need to consider whether they have to appoint an EU representative.

## SUMMARY

In conclusion, this chapter gives readers a better understanding of:

- the GDPR rules regarding the establishment of national regulators;
- the regulators' competences, tasks and enforcement powers;
- the EU 'one-stop shop' system for regulating cross-border data processing activities affecting two or more countries;
- the situations where the GDPR requires controllers and processors to appoint EU Representatives.

---

[24] GDPR, Recital 80.

# 8 TRANSFERRING DATA BETWEEN THE GDPR LAND MASS AND THIRD COUNTRIES

## Tuğhan Thuraisingam

This chapter provides an overview of the GDPR requirements for international data transfers. It explains the data transfer mechanisms available to organisations in order to legitimise transfers of personal data to third countries; how to identify the most appropriate mechanism to use; and the key characteristics of each mechanism including the benefits, issues and practical considerations.

## WHY REGULATE INTERNATIONAL TRANSFERS?

The GDPR acknowledges that flows of personal data to and from countries and international organisations located outside the EU/EEA ('third countries') 'are necessary for the expansion of international trade and cooperation'.[1] Therefore, a key objective of the GDPR is to ensure that the level of protection afforded to individuals under the regulation can be not 'undermined' when their personal data are transferred to third countries. Such protection can be undermined where, for example, third countries do not provide the same or essentially equivalent standards for data protection as those provided for under the GDPR. One of the biggest concerns is the risk that individuals may lose control over their personal data once it leaves the EU/EEA. Or they may not enjoy the same rights or protections as they do in Europe. As a result, organisations are typically under an obligation to implement appropriate safeguards before transferring personal data to such third countries in order to ensure and maintain 'a high level of protection of personal data'[2] that meets the expectations of the GDPR.

## WHAT IS A TRANSFER?

The GDPR does not provide a definition of what constitutes a 'transfer' of personal data. However, ICO guidance states that making personal data 'accessible' to a recipient located outside the EEA would constitute a transfer.[3] In addition, the definition of 'processing' under the GDPR is very wide and includes 'disclosure by transmission, dissemination or otherwise making available' of personal data and any 'adaptation or alteration' to personal data. So for example, if a controller located in the EEA engages

---

[1] GDPR Recital 101.

[2] GDPR Recital 6.

[3] ICO Guide to the General Data Protection Regulation (version 01 January 2021 – 1.1.106), page 253.

with a processor in India for outsourced IT support and that processor has view-only access to the personal data hosted in the controller's servers located in the EEA, this would still be considered a transfer. As such, the interpretation of what constitutes a transfer under the GDPR can be very broad.

The ICO guidance also makes it clear that 'transfer' does not mean the same as 'transit'. For example, if personal data are transferred from a controller in Germany to a processor in France (both countries in the EEA) via a server in India, there is no 'transfer' outside the EEA provided that the personal data are not 'accessed or manipulated' whilst transiting through India.[4] However, if there were to be any access or manipulation of personal data in India of any form, this would likely constitute a restricted transfer of personal data to India that would trigger the requirement to comply with the provisions in Chapter V of the GDPR, as further described below.

## GENERAL PRINCIPLES FOR TRANSFERS

As a general rule, the GDPR restricts transfers of personal data from the EU/EEA to third countries. For ease of reference, these transfers will be called 'restricted transfers' in this chapter.

This creates a default position whereby personal data cannot flow freely from the EU/EEA to third countries. Instead, further consideration is needed (including the implementation of an appropriate data transfer mechanism, where required) to ensure that restricted transfers can take place in compliance with the GDPR. Although transfers of personal data between countries located in the EU/EEA can flow freely (i.e. without the need to implement any further data transfer specific measures), the processing of such personal data (including the transfer) would still need to comply with all of the other provisions of the GDPR.

The GDPR rules on international data transfers start by introducing the 'general principle for transfers' under Article 44. The general principle requires transfers to third countries to only take place if the conditions laid down in Chapter V of the GDPR (i.e. Articles 44 to 50) are complied with. This also applies to any onward transfers of personal data.[5] Importantly, it requires that all provisions in Chapter V are applied 'in order to ensure that the level of protection' of individuals that are guaranteed by the GDPR 'is not undermined'.[6]

Chapter V of the GDPR provides a roadmap for organisations to follow when considering what measures (if any) are required to enable restricted transfers. In particular, it sets out a 'layered approach' as summarised in Figure 8.1.

---

[4] ICO Guide to the General Data Protection Regulation (version 01 January 2021 – 1.1.106), pages 253 and 254.

[5] Onward transfers refer to personal data (originally transferred from the EEA/EU to a third country) that are subsequently transferred from that third country to another third country.

[6] GDPR Article 44.

**Figure 8.1 Transfer roadmap**

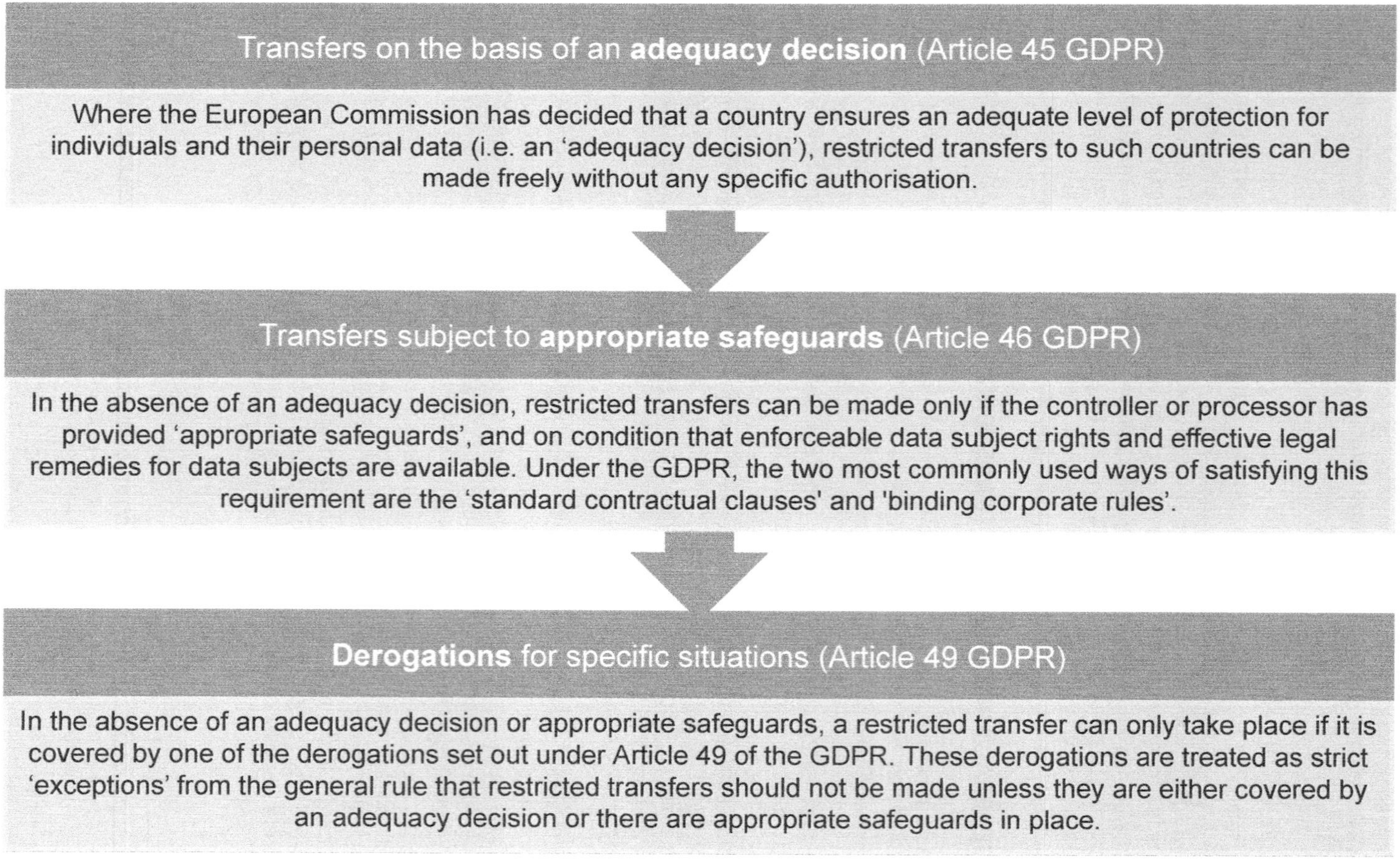

**Transfers on the basis of an adequacy decision (Article 45 GDPR)**

Where the European Commission has decided that a country ensures an adequate level of protection for individuals and their personal data (i.e. an 'adequacy decision'), restricted transfers to such countries can be made freely without any specific authorisation.

**Transfers subject to appropriate safeguards (Article 46 GDPR)**

In the absence of an adequacy decision, restricted transfers can be made only if the controller or processor has provided 'appropriate safeguards', and on condition that enforceable data subject rights and effective legal remedies for data subjects are available. Under the GDPR, the two most commonly used ways of satisfying this requirement are the 'standard contractual clauses' and 'binding corporate rules'.

**Derogations for specific situations (Article 49 GDPR)**

In the absence of an adequacy decision or appropriate safeguards, a restricted transfer can only take place if it is covered by one of the derogations set out under Article 49 of the GDPR. These derogations are treated as strict 'exceptions' from the general rule that restricted transfers should not be made unless they are either covered by an adequacy decision or there are appropriate safeguards in place.

## TRANSFERS ON THE BASIS OF AN ADEQUACY DECISION

Pursuant to Article 45 of the GDPR, a restricted transfer may take place where the European Commission has decided that the third country in question (or one or more specified sectors within that third country) 'ensures an adequate level of protection'[7] (commonly referred to as an adequacy decision).

Transfer of personal data to a third country that has been issued an adequacy decision does 'not require any specific authorisation'[8] or implementation of appropriate safeguards pursuant to Article 46 of the GDPR. However, the processing of such personal data (including the transfer) would still need to comply with all of the other provisions of the GDPR such as the principles of lawfulness, fairness and transparency as well as data minimisation, accuracy, purpose limitation, storage limitation and security principles.

### Elements considered in assessing adequacy

When assessing the level of protection provided in a third country with a view to issuing an adequacy decision, the European Commission is required to take particular account of the elements listed in Article 45(2) of the GDPR. These include the presence or absence of the elements (Figure 8.2).

### Figure 8.2 Considerations for adequacy

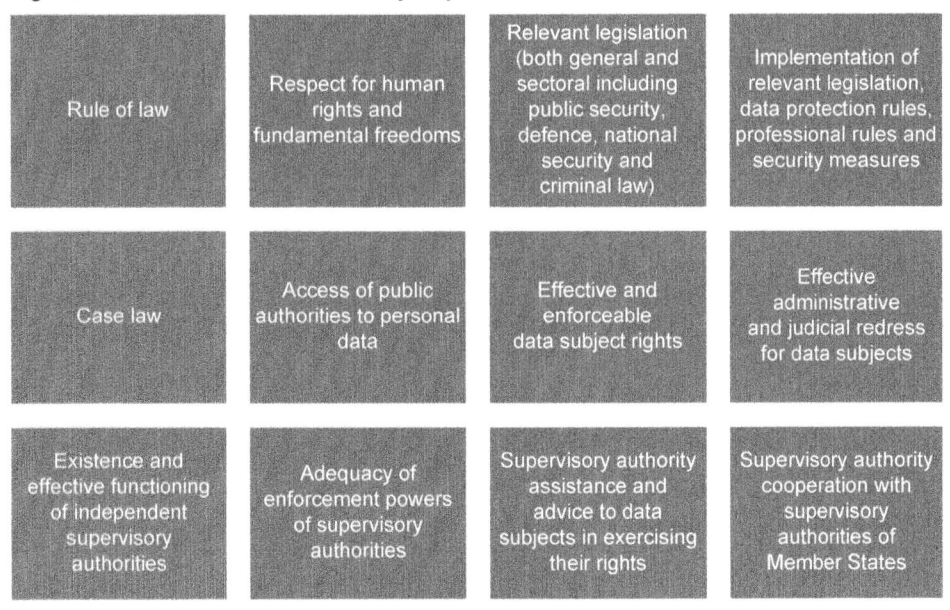

| Rule of law | Respect for human rights and fundamental freedoms | Relevant legislation (both general and sectoral including public security, defence, national security and criminal law) | Implementation of relevant legislation, data protection rules, professional rules and security measures |
|---|---|---|---|
| Case law | Access of public authorities to personal data | Effective and enforceable data subject rights | Effective administrative and judicial redress for data subjects |
| Existence and effective functioning of independent supervisory authorities | Adequacy of enforcement powers of supervisory authorities | Supervisory authority assistance and advice to data subjects in exercising their rights | Supervisory authority cooperation with supervisory authorities of Member States |

International commitments entered into particularly in relation to the protection of personal data

---

[7] GDPR Article 45(1).

[8] GDPR Article 45(1).

A third country must therefore have a legal system that can deliver effective protection for data subjects and their personal data that is 'essentially equivalent' (but not necessarily identical) to that guaranteed in the EU. Importantly, the EDPB guidelines (WP254 rev.01) highlight the following:

> It is ... necessary to consider not only the content of rules applicable to personal data transferred to a third country or an international organization, but also the system in place to ensure the effectiveness of such rules. Efficient enforcement mechanisms are of paramount importance to the effectiveness of data protection rules.[9]

It is therefore not sufficient to just identify evidence of the presence or absence of relevant legislation in a particular third country, as this may only indicate protections 'on paper'. Instead, there must be evidence of effective implementation of that legislation through mechanisms such as the existence of independent supervisory authorities. These authorities must have adequate enforcement powers to monitor and address non-compliance with data protection laws. Importantly, data subjects must have effective and enforceable data subject rights over their personal data (e.g. rights in relation to access, deletion and rectification of their personal data) to ensure that they do not lose control over their personal data once transferred to a third country. The loss of control can also occur through indiscriminate and disproportionate access to personal data by public authorities in third countries (e.g. through initiatives such as mass surveillance). In these circumstances, a third country is unlikely to be determined as adequate particularly if data subjects do not have effective administrative and judicial redress to challenge such public authority access to their personal data.

## Adequacy decisions issued

The European Commission has issued adequacy decisions to Andorra, Argentina, Canada, Faroe Islands, Guernsey, Israel, Isle of Man, Japan, Jersey, New Zealand, South Korea, Switzerland, UK and Uruguay, confirming that they provide adequate protection judged by the GDPR's standards.

Taking Japan as an example, the European Commission issued its adequacy decision on 23 January 2019. The European Commission noted that the adequacy finding was based on a number of factors and series of additional safeguards that Japan would apply to data subjects when personal data are transferred to its country, including:

- the recent modernisation of Japan's data protection legislation, as reflected in the recognition of data protection as a fundamental right;
- the expansion of the Japanese definition of sensitive data;
- a common set of safeguards including the facilitation of the exercise of data subject rights;
- the establishment in Japan of a system of handling and resolution of complaints, under the supervision of the Japanese data protection authority (the Personal Information Protection Commission), to ensure that potential complaints from Europeans as regards access to their data by Japanese law enforcement and national security authorities will be effectively investigated and resolved.[10]

---

[9] EDPB guidelines (WP254 rev.01), page 3.

[10] European Commission, 'Questions & Answers on the Japan adequacy decision' published on 23 January 2019, accessible here: https://ec.europa.eu/commission/presscorner/detail/en/MEMO_19_422

## UK adequacy

On 19 February 2021 and following the end of the Brexit transition period (whereby the UK became a 'third country' in the context of restricted transfers under the GDPR), the European Commission launched the process towards the adoption of two adequacy decisions for transfers of personal data to the UK (one under the GDPR and the other for the Law Enforcement Directive[11]). The Commission adopted final adequacy decisions on 28 June 2021, meaning that personal data can flow between the EU and the UK without impediments. These decisions are subject to four-year sunset clauses.

## Partial adequacy decisions

The European Commission can also issue what is known as 'partial' adequacy decisions. This is where an adequacy decision has a narrower application to a third country. A partial adequacy decision could be applied to certain categories of organisations, sectors or types of personal data rather than applying to the third country as a whole. Alternatively, it could involve organisations in the third country having to self-certify against a privacy framework that facilitates protections that are essentially equivalent to those guaranteed in the EU.

For example, in December 2001, the European Commission issued a partial adequacy decision regarding the Canadian Personal Information Protection and Electronic Documents Act (the PIPEDA). The PIPEDA applies to private sector organisations that collect, use or disclose personal information in the course of commercial activities. As a result, the adequacy decision issued by the European Commission only applies to restricted transfers to private sector organisations in Canada that are engaged in commercial activity. This adequacy decision is therefore considered as partial as it would not apply to all restricted transfers such as those to public sector organisations in Canada.

The European Commission also issued partial adequacy decisions for restricted transfers to the United States in the form of the Safe Harbor framework in July 2000 and subsequently the Privacy Shield framework in July 2016. However, both of these adequacy decisions have since been declared invalid through judgments of the CJEU handed down in 2015 and 2020 respectively (see the summary and impact of these judgments in 'Litigation on international data transfers' below).

## Ongoing monitoring of adequacy decisions

Once the European Commission issues an adequacy decision with respect to a third country, the decision must 'provide for a mechanism for a periodic review, at least every four years', which must take into account all relevant developments in that third country.[12] In particular, the European Commission must 'monitor developments' in that third country that could affect the functioning of the adequacy decision adopted.[13] If it is revealed that the third country no longer ensures an adequate level of protection

---

[11] Directive (EU) 2016/680 of the European Parliament and of the Council of 27 April 2016 on the protection of natural persons with regard to the processing of personal data by competent authorities for the purposes of the prevention, investigation, detection or prosecution of criminal offences or the execution of criminal penalties, and on the free movement of such data, and repealing Council Framework Decision 2008/977/JHA.

[12] GDPR Article 45(3).

[13] GDPR Article 45(4).

(based on available information or following a periodic review), Article 45(5) of the GDPR requires the European Commission to consider repealing, amending or suspending the adequacy decision to the extent necessary.[14]

It is important to note that unlike for transfers subject to appropriate safeguards (described in the following section), supervisory authorities are unable to invalidate or suspend adequacy decisions. However, they do have the power under Article 58(5) of the GDPR to bring infringements of the GDPR 'to the attention of the judicial authorities and where appropriate, to commence or engage otherwise in legal proceedings' in order to enforce the provisions of the GDPR. As such, if a supervisory authority considers a challenge to an adequacy decision well founded, it can exercise this power and 'put forward the objections which it considers well founded before the national courts'.[15] If the national court also shares doubts as to the validity of the adequacy decision, it can subsequently make a reference for a preliminary ruling to the CJEU for the purposes of examining the validity of the adequacy decision. It is then left to the CJEU to determine the question of validity.

## TRANSFERS SUBJECT TO APPROPRIATE SAFEGUARDS

In the absence of an adequacy decision, a restricted transfer may only take place where 'the controller or processor has provided appropriate safeguards, and on condition that enforceable data subject rights and effective legal remedies for data subjects are available'.[16]

The appropriate safeguards recognised by the GDPR under Article 46 are summarised in Table 8.1.

### Table 8.1 Appropriate safeguards for international transfers

| GDPR reference | Appropriate safeguards | Is specific authorisation required from a supervisory authority? |
|---|---|---|
| Article 46(2)(a) | Legally binding and enforceable instrument between public authorities or bodies. | No |
| Article 46(2)(b) | Binding corporate rules.[17] | No |
| Article 46(2)(c) | Standard data protection clauses adopted by the European Commission. | No |
| Article 46(2)(d) | Standard data protection clauses adopted by a supervisory authority and approved by the European Commission. | No |

*(Continued)*

---

**14** GDPR Article 45(5).
**15** Case C-362/14, *Maximillian Schrems v. Data Protection Commissioner*, 6 October 2015, paragraph 65.
**16** GDPR Article 46(1).
**17** In accordance with Article 47 of the GDPR.

**Table 8.1 (Continued)**

| GDPR reference | Appropriate safeguards | Is specific authorisation required from a supervisory authority? |
|---|---|---|
| Article 46(2)(e) | Approved code of conduct.[18] | No |
| Article 46(2)(f) | Approved certification mechanism.[19] | No |
| Article 46(3)(a) | Contractual clauses between the controller or processor and the controller, processor or the recipient of the personal data in the third country or international organisation. | Yes |
| Article 46(3)(b) | Provisions to be inserted into administrative arrangements between public authorities or bodies, which include enforceable and effective data subject rights. | Yes |

Although it appears that there are a number of appropriate safeguards for organisations to choose from to enable restricted transfers, this is not the case in practice. For example, certain mechanisms apply to public authorities or bodies only whereas others require an approved code of conduct or certification mechanisms that have not yet been developed (and even if developed, they are only likely to apply to certain types of organisations in certain industries). As such, the two most commonly used mechanisms to date under Article 46 of the GDPR to legitimise restricted transfers are:

- the standard data protection clauses adopted by the European Commission, often referred to as the 'model clauses' or 'standard contractual clauses' (SCCs);
- binding corporate rules.

**Standard contractual clauses**

The SCCs are standard contracts adopted by way of European Commission decisions. They are entered into between (1) an organisation that is sending personal data from the EU/EEA (the 'data exporter') and (2) an organisation receiving that personal data from a third country (the 'data importer'). Note that it is common practice for organisations to enter into intra-group data transfer agreements that are based on the SCCs. Such agreements are typically entered into between multiple entities that (a) form part of the same organisation; (b) are located in different countries globally; and (c) regularly transfer personal data between each other.

---

[18] Pursuant to Article 40 together with binding and enforceable commitments of the controller or processor in the third country to apply the appropriate safeguards, including as regards data subjects' rights.

[19] Pursuant to Article 42 together with binding and enforceable commitments of the controller or processor in the third country to apply the appropriate safeguards, including as regards data subjects' rights.

### Issues with previous versions of the SCCs
Historically and up until 4 June 2021, there were two versions of the SCCs that were adopted by the European Commission and that covered restricted transfers between a data controller (as data exporter) and data processor (as data importer)[20] or between two data controllers.[21]

However, there were certain features of these SCCs that had traditionally caused issues for organisations seeking to rely on them. For example, these SCCs did not cover restricted transfers between two processors or restricted transfers undertaken by data exporters that are subject to the GDPR but not based in the EU/EEA. In addition, since the introduction of the GDPR, the references contained in these SCCs were outdated as they referred to the directive. Many commentators agreed that the controller-to-processor SCCs would benefit from the inclusion of the mandatory Article 28 GDPR provisions that need to be included in a contract between a controller and a processor. Further, following the CJEU judgment in *Schrems II* certain provisions in the SCCs required updating to align with the expectations of the judgment (particularly regarding disproportionate access to personal data by public authorities in third countries).

### The new SCCs
As a result, in order to address these issues (and others) within the previous versions of the SCCs, the European Commission finally adopted a new set of SCCs on 4 June 2021.[22] The new set has four modules that cover the following types of restricted transfers:

- module 1 – controller-to-controller transfers;
- module 2 – controller-to-processor transfers;
- module 3 – processor-to-processor transfers;
- module 4 – processor-to-controller transfers.

The new SCCs also include Article 28 GDPR provisions for controller-to-processor restricted transfers and a number of provisions that impose additional obligations on data importers with respect to public authority access to personal data following the CJEU judgment in *Schrems II* (2020). Amongst other things, they include an optional 'docking clause' that enables additional entities to enter into SCCs that have already been executed. The additional entities can enter into the SCCs as either a data exporter or data importer and must complete information within the annexes relating to the list of parties, description of transfers and the technical and organisational measures. Once the list of parties annex is signed, new entities will be treated as parties to the SCCs with all the resulting rights and obligations.

### Content of the SCCs
The SCCs must be used in their entirety and without any amendment (however, note that additional clauses on business-related issues can be included provided that they

---

[20] European Commission decision 2010/87/EU.

[21] European Commission decisions 201/497/EC and 2004/915/EC.

[22] The standard contractual clauses adopted by the European Commission on 4 June 2021 for the transfer of personal data to third countries pursuant to Regulation (EU) 2016/679 of the European Parliament and of the Council (Commission Implementing Decision (EU) 2021/914).

do not contradict the SCCs).[23] For example, the controller-to-processor module imposes a number of non-negotiable contractual obligations on the data importer. They include the following:

- To process personal data only on documented instructions from the data exporter including with respect to any onward transfers of personal data from the data importer to a third party.
- To implement technical and organisational measures to ensure the security of the data, including with respect to personal data breaches. At a minimum, the data importer must implement the technical and organisational measures agreed between the parties and set out in Annex II of the SCCs.
- To promptly notify the data exporter about (1) any legally binding request from a public authority (including judicial authorities) under the laws of the country of destination for the disclosure of the personal data transferred; or (2) any direct access by public authorities to personal data transferred under the SCCs.
- To keep appropriate documentation about the processing activities carried out on behalf of the data exporter. At the data exporter's request, the data importer must allow for and contribute to audits of the processing activities covered by the SCCs, at reasonable intervals or if there are indications of non-compliance. In deciding on a review or audit, the data exporter may take into account relevant certifications held by the data importer.

The controller-to-processor SCCs also include:

- a third-party beneficiary clause that enables the data subject to enforce certain provisions of the SCCs against the data exporter and data importer;
- informing data subjects of the right they have to obtain a copy of the SCCs and making the same available to the data subject upon request;
- a right for any data subject who has suffered damage as a result of any breach of certain obligations in the SCCs to receive compensation from the data exporter and where applicable the data importer and sub-processors for the damage suffered;
- a right for the supervisory authority to make inquiries and conduct an audit of the data importer with respect to the restricted transfers.

The SCCs also include a number of sections that require completion by the parties to reflect the specifics of the restricted transfer, such as:

- details of the data exporter and data importer organisations including a description of their respective activities relevant to the restricted transfer;
- specification of a governing law clause (i.e. the Member State in which the data exporter is established);

---

[23] For example, commercial provisions could be agreed between the parties that enable the data importer to recover reasonable expenses from the data exporter for the data importer's support in responding to the exercise of data subject rights requests received by the data exporter.

- details of the restricted transfer including the categories of data subjects, categories of data, special categories of data (if any) and a description of the processing operations (Annex I(B) of the SCCs);
- description of the technical and organisational measures implemented by the data importer (Annex II of the SCCs).

An example of the type of information typically included in Annex I(B) of the SCCs is set out in Table 8.2.

**Table 8.2 Information required as part of SCCs**

| | |
|---|---|
| Categories of data subjects | The data exporter's employees |
| Categories of personal data transferred | • Names<br>• Date of birth<br>• Postal address<br>• Contact telephone number<br>• Email |
| Sensitive data transferred (if applicable) | N/A |
| The frequency of the transfer | The personal data are to be transferred on a continuous basis (i.e. not on a one-off basis). |
| Nature of the processing | Processing of personal data in the context of HR management, which includes access, storage, recording, retrieval and dissemination of personal data and as further described in the Master Services Agreement entered into between the data importer and the data exporter. |
| Purpose(s) of the data transfer and further processing | The data exporter is an insurance company with employees located in the UK and requires HR technology support with respect to its employees as further described in the Master Services Agreement entered into between the data exporter and data importer. |
| | The data importer provides HR technology support services and has agreed to provide the data exporter with the services described in the Master Services Agreement entered into between the parties, which requires the processing of the personal data described in this table. |
| Retention period | 7 years (unless compliance with a legal obligation requires further retention, in which case, the data importer shall inform the data exporter). |

With respect to Annex II of the SCCs (i.e. the description of the technical and organisational measures implemented by the data importer), descriptions of requirements for the following matters are typically included:

- pseudonymisation and encryption of personal data;
- ensuring ongoing confidentiality, integrity, availability and resilience of processing systems and services;
- the ability to restore the availability and access to personal data in a timely manner in the event of a physical or technical incident;
- processes for regularly testing, assessing and evaluating the effectiveness of technical and organisational measures for ensuring the security of the processing;
- user identification and authorisation;
- the protection of data during transmission;
- the protection of data during storage;
- physical security of locations at which personal data are processed;
- events logging;
- system configuration, including default configuration;
- certification/assurance of processes and products;
- data avoidance and minimisation;
- data quality;
- data retention;
- accountability;
- data portability and data disposal.

The provisions outlined above are illustrative of a number of other non-negotiable provisions in the SCCs that aim to provide contractual safeguards for data subjects over their personal data when subject to a restricted transfer under the SCCs.

### The UK International Data Transfer Agreement
Under section 119(A) of the UK DPA and in connection with Article 46 of the UK GDPR, the ICO has the power to issue a document specifying standard data protection clauses that the ICO considers provide appropriate safeguards for the purposes of transfers of personal data to a third country or an international organisation.

On 11 August 2021, the ICO launched a public consultation on a draft set of such clauses referred to as an 'international data transfer agreement' (IDTA). The purpose of the proposed IDTA is to replace the previous versions of the SCCs (adopted under the directive) for legitimising transfers of personal data from the UK to third countries that are not covered by UK 'adequacy regulations' (which currently include countries in the EEA and countries that have received an adequacy decision from the European Commission).

The proposed IDTA also takes into account the CJEU judgment in *Schrems II* (2020) by emphasising the requirement to conduct a transfer risk assessment. As part of its proposal, the ICO has issued a draft 'international transfer risk assessment and toolkit' to support organisations with such transfer risk assessments. In addition, the ICO has also issued a draft 'UK Addendum' to the new SCCs adopted by the European Commission for consideration and to also serve as an appropriate safeguard under Article 46(2) of the UK GDPR.

Following the conclusion of the public consultation and once the final forms of the ICO's standard data protection clauses are issued, the next step will be for the ICO to send a copy of the same to the UK Secretary of State who must then lay it before the UK Parliament. Provided that the UK Parliament does not object to the proposals within a 40-day period, the standard data protection clauses issued will be legally operative as a valid data transfer mechanism under Article 46(2) of the UK GDPR.

### *Binding corporate rules*

Binding corporate rules are an internal code of conduct operating within a multinational organisation's group of entities. They enable restricted transfers from an organisation's EEA entities to its non-EEA entities. As such, they do not cover restricted transfers to entities outside the organisation. BCRs also need to be approved by an EEA supervisory authority and can therefore take a lot of time and resource to put in place.

There are two types of BCR:

1. BCR-Controllers. This covers transfers of personal data from data controllers established in the EU/EEA to other data controllers or data processors (established outside the EU/EEA) within the same group of entities.
2. BCR-Processors. This applies to personal data received from an external third-party data controller (established in the EU/EEA) that is not a member of the group entity subject to the BCRs, and then further processed by the group entities as data processors and/or sub-processors.

BCRs require supervisory authority approval[24] based on the criteria set out in Article 47 of the GDPR. Table 8.3 contains selected parts of the Article 47 criteria. The table is not reflective of Article 47 in its entirety, which includes additional criteria. Some parts have also been amended for readability. As such, for any direct citations or references please consult the text of the GDPR directly.

Given the rigour of the criteria involved in obtaining BCRs (including the requirement for supervisory authority approval), BCRs are often viewed as a gold standard of compliance with the GDPR rules on international data transfers. Large organisations that have multiple group entities globally can benefit from having a common and binding set of rules that set a baseline of data protection compliance across the organisation's group. It can help to demonstrate a high level of data protection maturity to external stakeholders (e.g. customers and business partners), which can increase trust and can act as a competitive advantage in the market.

---

[24] In accordance with the consistency mechanism set out in Article 63 of the GDPR.

**Table 8.3 Criteria for supervisory authority approval of BCRs**

| Source | Criteria |
|---|---|
| Article 47(1)(a) | BCRs must be legally binding and apply to and be enforced by every group entity including their employees. |
| Article 47(1)(b) | BCRs must expressly confer enforceable rights on data subjects in relation to the processing of their personal data. |
| Article 47(2)(a) | BCRs must specify the structure and contact details of the group of entities. |
| Article 47(2)(b) | BCRs must specify the data transfers or set of transfers, including the categories of personal data, the type of processing and its purposes, the type of data subjects affected and the identification of the third countries in question. |
| Article 47(2)(c) | BCRs must specify their legally binding nature, both internally and externally. |
| Article 47(2)(d) | BCRs must specify the application of the general data protection principles provided for under the GDPR, in particular purpose limitation, data minimisation, limited storage periods, data quality, data protection by design and by default, legal basis for processing, processing of special categories of personal data, measures to ensure data security, and the requirements in respect of onward transfers to bodies not bound by the binding corporate rules. |
| Article 47(2)(e) | BCRs must specify the rights of data subjects in regard to processing and the means to exercise those rights, including the right to obtain redress and, where appropriate, compensation for a breach of the BCRs. |
| Article 47(2)(f) | BCRs must specify the acceptance by the controller or processor established in the EU/EEA of liability for any breaches of the BCRs by any group entity in a third country (unless it can prove that it is not responsible for the event giving rise to the damage). |
| Article 47(2)(g) | BCRs must specify how the information in the BCRs is provided to the data subjects in addition to the requirements to provide transparent processing information under Articles 13 and 14 of the GDPR. |
| Article 47(2)(h) | BCRs must specify the tasks of any designated data protection officer or any other person or entity in charge of monitoring compliance with the BCRs, as well as monitoring training and complaint-handling. |
| Article 47(2)(i) | BCRs must specify the complaint procedures. |
| Article 47(2)(j) | BCRs must specify the mechanisms within the group of entities for ensuring the verification of compliance with the BCRs. Such mechanisms shall include data protection audits and methods for ensuring corrective actions to protect the rights of the data subject. |
| Article 47(2)(k) | BCRs must specify the mechanisms for reporting and recording changes to the rules and reporting those changes to the supervisory authority. |
| Article 47(2)(n) | BCRs must specify the appropriate data protection training to personnel having permanent or regular access to personal data. |

Compared to data transfer mechanisms such as the SCCs, BCRs require significant investment, time and resource to put in place. They can easily take two years, or longer, to be approved. They also place organisations within the supervisory authorities' radar – for example, data protection audit reports (to verify compliance with the BCRs) can be accessed by supervisory authorities and, if required, supervisory authorities can conduct their own audits. Further, although BCRs have the potential to offer greater flexibility for complex processing, they require organisations to have a mature data protection programme in place. BCRs are therefore unlikely to be suitable for small and medium-sized enterprises. Ultimately, the decision as to whether to apply for BCRs will depend on an organisation's size, nature of the intra-group restricted transfers undertaken and overall strategy for data protection compliance.

## DEROGATIONS FOR SPECIFIC SITUATIONS

In the absence of an adequacy decision (pursuant to Article 45) or appropriate safeguards (pursuant to Article 46), a restricted transfer can only take place if it is covered by one of the derogations under Article 49 of the GDPR as set out in Table 8.4.

**Table 8.4 Derogations from the prohibition on transfers**

| GDPR reference | Description of derogation | |
| --- | --- | --- |
| Article 49(1)(a) | Consent | The data subject has explicitly consented to the proposed transfer, after having been informed of the possible risks to them and their data. |
| Article 49(1)(b) | Contract with the data subject | The transfer is necessary for the performance of a contract between the data subject and the controller or for the implementation of pre-contractual measures taken at the data subject's request. |
| Article 49(1)(c) | Contract in the interest of the data subject | The transfer is necessary for the conclusion or performance of a contract concluded in the interest of the data subject between the controller and another natural or legal person. |
| Article 49(1)(d) | Public interest | The transfer is necessary for important reasons of public interest. |
| Article 49(1)(e) | Legal claims | The transfer is necessary for the establishment, exercise or defence of legal claims. |
| Article 49(1)(f) | Vital interests | The transfer is necessary in order to protect the vital interests of the data subject or of other persons, where the data subject is physically or legally incapable of giving consent. |

*(Continued)*

**Table 8.4 (Continued)**

| GDPR reference | Description of derogation | |
|---|---|---|
| Article 49(1)(g) | Public register | The transfer is made from a register, which according to Union or Member State law is intended to provide information to the public and which is open to consultation either by the public in general or by any person who can demonstrate a legitimate interest, but only to the extent that the conditions laid down by Union or Member State law for consultation are fulfilled in the particular case. |

## Relying on the derogations in practice

The EDPB guidelines (2/2018) make it clear that 'data exporters should first endeavor possibilities to frame the transfer with one of the mechanisms included in Articles 45 and 46 GDPR, and only in their absence use the derogations provided in Article 49(1)'. This is because the derogations on their own 'do not provide adequate protection or adequate safeguards for the personal data transferred'.[25]

Further, given that no prior authorisation is required from supervisory authorities when transferring personal data on the basis of the derogations, this 'leads to increased risks for the rights and freedoms of the data subjects concerned'.[26] The Article 49 derogations are therefore 'exemptions from the general principle' and 'must be interpreted restrictively so that the exception does not become the rule'.[27]

The EDPB guidelines (2/2018) also explains the conditions and circumstances within which organisations can, in practice, rely on each of the Article 49(1) derogations. A summary of the EDPB's guidance on the consent and contract derogations is provided below to illustrate the high threshold and restrictiveness of the application of the derogations in practice.

### *Consent derogation*
The general conditions for valid consent under Article 7 of the GDPR (read together with Article 4(11)) apply to this derogation. However, there are additional elements required for consent to be considered a valid legal ground when relied on for international data transfers. For example, the standard of consent is stricter in that it requires 'explicit' consent. In addition, consent must be 'specific' in that data subjects should give their consent for a specific transfer at the time when the transfer is envisaged (i.e. not for future transfers that are not specified). Data subjects must also be appropriately 'informed' of the restricted transfer. Information must not only be provided about the

---

[25] EDPB guidelines 2/2018, page 4.

[26] EDPB guidelines 2/2018, page 4.

[27] EDPB guidelines 2/2018, page 4.

circumstances of the restricted transfer (e.g. purpose of transfer, recipient details, types of data and ability to withdraw consent) but also any specific risks resulting from the fact that personal data will be transferred to a third country.

The EDPB states that 'the GDPR sets a high threshold' for the use of consent as a derogation and therefore 'consent might prove not to be a feasible long-term solution for transfers to third countries'.[28]

### *Contract with the data subject derogation*
Restricted transfers under this derogation may take place 'where the transfer is occasional and necessary in relation to a contract'.[29] According to the EDPB, establishing necessity 'requires a close and substantial connection between the data transfer and the purposes of the contract'.[30] For example, if a corporate group has centralised its HR management functions for its employees in a third country, there would be 'no direct and objective link between the performance of the employment contract and such transfer'.[31] However, the EDPB distinguishes this from a scenario where a travel agent transfers personal data to a third country for the purposes of arranging accommodation in a hotel based in that third country. Unlike the corporate HR example, this scenario involves a close and substantial link between the restricted transfer and purposes of the contract (i.e. arranging the data subject's travel/accommodation).

With respect to establishing what constitutes an 'occasional' transfer, the EDPB states that this will require an assessment on a case-by-case basis. For example, an organisation could decide to share the personal data of an employee with its clients based in third countries for the purposes of arranging meetings between that employee and the clients. This would be considered as an occasional restricted transfer. However, if the organisation decides to establish an employee training centre in a third country that will require 'systematic transfers of personal data'[32] relating to employees attending training courses, this would not be considered as an occasional restricted transfer.

### Compelling legitimate interests

In the event that none of the derogations for a specific situation listed in Table 8.4 applies, Article 49(1) of the GDPR states that a restricted transfer 'may take place only if the transfer is not repetitive, concerns only a limited number of data subjects, is necessary for the purposes of compelling legitimate interests pursued by the controller which are not overridden by the interests or rights and freedoms of the data subject, and the controller has assessed all the circumstances surrounding the data transfer and has on the basis of that assessment provided suitable safeguards with regard to the protection of personal data'.

---

[28] EDPB guidelines 2/2018, page 8.
[29] Recital 111 of the GDPR.
[30] EDPB guidelines 2/2018, page 8.
[31] EDPB guidelines 2/2018, page 8.
[32] EDPB guidelines 2/2018, page 9.

If an organisation decides to rely on compelling legitimate interests as a last resort, the organisation is under an obligation to inform the supervisory authority of the restricted transfer. Further, the organisation must also 'inform the data subject of the transfer and on the compelling legitimate interests pursued' in addition to complying with the transparency requirements under Articles 13 and 14 of the GDPR.

## LITIGATION ON INTERNATIONAL DATA TRANSFERS

The application of the GDPR rules on international data transfers has been heavily influenced by two landmark (and related) CJEU judgments, namely the *Schrems I* (2015) and *Schrems II* (2020) cases respectively. *Schrems I* invalidated the Safe Harbor framework and *Schrems II* invalidated its successor, the Privacy Shield framework. Importantly, *Schrems II* also emphasised the need for organisations to take additional steps when considering the use of the standard contractual clauses to enable restricted transfers in accordance with the requirements of the GDPR.

### *Schrems I* – Safe Harbor decision declared invalid

The *Schrems I* litigation was triggered as a result of the Edward Snowden disclosures in 2013 that revealed the mass surveillance practices carried out by a number of public authorities including those located in the United States. In particular, Snowden exposed the operation of surveillance programmes such as PRISM and the extent to which US intelligence agencies had access to personal data held by some of the largest and most renowned technology, communications and social media companies in the world.

Following the disclosures, Max Schrems (a Facebook user and an Austrian law student at the time) filed a complaint with the Irish supervisory authority[33] regarding Facebook Ireland's reliance on the Safe Harbor framework to legitimise the transfers of his personal data to Facebook Inc. in the United States.

In his complaint, Schrems stated that 'documents published by the US National Security Agency (NSA) ... show that "Facebook Inc." is forwarding its user data to the NSA for reasons of espionage, national security and other matters. Facebook is listed in these documents as granting "mass access" to such data without any need for a probably cause since June 3rd 2009 under a program called "PRISM". The published documents indicate that "Facebook Inc." is participating (among other companies) in the PRISM program voluntarily.'

The complaint noted that changes in US legislation after the terrorist attacks in September 2001 facilitated these mass surveillance practices by US public authorities. In particular, it highlighted how 'mass confiscation of the EU citizens' data is ... not covered by protections under the US constitution, but instead expressly allowed ...' without effective judicial oversight. The complaint acknowledged that given the European

---

[33] Letter of complaint from Maximillian Schrems to the Data Protection Commissioner dated 25 June 2013.

Commission's Safe Harbor decision was issued in 2000 (i.e. before the changes in US surveillance legislation), it might have been within the limits of the directive. However, following the changes in the US legal system the complaint claimed that 'there are now serious doubts if the US is still giving "adequate" protection to the fundamental rights of European citizens on a legal and factual level'.

The Irish supervisory authority rejected the complaint on the basis that it was bound by the European Commission's Safe Harbor decision. Schrems filed for judicial review of the Irish supervisory authority's decision arguing that the regulator had the power to suspend the data transfer to the United States under the Safe Harbor decision and that, in any event, the Safe Harbor decision was invalid. The Irish High Court decided to refer the case to the CJEU to determine the validity of the Safe Harbor decision before making a final decision.

The CJEU subsequently declared the Safe Harbor decision as invalid. The CJEU concluded that a third country (e.g. the United States) must provide an 'essentially equivalent' level of protection to that provided under EU laws. In particular, laws that permit public authorities to have access on a general basis and the lack of redress available for individuals who are non-US persons went against the essence of the fundamental right to privacy and right to judicial remedy under the EU Charter of Fundamental Rights.

### *Schrems II* – Privacy Shield declared invalid and SCCs declared valid subject to certain conditions

Following the judgment in *Schrems I*, Schrems was informed by the Irish supervisory authority that Facebook was relying on the SCCs (not Safe Harbor) as a valid mechanism for transferring personal data from the EEA to the United States. As a result, Schrems reformulated his complaint to include the SCCs and any other legal basis for data transfers that could be relied on by Facebook. During this period, the Privacy Shield had also replaced Safe Harbor following *Schrems I* and was a data transfer mechanism that was also being relied on by Facebook.

The case ultimately made its way back to the CJEU, which handed down its landmark judgment in *Schrems II* on 16 July 2020. In summary, the key conclusions were as follows:

- Privacy Shield declared invalid. The CJEU declared the Privacy Shield invalid as a mechanism to transfer personal data from the EEA to entities in the US who had self-certified under the Privacy Shield framework. This was due to the lack of proportionality and limitations on the surveillance activities conducted by US public authorities in relation to personal data arriving from the EEA and the lack of redress for individuals caught up in those surveillance practices. As a result, the CJEU held that the Privacy Shield was unable to ensure a level of protection 'essentially equivalent' under EU law.

- SCCs remain valid subject to certain conditions. The CJEU held that the SCCs remain valid as they are still capable as a data transfer mechanism of ensuring a level of protection 'essentially equivalent' to that under EU law. However, in order to be able to rely on SCCs as a valid transfer mechanism, the CJEU emphasised that the data exporter needs to carry out an assessment of the legal system of the

third country, in particular the extent to which there is any access to personal data by public authorities of that third country.
- The transfer assessment should also take into account the factors considered by the European Commission in assessing third countries for an adequacy decision (as described earlier in this chapter). In particular, the assessment should consider the nature and context of the personal data transferred and determine, amongst other things, whether there is any disproportionate public authority access to such personal data.
- If the outcome of the transfer assessment identifies inadequacies in the level of protection afforded in a third country, the CJEU confirmed that it may prove necessary to supplement the guarantees contained in the SCCs with additional measures to address these deficiencies.
- Where additional measures cannot be put in place, it is the data exporter's responsibility to suspend or not go ahead with the transfer.
- If the data controller fails to suspend or goes ahead with the transfer and this issue is brought to the attention of a supervisory authority, it is the supervisory authority's responsibility to investigate the matter by taking into account all of the circumstances surrounding the transfer and subsequently decide whether to order a suspension of the transfer.

## NAVIGATING INTERNATIONAL DATA TRANSFERS

The CJEU decision in *Schrems II* caused many organisations to reassess the extent of their positions on international transfers of personal data and to take steps to align with the judgment. One of the key questions left unanswered by *Schrems II* was the additional measures that organisations should put in place to supplement the guarantees contained in the SCCs following the completion of a transfer assessment.

### EDPB's six-step recommendations

In order to provide more clarity for organisations, the EDPB adopted 'recommendations 01/2020 on measures that supplement transfer tools to ensure compliance with the EU level of protection of personal data'.[34] These recommendations are summarised in Table 8.5.

### Supplementary measures

Appendix 2 of the EDPB recommendations set out a list of example technical, organisational and/or contractual measures that organisations may consider to implement or impose on a data importer depending on the circumstances of the restricted transfer. Examples include the following.

---

[34] Adopted on 18 June 2021.

**Table 8.5 Six-step recommendations for supplemental transfer tools**

| Steps | Recommendation | More detail |
|---|---|---|
| Step 1 | Know your transfers | • Identify and map all restricted transfers.<br>• Verify that the restricted transfer is adequate, relevant and limited to what is necessary in relation to the purposes for the transfer. |
| Step 2 | Verify the data transfer mechanism relied on | • If the third country has an adequacy decision, there is no need to take any further steps other than monitoring that the adequacy decision remains valid.<br>• In the absence of an adequacy decision, the requirement is to rely on an appropriate safeguard under Article 46 of the GDPR for transfers that are regular and repetitive.<br>• Only in some cases of occasional and non-repetitive transfers can one of the derogations under Article 49 of the GDPR be relied on (provided the relevant conditions are met). |
| Step 3 | Assess the law or practice of the third country | • In the context of the specific restricted transfer, assess whether there is anything in the law and/or practices of the third country that may impinge on the effectiveness of the appropriate safeguards of the data transfer mechanism relied on.<br>• The assessment should be focused on third country legislation that is relevant to the restricted transfer in question and should be thoroughly documented.<br>• In addition, examining the practices of the third country's public authorities will help to verify whether the safeguards contained in the transfer tool can ensure, in practice, the effective protection of the personal data transferred. This examination will be particularly relevant where (1) the legislation in the third country is manifestly not applied/complied with in practice; (2) there are practices incompatible with the commitments of the transfer tool where relevant legislation in the third country is lacking; (3) the personal data transferred and/or data importer fall (or might fall) within the scope of problematic legislation that impinges on the transfer tool's contractual guarantee of an essentially equivalent level of protection. |

*(Continued)*

**Table 8.5 (Continued)**

| Steps | Recommendation | More detail |
|---|---|---|
| | | • For circumstances falling in points (1) and (2) above, the transfer will need to be suspended or adequate supplementary measures must be implemented in order to proceed with the transfer. For circumstances falling in point (3), an additional option is to proceed with the transfer without implementing supplementary measures if it is considered, demonstrated and documented that there is no reason to believe that relevant and problematic legislation will be interpreted and/or applied in practice that covers the personal data transferred and the data importer. |
| | | • The EDPB's Essential Guarantees[35] recommendations should be referred to for evaluating elements to be taken into account when assessing the law of the third country dealing with access to personal data by public authorities. |
| Step 4 | Identify and adopt supplementary measures | • If the assessment in Step 3 determines that the law or practice of the third country impinges the effectiveness of appropriate safeguards, the next step is to identify and adopt supplementary measures to enhance the level of protection of the personal data to the EU standard of essential equivalence. The assessment and outcome of the supplementary measures identified (if any) should be thoroughly documented. |
| | | • Some supplementary measures may be effective in some third countries but not others. In addition, it might be that several supplementary measures will require combining in order to achieve the necessary protections. |
| | | • In circumstances where no supplementary measure is suitable, the restricted transfer must be avoided, suspended or terminated to avoid compromising the level of protection afforded to the personal data. |
| Step 5 | Take any formal procedural steps | • If the adoption of any supplementary measure requires formal procedural steps, these should be followed. For example, there may be instances where the competent supervisory authority will need to be consulted before adopting certain supplementary measures. |
| Step 6 | Re-evaluate and monitor level of protection | • The level of protection afforded in the third country should be re-evaluated and monitored at appropriate intervals (e.g. if there are any developments in the law or practices of the third country in question that may impact the original assessments conducted in steps 3 and 4 above). |

---

[35] See EDPB Recommendations 02/2020 on the European Essential Guarantees for surveillance measures. https://edpb.europa.eu/sites/edpb/files/files/file1/edpb_recommendations_202002_europeanessentialguaranteessurveillance_en.pdf

### Contractual measures
- Inclusion of annexes to the contract with information that the data importer would provide (based on its best efforts) upon a request for access to personal data by public authorities.
- Inclusion of additional provisions in the contract whereby the data importer certifies that it has not purposefully (1) created back doors or similar programming that could be used to access the system and/or personal data, and (2) created or changed its business processes in a manner that facilitates access to personal data or systems.
- Contractually reinforcing the data exporter's power to conduct audits or inspections of the data processing facilities of the data importer to verify if data was disclosed to public authorities and under which conditions.

### Organisational measures
- Adoption of adequate internal policies with clear allocation of responsibilities for data transfers, reporting channels and standard operating procedures for cases of covert or official requests from public authorities to access personal data.
- Documenting and recording requests for access received from public authorities and the response provided together with the legal reasoning for the same.
- Regular publication of transparency reports or summaries regarding governmental requests for access to date and the types of replies provided.

### Technical measures
With respect to technical measures, the EDPB sets out a number of use cases and explained how certain technical measures (e.g. encryption and pseudonymisation) applied to these use cases would be deemed 'effective'. For example:

***Encryption***   The EDPB would consider encryption to be an effective supplementary measure if:

- personal data are processed using strong encryption before transmission, and the identity of the importer is verified;
- the encryption algorithm and its parameterisation conform to the state of the art and can be considered robust against cryptanalysis performed by the public authorities in the recipient third country;
- the strength of encryption takes into account the specific time period during which the confidentiality of the encrypted personal data must be preserved;
- the encryption algorithm is flawlessly implemented by properly maintained software;
- the encryption keys are reliably managed;
- the encryption keys are retained solely under the control of the data exporter.

***Pseudonymisation***   The EDPB would consider pseudonymisation to be an effective supplementary measure if:

- the personal data can no longer be attributed to a specific data subject, nor be used to single out the data subject in a larger group, without the use of additional information;
- additional information is held exclusively by the data exporter and kept separately in the EU or third country having an adequacy decision;
- disclosure or unauthorised use of that additional information is prevented by appropriate technical and organisational safeguards, that is, it is ensured that the data exporter retains sole control of the algorithm or repository that enables reidentification using the additional information;
- the controller has established by means of a thorough analysis of the data in question taking into account any information that the public authorities of the recipient country may possess that the pseudonymised personal data cannot be attributed to an identified or identifiable natural person even if cross-referenced with such information.

## A PRACTICAL APPROACH TO INTERNATIONAL TRANSFERS

Although the EDPB provides helpful steps for organisations to follow, the challenge lies in applying these steps in practice, particularly as part of running a multinational or international organisation. There could also be resource, time and cost implications of running a project that aims to address multiple restricted transfers at the same time.

As a result, a more tailored approach is typically required, one that can be risk based and that can help organisations prioritise compliance efforts in a way that realises the reduction of risk in a more effective and measurable manner. Figure 8.3 illustrates a *Schrems II* roadmap as an example of an approach to how organisations can channel efforts to comply with the judgment in practice.

### Getting to know your 'special characteristics'

It is important for an organisation to design an approach to international data transfers based on factors personal to that organisation and its stakeholders. Having a good understanding of the organisation's 'special characteristics' (such as business purpose, business operations and model, geographic locations, risk appetite, and culture and ethics) provides a strong foundation to help make reasoned decisions on international data transfers based on practical realities.

For example, an organisation based in Germany (where regulatory scrutiny of international data transfers has been traditionally stricter) may decide to take a more conservative approach to restricted transfers to the United States post-*Schrems II* compared to an organisation based in the UK. The organisation based in Germany may decide to either suspend such restricted transfers or move its data centres from the United States back into the EEA. These decisions may also be driven by the organisation's overall risk appetite if it operates in industries where risk tolerance is typically low (e.g. financial services). It may also be influenced by its track record of adverse regulatory enforcement action in the area of international data transfers. These are only a few illustrative examples of characteristics that are unique to an organisation that may lead to courses of action that are considered more conservative than market practice.

**Figure 8.3 A *Schrems II* roadmap for compliance**

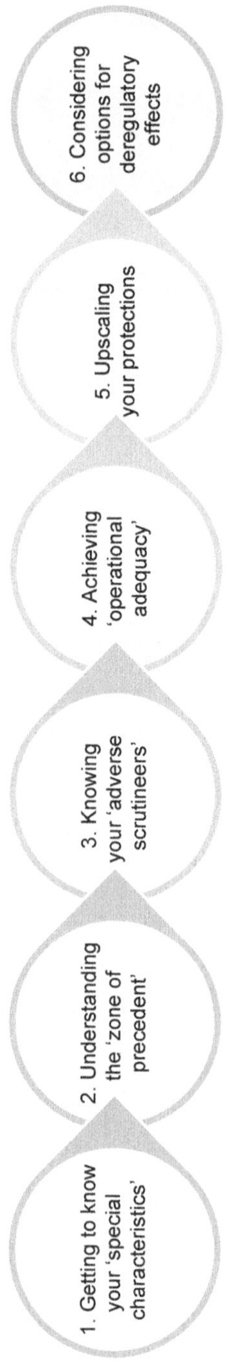

1. Getting to know your 'special characteristics'
2. Understanding the 'zone of precedent'
3. Knowing your 'adverse scrutineers'
4. Achieving 'operational adequacy'
5. Upscaling your protections
6. Considering options for deregulatory effects

## Understanding the 'zone of precedent'

Having a clear understanding of the scope of the *Schrems II* judgment can also help to prioritise compliance efforts. In forming its judgment, the CJEU took into account surveillance laws in the United States including the extent to which effective rights and remedies were available to individuals in that jurisdiction. It is therefore important to keep in mind that the CJEU did not opine on the levels of protection afforded in other third countries such as India, China or Brazil and the extent of the surveillance laws in those jurisdictions. As such, applying the 'zone of precedent' set by the *Schrems II* case, organisations may decide to prioritise compliance efforts in the order shown in Table 8.6.

**Table 8.6 Prioritising focus areas for international transfers through a 'zone of precedent' test**

| Priority | Focus area |
| --- | --- |
| Highest | Restricted transfers to the United States based on the Privacy Shield or SCCs |
| Medium | All other non-US restricted transfers based on the SCCs |
| Lowest | All other restricted transfers based on other data transfer mechanisms (e.g. BCRs, derogations, etc.) |

## Knowing your 'adverse scrutineers'

The nature of the internal and external challenge that organisations face from a data protection perspective is another factor that often influences decision making and prioritisation. In addition to regulatory scrutiny, organisations may face challenge from groups such as privacy activists, employees, works councils and/or customers (whether individuals or businesses). For example, following the *Schrems II* judgment many organisations received information requests from individuals on whether any of their personal data were being sent outside the EU/EEA particularly to the United States and on what legal basis. In particular, individuals wanted to know whether these transfers were caught by surveillance laws in the United States and, if so, what technical measures were in place to prevent exposure to the surveillance. Business customers also requested similar assurances from organisations around these questions. As a result, prioritising the restricted transfers that are subject to such adverse scrutiny is likely to help minimise immediate (and more pressing) data protection risk to the organisation.

## Achieving operational adequacy

Understanding and acknowledging the context of the restricted transfer can support organisations to deliver meaningful protections in operations. For example, is the nature of the personal data transferred actually at risk of public authority access? To what extent would technical measures such as cryptography really make a difference? Does the data exporter organisation have real operational control over the personal data or does control sit with the data importer organisation (with the only control exerted by the data exporter in the form of contractual provisions vis-à-vis the data importer)? Answers to these questions can help organisations to decide the extent to which additional measures are able to safeguard the personal data transferred in reality. Importantly, it can help to avoid purposeless activities that do not achieve meaningful risk reduction and protections in practice.

## Upscaling protections

Once an organisation gets a real sense of the compliance activities required to address its position with respect to international data transfers post-*Schrems II*, the next step will likely involve developing a business case to undertake a transformation plan to upscale existing protections. This transformation plan can act as a framework within which key compliance activities will be undertaken. Such activities could include, for example, reviewing existing third-party supplier management processes with a view to enhancing each stage of the process for international data transfers (e.g. due diligence during onboarding, data protection contracting, ongoing monitoring/audits and post-termination steps). It is within each of these stages where the identification, consideration and implementation of appropriate data transfer mechanisms and additional technical, organisational and contractual measures to safeguard personal data (where required) can operate.

## Considering options for deregulatory effects

As a final consideration, organisations may decide to explore options for deregulatory effects. This is where certain actions are taken to move the restricted transfer outside the scope of the GDPR's rules on international data transfers. This can include anonymising or deleting personal data or considering global relocation of servers from a third country back into the EU/EEA. Alternatively, an assessment can be made as to whether one of the derogations under Article 49 of the GDPR can be relied on instead of the need to rely on the SCCs and implementation of additional measures to safeguard personal data.

## SUMMARY

In conclusion, this chapter gives readers a better understanding of:

- how the GDPR regulates transfers of personal data to third countries;
- the principles that apply to these transfers, including the general prohibition against transfers to non-adequate countries;
- the safeguards and derogations that can be relied upon to overcome the prohibition against transfers to non-adequate countries;
- the priorities and urgency that attach to properly managing international transfers, in light of recent litigation and Brexit;
- the practical steps that organisations can take to manage their transfers and their operational risks.

# 9 DATA PROTECTION BEYOND THE GDPR LAND MASS

## James Drury-Smith and Simon Davis

This chapter provides an overview of key international data protection laws that have been adopted outside the GDPR land mass. It also explains how the GDPR has influenced global legislative reform and identifies some of the challenges faced by organisations operating on a global stage and the coping mechanisms that they might adopt.

## MULTI-JURISDICTIONAL FRAMEWORKS PROTECTING RIGHTS AND FREEDOMS INCLUDING DATA PROTECTION

There are approximately 195 sovereign states in the world, although the exact number is disputed and varies from time to time. The United Nations Conference on Trade and Development reported that as of April 2020, 128 of those states had put in place legislation to secure the protection of data and privacy, with a further 20 having legislation in draft. It therefore seems a near certainty that organisations operating internationally will need to consider a plethora of data protection laws as they go about their business. These can be multiregional, in the sense of frameworks that apply in more than one territory, of which Europe has three examples, namely the European Convention on Human Rights, the Data Protection Convention and the GDPR. Others to note outside Europe are the United Nations (UN) Declaration of Human Rights, the OECD Guidelines on the Protection of Privacy and Transborder Flows of Personal Data and the Asia-Pacific Economic Cooperation (APEC) Privacy Framework.

### The Universal Declaration of Human Rights

The United Nations adopted the Universal Declaration of Human Rights (UDHR) on 10 December 1948. Article 12 of the UDHR sets out that:

> No one shall be subjected to arbitrary interference with his privacy, family, home or correspondence, nor to attacks upon his honour and reputation. Everyone has the right to the protection of the law against such interference or attacks.

The UDHR is the foundation of international human rights law. Although the Declaration is non-binding, Article 12 has been a catalyst for the development of privacy laws and, subsequently, data protection laws internationally.

Article 12 of the UDHR is replicated in Article 17 of the International Covenant on Civil and Political Rights (United Nations, 19 December 1966). Whereas the UDHR is not legally binding on Member States, the covenant is.

## The OECD Guidelines on the Protection of Privacy and Transborder Flows of Personal Data

The Council of the OECD adopted the Guidelines on the Protection of Privacy and Transborder Flows of Personal Data (the 'Guidelines') in 1980. They were developed against a backdrop of:

- widespread use of computers for the processing of personal data, with vastly expanded possibilities of storing, comparing, linking, selecting and accessing personal data;
- increasing flows of information between countries because of the introduction of new computer and communications technology;
- member countries having developed or being in the process of developing their own laws for the protection of privacy;
- privacy protection laws taking different forms in different countries;
- concerns that disparities in the developing legislation would create obstacles to the free flow of information between countries.

The objectives of the Guidelines included helping to facilitate harmonisation of national legislation; setting minimum standards of protection for personal data; and reducing, as far as possible, interference with and restrictions on the transborder flow of personal data.[1] In its explanatory notes, the OECD noted that common features had materialised across various legal instruments and initiatives:

> Some core principles of this type are: setting limits to the collection of personal data in accordance with the objectives of the data collector and similar criteria; restricting the usage of data to conform with openly specified purposes; creating facilities for individuals to learn of the existence and contents of data and have data corrected; and the identification of parties who are responsible for compliance with the relevant privacy protection rules and decisions. Generally speaking, statutes to protect privacy and individual liberties in relation to personal data attempt to cover the successive stages of the cycle beginning with the initial collection of data and ending with erasure or similar measures, and to ensure to the greatest possible extent individual awareness, participation and control.

The Guidelines incorporate terms and principles that have subsequently become common parlance in data protection. This includes defined terms for 'data controller', 'data subject' and 'personal data'. The Guidelines also incorporate principles of data protection that address lawful and fair processing, transparency, data minimisation, data quality, purpose specification, data security, rights of access, erasure, rectification, accountability and international transfers of personal data.

The Guidelines were adopted the year before the Council of Europe's Data Protection Convention, but they were developed in parallel and the two bodies maintained

---

[1] Detailed background information about the development of the OECD guidelines can be found in the Explanatory Memorandum that accompanies the Guidelines.

close contact as they went about their work. They both wanted to avoid unnecessary differences developing between the texts of the two documents, which explains why the principles within them are similar. They are not identical, however. Other differences include the legally binding nature of Convention 108, its focus and terminology. For example, the Convention focuses on automatic processing of personal data, whereas the Guidelines apply to personal data that involves dangers to privacy and individual liberties, irrespective of the method of processing.

The first revision and updates to the Guidelines took place in 2013. Two themes emerged from the updates: first, a focus on the practical implementation of data protection through risk management and secondly, improved interoperability to help address globalisation. The update also introduced new concepts such as national strategies, which emphasise the need for data protection to be coordinated at the highest levels of government; privacy management programmes as operational mechanisms for implementing privacy protection; and data security breach notification to authorities and affected individuals.

## APEC Privacy Framework

The Asia-Pacific Economic Cooperation was established in 1989. Its members are Australia; Brunei; Canada; Chile; China; Hong Kong; Indonesia; Japan; South Korea; Malaysia; Mexico; New Zealand; Papua New Guinea; Peru; Philippines; Russia; Singapore; Chinese Taipei; Thailand; USA and Vietnam. The stated aim of APEC is to create greater prosperity for the people of the region by promoting balanced, inclusive, sustainable, innovative and secure growth and by accelerating regional economic integration.[2]

The first version of the Framework, adopted in 2005, was modelled on the OECD Guidelines. The latest version, 2015, builds on concepts introduced into the OECD Guidelines in 2013. It aims to protect privacy while maintaining information flows within the Asia-Pacific region. Like the European model for data protection, the Framework is based on a set of principles. However, APEC members do not enter binding commitments or treaty obligations. Participation in the Framework is on a voluntary basis.

## NATIONAL LAWS BEYOND THE GDPR LAND MASS

The GDPR has had a monumental impact on data protection law-making outside Europe. An obvious reason for the GDPR's influence in bringing about global change is that it has made data protection a front and centre policy issue for governments and businesses wishing to join the EU or trade with Europe. As a result of the GDPR's success in harmonising data protection legislation across the EU, there is also a clear desire in many nations outside Europe to consolidate their own laws to create a singular comprehensive data protection framework that aligns with the GDPR, often with the intent of seeking an adequacy decision from the European Commission in their favour. To achieve adequacy status, countries must, amongst other things, demonstrate that they provide a level of data protection that is essentially equivalent to that in EU law.

---

2   As described on the APEC website.

# DATA PROTECTION AND COMPLIANCE

Once a country is granted adequacy status by the European Commission, data can pass freely between it and the EEA without any further safeguards being required.

## Notable new legislation

Table 9.1 provides examples of notable data protection laws that other jurisdictions have recently passed, or are in the process of bringing into force, which bear similarities with the regime set out by the GDPR.

**Table 9.1 Notable new data protection legislation**

| Jurisdiction | Legislation | Description/status |
|---|---|---|
| **North America** | | |
| US (California) | The California Consumer Privacy Act 2018 (as amended) under Part 4 of Division 3 of the California Civil Code and the California Consumer Privacy Act Regulations (CCPA) | The CCPA came into effect on 1 January 2020 and became enforceable on 1 July 2020. |
| US (Virginia) | Consumer Data Protection Act 2021 (CDPA) | The legislature passed the CDPA in February 2021 and it is set to come into effect on 1 January 2023. |
| **South America** | | |
| Brazil | Brazil's Lei Geral de Proteção de Dados – The Law No. 13.709 of 14 August 2018, General Personal Data Protection Law (as amended by Law No. 13.853 of 8 July 2019) (LGPD). | The LGPD came into effect on 18 September 2020. It attempts to unify several existing statutory regimes relating to data protection in Brazil. Its enforcement provisions came into effect on 1 August 2021. |
| Argentina | The Personal Data Protection Bill 2018 ('the Bill') | Since GDPR, the Agencia de Acceso a la Información Pública (AAIP) has been working on the draft Personal Data Protection Bill 2018 to replace the current Act. |
| | | The Bill follows key GDPR principles but is yet to be passed as law. It lost its parliamentary status in March 2020, but could be reintroduced. |

*(Continued)*

**Table 9.1 (Continued)**

| Jurisdiction | Legislation | Description/status |
| --- | --- | --- |
| Chile | Bill No. 11144-07 Regulating the Processing and Protection of Personal Data and Creating the Personal Data Protection Authority ('Bill 11144-07') | Bill No. 11144-07 Regulating the Processing and Protection of Personal Data and Creating the Personal Data Protection Authority has similar concepts to GDPR, including establishing rights for individuals to access data, rectification, deletion/erasure and portability and would bring data protection to a comparable level to the GDPR in Chile.<br><br>The Bill is expected to be adopted in due course. |
| **Asia** | | |
| India | Personal Data Protection Bill 2019 (PDPB) | The PDPB was introduced before the Indian Parliament on 11 December 2019 but has not yet been adopted, although the legislative process continues. It will create a data protection authority (DPA) responsible for enforcement of the legislation. |
| People's Republic of China | Draft Personal Information Protection Law (PIPL) and<br><br>Data Security Law of the People's Republic of China (Draft) | PIPL came into effect on 1 November 2021. It clarifies processing rules, obligations and data subject rights in a manner analogous to the GDPR, whilst the Draft Data Security Law introduces data security requirements for data activities conducted within mainland China. |
| Japan | The Act on the Protection of Personal Information (APPI) (Act No. 57 of 2003 as amended in 2015) | APPI was passed by the Japanese Parliament in June 2020. Its transitional measures came into effect in October 2021, but its main provisions commence in April 2022. It introduces new obligations for data controllers, data subject rights, data breaches and data transfers. |
| South Korea | Personal Information Protection Act 2011 (as amended in 2020) (PIPA) | Amendments to South Korea's PIPA have led to a high degree of convergence between PIPA and the GDPR. On 30 March 2021, adequacy talks were concluded between the European Commission and South Korea. The European Commission adopted an adequacy decision for South Korea in September 2021. |

## COMPARATIVE REVIEW BETWEEN THE GDPR AND KEY INTERNATIONAL LAWS

Upon closer analysis of the different regimes outlined in Table 9.1, elements of the key principles and processes of the GDPR regime are present and can be clearly seen to have influenced the core foundations of the various privacy frameworks, including:

- substance and definitions of key terms used within the legislation;
- material and territorial scope of the laws (including in relation to extraterritorial scope);
- bases/grounds required for lawful processing of personal data;
- obligations imposed on processors/controllers of personal data;
- provision of greater rights to individuals and providing express mechanisms to enforce rights in the courts for non-compliance;
- establishment of regulatory authorities and increased powers of enforcement for non-compliance.

## UNITED STATES

The current position in relation to privacy rights and enforcement varies across the 50 US states, as there is no harmonising data protection legislation in force on a federal level (the level that applies law to all industries and states within the US).

As such, for businesses operating across the US to ascertain and comply with the relevant legal and regulatory requirements in relation to data protection, they must consider local data protection legislation in each state, along with any related sectoral federal laws that apply, such as:

- The Health Insurance Portability and Accountability Act of 1996 (HIPAA). This imposes requirements in relation to the privacy and security of health information.
- The Children's Online Privacy Protection Act of 1998 (COPPA). This imposes requirements in relation to the operation of websites and online services directed to children under 13 years of age.
- The Gramm-Leach-Bliley Act of 1999 (GLBA). This imposes requirements in relation to financial institutions' safeguarding of data and information sharing practices.

As referred to in Table 9.1, two notable states that have recently brought in data protection laws bearing similarities to the GDPR and are paving the way forward for data protection in the US are:

- California (California Consumer Privacy Act 2018);
- Virginia (Consumer Data Protection Act 2021).

It is anticipated that other states may follow a similar approach to these states and it is also possible that legislation on a federal level will be brought into effect in the future.

The establishment of a federal privacy law governing the private sector in the US has been discussed for some time but has yet to come to fruition.

Some of the key similarities and differences between the laws within these two jurisdictions and the GDPR are considered in more detail and outlined below.

## California

The California Consumer Privacy Act 2018 (as amended) came into effect on 1 January 2020 and became enforceable on 1 July 2020. The CCPA drastically increases consumer privacy rights in relation to 'personal information' of 'consumers' who are residents of California, in a way that has not been seen before in the US. The requirements of the CCPA are enforced by the California Attorney General (AG). The AG has the power to assess a violation of the CCPA and to bring a civil action before the court for civil penalties, including monetary penalties and injunctions.

### *The magnitude of processing in California*
California boasts the largest economy in the United States, with a gross domestic product (GDP) of approximately $3.09 trillion in 2020.[3] For this reason, data protection legislation passed in California has significance on both a national and global stage.

### *Key similarities between the GDPR and CCPA*
- Broadly speaking, the CCPA's obligations apply to the 'collecting', 'selling' and 'sharing' of personal 'information', whereas the GDPR applies to the 'processing' of 'personal data'. The definitions of 'personal data' and 'personal information' that are used in the legislation have strong elements of convergence. The CCPA defines 'personal information' as 'information that identifies, relates to, describes, is reasonably capable of being associated with, or could reasonably be linked, directly or indirectly, with a particular consumer or household'.

- The CCPA does not refer to 'data subjects', but 'consumers'. However, the practical effect and definition of these terms is also similar and there is overlap between the definitions applying to natural persons.

- The CCPA and GDPR both have extraterritorial effect. In a similar way to the GDPR's approach outlined in Article 3(2), which extends its application to the processing of personal data belonging to data subjects who are in the Union by controllers and processors that are not established in the Union,[4] the CCPA applies to businesses that are 'doing business in California', and despite this term not being defined within the CCPA, businesses that are out of state and carrying out the collecting, selling or sharing the personal information of Californian residents have the potential to fall within its scope.[5]

---

3   https://www.statista.com/statistics/248023/us-gross-domestic-product-gdp-by-state/

4   So long as the processing activities are related to the offering of goods or services or monitoring of the behaviour of data subjects within the Union.

5   The Californian Franchise Tax Board states that 'doing business in California' means: 'actively engaging in any transaction for the purpose of financial or pecuniary gain or profit' and if certain thresholds are met (see Section 23101 of the Revenue and Taxation Code).

- Like the data subject rights provided by the GDPR, consumers[6] are also granted several rights under the CCPA in relation to their personal information including:
    - A right to access (through request and disclosure) personal information that is processed.
    - A right to erasure/deletion regarding personal information that a business has collected from them (similar exceptions apply to those set out under the GDPR[7]).
    - A right to opt out of their personal information being sold. However, this right is not as expansive as the equivalent rights under the GDPR, as consumers are only able to opt out of the sale of personal information and not the collection or other uses that do not fall under the definition of 'selling'.
    - A right to data portability (considered as part of the right of access under CCPA).
    - Rights in relation to disclosure and transparency.
    - A right to be informed.
- Both the GDPR and CCPA are prescriptive about the information that must be provided to individuals when collecting and processing their personal information. Businesses that are subject to the CCPA must provide a notice to consumers before or at the point of collecting personal information. The privacy notice must include key information such as the category(ies) of personal information that is collected and a description of the reason why it is being collected.
- Like the GDPR's requirement for controllers to put in place contracts with their processors, the CCPA requires that personal information is disclosed to 'service providers' pursuant to a written contract.
- The CCPA establishes an enforcement regime in relation to the legislation. The Attorney General may bring civil lawsuits against businesses that breach the requirements of the CCPA (including a power to issue injunctions and fines).
- The CCPA provides an express ability for consumers to enforce privacy rights against private individuals and seek compensation in relation to data security breaches.

### Key differences between the GDPR and the CCPA

However, despite the strong similarities that exist between the two laws, they have their differences, including:

- The CCPA does not separately define or categorise 'special categories' of personal data.
- The CCPA does not include a list of lawful bases that businesses must establish to collect, sell and disclose personal information. It only provides that they

---

[6] 'Consumers' are defined as natural persons who are California residents currently living in California or outside the state for a temporary purpose.

[7] For example: freedom of speech, processing of personal data for research purposes if erasure of that data would impair the objectives of the research and complying with a legal obligation.

must obtain consumers' consent when they enter a scheme that gives financial incentives based on the personal information provided.

- In contrast to the GDPR terms such as 'controller' and 'processor', those responsible for compliance are instead referred to by the singular term of 'businesses' within the CCPA. There are elements of convergence between their meanings, but only businesses (for-profit entities) are covered under CCPA and in contrast to the GDPR not-for-profit organisations and public bodies fall outside its scope.

- The CCPA provides carve-outs in relation to its applicable scope including medical information, in addition to data related to health collected for clinical trials, publicly available information and employee data.

- The CCPA does not apply to the non-commercial activities of a person, including businesses, whilst the equivalent GDPR exemption only excludes individuals processing data in the context of a purely personal or household activity.

- Although the CCPA provides an express ability for consumers to enforce privacy rights against private individuals and rights to seek compensation in relation to data security breaches, under the GDPR a civil claim can be brought for failing to comply with any of its provisions, as opposed to only breaches of security measures.

## Virginia

The Consumer Data Protection Act 2021 is set to come into effect in Virginia on 1 January 2023. The Virginia Attorney General will be responsible for enforcing the terms of the CDPA. The Attorney General, amongst other things, will have the power to issue a civil investigative demand and may initiate an action in the name of the Commonwealth, to seek an injunction and/or civil penalties for violations of the CDPA.

### *Key similarities between the CDPA and the GDPR*
The CDPA and GDPR both apply in relation to 'personal data' and the two definitions are almost identical with 'personal data' defined in the CDPA as 'any information that is linked or reasonably linkable to an identified or identifiable natural person'.

The CDPA does not refer to 'data subjects', but instead 'consumers'. However, both definitions have strong elements of convergence with 'consumer' defined in the CDPA as 'a natural person who is a resident of Virginia'.

In comparison to the GDPR, and unlike the approach taken in the CCPA, the CDPA makes provision for special categories of data, in similar terms to the GDPR, in that it imposes a requirement for businesses to 'not process sensitive data concerning a consumer without obtaining the consumer's consent'.

Like the GDPR, the CDPA grants consumers several strengthened rights in relation to their personal data including:

- right of access;
- right to confirmation that personal data are being processed;

- right to correction;
- right to deletion/erasure;
- right to opt out of processing (in relation to targeted advertising, profiling and the sale of personal data);
- right to data portability.

**Key differences between the CDPA and the GDPR**
- Notably the CDPA does not apply to non-profits, government entities, or institutions of higher education but is instead limited to 'Persons that conduct business in Virginia or produce products or services that are targeted to residents of Virginia and that: control or process personal data of at least 100,000 consumers annually; or control or process personal data of at least 25,000 consumers and derive over 50% of gross revenue from the sale of personal data'.
- The CDPA specifies that a Virginia resident is only a consumer when they are acting in an individual or household context, and expressly excludes a natural person acting in a commercial or employment context.
- CDPA provides no express private right of action for individuals to bring claims for breaches of its obligations.
- CDPA imposes no requirement on organisations to appoint a data protection officer.

## BRAZIL

Brazil's Lei Geral de Proteção de Dados – The Law No. 13.709 of 14 August 2018, General Personal Data Protection Law (as amended by Law No. 13.853 of 8 July 2019) was passed in 2018 and entered into effect on 18 September 2020. Its enforcement provisions came into effect on 1 August 2021. The Brazilian National Data Protection Authority (ANPD) is responsible for enforcing the terms of the LGPD. The LGPD provides that the ANPD may, amongst other things, issue administrative sanctions and monetary penalties for non-compliance with its terms.

Brazil is Latin-America's largest economy, and its impact on the global data protection landscape is therefore very significant. The LGPD attempts to unify several different statutory regimes that existed in Brazil and its approach to doing so can be seen to have been strongly influenced by the GDPR.

**Key similarities between the LGPD and the GDPR**
- Both the GDPR and LGPD have strong similarities about scope. The LGPD applies to any processing operation of personal data and defines 'personal data' in almost identical terms to the GDPR as: 'information regarding an identified or identifiable natural person'.
- Both the LGPD and GDPR use the terms 'controller' and 'processor' and there is a high level of convergence between the two sets of definitions and important demarcations of the respective roles played.

- The LGPD has extraterritorial effect and applies to data processing operations carried out in Brazil regardless of where the headquarters of an organisation are, if the data being processed belongs to individuals located in Brazil or if the personal data being processed was collected in Brazil. In addition, the LGPD applies irrespective of the location of an entity's headquarters, or the location of the data being processed, if the purpose of an entity's processing activity is to offer or provide goods or services to individuals who are in Brazil.
- The LGPD makes accountability and transparency key principles and individuals must be provided with a detailed privacy notice setting out information regarding the processing of their personal data.
- The LGPD distinguishes between personal data and special category data in similar terms to the GDPR and like the GDPR there are specific requirements imposed for its processing. The LGPD refers to 'sensitive personal data' as 'personal data concerning racial or ethnic origin, religious belief, political opinion, trade union or religious, philosophical or political organisation membership, data concerning health or sex life, genetic or biometric data, when related to a natural person'.
- The LGPD provides individuals with enhanced rights including:
  - right of access;
  - right to be informed of processing activities based on personal data;
  - right of erasure;
  - right of rectification;
  - right to object;
  - right to data portability.
- The LGPD provides for the appointment of a data protection officer.
- The LGPD provides legal bases for processing personal data that cover consent, performance of a contract, compliance with legal obligation, protection of vital interests, public interest or exercise of official authority, and legitimate interests.
- The LGPD provides an express right for individuals to seek civil damages (pecuniary or moral) for non-compliance with its terms.
- Provision is made by the LGPD for the possibility of monetary penalties for non-compliance with its terms.

### Key differences between the LGPD and the GDPR

- The LGPD does not require processing that is undertaken on behalf of controllers by processors to be governed by a binding contract or other legal act; instead, the processor must only conduct processing according to the controller's instructions.
- There are four further legal bases for processing data set out within the LGPD, namely, for the conduction of studies by research bodies; the exercise of rights in judicial, administrative and arbitral proceedings; for the protection of health in procedures conducted by health professionals and health entities; and for the protection of credit.

- The LGPD's legal bases for the processing of sensitive data include fraud prevention.
- Although provision is made for the appointment of a DPO under both regimes, the LGPD does not specifically impose the obligation for processors.
- The LGPD provides a shorter timeframe to respond to DSARs than the GDPR.

## INDIA

India currently has no data protection legislation in force. However, the Personal Data Protection Bill 2019 was introduced before the Indian Parliament on 11 December 2019.

The PDPB's goal is to implement a comprehensive data protection regime in India that mirrors the approach of the GDPR in harmonising and increasing privacy rights and standards for individuals. It also establishes a data protection authority to enforce its terms. The PDPB provides for monetary penalties in the case of non-compliance (up to 4% of annual worldwide turnover of an organisation) and the DPA is empowered to enforce the terms of the PDPB by, amongst other things, inquiring into the affairs of a data fiduciary, issuing warnings, suspending or discontinuing business activities in violation of the PDPB and/or requiring data fiduciaries to take specified actions.

As a result of the size and significance of India's economy, and the popularity of India as an outsourcing destination for organisations, should the PDPB become enacted, it will have a profound impact on data protection on a global level.

The PDPB is comparable to the GDPR in many respects, including key provisions relating to accountability, data subject rights and scope.

### *Key similarities between the GDPR and the PDPB*
- The material scope of the PDPB is comparable to the GDPR and applies in relation to 'personal data'. The definition of personal data under each piece of legislation has strong elements of convergence. In the PDPB it is defined as: 'data about or relating to a natural person who is directly or indirectly identifiable, having regard to any characteristic, trait, attribute or any other feature of the identity of such natural person, or any combination of such features, or any combination of such features with any other information.'
- The PDPB applies to 'data fiduciaries' rather than controllers; however, there are strong elements of convergence between the two terms with the former defined as 'any person, including the State, a company, any juristic entity or any individual who alone or in conjunction with others determines the purpose and means of processing of personal data.'
- The PDPB also refers to 'processors' and sets out the role in similar terms to that under the GDPR. The PDPB defines a 'processor' as 'any person, including the State, a company, any juristic entity or any individual, who processes personal data on behalf of a data fiduciary.'

- The PDPB provides individuals with increased rights including:
  - right of access;
  - right to erasure;
  - right to portability;
  - right to correction/rectification.
- The PDPB specifies the lawful bases for the processing of personal data, including:
  - Consent (which must be freely given, informed, specific, clear, and capable of being withdrawn).
  - Functions of the state.
  - Compliance with law or any order of any court or tribunal.
  - Employment.
  - Reasonable purpose. The concept of reasonable purpose is comparable to the legitimate interests test under the GDPR.
- The PDPB makes a distinction between 'personal data' and 'sensitive personal data' and there are similarities in relation to the types of personal data categorised as 'sensitive' in the PDPB and special category data under the GDPR including genetic data, religious or political beliefs, sex life and sexual orientation, and biometric data. As is the case with the GDPR, explicit consent is required in cases where sensitive personal data are being processed and consent is required.
- The scope of the PDPB is extraterritorial and its application includes processing by 'data fiduciaries' who are not present within India, if the processing is in connection with any business, or systematic offering of goods or services to data principals, in India or with the profiling of data principals in the region.
- The PDPB requires 'significant data fiduciaries' to carry out a DPIA in relation to processing of personal data if the processing involves (a) new technologies, (b) large-scale profiling or use of sensitive data, or (c) any other activities that carry a significant risk of harm (as may be specified by regulations).
- The PDPB requires significant data fiduciaries to appoint a data protection officer.
- There is a requirement for data fiduciaries and processors to implement 'necessary security safeguards'.
- The PDPB introduces concepts of accountability, like the GDPR.
- The PDPB provides for monetary penalties and set out that maximum fines can be up to 4% of the annual worldwide turnover of an organisation.
- The PBPB expressly provides data principals with a private right of action to seek compensation from data fiduciaries and processors for any harm suffered because of the PDPB's provisions.

### Key differences between the PDPB and the GDPR
However, the bill differs to the GDPR in other respects, including:

- there is no right to object to profiling under the PDPB, unless the data subject is a child;

- under the PDPB, all DPIAs are required to be submitted to the DPA;
- the PDPB imposes data localisation requirements (further information in relation to data localisation is outlined below).

## CHINA

There are several relevant privacy provisions that are currently contained in different laws and regulations in force in the People's Republic of China (PRC).

However, on 21 October 2020 the National People's Congress of China released the Draft Personal Information Protection Law for public comment. The draft PIPL seeks to provide a comprehensive data protection system in the PRC and, amongst other things, sets out data subject rights and requirements for processors of 'personal information'. Those responsible for enforcement of its terms will include the Cyberspace Administration of China, departments of local government and the State Council. Data processors may receive fines of up to 50 million RMB or up to 5% of the prior year's revenue in serious cases of non-compliance.

### *Key similarities between the draft PIPL and the GDPR*
- The draft PIPL defines 'personal information' in similar terms to personal data within the meaning of the GDPR as 'various types of electronic or otherwise recorded information relating to an identified or identifiable natural person.'
- The draft PIPL makes provision for 'personal information processors', which are analogous to those undertaking the role of controller under the GDPR. Personal information processors are defined in similar terms as 'the organisations or individuals that independently determine the purposes, means and or any other matters relating to the processing of any personal information'.
- The draft PIPL distinguishes between 'personal sensitive information' and 'personal information' in similar terms to personal data and special category data under the GDPR and includes race, nationality, religious beliefs and health data as categories of such information.
- The draft PIPL has extraterritorial application in similar terms to the GDPR and applies both to the processing of personal information within the PRC and to cross-border processing activities of PRC individuals if, amongst other things, its purpose is to provide products or services to PRC individuals or to analyse and evaluate their activities.
- The draft PIPL creates the following seven data processing principles, which bear strong similarities to the GDPR's principles:
  - legality;
  - explicit purpose;
  - minimum necessity;
  - transparency;
  - accuracy;

DATA PROTECTION BEYOND THE GDPR LAND MASS

- accountability and data security;
- storage limitation.
- The draft PIPL creates a system of lawful bases analogous to the GDPR and outlines that personal information processors can process personal information based on:
  - consent (which must be voluntary and informed by full knowledge of the data subject);
  - response to a public emergency, a public health event or, if necessary, to protect the safety of an individual's life or property;
  - necessity to perform or execute a contract;
  - necessity to perform a legal obligation or legal duty;
  - news publication and supervision by public opinion for public interests within reasonable scope;
  - other circumstances required by law and administrative regulations.
- Under the draft PIPL, subjects are provided with the following rights:
  - right to object to automated decision making;
  - right to know/be informed of the processing of their data and related rules;
  - right to access and copy their personal information from data processors;
  - right to correction/completion of personal data;
  - right to withdraw consent;
  - right to deletion/erasure (in certain circumstances).
- Under the draft PIPL, obligations imposed on data processors include:
  - establishing internal administrative policies and operating procedures;
  - conducting regular training and education;
  - conducting regular audits of personal information processing activities;
  - requirement to appoint a DPO if the volume of personal information processed reaches the threshold level specified by Chinese regulators.

### *Key differences between the draft PIPL and the GDPR*
- The draft provides no right to data portability for data subjects.
- There is no legitimate interests justification for the processing of personal data.

## DATA LOCALISATION

The OECD Guidelines, the Data Protection Convention, the APEC Framework and the GDPR have aimed to create greater harmonisation between countries and facilitate the free flow of personal data. However, restrictions and protectionist behaviours in the form of data localisation measures can be observed in many countries.

Data localisation measures come in several forms. They can be deliberate attempts to prevent the movement of data from one jurisdiction to another. They can also be the unintentional consequence of rules designed to protect individuals. Irrespective of how they come about, the results of localisation measures are usually the same: organisations face restrictions on the free flow of data. They also create compliance, financial and operational burdens for international organisations, which must contend with a patchwork of data requirements across the jurisdictions they operate in.

The reasons that countries develop data localisation requirements include:

- concerns that data will not be protected to the same standard as it was in the exporting jurisdiction;
- governments and regulators wanting to remove barriers to their access to data;
- commercial decisions that organisations make about the way they structure their business operations;
- national agendas to support local economies by retaining data within the jurisdiction.

Localisation rules can take several forms. These include:

- data can only be transferred to a country that offers protection to personal data that is adequate or equivalent to protections provided in the exporting country;
- a copy of the data must be retained within the exporting country;
- restrictions are placed on outsourcing data processing;
- the transfer of certain types of personal data outside the jurisdiction is prohibited;
- requiring consent/authorisation from an individual or body before exporting personal data.

## Examples of localisation laws

Table 9.2 provides examples of countries and jurisdictions that have adopted or are adopting laws containing localisation requirements.

Each of the laws listed in Table 9.2 illustrates that barriers to the free movement of data, whether ultimately surmountable through the application of an exception or not, are commonplace within the global data protection environment. Sometimes they can seriously threaten civil liberties. Take Russia as an example. In November 2016, online

### Table 9.2 Examples of data localisation laws

| Localisation requirement | Country/jurisdiction – transfer restriction law |
| --- | --- |
| Transfers can only take place to a country offering adequate or equivalent protection (unless exceptions to the rule apply) | • EU – GDRP<br>• Brazil – Law on General Data Protection 2018<br>• Japan – Act on the Protection of Personal Information 2003<br>• Israel – Privacy Protection (Transfer of Data to Database Abroad) Regulations, 5761-2001<br>• Argentina – Personal Data Protection Act 2000<br>• Nigeria – Data Protection Regulation 2019<br>• Turkey – Law on Protection of Personal Data 2016 |
| A copy of personal data must be retained in the country | • China – Cybersecurity Law Article 37 of the Cybersecurity Law 2016 requires 'key information infrastructure' operators to store personal information and critical data within China.<br>• Russia – Federal Law of 21 July 2014 No. 242-FZ on Personal Data Processing sets out that databases that are used to record, systematise, accumulate, store, update, modify and retrieve personal data of Russian citizens must be located in Russia. |
| Restricting the export of certain data types | • India – the Data Protection Bill 2019 permits certain personal data to be designated as 'critical personal data'. If such a designation takes place, the personal data can only be processed in India unless very limited exceptions apply. |
| Consent/authorisation from an individual or body | • South Korea – Personal Information Protection Act requires that data transfers can only take place with the prior consent of the data subject.<br>• Algeria – Law No. 18-07 of 25 Ramadhan 1439 Corresponding to 10 June 2018, relating to the Protection of Individuals in the Processing of Personal Data – Data controllers cannot transfer data outside Algeria unless they have obtained authorisation from the Algerian data protection authority.<br>• Egypt – Personal Data Protection Law No.151 of 2020 – a licence from the Personal Data Protection Centre will be required unless exemptions apply. |

access to LinkedIn was blocked throughout Russia under a procedure for a breach of the data localisation law. Over 5 million users of LinkedIn in Russia were affected.

## COPING STRATEGIES FOR ORGANISATIONS OPERATING GLOBALLY

The global data protection landscape is likely to continue evolving and as the above analysis demonstrates, despite similarities existing between the laws of various regions and countries, important nuances and different considerations exist between them that global businesses must be mindful of.

The large number of nations that are choosing to apply extraterritorial scope/jurisdiction in relation to the application of their data protection regimes means that organisations operating across multiple jurisdictions need to be aware of the continuously changing environments in which they operate. As such, businesses must ensure that they deploy strategies to achieve regulatory and legal compliance globally, which might include:

- Monitoring the progress of legislation globally, including the introduction of draft bills and any key dates for the enforcement of provisions.
- Organisations should carefully study how new and emerging legislation compares to that of other jurisdictions and seek to highlight areas of convergence to align their operational approach.
- Monitoring the development of regulatory guidance. Being aware of the relevant enforcement bodies and accessing their guidance will be key to understanding legal requirements, particularly those that appear to be vague or poorly drafted.
- Monitoring judicial and common law developments, to keep up to date with key cases.
- Tracking regulatory enforcement decisions will help organisations to understand areas of risk and focus.
- Having a clear operating model, to identify who is in charge in each country and how reporting lines operate.

### Examples of coping mechanisms

Table 9.3 describes some of the steps that organisations might take to manage data protection compliance on the global stage.

**Table 9.3 Examples of coping mechanisms for global compliance**

| Coping mechanism | Description |
| --- | --- |
| Understand the data protection requirements in the jurisdictions that the organisation operates in | • Where an organisation operates in many jurisdictions, it may decide to adopt a risk-based approach to identifying data protection requirements that are relevant to its business. A risk-based approach may involve an organisation selecting key jurisdictions for which it intends to develop a strong understanding of their data protection requirements.<br><br>• The selection of the key jurisdictions may be influenced by a range of factors including the volume and types of personal data the organisation processes within/from a jurisdiction; the value of its business or strategic importance of its business within a jurisdiction; and the data protection enforcement and litigation culture within a jurisdiction. |
| Identify likely sources of adverse scrutiny | • In addition to understanding data protection requirements, organisations will often identify issues and topics that are typically scrutinised by regulators, individuals and stakeholders within a jurisdiction.<br><br>• For example, in the UK the ICO has historically brought enforcement action for breaches of direct marketing requirements and breaches of security, whereas complaints from individuals tend to focus on failures relating to direct marketing and the exercise of data subject rights. In other countries there has been a greater focus on surveillance in public and in the workplace. Yet others have expended more effort in enforcing the transparency rules that apply before the collection of data can begin.<br><br>• Understanding the likely sources of adverse scrutiny in a jurisdiction can assist an organisation to identify key issues that should be prioritised for action. This can help to determine whether a blanket or uniform approach to data protection compliance can be achieved across jurisdictions or whether certain topics require greater attention in some jurisdictions. |
| Set a baseline data protection standard | • A common approach adopted by organisations operating across jurisdictions is to assess the similarities between the data protection laws in the jurisdictions they operate within. Using this assessment, a baseline data protection standard can be developed and applied to the business globally. |

*(Continued)*

## Table 9.3 (Continued)

| Coping mechanism | Description |
|---|---|
|  | • Some parts of the business may be required to move up to the standard and adopt measures that go beyond their local requirements. Other parts of the business may need to adopt measures that go beyond the standard to meet stricter local legal and regulatory requirements. |
|  | • Overall, the baseline standard approach can lead to the global adoption of data protection measures, create certainty within an organisation and permit compliance to be monitored against the standard. The baseline can also prevent a patchwork of approaches and inconsistent data protection measures being adopted across the jurisdictions an organisation operates in. In turn, this can help to reduce risk to the organisation's business, allow for centralised oversight and create efficiencies through the deployment of group-level policies, procedures and processes. |
| Develop policies, procedures and processes | • Policies, procedures and processes are developed that accommodate and promote compliance with different international data protection requirements. |
|  | • Where a baseline data protection standard has been set, policies, procedures and processes are developed against that baseline. |
| Establish a global data protection function | • A global data protection function is responsible for promoting data protection within an organisation and developing and maintaining global policies, procedures and processes. |
|  | • It may also have responsibility for monitoring and enforcing compliance with data protection requirements within the organisation. In addition, it is likely to provide a range of information, guidance and tools to the organisation to support data protection compliance. |
| Develop regional and/ or country-level subject matter expertise | • The setting of a common baseline standard for data protection, developing related policies, procedures and processes and the establishment of a global data protection functions will not necessarily remove the need for local-level data protection support. |

*(Continued)*

**Table 9.3 (Continued)**

| Coping mechanism | Description |
|---|---|
| | • Such support may still be necessary at a regional (e.g. North America, Asia, and Europe, the Middle East and Africa) or country level, particularly where complex data protection requirements apply, or the level of data processing connected to a specific region or country will create significant demands for local support. |
| Create key performance indicators and undertake regular data protection reviews and auditing to monitor compliance | • Key performance indicators (e.g. to evaluate timely responses to subject rights requests or notification of data breaches) can be developed for different jurisdictions based on local requirements.<br>• These measures, when coupled with regular monitoring and reporting, can be used to assess and evaluate data protection risks arising in different jurisdictions.<br>• Regular reviews and auditing (including by external parties) can also support the assessment of compliance levels across jurisdictions. |
| Monitor for new and updated laws and guidance | • Organisations should build mechanisms to help them keep up to date on new and amended laws and guidance in the jurisdictions they operate in.<br>• Such mechanisms should also feed into processes for making any required updates to policies, processes and procedures following new or updated law and guidance being introduced. |
| Understand the data the organisation processes | • To understand the impact of the global data protection requirements, organisations must understand what data they process, why they process them and where they are processed.<br>• This understanding is key to assessing the territorial reach of different jurisdictional data protection requirements. |
| Accountability documentation | • Organisations should document the steps they are taking to comply with regional requirements. For example, they might document policies, processes and procedures, processing activities, data protection impact assessments, contracts with data processors, security measures implemented by the organisation and records of data breaches.<br>• Such documentation helps organisations to implement data protection requirements within different jurisdictions, monitor compliance and demonstrate how they are complying with jurisdictional requirements. |

*(Continued)*

**Table 9.3 (Continued)**

| Coping mechanism | Description |
|---|---|
| Implement training and awareness | • Undertaking appropriate training and awareness can help an organisation to ensure that its personnel understand the data protection requirements it is subject to and their responsibilities for compliance with them.<br>• Training that is tailored for specific jurisdictions or roles within jurisdictions can further support these aims. |

## SUMMARY

In conclusion, this chapter gives readers a better understanding of:

- the multiregional schemes for data protection that have been adopted outside Europe;
- some of the national laws adopted outside Europe in the wake of the GDPR;
- the differences and similarities between those laws and the GDPR;
- data localisation rules and the impacts for global data processing;
- strategies that can be adopted to cope with global data protection laws.

# PART IV
# DELIVERY

# 10 MECHANISMS TO SUPPORT OPERATIONAL COMPLIANCE

## Tuğhan Thuraisingam

This chapter outlines some of the mechanisms within the GDPR that are designed to help controllers and processors to achieve operationally required standards of data protection. As well as supporting the achievement of operational outcomes, these mechanisms constitute standalone legal duties in their own right, meaning that a controller or processor could face regulatory action or legal proceedings for failing to implement the compliance mechanisms, regardless of the actual consequences for data processing.

### MECHANISMS WITHIN THE GDPR

One of the most impactful innovations of the GDPR is the requirement for controllers to be able to demonstrate compliance. This covers the entirety of the regulation, due to the requirements of Article 5.2 (i.e. the accountability principle) and Article 24.1 (called 'responsibility of the controller'). These requirements are extended by A.32.1, concerning security, the provisions of which apply to both controllers and processors.

Together, these provisions underpin a collection of mechanisms that are intended to provide the structures for delivering compliance, namely:

- data protection policies;
- records of processing activities;
- Data Protection by Design and Default;
- data protection impact assessments;
- data protection officers;
- contracts.

These mechanisms are event agnostic, in the sense that they are not contingent on an event arising, but, rather, they flow from the data nature of the processing activities that are performed. In contrast, the compliance mechanisms that need to be adopted after the exercise of a data subject rights request or a personal data breach, which are discussed elsewhere in this book, are dependent on these events happening.

## TECHNICAL AND ORGANISATIONAL MEASURES

The compliance obligations in A.24 and A.32 centre on the taking of 'appropriate technical and organisation measures', which should be commensurate to the risks presented by the processing activities.

### Organisational measures

Organisational measures are typically those that centre on the activities of people or that are contained in documentary form (physical or electronic). A measure that centres on the activities of people would include staff training on how to handle data subject access requests. A documentary measure would be the policy governing those activities.

### Technical measures

Technical measures cover those that have a technical effect, which can be either a physical measure or a technological measure. A safe door or a locked window are examples of physical measures having a technical effect. Encryption software is an example of a technological measure that has a technical effect.

### Codes of conduct and certification mechanisms

Codes of conduct and certification mechanisms can act to demonstrate compliance with the GDPR, due to the provisions in A.40–43. The ICO describes codes of conduct as 'voluntary accountability tools enabling sectors to identify and resolve key data protection challenges in their sector with assurance from ICO that the code, and its monitoring is appropriate'.[1] In particular, ICO considers that they can help organisations to ensure that they 'follow rules designed for [their] sector to achieve good practice'.[2] Certifications on the other hand are described by the ICO as 'a way for an organisation to demonstrate compliance' with the GDPR. They involve a certification body assessing and approving an organisation against a particular certification scheme and subsequently issuing the organisation with 'a certificate and a seal or a mark relevant to that scheme'.[3]

At the time of writing, codes of conduct and certification mechanisms are still in their infancy, so they are not the focus of this chapter. However, they are likely to take on more importance over time, as the GDPR continues to mature.

### Risk assessments

The nature of the technical and organisational measures that need to be adopted under A.24 and A.32 are dependent on the overall circumstances of the processing, that is, the nature, scope, context and purposes of processing and the risks to the rights and freedoms of individuals that are involved, which can be of 'varying likelihood and severity'.

---

[1] ICO Guide to the General Data Protection Regulation (version 01 January 2021 – 1.1.106), page 202.

[2] ICO Guide to the General Data Protection Regulation (version 01 January 2021 – 1.1.106), page 202.

[3] ICO Guide to the General Data Protection Regulation (version 01 January 2021 – 1.1.106), page 207.

Therefore, A.24 and A.32 both require risk assessments to be performed, making them critical compliance mechanisms within the overall framework of accountability. A.35 requires data protection impact assessments to be performed in various high-risk situations.

Risk assessments can begin with a preliminary set of questions that identify the nature and scope of a particular processing activity in a broad sense, which can act as a guide for further decision making about the performance of more detailed risk assessments, including DPIAs. Where a DPIA is mandatory, the risk assessment should enable the controller to reach an informed conclusion on whether to refer the processing to the regulator for further assessment under A.36.

Processing that takes place without a risk assessment being carried out is unlikely ever to be compliant with the GDPR, at least insofar as the question of accountability is concerned.

## DATA PROTECTION POLICIES

Article 24.2 states that the appropriate technical and organisational measures should include the 'implementation of appropriate data protection policies' by the controller where proportionate in relation to its processing activities. Data protection policies are typically internal documents that explain how an organisation complies with its data protection obligations. Such policies should be distinguished from 'privacy notices' (sometimes referred to by some organisations as their 'privacy policy'), which are external to the organisation and provide data subjects with the necessary transparency information required by A.13 and 14. The nature, number and content of data protection policies will differ from organisation to organisation, but, in general, an organisation would typically have the following in place.

### An overarching data protection policy

This describes, at a high level, the data protection outcomes that an organisation is required to meet. The GDPR does prescribe mandatory content for a data protection policy, but it could include information about the organisation's vision and strategy for data protection compliance, contact details of key staff members involved in processing and an overview of the data protection principles and obligations applicable to the organisation, including how the organisation is set up to comply with them in the context of its processing activities.

### Policies covering specific GDPR obligations

These specific policies provide the next level of detail and are often cross-referenced or linked to the overarching policy. For example, an organisation might have a separate policy describing its approach to data subject access requests, which would provide detailed information about the organisation's obligations with respect to responding to such requests and guidance to staff on how to identify a request and the steps they should take when preparing the response.

### Procedures

An organisation could also have detailed written procedures in place that facilitate compliance with specific GDPR obligations. For example, a procedure might contain detailed step-by-step processes perhaps supported by flowcharts, diagrams and similar instructions. In the case of data subject access requests, for example, the procedures outlined would be those necessary to achieve a timely, consistent and comprehensive response. Elements might include:

- steps to take in order to verify the data subject's identity;
- timelines for actions and recording statutory deadlines for responses;
- initial meetings to discuss the nature of the request and agree search terms;
- involvement of technical teams to search and retrieve the data;
- guidance on whether any exemptions apply to the disclosure of certain types of information (e.g. information subject to legal professional privilege or management information);
- guidance on how to determine whether or not it is reasonable to disclose third-party personal data as part of the request;
- rules around engaging external support or legal counsel if the request cannot be complied with using the in-house resources;
- guidance on circumstances where the organisation can reasonably request to extend the time to respond by a further two months (e.g. if the request is complex or if the organisation has received a number of requests from the individual);
- template response letters to data subjects;
- methods by which the information can be provided to the data subject (e.g. if electronic, guidance on how to share the information securely);
- post-response wash-up mechanisms to incorporate any new leanings in future responses or updates to procedures;
- escalation procedures, if the data subject is not happy with the response.

## Reflecting operational realities

Irrespective of the nature, number and content of data protection policies and procedures, it is important that they reflect the operational realities of the organisation and what happens on the ground. Organisations that have comprehensive procedures that link to a set of overarching policies are likely to be better placed to demonstrate compliance with their data protection obligations in practice compared to those organisations that only have high-level information or off the shelf documents. In addition to having these policies and procedures in place, it is equally important to demonstrate that they are implemented and adhered to. According to the ICO, this could include 'awareness raising, training, monitoring and audits'.

Although data protection policies are aimed at internal activities, they can be subject to disclosure to supervisory authorities during investigations into an organisation's practices. In the context of regulator scrutiny, policies are one of the first layers of defence for an organisation, acting as its 'paper shield' and initial evidence of its compliance with the law. When looking at the history of enforcement actions taken by the ICO, it is common for the ICO's decisions to not only reference the provisions of the GDPR or UK

DPA that have been violated, but to also consider the relevant data protection policies adopted by the organisation. The existence of a relevant policy and/or procedure, the comprehensiveness of it and the extent to which an organisation followed it in practice can act as either an aggravating or mitigating factor when the ICO starts to determine the severity of the enforcement action, such as the level of fine issued.

## RECORDS OF PROCESSING ACTIVITIES – A BASELINE FOR ACCOUNTABILITY

Article 30 of the GDPR introduces the requirement for controllers and processors to maintain records of processing activities that are under their responsibility. A.30.4 requires organisations to 'make the record available to the supervisory authority on request'. Recital 82 also states that organisations need to 'cooperate with the supervisory authority' in this regard and that making such records available 'might serve for monitoring those processing operations'.

Recital 82 further states that ROPAs should be in place 'in order to demonstrate compliance with' the GDPR. The requirement to maintain ROPAs provides a starting point for any organisation looking to build a strong accountability framework. It requires them to really understand the personal data that they hold and process and to maintain up-to-date records throughout the data life cycle.

Not all organisations have to maintain ROPAs as a mandatory requirement. Article 30.5 makes it clear that organisations 'employing fewer than 250 persons' are exempt unless the processing it carries out 'is likely to result in a risk to the rights and freedoms of data subjects'; 'is not occasional'; or includes 'special categories of data'.[4]

### Minimum content of ROPAs

Article 30.1 sets out the minimum content requirements of ROPAs maintained by controllers. Article 30.2 does the same for processors and, where applicable, the processor's representative. Table 10.1 provides a summary of these requirements.

**Table 10.1 Minimum contents of ROPAs**

| Topic | Controllers – minimum ROPAs content Article 30(1) | Processors – minimum ROPAs content Article 30(2) |
|---|---|---|
| Contact details | Name and contact details of the controller and where applicable:<br>• any joint controllers;<br>• the controller's representative; and/or<br>• the data protection officer. | Name and contact details of the processor or processors and of each controller on behalf of which the processor is acting and where applicable:<br>• the controller's or the processor's representative; and/or<br>• the data protection officer. |

*(Continued)*

---
4 Including personal data relating to criminal convictions and offences referred to in Article 10.

**Table 10.1 (Continued)**

| Topic | Controllers – minimum ROPAs content Article 30(1) | Processors – minimum ROPAs content Article 30(2) |
|---|---|---|
| Categories of processing | No mandatory requirement. | The categories of processing carried out on behalf of each controller. |
| Purpose | Purposes of the processing. | No mandatory requirement. |
| Data subjects | A description of the categories of data subjects and of the categories of personal data. | No mandatory requirement. |
| Recipients | The categories of recipients to whom the personal data have been or will be disclosed including recipients in third countries. | No mandatory requirement. |
| Retention | Where possible, the envisaged time limits for erasure of the different categories of data. | No mandatory requirement. |
| Transfers | Where applicable, transfers of personal data to a third country, including the identification of that third country and, where necessary, the documentation of suitable safeguards where a derogation is relied on under Article 49(1) of the GDPR. | |
| Security | Where possible, a general description of the technical and organisational security measures under Article 32(1) of the GDPR. | |

In addition to the mandatory information above, organisations typically record further information including:

- the legal basis for processing linked to each of the purposes of processing;
- whether the personal data are processed in the capacity of a controller, processor or joint controller;
- the data subject rights available to individuals taking into account the legal basis and purposes of processing;
- the systems within which personal data are processed and the business units that make use of such systems;
- the source of the personal data (i.e. direct collection from individuals or from a third-party source);
- the relevant retention periods for the personal data stored in specific systems.

**Wider benefits of ROPAs**

If done properly, ROPAs aid compliance with other key requirements within the GDPR. For example, knowing in which systems personal data are held can help responses to data subject access requests. Understanding the data processing landscape and the purposes for which processing is done can help with the development of comprehensive data protection policies and public-facing privacy notices.

The ICO's guidance on 'Accountability and Governance' points out that having comprehensive and well maintained ROPAs is 'not just about legal compliance with the GDPR'. It helps to 'improve data governance' by giving 'assurance as to data quality, completeness and provenance'. It can also 'increase businesses efficiency' to help 'develop more effective and streamlined business processes'.

## DATA PROTECTION BY DESIGN AND DEFAULT

The controller's duty to achieve the outcomes of the GDPR is set by Articles 5 and 24, which both require the outcomes to be provable. The questions that naturally arise are these:

- At what point in time do the outcomes need to be achieved?
- At what level of quality do the outcomes need to be achieved?

These points are addressed by Article 25.

### A formula for compliance

Article 24 sets a general formula for compliance and Article 25 expands upon this, by setting rules for Data Protection by Design and Default, which is sometimes called 'Privacy by Design'.

Article 25.1 contains a 'state-of-the-art' component for judging the appropriateness of the measures taken for compliance. This has a far-reaching effect, as it requires the controller to keep abreast of developments for data protection, meaning that compliance cannot be viewed as a moment-in-time issue. The result is that the controller will need to implement measures that deliver continuous improvement, to keep up to date with the state of the art. The need for continuous improvement is reinforced by the focus on the full continuum of processing within these words of Article 25.1: 'the controller shall, both at the time of the determination of the means for processing and at the time of the processing itself, implement appropriate technical and organisational measures ...'

Another component for judging the appropriateness of the measures for compliance is a 'cost of implementation' provision. This might provide the controller with an argument that a data protection measure that forms part of the state of the art would not be appropriate for implementation on the grounds of cost compared to risk, but the provision is more likely to be about budgeting and cost recording, so that the financial and resource costs of DPbDD are not overlooked in planning. The GDPR does not address head-on the issue of a controller's impecuniosity, but it is unlikely that a controller will be excused an appropriate measure simply because they cannot afford it, when a better solution would be to avoid undertaking risky processing. This view is supported by the

European Data Protection Board's guidelines[5] ('the DPbDD guidelines'), which say that 'incapacity to bear the costs is no excuse for non-compliance with the GDPR'. At the same time, the guidelines also state that 'effective implementation of principles must not necessarily lead to higher costs'. In other words, 'spending more on technology does not necessarily lead to more effective implementation of the principles' and 'in some instances, there may be simple low-cost solutions that can be just as or even more effective than their costly counterparts'.

## Design

At the heart of the requirement for DPbDD is the need for there to be a 'design' to implement the data protection principles. The GDPR does not give a precise definition of the meaning of 'design'. However, some insight can be derived when considering:

- the ordinary meaning of the word 'design';
- the required outcomes as set out in Article 25 (i.e. that the design must result in the implementation of the principles 'in an effective manner' with the integration of 'the necessary safeguards into the processing');
- the naming of 'pseudonymisation' as an example of the type of measure that may be required.

Therefore, it is likely that the process of design should involve a detailed planning exercise that will incorporate at a bare minimum:

- a complete understanding of the nature of the personal data that are to be processed;
- the purpose of the processing;
- the outcomes to be achieved;
- the transformation that needs to occur throughout the controller's organisation and within its supplier base to achieve the objectives of DPbDD.

The amount of design work that needs to be done will vary from case to case, but the DPbDD guidelines reinforce the need for detailed planning by implication. This is demonstrated by the approach that they take to the 'default' concept within DPbDD and through the illustrations given on best practice for transparency, which address matters such as semantics, multichannel communications and universal design.

## Default

Also at the heart of the requirement for DPbDD is the need for data protection to be delivered by 'default'. The two central requirements run together, meaning that the design should deliver the necessary data protection outcomes by default. In other words, the design should incorporate default settings that protect and preserve privacy. The DPbDD guidelines provide helpful advice around the meaning of default in the context

---

[5] Guidelines 4/2019 on Article 25 Data Protection by Design and by Default Version 2.0, adopted on 20 October 2020.

of technology and software settings by saying, in reference to computer science, that default 'refers to the pre-existing or preselected value of a configurable setting that is assigned to a software application, computer program or device. Such settings are also called "presets" or "factory presets", especially for electronic devices.' The duty to deliver data protection by default is not limited to technology matters, however; it applies to all measures for data protection.

## DATA PROTECTION IMPACT ASSESSMENT

DPbDD addresses the questions relating to when and to what level of quality the GDPR outcomes need to be achieved. Connected to this are the questions around how such outcomes need to be identified and what steps need to be taken in order to achieve those outcomes. These points are addressed by Article 35.

Article 35.1 sets the requirement for the controller to carry out a data protection impact assessment 'where a type of processing ... is likely to result in a high risk to the rights and freedoms' of individuals. Recital 84 says that a DPIA is a mechanism to 'enhance compliance with the Regulation' by evaluating 'the origin, nature, particularity and severity of that risk'. The conclusions of a DPIA are to then be considered when determining the appropriate measures to put in place to demonstrate that the processing activity complies with the GDPR.

Putting these concepts together, the EDPB guidelines on data protection impact assessments[6] ('the DPIA guidelines') define a DPIA as 'a process designed to describe the processing, assess its necessity and proportionality and help manage the risks to the rights and freedoms' of individuals resulting from such processing by 'assessing them and determining measures to address them'. A DPIA is therefore 'a process for building and demonstrating compliance' and is one of the most important tools for accountability introduced by the GDPR.

A DPIA is also valuable in many ways from a practical perspective. For example, it can serve to evidence the organisation's decision-making process. It brings a degree of rigour to those decisions and can prove invaluable in justifying why certain actions or measures were, or were not, taken. This can prove useful should a regulatory investigation take place into high-risk processing activities undertaken by the organisation. A DPIA can also help an organisation with contractual negotiations with third parties who are involved in the processing of personal data that is subject to the DPIA. It can help the organisation to better understand and allocate appropriate roles and responsibilities between the parties and to ensure that this is accurately reflected in the contract.

### Likely to result in a high risk

A DPIA is only mandatory when a processing activity is 'likely to result in a high risk' to individuals, which, according to the DPIA guidelines, is 'in line with the risk-based approach embodied by the GDPR'.

---

[6] Guidelines on Data Protection Impact Assessment (DPIA) and determining whether processing is 'likely to result in a high risk' for the purposes of Regulation 2016/679, WP 248 rev.01

A.35.3 sets out a non-exhaustive list of circumstances where a processing activity is 'likely to result in a high risk'. This includes activities that involve:

- the 'systematic and extensive evaluation of personal aspects' relating to individuals based on automated processing (including profiling) on which decisions are based that 'produce legal effects' concerning the individual or that have a similarly significant effect;
- the processing on a 'large scale of special categories of data';[7]
- the 'systematic monitoring of a publicly accessible area on a large scale'.

To bring some of these circumstances to life and to provide organisations with a more concrete set of processing activities that require a DPIA, the DPIA guidelines set out nine criteria that should be considered when the duty to undertake a DPIA is being addressed:

- evaluation or scoring;
- automated decision making with legal or similar significant effect;
- systematic monitoring;
- sensitive data or data of a highly personal nature;
- data processed on a large scale;
- matching or combining data sets;
- data concerning vulnerable data subjects;
- innovative use or applying new technological or organisational solutions;
- refusal of rights or use of a service or contract.

According to the DPIA guidelines, in most cases 'a data controller can consider that a processing activity meeting two criteria would require a DPIA to be carried out'. Therefore, the more criteria that a specific processing activity meets, 'the more likely it is to present a high risk to individuals and therefore require a DPIA'. Nevertheless, the EDPB did not exclude the possibility of the need to carry out a DPIA if only one of the criteria are met. It follows for accountability purposes that controllers should document their assessment and decisions when determining whether a DPIA is required.

## Minimum features of a DPIA

The minimum features of a DPIA are set out under Article 35.7 and Recitals 84 and 90. They say that a DPIA should contain:

- a description of the envisaged processing operations and the purposes of processing;
- an assessment of the necessity and proportionality of the processing;

---

[7] Including personal data relating to criminal convictions and offences referred to in Article 10.

- an assessment of the risks to the rights and freedoms of data subjects;
- the measures envisaged to (1) address the risks, and (2) demonstrate compliance with the GDPR.

According to the DPIA guidelines, the 'GDPR provides data controllers with flexibility to determine the precise structure and form of the DPIA in order to allow for this to fit with existing working practices'. However, the EDPB guidelines highlight that 'whatever its form, a DPIA must be a genuine assessment of risks, allowing controllers to take measures to address them'.

## DATA PROTECTION OFFICER

The requirement to appoint a data protection officer is one of the most instrumental compliance mechanisms introduced by the GDPR. According to the EDPB Guidelines on Data Protection Officers[8] ('the DPO guidelines') the 'GDPR recognises the DPO as a key player in the new data governance system' who 'will be at the heart of this new legal framework for many organisations, facilitating compliance with the provisions of the GDPR'.

The GDPR fiercely protects the position of a DPO within an organisation and provides an extensive set of minimum tasks as part of the job specification. It ensures that the DPO plays a critical role with respect to data protection both internally, within an organisation's management structures, and externally, as the organisation's main point of contact for supervisory authorities and data subjects. The DPO also must be 'a person with expert knowledge of data protection law and practices'[9] who, at a minimum, has the professional ability to fulfil the tasks of a DPO as set out under the GDPR.

Their role is limited to facilitating compliance, however, through advisory and reviewing functions. Achieving compliance in an operational sense remains the responsibility of controllers (and in certain circumstances, processors). The legislative intent of the DPO role is nevertheless clear: by embedding an expert advisor and reviewer, with point of contact functions for regulators and data subjects, the scope for non-compliance (including a lack of transparency after non-compliance) is lessened, to the ultimate benefit of data subjects.

### Requirement to appoint a DPO

Not all organisations are obliged to appoint a DPO. Article 37.1 requires controllers and processors to appoint a DPO if their 'core activities' consist of processing operations that 'require regular and systematic monitoring of data subjects on a large scale' or where they consist of 'processing on a large scale of special categories of data'.[10] In addition, all public authorities and bodies[11] are required to appoint a DPO irrespective of

---

8 Guidelines on Data Protection Officers ('DPOs'), WP 243 rev.01.

9 Article 37.5 of the GDPR.

10 Including personal data relating to criminal convictions and offences referred to in Article 10.

11 Except for courts acting in their judicial capacity.

the nature of data subject monitoring activities, scale of data processing or categories of personal data.

In practice, the following terms are frequently analysed and applied within organisations that are unsure as to whether a mandatory DPO is required:

- Regular and systematic monitoring of data subjects. This can include all forms of tracking and profiling online and offline, including for the purposes of behavioural advertising. The DPO guidelines interpret 'regular' as meaning one or more of the following: ongoing or occurring at particular intervals for a particular period; recurring or repeated at fixed times; constantly or periodically taking place. As for the term 'systematic' the guidelines interpret it as one or more of the following: occurring according to a system; prearranged, organised or methodical; taking place as part of a general plan for data collection; carried out as part of a strategy.
- Core activities. Recital 97 states that the core activities of a controller relate to 'primary activities and do not relate to the processing of personal data as ancillary activities'. As such, the DPO guidelines consider 'core activities' to be 'the key operations necessary to achieve the controller's or processor's goals'. The guidelines also acknowledge that a core activity could include processing personal data that is an 'inextricable part' of an organisation's processing activity. For example, a hospital's processing of patient health records may not necessarily constitute a core activity of the hospital, but it is an inextricable part of its services and therefore the processing of such data would be considered as a core activity.[12]
- Large scale. There is no exact figure that constitutes 'large scale'. However, the DPO guidelines provide several factors that can help to make this determination such as the number of data subjects concerned; the volume of data and/or the range of different data items being processed; the duration, or permanence, of the data processing activity; and the geographical extent of the processing activity.

Further, the DPO guidelines state that 'unless it is obvious that an organisation is not required to designate a DPO', organisations should 'document the internal analysis carried out to determine whether or not a DPO is to be appointed, in order to be able to demonstrate that the relevant factors have been taken into account properly'. Importantly, the EDPB goes on to state that 'this analysis is part of the documentation under the accountability principle'.

Controller and processors can elect to appoint DPOs, if a mandatory duty to do so does not exist. If a DPO is appointed on a voluntary basis, the GDPR requirements with respect to the designation, position and tasks of a DPO[13] will apply as if the appointment had been mandatory.

## Tasks of the DPO

The tasks of the DPO are set out in A.39.1:

---

[12] Note that certain hospitals are likely to be public authorities. If so, there would be an automatic requirement to appoint a DPO due to the status of the hospital as a public authority.

[13] Articles 37–39.

- inform and advise the organisation of their GDPR obligations;
- monitor compliance with the GDPR and with data protection policies of the organisation;
- provide advice on data protection impact assessments;
- cooperate with the supervisory authority;
- act as the contact point for the supervisory authority.

When performing these tasks, the DPO must 'have due regard to the risk associated with processing operations taking into account the nature, scope, context and purposes of processing' (Article 39.2). According to the DPO guidelines this requires DPOs to 'prioritise their activities and focus their efforts on issues that present higher data protection risks' as part of a 'selective and pragmatic approach' that will help to devote time and resources to areas that matter the most. This is in line with the GDPR's risk-based approach to compliance.

The GDPR requires organisations to appoint a DPO 'on the basis of [the DPO's] professional qualities and, in particular, expert knowledge of data protection law and practices and the ability to fulfil the tasks under Article 39'.[14] The GDPR does not describe the professional qualities or level of expert knowledge required, but the DPO guidelines provide additional context, saying that:

- The level of the DPO's expertise must be 'commensurate with the sensitivity, complexity and amount of data an organisation processes'.
- The DPO must have 'expertise in national and European data protection laws and practices and an in-depth understanding of the GDPR'.
- A DPO with 'knowledge of the business sector' and of the organisation including its processing operations is useful.
- The DPO should have personal qualities that include, for example, 'integrity and high professional ethics'.

There is no specific requirement for the DPO to be legally qualified or to have any other type of qualification or certification, but they can serve as evidence that the appointee has a certain level of expertise.

## Position of the DPO

Article 38 describes more the position of the DPO, covering the protections that the office is afforded, their place within the data protection operating model and resources:

- The DPO must be involved properly, and in a timely manner, in all issues that relate to data protection.
- The DPO must be provided with the necessary resources to carry out their tasks, have access to personal data and processing operations, and must maintain their expert knowledge.

---

**14** Article 37(5).

- The DPO must not receive any instructions on the exercise of their tasks.
- The DPO must not be dismissed or penalised for performing their tasks.
- The DPO must report directly to the highest management level of the organisation.
- Data subjects may contact the DPO regarding all issues relating to data protection and exercise of their data subject rights.
- The DPO must be bound by secrecy or confidentiality regarding the performance of their tasks.
- The DPO may fulfil other tasks and duties. The organisation shall ensure that such tasks and duties do not result in a conflict of interest.

The DPO guidelines provide additional guidance on each of these elements, some of which are discussed below.

### *Involvement and reporting*
According to the DPO guidelines, it is 'crucial that the DPO ... is involved from the earliest stage possible in all issues relating to data protection'. Doing so is likely to put the organisation in a far better position to comply with its GDPR obligations and to help facilitate DPbDD. The guidelines provide examples of ways in which this requirement can be met:

- ensuring that the DPO is regularly invited to attend and participate at relevant senior and middle management meetings;
- providing the DPO with all relevant information in a timely manner so that the DPO can provide adequate advice;
- always giving due weight to the opinion of the DPO and where there are any disagreements, documenting reasons for not following the DPO's advice;
- ensuring that the DPO is promptly consulted in the event of a personal data breach.

Connected to the concept of the involvement is ensuring that the DPO has a strong voice within the organisation by reporting directly to the highest management level (e.g. the board of directors). This ensures that senior individuals are 'aware of the DPO's advice and recommendations as part of the DPO's mission to inform and advise' the organisation on issues that have a data protection impact. Another example of direct reporting provided by the guidelines is 'the drafting of an annual report of the DPO's activities provided to the highest management level'.

### *Dismissal*
The DPO guidelines note that the requirement to ensure that the DPO is not dismissed or penalised by the organisation for performing their tasks 'strengthens the autonomy of DPOs and helps ensure that they act independently and enjoy sufficient protection in performing their data protection tasks'. With respect to the potential penalties that could be imposed by an organisation on the DPO, the guidelines highlight the following points:

- Penalties are only prohibited under the GDPR if they are imposed as a result of the DPO carrying out their duties as a DPO.

- Penalties may take a variety of forms and may be direct or indirect. They could consist, for example, of absence or delay of promotion, prevention from career advancement or denial of benefits that other employees receive.
- It is not necessary that these penalties be actually carried out. A mere threat is sufficient as long as they are used to penalise the DPO on grounds related to their DPO activities.

*Instructions*
The requirement that the DPO should not receive any instructions regarding the exercise of their tasks is linked to the idea of the 'independence' of the DPO. Recital 97 of the GDPR makes it clear that the DPO 'should be in a position to perform their duties and tasks in an independent manner', irrespective of whether or not the DPO is an employee of the organisation.

According to the DPO guidelines, 'this means that, in fulfilling their tasks under Article 39, DPOs must not be instructed on how to deal with a matter, for example, what result should be achieved, how to investigate a complaint or whether to consult the supervisory authority … they must not be instructed to take a certain view of an issue related to data protection law, for example, a particular interpretation of the law'.

However, DPOs do not have decision-making powers that extend beyond the tasks they are required to fulfil under Article 39 of the GDPR. As explained earlier, the organisation itself is responsible for complying with the GDPR and demonstrating the same. DPOs can make their opinion on a matter clear (including reporting the same to the highest management level) but it is the organisation that ultimately has the decision-making power as to whether or not to follow that opinion.

## CONTRACTS

The obligation to directly comply with the provisions of the GDPR weighs heavily on the controller. There are also a number of GDPR provisions that apply directly to the processor, with examples including:

- maintaining records of processing activities (A.30.2);
- implementing appropriate security measures (A.32.1);
- notifying the controller without undue delay if it suffers a personal data breach (A.33.2);
- designating a data protection officer where necessary (A.37.1).

### Article 28 processor contracts

The full scope of a processor's responsibilities become apparent through its mandatory contractual obligations. Article 28.3 requires the processing of personal data on behalf of a controller to be governed by a contract that is binding on the processor. This contract must set out the subject matter and duration of the processing; the nature and purpose of the processing; the types of personal data and categories of data subjects; and the obligations and rights of the controller.

The contract must also, at a minimum, require the processor to comply with the obligations set out in Table 10.2.

**Table 10.2 Contractual obligations and requirements for processors**

| Topic | Processor's minimum Article 28(3) contractual obligations |
|---|---|
| Instructions | Process personal data only on documented instructions from the controller (including with regard to transfers of personal data to a third country). |
| Confidentiality | Ensure that individuals authorised to process the personal data have committed themselves to confidentiality or are under an appropriate statutory obligation of confidentiality. |
| Security | Take all measures required pursuant to Article 32 (security of processing). |
| Sub-processor appointment and contracting | Ensure that another processor (i.e. 'sub-processor') is not engaged to carry out specific processing activities on behalf of the controller without prior specific or general written authorisation of the controller. Where authorisation is provided, a processor must ensure that a contract is in place with the sub-processor that contains the same data protection obligations agreed to between the processor and controller. |
| Data subject rights support | Assist the controller with its obligations to respond to requests for exercising the data subject rights in Chapter III of the GDPR. |
| Support with controller's GDPR obligations | Assist the controller with its GDPR obligations in relation to security of processing (Article 32); personal data breach notification to the supervisory authority and communication of the same to data subjects (Article 33 and 34); data protection impact assessments (Article 35); and prior consultation with the regulator with respect to high-risk data protection impact assessments (Article 36). |
| Return or delete data | Ensure that at the end of the provision of services relating to the processing and at the choice of the controller, all personal data are either deleted or returned to the controller. |
| Audits | Make available all information necessary to demonstrate compliance with the obligations under Article 28 and allow for and contribute to audits, including inspections, conducted by the controller or another auditor mandated by the controller. The processor must also immediately inform the controller if, in its opinion, an instruction infringes the GDPR. |

In addition to the minimal contractual obligations, it is common for such contracts to also include liability and indemnity provisions. For example, the controller may want to ensure that it will be indemnified from and against all losses suffered by the controller arising from action taken by a supervisory authority or data subject due to a breach by the processor of its contractual obligations. Given the high fining powers that supervisory authorities have under the GDPR and the fact that there are no financial limits to the compensation that data subjects may be awarded by the courts, it is not surprising that these contractual provisions are fiercely negotiated between the parties.

Often, processors will agree to an indemnity in favour of the controller provided that it is subject to a liability cap. Depending on the nature and context of the processing activity, including the personal data types involved, the processor could be in a reasonable position to argue that its liability to the controller should not exceed a certain value.

In addition, Article 28.4 makes it clear that where the processor engages a sub-processor for carrying out specific processing activities on behalf of the controller, and that sub-processor fails to fulfil its data protection obligations, it is the processor that will 'remain fully liable to the controller for the performance of' the sub-processor's obligations.

Article 82 builds in a mechanism for apportioning liability for damage caused by the processing of personal data. A.82.5 says that where a controller or processor has paid full compensation for the damage suffered, that controller or processor 'shall be entitled to claim back from the other controllers or processors involved in the same processing that part of the compensation corresponding to their part of responsibility for the damage'.

### *Processor due diligence*
A signed agreement complying with A.28.3 is not sufficient on its own to achieve the outcomes envisaged by the GDPR. Additionally, pursuant to Article 28.1, the controller must 'use only processors providing sufficient guarantees to implement appropriate technical and organisational measures in such a manner that processing will meet the requirements of' the GDPR including ensuring the protection of the rights of individuals. Read together with the processor's Article 28.3.(h) contractual obligation regarding audits, controllers must carry out appropriate due diligence to satisfy themselves that the prospective processor is able to meet both its legal and contractual obligations in an operational sense. This prevents the Article 28.3 contract from being merely a 'tick-box' exercise.

### **Joint controller contracts**

Article 26 governs the arrangements that need to be in place when two or more controllers jointly determine the purposes and means of processing. For example, a bank could partner with a third-party company to offer loyalty services to the bank's cardholders through the third-party company's platform and customer registration system. In this scenario, A.26 requires that both the bank and the third party should 'determine their respective responsibilities for compliance with the obligations' under the GDPR. These responsibilities include determining which party is responsible for obligations such as responding to data subject rights requests (and the level of support required from the other party), and providing fair and transparent processing information through a privacy notice.

Article 26.1 states that 'the essence of the arrangement [between the controllers] shall be made available to the data subject'. There is no explicit requirement to have a contract in place to govern these responsibilities, but, in practice, it is common for joint controllers to enter into an agreement that makes the division of responsibilities clear from a data protection perspective. Additional obligations would also be addressed, such as data breach notification, security of processing, data retention and appointment of third-party sub-processors, where relevant. Such contractual arrangements allow each organisation to hold the other to account for their respective responsibilities and to rely on contractual remedies where necessary for any breaches of such responsibilities. Irrespective of whether a contract governs the joint controller relationship, organisations must document and agree their respective responsibilities.

### *Contracts between two independent and separate controllers*

Where organisations are sharing personal data in their capacity as independent and separate controllers, the GDPR does not specifically require written agreements or any non-contractual arrangements to be put in place to allocate responsibility.

However, supervisory authorities will consider having a data sharing agreement as good practice. For example, in the UK, the ICO has issued a data sharing code of practice that recommends having a data sharing agreement in place where independent controllers share personal data with each other. According to the code, data sharing agreements can be helpful in the following ways:

- setting out the purpose of the data sharing;
- covering what happens to the data at each stage;
- setting standards (e.g. technical and organisational measures to safeguard personal data);
- helping the parties to be clear about their roles and responsibilities;
- helping to demonstrate that each of the controllers are meeting their respective accountability obligations under data protection law.

## SUMMARY

In conclusion, this chapter gives readers a better understanding of:

- the range of compliance mechanisms within the GDPR that are intended to support controllers and processors to achieve the required operational outcomes of the law;
- the key requirements of these compliance mechanisms and what they require organisations to do;
- how these compliance mechanisms are intended to help controllers and processors with operational and legal risk management;
- the situations where these compliance mechanisms do, or do not, apply.

# 11 PROGRAMMATIC APPROACHES FOR DELIVERING DATA PROTECTION BY DESIGN AND DEFAULT

## James Drury-Smith

This chapter provides an overview of the concepts of Data Protection by Design and Default, identifying how their requirements can be operationalised through business transformation programmes and projects and the essential elements of these works. This chapter also provides insights into the importance of establishing data protection governance frameworks and some of the considerations that arise.

### THE ORIGINS OF DATA PROTECTION BY DESIGN AND DEFAULT

The concept of Privacy by Design was developed in the 1990s in Canada, spearheaded by Ann Cavoukian during her time as the Information and Privacy Commissioner of Ontario. It consists of seven foundational principles that focus on the need for proactive measures to embed privacy into the design of IT systems and business practices. Formal international recognition for the concept came in 2010, when the 32nd International Conference of Data Protection and Privacy Commissioners adopted the Resolution on Privacy by Design. The resolution invited the data protection authorities to promote Privacy by Design and foster its incorporation into policy development and legislation within their respective jurisdictions.

The draft GDPR, published in 2012, was the first piece of major international legislation to build on the Privacy by Design idea. However, recognising the more expansive focus of the GDPR, which is concerned with all fundamental rights and freedoms, not just the right to privacy, the legislation is concerned with Data Protection by Design and Default, the rules for which are contained in Article 25. Many people use the phrase Privacy by Design as a substitute for the A.25 concept, however.

### DATA PROTECTION BY DESIGN AND DEFAULT IN THE GDPR

As its name makes clear, the concept of Data Protection by Design and Default consists of two distinct elements.

#### The design element

Article 25.1 of the GDPR sets out the 'design' element of DPbDD:

> The controller shall, both at the time of the determination of the means for processing and at the time of the processing itself, implement appropriate technical

and organisational measures, such as pseudonymisation, which are designed to implement data-protection principles, such as data minimisation, in an effective manner and to integrate the necessary safeguards into the processing in order to meet the requirements of this Regulation and protect the rights of data subjects.

Article 25.1 contains two requirements. The first relates to the temporal element of the design requirement. The second relates to the measures that must be adopted to achieve the design element. The temporal element says that the design requirement applies both before processing starts and during processing, which covers all of the data processing life cycle. In other words, DPbDD requires 'end-to-end' data protection. The measures element is a broad requirement to adopt all necessary measures deemed appropriate to achieve the outcomes required by the GDPR, which means across all layers of the organisation (i.e. the people layer, the paper layer and the technology and data layer).

## The default element

The 'default' element of DPbDD is contained in A.25.2:

> The controller shall implement appropriate technical and organisational measures for ensuring that, by default, only personal data which are necessary for each specific purpose of the processing are processed. That obligation applies to the amount of personal data collected, the extent of their processing, the period of their storage and their accessibility. In particular, such measures shall ensure that by default personal data are not made accessible without the individual's intervention to an indefinite number of natural persons.

A.25.2 has two effects. First, it ties together the second, third, fifth and sixth data protection principles within an overarching minimisation requirement. Secondly and most importantly, it creates legal and operational presumptions about the starting point for data protection, which is that minimisation is the default setting.

For many organisations, significant technical and operational change is required to establish a DPbDD approach within their daily operations. A process of business transformation, or what could be called 'data transformation', is therefore often required for these purposes.

## THE NEED FOR DPBDD – COMPELLING EVENTS THAT TRIGGER DATA PROTECTION TRANSFORMATION

Organisations that have managed to successfully embed DPbDD throughout their approach to data protection will have implemented a data protection programme for this purpose. This does not happen spontaneously. Usually it requires a compelling event for the wheels of transformation to start turning. Compelling events will typically fall within the categories described in Table 11.1.

**Table 11.1 Compelling events that trigger data protection transformation**

| Compelling events | Description of compelling event |
| --- | --- |
| Legislative change | • An obvious example was the adoption of the GDPR in 2016, which required changes to data protection controls to be implemented before the law came into effect in May 2018.<br>• It can also include laws and guidance that are not focused on data protection, but which affect the processing of personal data nonetheless. For example, the Second Payment Services Directive requires banks to make changes to their data controls to meet the directive's requirements in relation to open banking. |
| Case law | • The need to make changes to technical and organisational measures can be driven by decisions of the courts (both nationally and supranationally).<br>• For example, the CJEU decision in *Schrems II* (2020) has caused organisations to commence new data protection programmes and projects to manage international transfers of personal data. |
| Operational failure | • Changes to technical and organisational measures may need to be made after the exposure of weaknesses or failings in an organisation's data protection controls.<br>• For example, a process failure that allows a marketing campaign to include email addresses that are on an organisation's suppressions list will need a transformation exercise to remedy the problem.<br>• A security breach that causes a personal data protection breach will have to be remediated following detection and the establishment of root cause. |
| Regulatory action | • Changes to technical and organisational measures might be required because of regulatory action, for example after the imposition of an Enforcement Notice.<br>• The UK Information Commissioner's investigation into the use of data analytics in political campaigns has far-reaching implications for data brokers, political parties and online platforms in relation to the sale and use of personal data. This has triggered many requirements for data transformation. |
| Data subject and privacy advocate scrutiny | • Cases such as *Google Spain SL, Google Inc. v. Agencia Española de Protección de Datos, Mario Costeja González* (2014) (about the right to be forgotten) illustrate how a data subject can force organisations to develop new procedures in relation to their data processing activities, supported by the legal process.<br>• Privacy activists can draw attention to significant issues of concern. Due to their reach, press publicity, network effects and their mastery of legal processes, their actions can trigger a 'domino effect' of data transformation programmes and projects. |

*(Continued)*

**Table 11.1 (Continued)**

| Compelling events | Description of compelling event |
|---|---|
| Threat actors | • This relates to changes to technical and organisational measures that are required to address criminal threats or state sponsored threats to personal data.<br><br>• For example, this could include operational changes required to counter risks from phishing emails from criminal gangs attempting to gain an individual's credentials for fraudulent activity, or the hacking of computer systems by state backed groups to gain information on persons of interest. |
| Technological change | • The adoption of new technologies provides a common reason for organisations to start new projects relating to the processing of personal data, which in turn triggers a data protection programme or project to aid compliance. |
| Organisational change | • A structural change within an organisation, such as the sale of a business or asset, or the integration of an acquired business or asset, or the internal restructuring of a business, may have data protection implications, thereby requiring a data transformation exercise. |
| Societal requirements | • As the COVID-19 pandemic has shown, there can be upheavals in society that have profound data protection impacts, which in turn require new approaches to data processing to be adopted.<br><br>• Other examples include equal opportunity monitoring, gender pay gap reporting or the use of facial recognition technologies to prevent crime. |
| Environmental conditions | • It is likely to become increasingly apparent that environmental conditions will have data protection impacts.<br><br>• For example, locating data centres to places with cooler climates to reduce energy expended on cooling servers, or relocations to maintain business continuity and access to personal data following a climate disaster, will inevitably result in accompanying data protection compliance programmes. |

## EMBARKING UPON A TRANSFORMATION JOURNEY TO ACHIEVE DPBDD

An organisation's transformation journey should begin with an understanding of where it will end. An organisation could ask itself:

- When we have finished embedding our DPbDD approach within the business, what outcomes will we want to have achieved?
- What is our vision for data protection within the business at the end of this journey?

## A vision statement – laying the foundations for DPbDD

The answer to these questions is often captured in a 'vision statement', which sets an executive mandate for what the organisation wishes to achieve over the long term. This in turn guides the organisation when making decisions and setting priorities for activities.

An organisation's vision for data protection does not have to consist of a singular aim. It might have multiple objectives. However, a vision should not simply repeat the legal requirements of the GDPR or other relevant laws. For example, a vision statement would not be that the organisation intends to provide privacy notices when it collects personal data or that it will respect a data subject's right to object to direct marketing. A vision for data protection should be greater than the sum of its regulatory parts and should take account of the organisation's overarching business purpose.

Example vision statements for data protection could include:

- To create opportunity through the data we hold whilst maintaining the trust of our customers.
- To be the best at communicating with our customers and colleagues.
- To understand our users and anticipate their needs.

### *Avoiding purposeless activity*
Without a vision, compliance can often become a box-ticking exercise, made up of a list of the GDPR's requirements that the organisation works its way through. This approach does not appropriately target risks or strategic priorities and can often result in an organisation undertaking purposeless activity.

Take the example of 'data mapping'. Despite the contents of Article 30 on records of processing activities, nowhere in the GDPR is there an explicit requirement to create detailed maps of systems containing personal data or how those systems share personal data between themselves. However, many GDPR programmes get stuck in a quagmire of data mapping. This can cause unnecessary financial expense and be at the expense of the organisation achieving GDPR compliance in more strategically important and high-risk areas of data processing.

This is not to say that data mapping has no place and no utility in an organisation's approach to data protection, but it should illustrate that without setting a vision for data protection at the start of a transformation journey, it is easy to lose sight of what is actually important to the business, thereby causing a failure to prioritise activities towards achieving meaningful business outcomes.

Vision setting requires an organisation to understand its special characteristics and those of potential challengers and scrutineers. Vision setting must involve consideration of those features to ensure that it reflects the realities of the operational environment and mitigates against the risk of data processing activities being challenged.

## Difference between data protection programmes and projects

There are numerous views on what distinguishes a data protection programme from a project and in practice organisations will make their own internal distinctions. What is considered a programme in one organisation may not deliver sufficient change, or be of sufficient complexity, to be a programme in another. However, to help understand the roles that programmes and projects play in data protection transformation, the descriptions below are useful reference points.

### *Programmes*
A programme is a group of related projects that have been brought together to ensure they are coordinated and controlled to achieve efficiencies and outcomes that would not be available if managed separately. A programme typically aims to deliver strategic objectives for an organisation through a process of business transformation. Although the organisational structures put in place for the management of a programme may be temporary, they have more permanence than those established for a project. A programme may take years to reach its conclusion.

### *Projects*
A project will usually deliver smaller levels of change to an organisation than an overarching programme. Its focus will typically be on providing certain deliverables or outputs, on time, to budget and meeting the specification for those outputs as set at the start the project. A project will also usually run for a defined period of time, in contrast to a programme that may run indefinitely until its objectives are achieved.

### *GDPR readiness programmes*
Many organisations conducted 'GDPR readiness' programmes between 2016 and 2018, to get ready for the coming into force of the law in May 2018. Many of these have concluded, but this does not mean that data protection programmes are complete and gone for good. For as long as data protection requirements continue to develop both in the UK and globally, as driven by the various compelling events identified earlier, there will be data protection programmes. Therefore, people working in the data protection field will need to understand what they involve, to achieve success in their organisations.

## The beginning of work – building a business case

A business case for a data protection programme or project can be as much about 'winning hearts and minds' as it can be about documenting what the work will entail. For many organisations data protection remains a compliance burden that at best stops an organisation being subject to regulatory action or legal claims and at worst inhibits the achievement of profit. In the past, the data protection community may not have necessarily helped with this viewpoint, particularly when it has focused on the potential for fines, sanctions and litigation to persuade senior stakeholders to support a programme or project.

The negative consequences that result from failure to comply with data protection laws should not be ignored but when attempting to elicit support for a programme or project, this should be balanced by stating the positive outcomes that the work could bring to the organisation in question.

It is therefore important to align the business case with the organisation's strategic objectives, purpose and values. A business case is more likely to receive support when it can demonstrate how it will support growth, profitability, or other issues of importance to the organisation.

The politics of making a business case and gaining executive support should also be considered. Identifying and engaging with supporters and stakeholders within the business early on can help to increase the prospects of success, by taking them on the journey.

**The beginning of work – developing the brief**

A data protection programme or project will often start with the development of a written brief. The brief will set out why the work is needed, the outcomes the work is to achieve and who should be involved.

The brief will usually be developed by the programme/project sponsor working alongside an initial team to gather information required to decide whether or not the work should actually be initiated.

A brief will contain information such as:

- the background to the programme/project, including why is it needed;
- the objectives for the work;
- the scope of the work, covering what it will do and what is excluded from scope;
- the business benefits that the work will bring;
- list of deliverables to be achieved;
- known assumptions that the work will proceed on;
- risks to success, that is, the risks to the successful completion of the work and the risks to the organisation from undertaking the work;
- known constraints on achieving the desired outcomes;
- identification of areas of the business that will be impacted by the work;
- any dependencies that the work is reliant on, such as dependencies on other projects, processes or decisions;
- the resources that are required to deliver the work;
- stakeholders that should be involved in the work;
- the timeframe that the work will run over;
- an estimate of costs.

**Managing the work**

The programme/project will need to establish its own management structures. Typically, they will typically require a multidisciplinary approach, calling on skills and experience from across the organisation.

An organisational chart for a data protection programme/project may include:

- The sponsor. Their role is to lead the work and have overall accountability for its successful delivery.
- Steering committee. This consists of the sponsor and other stakeholders who can make decisions; provide resources; represent areas of the business affected by the work; and/or lead workstreams.
- Director. A person who has day-to-day responsibility for delivery against the plan. Tasks include submitting management documentation to the steering committee; monitoring and reporting on progress; maintaining risk logs; managing stakeholder engagement and communications; managing budgets; and escalating issues and risks to the steering committee as necessary.
- Workstream teams. These are teams who have been allocated responsibility for completing specific workstreams, deliverables or outcomes.
- Assurance. Undertaken through an individual or team, this has responsibility for assessing whether the work is properly organised, planned and controlled.

## Initiating the work

The move to programme/project initiation results in the development of the programme/project initiation documentation or PID. The PID may be a single document or multiple documents combined. Regardless of the form it takes, it is one of the most important artefacts in the work, as it builds on the brief and sets out how the objectives will be achieved; who will have responsibility for activities within the work; and when those activities will take place.

For example, the PID will include:

- the business case;
- workplans, detailing what will be done, by whom and when; dependencies for achieving the activities in the plans; and key milestones in the work;
- defined roles, responsibilities and accountabilities for the people involved in the work;
- how the work will be governed, monitored and reported on;
- a review of the risks, including analysis of the likelihood and consequences of the risks and risk reduction plans;
- a cost/benefits analysis, which covers resource requirements across the lifetime of the work and considers how it all measures against the benefits that the work will bring;
- a communication plan, which sets out how internal and external stakeholders will be communicated with about the work.

## The workplans and workstreams

Programme and project workplans are important tools for ensuring the delivery of desired objectives, outcomes and outputs against predicted costs, resources and timelines. They will be referenced throughout the programme/project, to understand if things are on track and going to plan. When necessary, they will be amended to reflect changing circumstances, to keep things up to date.

These plans are likely to consist of a number of common workstreams such as:

- Transparency. Developing notices and other transparency information for data subjects.
- Lawful grounds. Identifying the lawful basis that data processing is based on. This may include activities relating to consent management.
- Data mapping/records of processing. Creating records of data processing activities and data maps.
- Risk management. Developing risk management processes, methodologies and registers.
- Rights and complaints. Processes for handling data subject rights requests, complaints and similar escalations.
- Security. Implementing security measures that are to be applied to data processing systems and personal data.
- Breach notification. Developing personal data breach notification and communication processes.
- International transfers. Identifying where personal data are being transferred internationally and the lawful basis the transfer is to be made on. Putting in place appropriate safeguards.
- Training and awareness. Developing training and awareness campaigns for workers.
- Governance. Designing and embedding appropriate data protection management structures, monitoring and reporting.
- Regulators and registrations. Identifying data protection regulators with authority over data processing activities. Lodging necessary notifications and registrations with regulators.

For each of its constituent workstreams, the plan should include:

- Roles and responsibilities. Who will do what?
- What needs to be done. The activities and tasks that need to be completed.
- Timeframe and duration. Start and end dates showing how long each activity or task within the plan will take to be completed.
- Milestones. Key events or points within the timeline that demonstrate that major progress has been made.

- Deliverables. The products of the workstream (these may be tangible or intangible).
- Dependencies. The critical links between different elements of the workstream.

## GOVERNANCE FRAMEWORKS REQUIRED BY DPBDD FOR ACCOUNTABILITY PURPOSES

The accountability principle in GDPR Article 5.2 says that the controller is responsible for complying with the data protection principles, which includes that they should be able to demonstrate their compliance. Article 24.1 expands upon this by saying that controllers should be able to demonstrate that their processing is performed in accordance with the regulation, which includes the requirements of DPbDD.

One implication of these rules is that the controller's data protection programme and its projects should achieve the outcome of continual governance over data processing. This means that controllers need to pursue data protection programmes and projects to deliver governance frameworks by design and default.

Critical elements that should fall within the purview of the governance framework include the following.

### Roles and responsibilities – who will do what?

The governance framework should identify the roles needed to deliver the required data protection outcomes within the organisation and the responsibilities those roles will have.

A key question will be whether the organisation is required to appoint a DPO and, if not, whether it will appoint one voluntarily or not at all. In the absence of a DPO, or in addition to a DPO, the organisation should also decide whether it will appoint any other functional heads who will have responsibility for the organisation's strategic approach to data protection and operational delivery (in contrast to the regulatory reviewing and advisory functions of the DPO). Some organisations have appointed chief privacy officers, a role that is seen as separate to and distinct from the DPO. Others have general council operating alongside the DPO, but, again, in a separate and distinct function.

An organisation should also consider what roles will support the DPO and other function heads. Considerations include:

- Will a data protection team be appointed and what will their responsibilities be?
- Will formal responsibilities for data protection be created in roles outside the data protection team such as in HR, the marketing team or IT security team?
- Will the organisation develop 'data protection champions' within different parts of its business to help integrate data protection into business-as-usual activities and to be spotters for data protection issues?
- What responsibilities will sit at senior management levels?

- What responsibilities will board members have?
- Are there any personal liabilities for senior executives?

An organisation may wish to capture the roles and responsibilities that support its data protection framework in a RACI matrix. The matrix should describe the roles that are involved in the completion of tasks, which roles are 'responsible' or 'accountable' for specific tasks and whether a role holder should be 'consulted' about a task or kept 'informed' about progress against a task.

## Management structures and reporting lines

There is no perfect template for data protection management structures. The final form that an organisation adopts will be influenced by multiple factors including the efficiency of the proposed structure to deliver the required outcomes; budget considerations; the teams that relevantly skilled individuals already sit in; and internal politics. From an accountability perspective, it will be important for the management structure to clearly demonstrate that data protection is supported by and reported to the highest levels of the organisation.

Considerations within the development of management structures include:

- Reporting lines. Who will report to whom and where will they sit within the organisation's structure? Where should the data protection team be placed, who should report to them and who should they report to?
- Will a three lines of defence model be deployed, with personnel in the first line of defence having operational duties for risk management, with a data protection team in the second line providing them with advisory support and tools to do their jobs, and a third line that provides independent assurance in relation to the organisation's compliance with data protection requirements?

## Setting a target operating model

In practice, organisations often talk about setting a target operating model (TOM) to bring all of the governance and operational responsibilities for data processing together, within a single design. This can be a very helpful exercise, as it helps not only with accountability, but with understanding the dependencies that exist within different roles and responsibilities, which, if ignored or unaddressed, can result in 'broken processes' and other problems that can contribute to operational failure and therefore a failure to protect rights and freedoms. Of course, a single design will not alter the fact that data protection governance and roles and responsibilities need to exist across all areas of the business that play a role in data processing, as the lines of defence model assumes.

## SUMMARY

In conclusion, this chapter gives readers a better understanding of:

- the requirements for Data Protection by Design and Default and the elements that need to be operationalised;
- the range of events that can trigger the need for business transformation programmes, to operationalise data protection requirements;
- the issues that need to be considered with the development of business transformation programmes;
- how to initiate business transformation programmes and manage the work;
- the governance structures that are required to achieve accountability for business transformation.

# 12 BEING ACCOUNTABLE FOR RECORDS OF PROCESSING, LEGITIMATE INTERESTS AND RISK MANAGEMENT

## Mark Hendry

This chapter considers the accountability principle and identifies some of the keys ways in which accountability can be delivered and demonstrated in practice, highlighting the importance of maintaining records of processing, legitimate interests assessments and risk management.

### ACCOUNTABILITY FOR OUR DECISIONS, ACTIONS AND BEHAVIOURS

Accountability, whatever the topic in question, is about the fulfilment of obligations and the ability to account for decisions, actions and behaviours. In an individual context this is a familiar concept normally introduced to us when we are young children; the idea is that we are answerable for and must live with the consequences of the decisions we make and actions we take.

If we translate this familiar idea into the modern digital economy and of data subjects, controllers and processors, who may sometimes be removed from the immediate and downstream benefits, harms, or other consequences of data processing, the idea of accountability can start to become quite opaque. However, in legislative terms the idea of accountability for data protection is easy to understand: controllers must comply with the law and be able to prove that they have done so.

As each data processing decision and action taken can have an effect on data subjects and because there is a strong regulatory system in place that gives supervisory authorities as well as data subjects broad powers and means to hold data controllers to account, demonstrating strong accountability is not just an obligation for controllers. It is also a benefit.

### ACCOUNTABILITY AS A CORE PRINCIPLE OF DATA PROTECTION

With respect to the data protection principle of accountability and the implementation of the GDPR, accountability has perhaps been miscomprehended as simply being about the generation and maintenance of basic compliance documentation, such as policies, and not a great deal else. Of course, the ability to produce documentary evidence is a key part of accountability and often it can be the most reliable or convenient evidence that can be provided, but taking a broader view reveals that it can also be oriented toward the achievement of a mandate that can be societal, ethical and professional, or a combination of all these factors. One approach to accountability can be the achievement broadens and deepens the records' service as an important accountability artefact. For instance, the following additional data points could be included within the records of processing (within the records themself, or as links to other records and/or systems) and take the records into a position of greater usefulness to the organisation:

- the lawful basis of the processing;
- the systems and environments in which the personal data are processed;
- what data subject rights attach to the processing (because of the lawful basis for the processing);
- links to assessments or other evidence supporting the lawful basis, for example, contract, legitimate interests assessment, consent record, and so on;
- details of specific third parties who are involved in the processing and their status (controller, joint controller, processor), along with links to information regarding the data processing agreement between parties;
- links to risk assessments relating to the processes, systems, processors, other third parties, and so on;
- links to the data retention schedule for the processes;
- details regarding incidents and breaches that have occurred relating to the processing and systems.

Clearly it is more difficult to create extended A.30 records than basic ones, but the benefit of doing so is to facilitate the delivery of positive data protection outcomes and outputs, that is, the delivery of accountability.

## Developing records of processing – discovery and analysis

Acknowledging the practical reality that most organisations are already operating and processing personal data by the time the need for data protection accountability becomes any kind of an imperative, what are the most common methods of discovering, recording and mapping the personal data across its life cycle? Essentially there are four main routes to 'data discovery'. These are:

- manual effort;
- technology-assisted effort;
- interfaces with other businesses processes;
- a combination of all of the above.

### *Manual data discovery*
Manual data discovery involves asking stakeholders from across a business questions about the data processing they undertake and writing their answers down. The benefits and drawbacks of manual data discovery are summarised in Table 12.1.

**Table 12.1 The benefits and drawbacks of manual data discovery**

| | |
|---|---|
| Benefit – cost | It tends to be low cost to execute, if processing is reasonably straightforward and stakeholders can readily provide information. |
| Benefit – skills | It does not require significant upskilling or training to perform. |
| Benefit – speed | The records produced often provide instant insight into issues that can then be addressed. |
| Benefit – induction | Engaging a network of business stakeholders provides an opportunity to induct them into the basics of data protection and information governance, which can be used to good effect in delivering ongoing accountability, governance and control outcomes. |
| Benefit – context | Mining human-held knowledge can quickly yield or generate context and provide vital information regarding use cases, value and therefore 'purpose' of processing. |
| Drawback – stakeholder management | It can be difficult to determine which stakeholders to involve and to engage them sufficiently that they do what is required. |
| Drawback – effort | The effort can become very long-winded and exhausting or draining for those involved, especially in large and complex organisational structures. |
| Drawback – completeness | Stakeholders may only understand or know about the specific part of the data life cycle they interact with in their role. |
| Drawback – repetition | Information can be captured multiple times and it can be difficult to determine whether the entry relates to one or more data processing operations. |
| Drawback – engagement | Some stakeholders may not engage, leaving the knowledge they hold unrecorded. |
| Drawback – inaccuracy | Stakeholders may omit important information for a variety of reasons (typically that they do not know, they forgot to mention it, or they are motivated for some reason to conceal information regarding data processing). |

### *Methodology of manual discovery*

Manual data discovery is typically performed in a logical and phased approach:

- high-level assessment of the segments of the organisation that process data and teams involved in data processing;
- identification of stakeholders within teams with suitable knowledge and organisational standing to act as a source of authority regarding data processing;
- engagement of identified stakeholders including basic training relating to topics such as definitions of personal data, controller and processor, data processing, records of processing, data transfers, third parties, systems, controls, governance and retention;

- discovery and records production by identified stakeholders, supported by knowledge and subject matter experts;
- review of the records produced, followed by rationalisation to remove duplicate entries relating to the same data processing operations and to determine linkage of data processing chains that span departmental boundaries;
- consideration of identifiable information and data gaps and anomalies remaining (commonly these take the form of empty fields in the records of processing, or multiple contradictory entries in the same field);
- deciding upon and executing necessary steps to improve the records.

## Technology-assisted data discovery

Technology-assisted data discovery takes advantage or one of more technology systems to identify data within an environment and generate records. There is myriad technology solutions that can be used to perform technical data discovery, many of which were developed for the purpose of eDiscovery forensic and technical investigations and have found utility in everyday data management. Table 12.2 summarises some of the benefits and drawbacks of technology-assisted data discovery techniques.

**Table 12.2 The benefits and drawbacks of technology-assisted data discovery**

| | |
|---|---|
| Benefit – speed | Depending on the environment in which it is deployed, it can very rapidly provide results. |
| Benefit – dynamic | Some technologies can re-scan the environment on a frequent or dynamic, ongoing basis, providing a real-time view of the data processing environment and highlighting changes to a reviewer. |
| Benefit – functionality | Some technologies with the capability to discover data also possess other functionality that is valuable in data management and data protection, such as the ability to retrieve data and/or suppress data. |
| Benefit – completeness | It is possible to obtain very comprehensive results with reliable technology and well-designed search parameters. However, the scope of the data environment that is covered will be determined by the choice of technology and how it is configured and used. |
| Benefit – reliability | Some data search technologies can produce forensically reliable evidence if such is needed in an investigation or resultant proceedings (however, such technologies are commonly expensive, highly specialised and so adopted and used on a case-by-case basis and only deployed as and when needed). |

*(Continued)*

## Table 12.2 (Continued)

| | |
|---|---|
| Drawback – suitability | There is a range of different technologies available with different ways of operating, for example technologies that examine data in transit, technologies that examine data *in situ*, technologies that search servers, technologies that search end user computing devices and technologies that are capable of some combination of these. It may be that any individual method may not be suitable or reliable for any given business. |
| Drawback – cost | The deployment of specialist technology can be expensive. The use cases need to be very carefully considered and a determination made over whether the cost can be justified, for example through the inclusion of supplementary functionality on top of discovery, or intended repeated use over time. |
| Drawback – intelligibility | Making the results intelligible can sometimes be a much longer process than the performance of the technical discovery itself and requires the interpretation of business stakeholders in much the same way as manual data discovery does. |
| Drawback – functionality | Some technologies are limited regarding the discovery they perform. Common pitfalls to be aware of are: technologies that cannot 'read' files types that are commonly used within the operating environment for the processing of personal data, and technologies that only read the filename or the first few characters of text within a file to determine whether or not it contains matches against the search terms before dismissing it and moving on. |
| Drawback – selection | As a result of the above, determining the most suitable technology or technologies to meet the needs of a particular environment, or to serve the particular use cases, can be challenging. |
| Drawback – deployment | Getting approval from IT stakeholders to deploy discovery agents onto a corporate IT network in a non-crisis or incident situation can be very challenging. |

## ROPAs and Data Protection by Design and Default

Integrating data protection considerations into these other business processes is an important step in achieving accountability. The phrasing of Article 25 GDPR (data protection by design and by default) requires that 'appropriate technical and organisational measures' to implement the data protection principles are implemented at the determination of the means of processing as well as at the time of processing itself. Embedding Data Protection by Design and Default considerations within existing business change processes is key to achievement of this obligation. As we have already set out, developing and maintaining records of processing is a key foundation and one of the core technical and organisational measures required to achieve the data protection principles.

Example business processes that could feed into records of processing updates and other data protection processes include:

- IT systems change processes;
- contracting, outsourcing, or other supplier agreements;
- project management stage gates;
- financial control gates for business initiatives;
- internal audit reviews;
- operational security processes such as data leakage prevention programmes, controls testing or system access reviews;
- security alerting and incident management;
- enterprise risk management;
- data protection processes such as risk assessments, data protection impact assessments or legitimate interests assessments.

Maintaining records of processing is an ongoing process and in our modern digital society, change is constantly under way, including changes to data processes carried out by organisations. This necessitates the continual review and maintenance of records of data processing, and this can in large part be achieved through interfacing those records of processing with these other business processes.

## Gated development – upskilling

It is noteworthy that for many organisations, even those that are very technologically advanced, having data protection 'gates' embedded into these processes is the primary way in which data protection risks are managed for new initiatives, and new data collection, creation, or use is identified. Of course the insertion of data protection involvement into these business processes also requires that practitioners responsible for such integration roles need to be equipped with suitable working knowledge of data protection concepts, tools and templates in order to properly to triage and assess the data protection considerations arising and to take appropriate action thereafter.

## Organisation type

Depending on the organisation in question, the way records of processing are developed may vary. For instance in a global organisation it may be necessary to adopt a combined approach to developing and maintaining records of processing spanning manual effort, technology-assisted effort and maintenance effort through integration of wider business processes with data protection processes. In smaller organisations where there is good awareness of the data processing activities, a straightforward technology environment and relatively unchanging data processing environment, it may be deemed appropriate to only perform manual discovery and ongoing maintenance through periodic efforts.

## A combination of all the above

Most organisations will need to undertake some combination of all the above to develop complete and robust records of processing. For instance, stakeholders involved in manual data discovery will most likely need to log into the processing systems to search for data and double-check the data fields within it. Organisations that have completed a technical data discovery exercise will need to engage system and data owner stakeholders to understand and record the purposes of the processing and to help determine the lawful basis for processing (which will generally not be clear from the immediate results of a technical search for data). Maintaining the records and keeping them accurate and complete will almost always require interfacing with other business processes, as well as regular reviews of the records and re-engagement with business stakeholders and further technical searches (where available) to find and record changes to processing.

## Exemptions

Article 30.5 states that organisations employing fewer than 250 persons are exempt from the obligation to maintain records of processing unless the processing it carries out 'is likely to result in a risk to the rights and freedoms of data subjects', 'is not occasional', or includes 'special categories of data'. In modern businesses careful consideration should be taken over whether this exemption truly applies or not. In fact, performing an information audit or data discovery process (and in so doing developing records of processing) may be necessary in order to properly assess whether the exemptions applies.

## BEING ACCOUNTABLE FOR LEGITIMATE INTERESTS

The lawful bases for processing within A.6 include the controller's legitimate interests.

As already discussed, acting accountably is about fulfilling obligations and being able to account for decisions taken, so when considering data processing based on legitimate interests it is necessary to apply a test to check whether it is an appropriate basis to rely upon. This involves an examination of the interest that is being pursued and balancing it against the interests that data subjects have in the maintenance of their rights and freedoms. In other words, the use of the legitimate interests basis for lawful processing has a proportionality test at its heart.

This performance of the test is often called a legitimate interests assessment and its completion is required to deliver accountability in practice. For example:

- Articles 13 and 14 GDPR require that the legitimate interests pursued by the controller or third party must be disclosed to the data subject. It would not be considered appropriate to simply state that the controller or third party has legitimate interests to process the data for the given purposes, without stating what the legitimate interests are.
- Recital 47 provides further detail regarding the use of the legitimate interests basis, including that the reasonable expectations of the data subject should be taken into account based on their prior relationship with the controller.

- The GDPR confirms that the legitimate interests basis can be used for certain specified purposes including marketing, fraud prevention, intra-group transfers and IT security. However, it should not be taken that legitimate interests is the only, or even the correct, lawful basis for all data processing that supports these functions of the organisation.

## Being accountable for the balancing exercise

With these ideas in mind, the LIA must consist of a balancing exercise that considers (a) the purpose of the legitimate interests of the controller or third party, (b) whether the processing itself is necessary to achieve the legitimate interests, and (c) the fundamental rights and freedoms of the data subject based on the relationship of the data subject and the controller. Consider some examples.

### *Utilities example*
A scenario might involve these situations:

- A data subject has a contract with a utility supplier (the controller) for the provision of electricity supply to their home.
- The controller wishes to process the data subject's personal data for the further purpose of directly marketing similar goods and services to the data subject.
- The data subject has not supplied their explicit consent for direct marketing and has not opted out of direct marketing communications.

In this scenario the controller could perform an LIA and reasonably conclude that they have legitimate interests to perform the further processing to promote any similar goods and services that they offer; that the data subject may have a reasonable expectation for them to do so, based on their existing relationship; and that to do so would not constitute a breach of the data subjects' fundamental rights and freedoms.

### *Site scraping example*
A scenario might involve these situations:

- A marketing agency has searched open internet pages to harvest contact details of individuals with whom they have no prior relationship, which they extract from websites administered by third parties.
- The agency wishes to process the data subjects' personal data for the purpose of indiscriminately marketing goods and services from across their own client base, which includes companies ranging from adventure holiday specialists to care home providers, to the data subjects.

The agency might be able to describe that they have legitimate interests to directly market the goods and services of their own customers, but it would be difficult to justify the necessity of harvesting data from open internet pages to do so, or to argue that there are no other less privacy-invasive methods of performing the direct marketing. Therefore in this scenario the fundamental rights and freedoms of the data subject would override the legitimate interests and the LIA balancing test would not be passed – that is, the controller would not have legitimate interests to rely upon – with the result that the processing as described would be unlawful.

## Considerations within legitimate interests

In every scenario where legitimate interests is being considered as the lawful basis for processing there are a range of factors to consider in terms of delivering accountability in practice. For instance, in the given scenarios some of the key considerations include:

- Whether the personal data are sourced directly from the data subject, or indirectly.
- How the source of the data engages different transparency obligations. A.13 covers information to be provided where personal data are collected from the data subject, whereas A.14 covers information to be provided where personal data have not been obtained from the data subject.
- The status of the organisations in terms of controller, joint controller, or processor and the obligations held as a result, for instance what ATOM need to be implemented to protect the rights and freedoms of the data subjects.
- The three elements of the LIA.
- Developing a trail of evidence that demonstrates the accountability of the data controller in the decisions and actions taken throughout to deliver against the data protection principles.

## Legitimate interests and the right to object to direct marketing

Most direct marketing in today's economy is undertaken by electronic means, such as by SMS and email. It is very important, therefore, to note that specific laws relate to such electronic marketing. The UK ICO provides the following guidance:

> If you intend to process personal data for the purposes of direct marketing by electronic means (by email, text, automated calls etc.) legitimate interests may not always be an appropriate basis for processing. This is because the e-privacy laws on electronic marketing – currently the Privacy and Electronic Communications Regulations (PECR) – require that individuals give their consent to some forms of electronic marketing. It is the UK GDPR standard of consent that applies, because of the effect of Article 94 of the UK GDPR.

Depending on the circumstances, including the means by which direct marketing is to be delivered, legitimate interests may still be an appropriate lawful basis for such processing.

When using legitimate interests as the lawful basis for direct marketing, the right to object to processing is absolute. This means that in all direct marketing communications the right to object must be made available. Controllers must also manage a suppressions list and check against this to ensure that data subjects who have objected to receiving direct marketing are removed from direct marketing outreach lists before their data are processed for these purposes. In some countries, including the UK, data subjects are able to subscribe to telephone and mail preference services. These are official registers for people and businesses to register their preference to opt out of sales and marketing via telephone calls and unsolicited (personally addressed) postal mail.

Controllers must respect the preferences of data subjects not only expressed directly to the controller and managed via the controller's suppressions list, but also those expressed by data subjects via subscriptions to official services such as those mentioned. Performance of these searches would need to be evidenced within an accountability framework for direct marketing based on legitimate interests.

### Legitimate interests and data subject rights

It should be noted that the right to data portability does not apply to data processing operations that rely upon legitimate interests as the lawful basis. In practical terms this is important, because it means that where systems are in use that are solely used for processing operations relying on legitimate interests, these need not be designed and configured in a manner that achieves compatibility with the data controller's other systems, because the controller is not obliged to 'port' or transfer these data. This stands to illustrate the need for the lawful basis of processing to feed into LIAs, in order to deliver accountability.

## BEING ACCOUNTABLE FOR RISK MANAGEMENT

Risk is a term that features regularly throughout the GDPR. It is often used in the context of considering the risk to the rights and freedoms of data subjects that may be posed by the processing of their personal data (including in Articles 24, 25, 32 and 35) and when a data breach has occurred (Articles 33 and 34).

Processing of personal data carries inherent risk and most risk management methodologies adopted by organisations cause the risk assessor to consider risk in terms of the severity of impacts on the business (regulatory, financial, reputational, operational, etc.). When considering data protection risks, those factors must be considered alongside the risks to rights and freedoms of individuals. For the individuals whose data are being processed, the main consideration is the risk of harm that might be caused to their fundamental rights and freedoms by the processing, such as the possibility of physical harm, discrimination, disadvantage, loss of damage to finances or property, and so on.

This is why proper consideration and response to risk in all aspects of data processing is a key component of accountability in practice; if the processing of personal data had little or no risk of harm to individuals attached to it, the emergence of regulation and introduction of increased regulatory powers would not have taken place in this field and then continued across the globe over the past 50 years. This is an important context-setting consideration for all practitioners who are involved in data protection risk identification, assessment and management in practice.

### Being accountable for ATOM

Most organisations have risk management practices in place, but they can vary dramatically in their rigour, approach, formality and effectiveness. The practice of data protection risk management is a topic that can be subjectively thought of in terms of the taking of appropriate technical and organisational measures for data protection

(ATOM). The following might be considered important elements within a determination of whether a risk management approach is appropriate:

- Do staff involved in data processing understand how to consider and identify data protection risk?
- Is there a clear method for such staff to highlight their concerns for further consideration and assessment?
- Are such staff equipped with aide-memoires or similar to help them consider the characteristics of and triage a potential risk and move it through to the correct next step?
- Is there a risk assessment process that causes a suitably expert risk practitioner to consider the risk in detail, including the likelihood, impact and proximity of the risk, and make suitable recommendations to respond to the risk?
- Does the risk assessment and/or triage process link to and facilitate the performance of a DPIA where one is deemed necessary or prudent?
- Are risk decisions escalated to an appropriate governance body according to the outcomes of the assessment?
- Are risk assessments and supporting documentation captured and maintained?
- Do risk responses within registers also contain information that drives accountability in practice, such as responsible individuals, due dates for actions or further reviews, and kept up to date?
- Are identified risks linked to the records of processing?

Further, the outcomes of the risk management process itself must also be considered in terms of ATOM, because for each risk and scenario any number and combination of technical and organisational measures may be devised to respond to each risk, but only certain combinations of technical and organisational measures will be considered appropriate.

## Risk of failure baked into design

When considering data protection risk, it should be remembered that for the most part the risk of harm to individuals arises as a result of the data processing itself, or issues and failings within the processing mechanisms and means. That is to say that failure, risk and non-compliance can be designed-in. If that is so, this will be demonstrated in the paperwork supporting the design or it will be rendered apparent through issues in the technical and operational layers of the processing.

These issues of design and operation then manifest as risk to the organisation performing the processing and, if the risk is realised, may result in business impacts such as financial cost, regulatory impact, or operational impacts.

For instance, a failure relating to inadequate transparency may mean that an individual's data are processed in a way that they feel is unfair and gives rise to a complaint and regulatory scrutiny; or an inadequate access control design may result in a situation where data are processed without sufficient confidentiality and a security or purpose limitation breach manifests. The accountability principle can render these design failures obvious.

## Being accountable for the 4-Ts

Therefore, when considering risk responses the question arises of what is meant by appropriate technical and organisational measures. The first consideration must be that common risk methodologies, including those recognised by the supervisory authority community, adopt the '4-Ts' for risk response:

- Treat – do something to adjust the likelihood of impact of the risk.
- Tolerate – do nothing or 'accept' the risk.
- Terminate – stop doing the thing that causes the risk to manifest in the first place.
- Transfer – move the risk somewhere else, most commonly seen as the adoption of insurance coverage or contractual indemnities.

Table 12.3 provides examples of how a controller might consider risk triggers and responses in practice.

**Table 12.3 Risk trigger and treatment considerations**

| Risk considerations | Response options |
|---|---|
| • Where does the risk arise from; paperwork, processes, or technology? | Tolerance of anything other than low risk is problematic given the obligations within GDPR requiring implementation of ATOM to deal with risks arising from the processing. |
| • Does the risk relate to the design only (and can therefore be fixed through a redesign), or does it relate to a process that is operational currently therefore requiring an operational change to take place? | Transference of risk, for instance through insurance cover, may help to soften the business impact if a risk occurs (for example, through a premium payout) but insurance does nothing to limit the risk of harm to individuals and it is expressly prohibited in some countries to insure against regulatory fines. |
| • What other actors are involved (e.g. third-party data processors), and what mechanisms exist to engage their cooperation in risk treatment? | Termination involves stopping the activity from which the risk emerges. For many businesses involved in data processing this would involve a fundamental rethink of the business model or method of operation, and therefore would be a last resort. |
| • Which adverse scrutineers are in play (e.g. hackers, rogue employees, data subjects, privacy activists, regulators) and what measures can be taken to limit the likelihood of them causing the risk to manifest, or limit the impact should they cause it to manifest? | Treatment of risk therefore becomes the main subject of consideration when delivering accountability in practice through risk management techniques. |

*(Continued)*

**Table 12.3 (Continued)**

| Risk considerations | Response options |
|---|---|
| • When deciding upon ATOM, what reference points can be used to determine appropriateness (e.g. regulatory guidance, recognised standards, case law, or prior regulatory sanctions or codes of conduct)? | Combined response: Even after treatment has been planned, designed or applied, some residual risk is likely to remain. It is for the controller to then determine how to respond to that residual risk. If the assessed risk to data subject rights and freedoms remains high even after the planned treatment, the controller can consult with the supervisory authority (Article 36 prior consultation), or seek to further treat the assessed risk to reduce it through redesign or further controls prior to commencing the processing, or terminate the risk by not going through with the processing. In other cases where the assessed risk is lower, it would be typical for the controller to use a combination of tolerance and transfer (through insurance) to respond to the residual risk. |

If these lenses and filters are applied in practice, a more practical approach to risk management that is oriented toward achievement of positive outcomes for data subjects and data processing organisations can be achieved when compared to the application of generalised risk management practices.

## Being accountable for embedding data protection risk management into change methodologies

The first step towards being able to effectively respond to risk is to identify risk. It is, therefore, important to embed risk identification and triage gates into business processes that are likely to involve the initiation of new personal data processing activities, or the making of alterations to existing data processing, or the undertaking of further processing on existing data.

For instance, data protection risk identification and triage gates may be designed into:

- business change methodologies;
- IT change stages;
- procurement stages;
- marketing planning.

In doing so, it is important to create a methodology that effectively identifies whether the changes or initiatives involve personal data, and the main characteristics of the proposed activity, in order that proportionate scrutiny can be applied and risks identified and responded to across the initiative's life cycle. Ultimately, to embed data protection risk considerations from an early stage and then throughout change initiatives has the potential to result in an end solution going into production that embodies and demonstrates the requirements of Data Protection by Design and Default and the accountability obligations that go with it.

## Being accountable for recognised controls

Recognised standards play a very important role in ATOM. There are many to choose from and determining which are suitable for the organisation should be the subject of careful consideration.

Examples of standards that are recognised and referred to by parties including supervisory authorities include the NIST,[1] ISO 27000 series[2] and ENISA[3] frameworks and standards for Information Security and Privacy Information Management. The requirements of these standards span management, paperwork, processes and technology controls and techniques that can be interpreted and implemented in most modern business settings. With the state-of-the-art requirements within the GDPR, it is becoming increasingly important to develop and deliver controls in the technical and data layers of processing.

## Being accountable for assurance

Assurance in the context of data protection is about achieving a state of confidence in the risk and compliance status of the data processing environment. Assurance can be achieved in a variety of manners. For example, assurance may be derived in varying degrees through, for instance:

- Governance reporting, such as that provided to the board of the organisation.
- Achievement and maintenance of certifications or marks of accreditation, such as those from the ISO. Most notable for data protection are those within the ISO 27000 series.
- Audit work, such as that performed by internal audit functions and practitioners, third parties (data controllers in controller/processor relationships) and by supervisory authorities.
- Monitoring, such as that performed by the data protection officer.

Another mechanism through which assurance could be achieved would be signing up to an approved code of conduct that is relevant to the industry to which the processing organisation belongs. These are intended to act as a means of demonstrating accountability and offer practical solutions to addressing the particular data protection challenges arising from the special characteristics of particular industries. However, signing up to such a code of conduct also requires that the organisation implements the

---

1  See https://www.nist.gov/cyberframework and https://www.nist.gov/privacy-framework

2  For example, ISO 27001:2013 (Information security management systems), ISO 27002:2013 (Security controls framework), and ISO 27701:2019 (Privacy information management).

3  See https://www.enisa.europa.eu/publications/handbook-on-security-of-personal-data-processing and https://www.enisa.europa.eu/risk-level-tool/

rules and standards in practice and subjects itself to monitoring mechanisms operated by assigned and accredited monitoring bodies.

Each of the means outlined above can provide a different focus, level of detail, and therefore affecting the degree of insight and confidence (or assurance) that can be taken.

### *Governance reporting*
This typically involves the presentation of data relating to key performance and risk indicators, with supporting statements regarding operational performance and particular topics of note for the reporting period.

### *Externally recognised certifications and accreditations*
Such as those of the ISO family of standards. These can demonstrate to external stakeholders, such as customers and third-party business relationships, that the organisation has achieved a particular level of control within their data processing environment and is a trustworthy party to interact with. To select, implement and then certify to such a standard can be a significant and complex undertaking. When seeking to place assurance in such a certification (for instance when considering a partnership with a third party) care should be taken to understand the scope of the certification, as it may only apply for a particular area of the organisation in question.

### *Audit work*
This involves checking and testing. It can be a significant contributor to both the attainment of assurance and also the removal of false assurance and confidence, due to the issues it can expose through scrutiny and testing. Auditing, by any party, normally involves the establishment of the scope and focus of testing; the establishment of the testing methods, such as reviewing policies and assessing against regulatory requirements and regulator guidance; reviewing management data and reporting; operational adequacy testing of procedures and controls in practice, and so on. The GDPR specifically mentions audit in relation to:

- processors allowing and contributing to audits by the controller (Article 28);
- one of the means by which a data protection officer shall monitor compliance with the regulation (Article 39);
- a mechanism for verification of compliance with BCRs (Article 47);
- one of the investigative powers of the supervisory authority (Article 58).

### *Monitoring*
Monitoring is performed as part of the duties of the DPO. A task of the DPO is to inform and advise the controller or processor and their employees of their data protection obligations. Such monitoring can act as an early warning signal of non-compliance or emerging risk and be used to stage interventions, inform risk management and inform a more detailed audit planning and execution, all for the purposes of assurance.

Other assurance mechanisms and methods exist, such as the seeking of an expert second opinion, or the engagement of a specialist third party to design and implement elements of a data processing and control environment from which some assurance can be automatically derived.

Each of the assurance mechanisms described, if adopted effectively, act to peel back layers of detail and provide insight into the design and operation of the data processing environment. When these insights are used to compare against the obligations held by the organisation and derive assurance, or identify opportunities for improvement and stage interventions, they are working towards accountability outcomes.

## BEING ACCOUNTABLE FOR ADVERSE SCRUTINY

A good way to test whether accountability methods operating in practice are fit for purpose is to apply a test of adverse scrutiny. When it comes to accountability, perhaps the most obvious adverse scrutineer to consider is the data protection regulator, for in certain circumstances (such as a request for cooperation or an audit) it is they who will expect you to be able to produce your evidence of compliance with obligations. That said, a regulator will typically only request to examine your accountability records if they have reasonable cause to focus their limited resources in your direction, so you could test your accountability from the perspective of another adverse scrutineer, such as a customer or employee (data subjects).

Data subjects have numerous and often ongoing opportunities to scrutinise data processing activities and practices throughout the data life cycle and relationship with the data controller. This provides opportunities for adverse scrutiny, especially regarding the fulfilment of accountability in practice. For instance, the data subject will be presented with information to fulfil transparency requirements (in the form of a privacy notice) and this may cause them to have concerns over what this reveals regarding the controller's fulfilment of their obligations. Equally, when exercising data subject rights an employee may have specific detailed knowledge of the data being processed and may be casting a sharp eye over the accuracy and completeness of the fulfilment of the request.

It is for these reasons that accountability in practice needs to be far more than a thin layer of paperwork. Rather it must be embedded deeply through appropriate technical and organisational measures that constantly supplement and bolster the evidence record.

## BEING ACCOUNTABLE FOR AN ACCUMULATION OF EVIDENCE

It is both interesting and vital to note that in modern business, evidence trails are generated both overtly (through the manual generation and recording of evidence) and covertly (by intended or automated consequence of the way processes and systems of data processing operate). Examples of each might include:

- *Overt:*
    - Policies, standards, and guidance demonstrating the organisation's attitude towards and rules for data processing.
    - Organisational charts showing governance arrangements and decision making authorities for data.
    - Meeting minutes showing what decisions were taken, in what context, when and by whom.

- Evidence of audits and other tests undertaken, as well as action taken to remediate deficiencies or issues discovered.
- *Covert:*
  - System event logs, for instance those showing what data was accessed, when and by whom.
  - Message logs, for instance those saved from person-to-person instant messaging or emails that often provide a contemporaneous account of decisions and actions taken.

This has the effect of producing a paper trail that can be detected and followed by a party with sufficient interest and access to the material to understand what has taken place (actions taken, decisions made) over time. This can then be used for a variety of purposes, not least to infer or determine to what extent an organisation has acted accountably with regard to the obligations it holds.

### Production of evidence under pressure and scenario testing

It is important to consider the scenarios in which an organisation may be required to deliver or provide access to accountability evidence when under pressure. Scenario planning can be a helpful tool and technique by which adverse scrutineers, areas and topics of scrutiny, representative or specific types of evidence that may be requested, and the organisation's ability to provide them quickly, might be identified and assessed.

When considering what evidence can be produced under pressure, the evidence produced in scenario planning and testing should be assessed not only in terms of timeliness of provision, but also to determine whether, from the perspective of the adverse scrutineer, it tells a good story regarding the controller's fulfilment of obligations. In some cases records of evidence produced and disclosed may act as a smoking gun, revealing issues that could impact the outcomes of regulatory investigations or litigation. Scenario testing provides an opportunity to identify issues of evidence collection, production and suitability and to undertake improvement actions as necessary in preparation for a live adverse scrutiny event.

## SUMMARY

In conclusion, this chapter gives readers a better understanding of:

- the meaning of accountability and how it covers the end-to-end continuum of data processing;
- critical areas of data processing where accountability often has to be demonstrated;
- how to develop records of processing activities, including through the use of manual and technology-assisted techniques;
- how to progress operational thinking about use of the legitimate interest grounds for processing;
- how to progress operational thinking about risk management.

# 13 'THE JOURNEY TO CODE'

## Mark Hendry and Stewart Room

This chapter expands on the idea of The Journey to Code. It looks further into the core privacy value chain within the technology reference architecture described in Chapter 4 to illustrate some of the situations where privacy management, data intelligence and principles and rights technologies can be used today within a system for Data Protection by Design and Default and accountability.

### THE JOURNEY TO CODE – WORKING TOWARDS ACHIEVING COMPLIANCE WITHIN TECHNOLOGY AND DATA THEMSELVES

To recap, it is a central proposition of this book that the trajectory of data protection law is one where the traditional lawmakers of the state, namely the regulators and the courts (prompted by data subjects, privacy activists, litigators and the challenges of adverse scrutiny), will have ever-increasing concern about the technology and data layer within controller and processor environments, which will lead to increasing expectations about the need for data protection requirements to be operationalised through the computer code that controls technology and data. This is called 'The Journey to Code'.

The thinking behind this proposition, inspired by 'Lessig's Code', stems from the philosophical root of data protection, which is that advanced technologies and data processing techniques present grave risks to the rights and freedoms of individuals. The logical consequence must be that if the risks that data protection law is intended to address stem from the use of technology and data, the solution to those risks must lie in technology and data themselves.

This is not to deny the centrality of the roles of people and paperwork within the achievement of desired operational outcomes, but controllers and processors have largely over-invested in these areas and under-invested in technology and data themselves. The status quo cannot be maintained, because people and paper-based solutions will never keep up with the ever-accelerating pace of technological development.

### THE JOURNEY HAS COMMENCED

The need to go on The Journey to Code is not an issue for tomorrow. The Journey has already begun. Evidence of this is all around us. For example, Apple's iOS has recently been updated, to enable users to easily configure app tracking functions. In the field of security, which is covered by the GDPR's data protection principles, the market for technology solutions is massive[1] and it seems inevitable that the market for wider data protection technology will develop exponentially.

In a purely legal sense, the beginning of The Journey to Code was signalled by the adoption of the GDPR, which put the concepts of Data Protection by Design and Default and accountability on a legislative footing. It is impossible to interpret these requirements in any other way than as to require the code-based solutions that The Journey to Code promotes. All that stands in the way of the legal principle and the actual operationalisation of these solutions is the current state of the art for technology and the appetite and willingness of parties to scrutinise the technology and data layers of controllers and processors for operational compliance with the data protection principles.

## THE NATURE OF THE PROBLEM

Considering for a moment how pervasive the use of technology and data in society has become, the reasons why code-based control are needed to achieve the desired outcomes of data protection law becomes clear.

### Email example

The use of email as a business tool is endemic at this point in history, as an enabler of instantaneous communications and the sharing of ideas and information. In this sense the use of email has been overwhelmingly positive for society.

However, when you consider email from a data protection standpoint, with risk to rights and freedoms of data subjects in mind, other perspectives arise. Email functionality is commonly put into the control of all types of user, from the very senior to the very junior. This can lead to a wide variety of data protection problems, without suitable controls being in place, through erroneous data sharing. Problems include:

- ungoverned international transfers of personal data;
- confidentiality breaches;
- data minimisation problems, such as creating multiple copies of data in multiple inboxes and archives/backups;
- lawfulness, fairness, transparency and purpose limitation problems.

Similar problems arise through the increased use of convenient, on-demand collaboration and productivity technology, such as cloud-based software-as-a-service (SaaS) and storage-as-a-service (STaaS) solutions that can arise in the form of 'shadow' or ungoverned IT (i.e. those technologies that are adopted without the oversight, authorisations, or control standards insisted upon by those charged with governance and control within an organisation). A relevant and modern example is the increasingly common use of WhatsApp and similar messaging and chat platforms by business stakeholders for business purposes, in preference to better-governed and controlled alternatives.

---

1 For example, on 26 June 2021, Symantec, McAfee and Fireye's market capitalisations were valued at $15.65B, $12.22B and $4.97B respectively.

## Malicious technology and code

In the field of information and cybersecurity, practitioners often talk about threats, in the sense of the 'threat landscape' and 'threat actors'. Security breaches and incidents commonly arise because of the actions of a threat actor, and threat actors can broadly be categorised as:

- Malicious insiders. Those with legitimate access to data and technology, but who choose to cause an issue or an incident.
- Accidental insiders. Those with legitimate access to data and technology, who accidentally misuse or disclose data through human error, thereby causing an issue or an incident, such as a misaddressed email.
- External actors. These can be further sub-categorised by capability and motivation, from (generally speaking) those with the greatest level of sophistication to the least:
  - State-sponsored advanced persistent threat groups (APTs). Examples include APT29, sometimes called 'Cosy Bear', who are believed to be associated with the intelligence agencies of Russia. A number of significant cyberattacks against governments, militaries and associated entities have been attributed to them.
  - Cyberterrorists and cybercriminals. Examples include the Darkside ransomware gang, who generally seek to generate profit and revenue from cyber-enabled crime and who can use the funds raised through cybercrime to develop further offensive cyber technology.
  - Hacktivists. Examples include the Anonymous hacking group, who are typically out to prove an ideological point. They may have significant computing power and capability, such as control of botnets.[2]
  - Script kiddies. This is a term to describe individuals who have adopted often powerful offensive technology that has been developed by others and use it to target and attack technology assets belonging to others, for fun, kudos, or other reasons.
  - White hat hackers/security researchers. These are individuals or organisations that seek to identify vulnerable infrastructure by scouring the internet for connected devices, databases and so on. Rather than exploiting those vulnerabilities, a white hat hacker would follow a set of rules of engagement called 'responsible disclosure rules' to notify the operator of the vulnerable system and encourage them to remediate the issues found. White hat researchers are typically motivated by kudos and bug bounties (payments offered by companies in return for responsible notifications of vulnerabilities found).

As described by their name, APTs are advanced in terms of their technological ability. They often have the funding of nation states to develop and deploy offensive cyber technologies to perpetuate attacks against their chosen or given targets. Those targets might include other governments or militaries, critical national infrastructure providers of other countries, or other targets. The UK has a National Cyber Force that is dedicated

---

[2] A botnet is a collection of internet-connected devices that have a 'bot' (a software program) installed to run automated scripts and which can be controlled by central command and control software to perform specific tasks.

to offensive action to combat security threats and is organised as a joint initiative between the Ministry of Defence and GCHQ (the UK government intelligence agency tasked with signals intelligence). What the UK designates as a cyber force would likely be classed as APTs by unfriendly states. Viewpoints aside, the common denominators of APTs around the world is that they develop very advanced technological means to attack enemy technology assets and data for the purposes of stealing information or causing disruption to technology-reliant services, often with state backing.

Likewise, cybercriminal organisations have the ability to use the funds generated by cybercrime and other criminal enterprises to develop new offensive technology to execute cyberattacks. The research and development that is undertaken by APTs and other threat actors includes work such as research into technical vulnerabilities, normally in the computer code of internet-facing technology devices, and the development of technology tools that can be used to exploit such vulnerabilities and perform unauthorised actions. As this description indicates, threat actors are themselves using state-of-the-art technology to cause harm.

Another key aspect of the development and use of malicious technologies to cause harm is that the intellectual property (i.e. the malicious code itself and instructions for its use) can pass through various hands over time. A state-of-the-art attack developed by an APTs might include advanced methods to obfuscate itself so that detective cyberthreat hunting technology cannot detect it. Sooner or later, the vulnerability and exploit will be identified by legitimate security researchers and developers, after which defensive technology will be updated to detect the attack method (such as malicious code) and defend against it (such as patches released to fix the code vulnerability that the attack seeks to exploit). At this point the APTs may decide that the malicious code has exceeded its useful lifespan for their own purposes and sell it to a criminal group who can use it for their purposes. Later that group may make it freely available on hacker forums on the Dark Web, where it is picked up and made use of by hacktivists and script kiddies.

The code being passed down and across to malicious actors is also picked up and further developed by white hat security researchers for use by them. Organisations need to be able to identify when they are being notified of a vulnerability by a white hat security researcher, in order to respond maturely and effectively and avoid pushing such researchers into a potentially harmful course of action. Such researchers often consider it their moral and social duty to disclose vulnerabilities publicly should the organisation being notified respond aggressively or fail to act promptly to remediate or fix the issue disclosed. The UK National Cyber Security Centre has published a responsible disclosure toolkit that contains useful guidance about how organisations can respond appropriately to vulnerabilities disclosed by security researchers.

It is against this backdrop of state-of-the-art malicious code development and hand-me-downs of advanced technological threats that the need to adopt technology and data-focused control solutions in order to treat technology and data-related risks should be considered.

## A TECHNOLOGY REFERENCE ARCHITECTURE FOR THE JOURNEY TO CODE

The 'Core Privacy Technology Value Chain', illustrated in Figure 4.2, is represented by three segments. Those segments alone will not deliver all the required outcomes of data protection by themselves. Instead, they need to interact with all elements of the wider technology and data landscape that supports data processing activities.

### The Core Privacy Technology Value Chain

To briefly elaborate on the segments within the architecture, Table 13.1 provides high-level descriptions for technology segments that support Data Protection by Design and Default.

**Table 13.1 Technology segments within a technology reference architecture for DPbDD**

| Technology segment | Description |
| --- | --- |
| Privacy management technology | Technical tools that generally do not interact directly with personal data, or systems that process personal data themselves, but which provide a workflow to assist individuals and teams to manage data protection tasks and risks. |
| Data intelligence technology | Technology solutions that perform functions on data processing systems and personal data, for instance to search and retrieve data in order that data protection tasks, and processing for other business purposes, can be performed. In large organisations with multiple data processing systems, data intelligence technologies are often overlaid so that they can deliver their functionality across the whole environment. |
| Principles and rights technology | Technology that facilitates the operational delivery of data protection principles and rights in the technology and data layer of the organisation, for instance technologies that deliver technical solutions to protect the confidentiality and integrity of data, or which facilitate storage limitation. |

### PRIVACY MANAGEMENT TECHNOLOGY

The privacy management technology marketplace has seen perhaps the largest increase in uptake in recent years, driven by the emergence of new regulations such as GDPR. These technologies have been adopted at pace by organisations seeking to standardise workflows and operational data protection management processes such as:

- developing and managing records of processing;
- performing assessments, such as risk assessments and lawful basis analyses;
- tracking the progress of time-limited obligations, such as responding to data subject rights requests;

- distribution of policies and training to staff and third parties;
- managing incidents;
- maintaining accountability records.

## The rise of privacy management technologies

Such processes, practices, methodologies and records can, and have for many years, been performed by data controllers and data processors without reliance on privacy management technologies. The GDPR does not mandate or even suggest their use. In fact, the company that is probably the most ubiquitous provider of pure-play privacy management technology globally as of 2021, OneTrust, was not even founded until 2016, the year that the EU adopted the GDPR. OneTrust became the first 'privacy tech unicorn' when it reached a US$1.3 billion valuation in 2019.

The fact that OneTrust has achieved such a rapid and widespread adoption can be seen as part of the evidence of increasing professionalisation within the delivery of data protection operations, driven by new laws and the rising maturity of privacy as a governance function. Other examples of the increasing professionalisation include the rise of the data protection officer and the vast expansion in the size of the professional services community and the reach of membership forums such as the IAPP and Data Protection World Forum. This state of increasing professionalisation creates inevitable momentum for the development of privacy management technologies by technology companies, which are very adept at sensing the commercial opportunities and expert at marshalling their resources to increase awareness levels and then the size of their installed user bases.

## Arguments for the use of privacy management technology

Many privacy management technology solutions come supplied with pre-built processes, templates, forms and access to similar materials that, if adopted and operationalised correctly, can provide a rapid boost to an organisation's ability to manage workflow and complete work to a consistent high standard.

Table 13.2 highlights some of the issues commonly experienced by organisations and data protection practitioners using traditional privacy management techniques, such as spreadsheets and other document-based artefacts and trackers, and how privacy management technology solutions seek to address them.

Considering the issues and the solutions highlighted, it can be argued that if a privacy management solution is used to a broad extent and integrated with other privacy management methods in use by an organisation, it can help to achieve data protection outcomes in practice in a way that is difficult, if not impossible, to achieve via more traditional methods. This is particularly the case for complex modern businesses that may derive the greatest benefits from a technology solution that facilitates the collecting together of information about, or necessary for, compliance into a single source with added intelligibility and usability for the user.

**Table 13.2 How privacy management technology improves on traditional methodologies**

| Topic | Common issues experienced using traditional privacy management methods | Privacy management technology solution |
|---|---|---|
| Records of processing | Spreadsheet-based records of processing can result in version control issues and require significant coordination to complete and manage. | • Intelligible and user-friendly forms can be issued to business teams to gain insight into processing operations, making it easier for them to understand requirements and provide their answers.<br><br>• In turn, this makes it easier for data protection teams to track completion.<br><br>• Some privacy management technologies incorporate, or integrate with, data intelligence technologies to auto-populate (to some extent) records of processing and/or data flow maps and diagrams. |
| Visibility and oversight, for example for risk management | Business teams failing to share status or insights regarding risk triage or assessments over new processing, or changes to existing processing. | • Data protection risk triage and further assessments are conducted within the system, by way of forms that business teams complete.<br><br>• Review alerts can be generated, or tasks added to the data protection team's workflow. |
| Connectivity between processes | Individual artefacts, such as records of processing, risk assessments and so on, sit as standalone artefacts and it can be difficult (especially after the passage of time, such as in an investigation) to tie them together to form a holistic view | • The system supports hyperlinking between modules, artefacts and processes.<br><br>• For instance, the records of processing may contain hyperlinks to associated risk assessments, lawful basis evidence (consent records, legitimate interests assessments, etc.). |

*(Continued)*

## Table 13.2 (Continued)

| Topic | Common issues experienced using traditional privacy management methods | Privacy management technology solution |
|---|---|---|
| Information rights management | Hand-offs between business teams that are each responsible for different elements of a process can be difficult, clunky, time-consuming and ultimately lead to missed deadlines or poor quality outcomes. | • Workflow automation for data search, retrieval and redaction.<br>• Some workflow tools enable users to work concurrently on different elements of the same process.<br>• Other workflow tools enable users to effectively forecast their completion of tasks so that downstream teams can prepare for their element of the work. |
| Reporting | Reporting on key performance and risk indicators can be difficult when data are not available, need to be created manually, or are held in disparate places. | Provides inbuilt dashboard and reporting functionality that draws from data created as a matter of standard operational use. |

## Drawbacks associated with privacy management technology

The adoption of a privacy management solution involves time, effort and cost. It is often the case that the solutions are offered as modular (e.g. data subject rights handling modules, records of processing modules, risk assessments modules) and access to each of them requires licences to be purchased on a per-user or a time-period basis. This can involve significant cost over time. If the individual or team responsible for data protection in any given organisation is already over-stretched and struggling to keep on top of their day job, they are not likely to have the spare time to develop or adopt privacy management technologies.

Another reason that costs may escalate is that the provider alters their pricing or changes their licencing model. By way of market evidence, changes to licencing pricing models have caused significant issues for clients of major ERP and governance risk and compliance solutions in recent years.

There is a further issue to consider, familiar to many users of many different types of technology, which is being locked in to the supplier technology ecosystem. That is to say that once adopted, it may be difficult to reduce reliance on, or move away from, such a supporting technology. Moving away from a privacy management technology solution may become desirable for any number of reasons including mergers and acquisitions, or finding that the solution does not, or no longer, supports business requirements, or the costs become prohibitive.

## DATA INTELLIGENCE TECHNOLOGY

Data intelligence technology is a broad term that encompasses technologies that are used to deliver analysis and integration of data for a variety of business purposes. In contrast to privacy management technology, they have often been developed and adopted for broader reasons than data protection risk management and compliance (although some of the more recent entrants to the market claim to have been developed specifically for data protection use cases), including investigations and forensic analysis, fraud management, data integration, business intelligence and predictive analytics. From 2016 onward they have found additional utility in data protection use cases, particularly for performing data discovery and searches to assist with the development of Article 30 records.

In comparison to privacy management technology, there is a stronger argument for the existence of a legal requirement for data intelligence technology to be in place for technology environments that process data in digital form. For example, any valid data subject rights request would require the controller to take action, but it would not be possible to do so in most cases without the ability to, at a bear minimum, search for and retrieve data concerning the data subject from the data estate (see the *Dawson-Damer* (2017)[3] case, about searches for subject access purposes). In a digital data environment, a technology solution is the only answer to this legislative requirement.

Data intelligence technologies may also be used to facilitate other important data protection obligations, such as those relating to accuracy (GDPR A.5.b), for instance by delivering data reconciliation functionality to compare a variety of data records held about a specific individual and highlight instances where they do not conform, to help the controller to determine whether this is an issue and to resolve it, if necessary.

### Native and third-party data intelligence technology

Data intelligence technology can often be found natively within systems that process personal data, or it might be designed and implemented as add-on systems that integrate with a variety of technology systems to provide their functionality across a broad technology estate.

Examples of native data intelligence functionality include:

- find and replace functionality in Microsoft Office software, such as Excel;
- search functionality provided by Microsoft Explorer or other filing systems, that can be used to search local drives and shared drives;
- email search functionality, such as that available to standard users and the more powerful functionality commonly available to administrators;

---

[3] *Dawson-Damer v. Taylor Wessing LLP* (2017) EWCA Civ 74.

- functionality allowing for search, retrieval and querying of data built into ERP systems, such as SAP and Oracle.

Issues with relying on native data intelligence functionality include:

- Search functionality only works on the individual system, meaning that the user must repeat the same operation multiple times if they need to search across multiple systems.
- Effort to collate and take further actions is time-consuming and labour intensive.
- Functionality is often lacking, weak or partial in comparison to that provided by systems developed specifically for data intelligence purposes.
- If functionality is weak or not available, after search and retrieval has been performed the user may need to apply third-party functionality, that is, take a hybrid approach.

Given that most organisations use a variety of data processing systems, it is increasingly common for large and complex organisations to rely upon an integrated system to provide a common level of functionality spanning the entire data and technology estate. Use cases for such technology arise most strongly when data processing systems do not possess suitable functionality natively. For large organisations, there is a reasonable chance that data intelligence technology may already have been adopted to support other business purposes, such as those already mentioned, the use of which could be expanded to support data protection purposes.

Small organisations, by comparison, may not have the means to adopt specialist data intelligence technology, or they may not find the benefit proportionate to the cost and effort.

**Small and medium-sized enterprise challenges – employment agency example**
A scenario might involve these situations:

- an employment agency stores spreadsheets and Word documents containing worker availability information, background checks, CVs and contracts between schools and agency staff on a shared network drive;
- it manages invoicing, payments and accounts through third-party cloud-based software;
- it uses email for everyday business matters such as confirming staff placements, including personal data of agency staff.

This organisation investigated the need for data intelligence technology after receiving some complaints from schools and agency staff, with data subject rights requests attached to some of them. Whilst these were difficult to deal with using the native functionality provided by the systems used by the company, they were low in volume and the company decided that having learned lessons from their experience they would be able to manage any future rights requests effectively using the same tools. This would be a proportionate conclusion.

### Small and medium-sized enterprise challenges – furniture retailer with online and physical stores

A scenario might involve these situations:

- the store outsources the processing of website payments to a third party, including the hosting of payment pages;
- the store operates two sales order systems, one for online orders that was adopted 18 months ago and one that was adopted 20 years ago to support physical stores;
- HR data are processed using cloud-based software-as-a-service.

This store needed to develop records of processing for the purposes of GDPR A.30. It realised that it was taking store staff a disproportionate amount of time to find information about customer orders compared to staff supporting online sales. The store defined their requirements and investigated data intelligence technology, finding a solution that met its needs. The solution enabled the organisation to search for and retrieve data records from all major processing environments and to alter data within the third-party cloud systems (i.e. online sales data and HR data) if necessary. This would seem to be a proportionate response to the opportunity to introduce data intelligence technology.

### Third-party integrated data intelligence technology

There are many providers of this type of technology solution, some with a background in forensics, or eDiscovery, use cases. Examples include Nuix and Relativity, which can be used to aid investigations and gain insights from vast quantities of data. For example, Nuix was reportedly used by the International Consortium of Investigative Journalists to analyse the 'Panama Papers', and Relativity is often used to query, search and analyse large data sets in support of large, complex cybersecurity and legal investigations.

Providers such as Big ID provide workflows and functionality to enable the fulfilment of a variety of data protection obligations by integrating with the data processing systems and technologies themselves, within the environment in which the data processing takes place.

The types of functionality that are advertised in the market are illustrated in Table 13.3.

**Table 13.3 Data intelligence functionality mapped to GDPR requirements**

| Supported functionality | Data protection issue | Associated GDPR articles |
|---|---|---|
| Data discovery and cataloguing | Records of processing | A.30 |
| Data correlation | Accuracy | A.5d |
| Data flow analysis and visualisation | Processors | A.28 |
|  | International transfers | A.44 |

*(Continued)*

## Table 13.3 (Continued)

| Supported functionality | Data protection issue | Associated GDPR articles |
|---|---|---|
| Data search, retrieval, rectification, deletion | Data subject rights | A.12–23 |
| | Purpose limitation | A.5b |
| | Storage limitation | A.5e |
| | Security | A.32 |
| | Incident management | A.33 |
| Data categorisation | Purpose limitation | A.5b |
| | Security | A.32 |

Just as with privacy management technology, the adoption of any new technology normally requires time, effort and skill. If the individual or team responsible for data protection cannot afford to invest sufficient time and effort in the deployment, or if it lacks the ability to describe the functional requirements and scope of deployment, it will be exceedingly difficult to adopt a data intelligence solution that is fit for purpose. Budget is also an important factor when considering a third-party data intelligence technology, because they can be very costly to deploy and manage. Other considerations for selecting a third-party data intelligence technology are shown in Table 13.4.

### Table 13.4 Example issues to consider when selecting data intelligence technology

| | |
|---|---|
| Functionality | • What 'off the shelf' functionality needs to be available and what are you willing to configure? |
| | • This may include, for instance, inbuilt search terms for common types of personal data (government ID numbers, credit card data, etc.) whereas if you use a specific 'regular expression'[4] numbering or naming convention for staff or customer identifiers it is likely that this would need to be configured as part of deployment. |
| Scope and nature of deployment | • Does the technology need to operate to provide functionality over corporate systems, file shares, cloud systems, user endpoints (such as laptops), or some combination thereof? |
| | • Does the technology need to cover only data at rest, or also data in transit across (and in and out of) the network? |
| Interoperability | • Does the technology solution interoperate with the systems where data are being processed, or are there interoperability gaps that need to be considered? |

*(Continued)*

---

[4] A regular expression is a specific sequence of characters that specifies a search pattern. For example, a UK national insurance number is two letters followed by six numbers followed by a character. This regular expression can be used to define a search pattern, that is, to command a data intelligence technology solution what to look for.

## Table 13.4 (Continued)

| | |
|---|---|
| Encryption | • Is data at rest or data in transit encrypted, and if so, will the solution be able to 'read' the data it is intended to? |
| Security | • The functionality available through data intelligence technologies is powerful, including the ability to alter and delete data from production systems. |
| | • Significant issues, including risks to rights and freedoms of data subjects and business interruption, could result from incorrect, accidental or malicious use. |
| Authorisation | • Given all the above, will the IT department allow data intelligence endpoint agents or network monitors to be deployed? |

## PRINCIPLES AND RIGHTS TECHNOLOGY

Principles and rights technology facilitate the operational delivery of the data protection principles in the technology and data layer of the organisation.

To a certain extent, both privacy management technologies and data intelligence technologies might be considered to also be principles and rights technologies, if they deliver principles and rights functionality with respect to data and achieve principles and rights outcomes. For example, a privacy management technology that facilitates reporting via dashboards could be considered to be an accountability tool. A data intelligence technology that searches for and retrieves data could be considered a data subject access or portability tool, that is, a rights tool. Table 13.5 gives examples of technologies that support and help to deliver data protection principles.

### Table 13.5 Examples of principles and rights technology

| Principle | Facilitating technology |
|---|---|
| Lawfulness, fairness and transparency | • Consent and preference management technology, such as those offered by OneTrust, SAP, Akamai and other providers provide technological methods of making data processing transparent to the data subject and giving them direct control over the ways in which it can be processed. |
| | • Some consent and preference management solutions even provide automated data subject rights functionality. These are commonly presented to the data subject by way of a web interface providing toggles to precisely configure their preferences about use of the data. |

*(Continued)*

### Table 13.5 (Continued)

| Principle | Facilitating technology |
|---|---|
| Accuracy | See data intelligence technology (data correlation and reconciliation). |
| Storage limitation | Data that no longer have a lawful basis for retention (such as that which are subject to a valid request for erasure from a data subject) must be deleted or otherwise made irreversibly non-personal through an anonymisation process. Technological means through which these outcomes are commonly achieved include:<br><br>• Applying natively available or third-party data intelligence search and deletion functionality to data in production systems to alter or remove data such that they can no longer be used to identify data subjects<br><br>• Scheduled deletion of backups,[5] which can be programmed and automated such that backups are deleted after a set period of retention. It should be noted, however, that it can be operationally difficult to fulfil erasure obligations over individual data records, because backup solutions often do not possess native search and alteration functionality and data intelligence deployments are not commonly extended to backup archives. |
| Integrity and confidentiality (security) | Security is possibly the data protection principle most supported by existing technology. Examples of security enabling technologies include:<br><br>• identify and access management tools and systems;<br>• anti-virus;<br>• threat detection;<br>• automated code review tools;<br>• data leakage prevention;<br>• virtual private networks;<br>• multifactor authentication;<br>• encryption. |

---

5  A backup is a copy taken of computerised data, which is stored in a non-production environment in order that it can be used to restore services if the original data are lost or corrupted.

## PRODUCERS OF TECHNOLOGY AND DATA PROCESSING SYSTEMS

During the legislative process that led to the adoption of the GDPR in 2016 it was proposed that the producers of technology and data processing systems should be regulated by the law. This proposal did not make its way into the final version of the regulation, although when these producers are involved in the determination of the purposes and means of data processing, they will be regulated as controllers, or if they process personal data on behalf of controllers they will be regulated as processors. Many producers of technology and data processing systems will be captured by the law through these routes. However, if they are not captured, does this leave a regulatory gap?

### A regulatory gap

The arguments have been finely balanced for many years, but as the pace of technological development advances, the risk of a serious regulatory gap emerging increases. This risk arises from the fact that the users of advanced technologies might not have meaningful powers, skills and resources to truly influence the design and operation of them. Take AI as an example. This is an impenetrable area for most people to comprehend and deal with. Moreover, as the markets concentrate around 'big tech' companies, the imbalance in powers can only widen further.

None of these risks absolve controller and processors of their duties, however. Instead, they will somehow have to adjust their risk management processes to cater for the situation before them.

Unfortunately, developing fit-for-purpose risk management systems for new technologies is easier to write about than to operationalise in practice. If the status quo pertains there must be a real likelihood of risks being untreated, to the ultimate detriment of the users of the controller and processors involved and the data subjects whom the law is meant to protect.

### Solutions to the regulatory gap

Among the practical solutions to these problems are for the producers of technology and data processing systems to be brought within the scope of the law as originally proposed, either through the amendment of the GDPR or through the adoption of other laws that fill the gap, or for them to take more proactive responsibility for baking data protection into their products and services.

The former solution is hinted at in new laws, such as the EU's proposed Regulation on digital operational resilience,[6] which will put critical information and communications technology service providers under regulatory supervision, giving hope to the ambition for legislation to fill some of the gaps that the GDPR has left in its wake at some point in the future.

The acceptance of the need for the producers to take greater responsibility for data protection is also starting to emerge as a business fact. For example, during the COVID-19

---

[6] Proposal for a Regulation of the European Parliament and Council on digital operational resilience for the financial sector and amending Regulations (EC) No 1060/2009, (EU) No 648/2012, (EU) No 600/2014 and (EU) No 909/2014.

pandemic, Apple and Google joined together to support a more rights-friendly approach to contact tracing apps than had been proposed by some governments. Other examples include Apple's approach to online tracking and the development of alternative browser systems that put privacy interests ahead of the goal of unmitigated tracking. These developments are responsive to market needs and the increasing awareness of data protection rights in society, which gives hope for increasing enlightenment in the field of technology production in the years ahead.

Pending a new era of full enlightenment in the technology sector, perhaps the best that most controllers and processors can do is to stay alert to the risks and to apply pressure wherever they can, to gain better insights from the producers into their approaches to data protection, while keeping a distance (insofar as that is possible) from producers that do not have a compelling data protection narrative. Alongside this, the regulators, politicians, industry groups and other powerful stakeholders can take on more of the responsibility to identify data protection-safe vendors and to educate the communities around them on good and bad practices.

In the medium term, perhaps some of the burden can be carried by certification schemes and codes of conduct. Elsewhere in this book it has been observed that these compliance mechanisms have not yet delivered meaningful outcomes, but the potential for them to do so is obvious. Hopefully, a system of certification and codes will emerge in due course that results in compliance Kitemarks being appended to deserving technologies and their producers.

### The risk of a litigation culture emerging

However, in the short term at least, controllers and processors will continue to rely upon technology and data processing systems that will not be fit for purpose from a data protection standpoint. In that case they will be liable to the regulatory system and data subjects during the exercise of their rights, which include the right to judicial remedies for compensation for damage and distress suffered. Controllers and processors will then have to turn to their contractual remedies against the producers. A litigation culture around these matters now seems almost inevitable.

## WHAT COMES NEXT ON THE JOURNEY TO CODE?

This chapter has largely given an account of the privacy management, data intelligence, and principles and rights technology solutions that are available today, corresponding to the data protection operational issues that they address. At one point in time, all of these would have been considered beyond the state of the art, but they are now commonplace and therefore would generally be considered to be within the GDPR requirement for appropriate technical measures. Looking to the state of the art, it is worth remembering that most of the time technological progress is about evolution, and rarely about revolution. It seems reasonable to predict that the uptake of the types of technology already discussed will increase as a result of them becoming more affordable, easier to integrate and easier to manage, most probably as a result of legal interventions by regulators, data subjects, civil society organisations and privacy activists.

## 'Your mission, should you choose to accept it'

In the late 1960s and early 1970s there was a *Mission Impossible* television show. Towards the beginning of each episode the protagonist would get hold of a recording that always contained the phrase 'Your mission, should you choose to accept it ...' before disclosing the dangerous tasks that lay ahead. At the end of the recording, the tape on which the message was playing would evaporate in a puff of smoke or a small explosion, effectively destroying the recording and the information it contained, thereby preventing its further use, the chance of it falling into the wrong hands and the risks of harm being caused.

On reflection, it might be considered somewhat remarkable that this sort of time-bombing of data and information has not become commonplace, given that its usefulness was shown to us with dramatic effect 50 years ago. Of course, time-bombing code is a technique sometimes used to stop trial-release software from working after a predetermined period of use, but the equivalent outcome has not yet been developed such that it can be applied on individual data sets or records, or, at least, not on a commercially viable basis at enterprise scale for data protection law compliance purposes. However, the automated, programmed destruction of data according to preset rules or by remote control is exactly the type of control that The Journey to Code envisages as forming part of the state of the art in due course.

The range of issues that the Journey to Code covers in the technology and data layer is seemingly infinite, such as the continuing development of trusted research environments, where personal data dependent business innovations can be safely tried and tested; the co-development with the regulators of innovative technology ideas (per the intent of regulatory sandboxes); the data protection application of technologies that are gaining traction for other purposes, but have not been developed for rights outcomes (such as blockchain); the enabling of rights relevant auditing of the technology and data layer (such as for data minimisation); the use of metadata to drive automation and new products and services; the testing of code itself, to ensure quality outcomes and the reduction of unintended consequences (such as biases and discrimination). The nature of this list supports another insight: the involvement of technologists, data scientists and similar technical experts in the delivery of DPbDD will increase.

## SUMMARY

In conclusion, this chapter gives readers a better understanding of:

- the importance of achieving data protection outcomes within technology and data themselves;
- how the use of technology reference architecture can help controllers and processors to understand the technology and data layers of their organisation where data protection outcomes need to be achieved;
- elements of technology that form part of the Core Privacy Technology Value Chain for achieving these outcomes;
- the responsibilities that controllers and processors have for technology and data processing systems developed by others.

# PART V
# ADVERSE SCRUTINY

# 14 HOW TO PREPARE FOR THE RISKS OF CHALLENGE AND 'ADVERSE SCRUTINY'

## Stewart Room

This chapter explores the issues of challenge and scrutiny, identifying when these situations may arise, their impacts and the steps that can be taken to deal with them.

### CHALLENGE AND SCRUTINY ARE INEVITABLE

An unavoidable truth of data protection is that processing activities will be regularly subjected to challenge, criticism and scrutiny, often by people who are adverse to the controller, the processor, or the purpose that the processing serves. This can happen not only when there is operational failure, such as after a security breach, but even when the processing results from good intentions, such as an aim to serve the wider interests of humankind. For example, the processing initiatives that were adopted for virus control during the COVID-19 pandemic, such as contact tracing apps and vaccine passports, which have the noble aim to protect public health, have been subject to significant scrutiny on proportionality grounds relating to civil liberties, including data protection.

Therefore, as part of Data Protection by Design and Default and proper risk management, controllers and processors need to understand and factor in the risks of challenge and scrutiny. This means:

- understanding who is likely to raise challenge and scrutiny, when and why;
- understanding the modus operandi of the challenger and scrutineer, what their motivations and motives look like, how they operate and what they are looking for;
- being ready and prepared for challenge and scrutiny, including knowing what an effective response looks like, including when to cooperate and when to push back;
- understanding the strengths and weaknesses of their position and having key accountability evidence to hand, ready to disclose at appropriate points where necessary;
- understanding the linkages between different types of risk and challenge and the potential domino effects;
- understanding how to use legal professional privilege and other mechanisms to enable confidential communications and discussions to take place during times of challenge and scrutiny.

## CHALLENGE AND SCRUTINY DESIGNED INTO REGULATORY LAW

The purpose of regulatory law, which the GDPR and PEC are examples of, is to deliver predefined behavioural outcomes within the regulated community. These outcomes are the achievement of the public policy objectives described in the law, including risk mitigation through adherence to the data protection principles, to reduce the potential of harm being caused to the rights and freedoms of individuals.

Data protection law therefore has challenge and scrutiny baked in as a key design feature.

### Adverse scrutiny

While much of the work that regulators undertake with controllers and processors comes from a neutral or benign standpoint (publication of guidance, codes of practice, etc.) in many situations the challenge and scrutiny is adverse:

- Formal regulatory investigations, enforcement actions and monetary penalties. UK law accepts that the exercise of these regulatory powers are forms of adversarial legal proceedings, akin to litigation and prosecutions.

Data subjects have their own regulatory powers, which are sometimes used in an adversarial manner:

- Weaponised exercise of rights. When data subjects exercise their rights, sometimes this is motivated from an adversarial position. Indeed, people often talk about the use of data protection rights as being 'weaponised', when they are used to further another agenda that may not be just about data protection. For example, some data subjects do the rounds of controllers, seeking compensation for alleged distress caused by alleged contraventions of the law.

### The supervisory authority

The main reasons for why the regulator will apply challenge and scrutiny are shown in Table 14.1.

**Table 14.1 Forms of challenge and scrutiny by the regulator**

| | |
|---|---|
| To understand things | • The regulators will apply challenge and scrutiny to understand the nature of data processing in society and the economy. |
| | • This is done by holding controllers and processors to account, through the use of information-gathering and investigatory powers. |
| | • In the UK, these powers include Assessment Notices and Information Notices. |

*(Continued)*

**Table 14.1 (Continued)**

| | |
|---|---|
| To cause behavioural change | • Regulators seek to change the ways that controllers and processors operate, through the giving of guidance, advice and recommendations.<br>• In the most serious cases they can use Enforcement Notices.<br>• These notices may require controllers and processors to take specific steps, or to desist from specific steps. |
| Fines to cause change | • Regulatory fines have three ideas within them:<br>  ▪ Discipline – they intend to change behaviours through the disciplinary effect of punishment.<br>  ▪ Disgorgement – by extracting a fine, the punished party does not gain an advantage from their unlawful behaviours.<br>  ▪ Deterrent – the imposition of fines teaches other would-be infringers of the law that they will not gain from their unlawful behaviours. |

## The data subject

Data subjects' rights and powers for challenge and scrutiny serve these key purposes:

- to provide them with transparency (e.g. the information rights within GDPR A.13–15 and 34);
- to give them powers over data processing (e.g. the right to object to processing, or the power to withdraw consent);
- to give them remedies for unlawful behaviours affecting them.

The impact that these rights and powers can have in combination makes them highly effective weapons.

## A legal duty to understand the risks of challenge and scrutiny

As already mentioned, the risks of challenge and scrutiny form part of the law's design. Therefore, the need to understand and deal with these risks forms part of the legal duty of data protection. The rules on accountability and regulatory cooperation further illustrate this point, as do the rules on data subject rights.

## THE CONTINUUM OF CHALLENGE AND SCRUTINY

Challenge and scrutiny can occur during the design phases of data processing and after it begins. Challenge and scrutiny can arise internally, from within the controllers' or processors' organisations, or externally, from outside. The motives might be neutral, benign, self-serving, or malign. It can focus on legacy issues of data protection, or new and emerging issues. Figure 14.1 provides an illustration of the continuum of scrutiny with examples of the kinds of scrutineers that an organisation may encounter.

**Figure 14.1 The continuum of scrutiny**

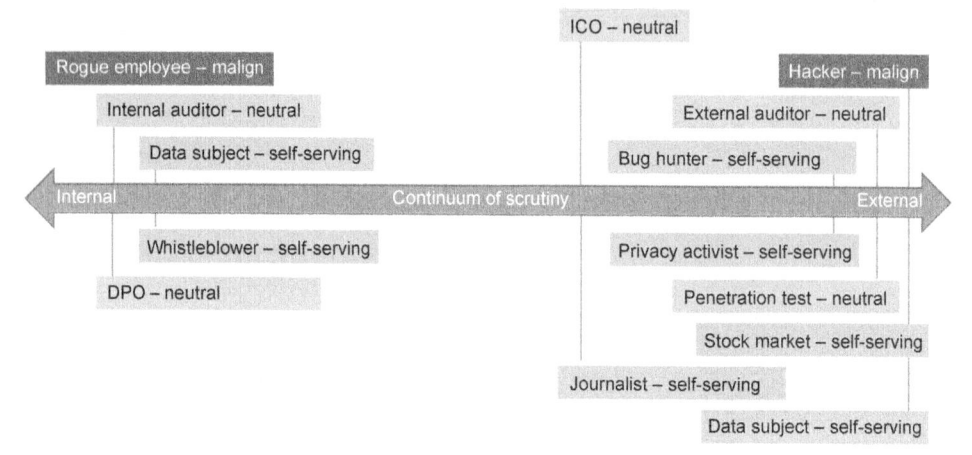

- ICO – neutral
- Rogue employee – malign
- Hacker – malign
- Internal auditor – neutral
- External auditor – neutral
- Data subject – self-serving
- Bug hunter – self-serving
- Internal ← Continuum of scrutiny → External
- Whistleblower – self-serving
- Privacy activist – self-serving
- DPO – neutral
- Penetration test – neutral
- Stock market – self-serving
- Journalist – self-serving
- Data subject – self-serving

### Why a continuum?

The *Oxford English Dictionary* defines a continuum as 'a continuous sequence in which adjacent elements are perceptibly different from each other, but the extremes are quite distinct'. This is apt to describe challenge and scrutiny in data protection: they can be hard to compartmentalise in practice. In real-life situations they often bleed into one another.

For example, the actions of a rogue employee (an internal, malign scrutineer) may trigger a regulatory investigation by the ICO (a neutral, external scrutineer) and then lead to civil litigation by compensation claimants (self-serving, external scrutineers). This domino effect, of an initial form of challenge and scrutiny leading to others, explains why the idea of real-life challenge and scrutiny is described here as a continuum. Understanding that there is a continuum and how it operates is part and parcel of data protection risk management and discharge of legal duties.

### Examples of internal challengers and scrutineers

Some of the types of internal challengers and scrutineers that a controller and processor may encounter are identified in Table 14.2.

## Table 14.2 Types of internal challenger/scrutineer

| | |
|---|---|
| Lines of defence | • People operating in a lines of defence model for risk management purposes.<br>• Examples include named officers with designated functions, such as a data protection officer or a chief information security officer, and those with assurance functions, such as internal audit. |
| Expert advisors | People operating in an expert advisory capacity, for example general counsel. |
| Executives and governance | People with executive powers and governance roles, including company secretaries and non-executive directors. |
| Workers | Workers and their representatives (e.g. trade unions). Situations include:<br>• Workers acting as data subjects.<br>• Workers acting as whistle-blowers.<br>• Workers acting in rogue fashion. |

## Moral spectrum

The continuum can also be envisioned from a moral perspective, because sometimes challenge and scrutiny is defined not by role type or position, but by the motives of the actor and what is done.

The worker example in Table 14.2 shows two examples that arguably operate at opposite ends of a moral continuum, namely whistle-blowers and rogue insiders. These actors can be drawn from any part of the organisation, at any level of seniority. A recent example of a high-profile data protection case involving a whistle-blower is the Cambridge Analytica scandal (Christopher Wylie). Perhaps the most famous whistle-blower of modern times is Edward Snowden, whose disclosures about mass surveillance in 2012 involved one of the central concerns of data protection. In contrast *WM Morrison Supermarkets Plc v. Various Claimants* (2020)[1] concerned a rogue insider who committed a personal data breach against his colleagues that was designed to hurt his employer.

## Examples of external challengers and scrutineers

External challengers and scrutineers may include:

- in addition to the data protection regulators, there are others with overlapping duties, such as the Competition and Markets Authority, the Financial Conduct Authority and Ofcom;

---

[1] (2020) UKSC 12.

- customers and users of services;
- the press and news media;
- claims management companies, which help people to bring compensation claims, sometimes through litigation;
- insurance companies, due to their underwriting of risks;
- business competitors;
- civil society organisations;
- stock markets, investors and shareholders;
- politicians;
- business competitors.

### The regulatory bear market

The range of challengers and scrutineers potentially facing controllers and processors therefore is vast. By bringing challenge and scrutiny, these actors can foster a sense of negativity about data protection, which can be difficult to break. This gives rise to a regulatory bear market, a time of negative sentiment and loss of confidence, leading to sustained negative outcomes, that is, complaints, regulatory investigations, compensation claims, litigation and 'bad news' stories in the media. In some areas of data processing, the negative sentiment is seemingly unbreakable, with AdTech and AFR being obvious reference points. From time to time, major US technology companies have struggled to break the cycle of negativity within the cycles of scrutiny and challenge that they face.

### Civil society organisations

Civil society organisations are empowered by the GDPR to represent data subjects in the bringing of complaints to the regulators and to the courts (Article 80). The hallmarks of these organisations are their not-for-profit status; that they act in the public interest; and they are active in the field of data protection. These organisations can include bodies that are sometimes known as privacy activists, or advocates, or champions.

There is a long track record of privacy activists delivering substantial change in data protection. High-profile cases include the ones led by Max Schrems, about international data transfers. In the UK, the Hacked Off campaign played a leading role in widening understanding about the phone-hacking scandal. Digital Rights Ireland played a leading role in litigation before the CJEU that brought an end to the Data Retention Directive 2006[2] and in the first case about the right to be forgotten and the duties that apply to search engines as controllers (the *Google Spain* (2014) case).

## MODELLING CHALLENGE AND SCRUTINY RISKS

An effective approach to data protection therefore needs the controller to model its challenge and scrutiny risks and then to put in place appropriate technical and organisational measures to address those risks. These requirements arise both directly and indirectly from the wording of the legislation.

---

2   Cases C-293/12 and C-594/12, 2014.

For example, if adverse scrutiny is caused by a rogue actor and it manifests as a personal data breach, in certain situations Article 33 of the GDPR will require the controller to inform the regulator of 'the measures taken or proposed to be taken by the controller to address the personal data breach, including, where appropriate, measures to mitigate its possible effects'. The obligation to mitigate 'possible effects' cannot be satisfied without the modelling of the risks. These risks might include:

- the risk of distress that impacted individuals may suffer when they discover that there has been a personal data breach and a loss of control over their data;
- identify theft;
- fraud risks.

**Situations in the GDPR calling for risk assessments**

The modelling of risk requires an assessment of:

- the nature of the risk under contemplation;
- the likelihood of the risk crystallising as an event or incident;
- the possible impacts if an event or incident were to happen.

Table 14.3 identifies some of the situations in the GDPR where the need for risk modelling arises.

**Table 14.3 Situations in the GDPR that require modelling of risk**

| | |
|---|---|
| Article 24.1 | • This is part of the general obligations of the controller. |
| | • It requires the controller to take account of 'the risks of varying likelihood and severity for the rights and freedoms of natural persons' when implementing measures for compliance. |
| Article 25.1 | • The rules on Data Protection by Design and Default repeat Article 24.1's focus on 'risk of varying likelihood (etc.)', to provide a timeframe for when the modelling needs to be done. |
| Article 32.1 | • This is about the security of processing and it repeats the previous examples' focus on 'risk of varying likelihood (etc.)', for the purpose of identifying the necessary security measures. |
| Article 33.1 | • This is about breach notification to the regulator, which requires the controller to consider whether a personal data breach is 'unlikely to result in a risk to the rights and freedoms of natural persons' before departing from the default position of giving notice to the regulator. |
| Article 34.1 | • This is about breach notification to people affected. It requires the controller to give notification where the breach 'is likely to result in a high risk to the rights and freedoms of natural persons'. |

*(Continued)*

## Table 14.3 (Continued)

| | |
|---|---|
| Article 35.1 | • This is about data protection impact assessments.<br>• It requires the controller to consider whether its processing activities are 'likely to result in a high risk to the rights and freedoms of natural persons' and, if they are, to 'carry out an assessment of the impact of the envisaged processing operations on the protection of personal data'. |

## Risk scenarios and context-specific risk modelling

Risk modelling can be performed by reference to risk scenarios, but risk scenarios are context-specific, differing from organisation to organisation, so a one-size-fits-all approach does not really exist.

Something more bespoke is required in practice. There are many starting points for developing an understanding of the risk scenarios that an organisation needs to address. Two examples include:

- The special characteristics. These are the operating and environmental features of the organisation that influence or determine its behaviours, thereby making it unique.
- The tiers of visibility. Generally speaking, challengers and scrutineers are reactive to the things that they see.

## The special characteristics and how they relate to modelling

Data protection law recognises the significance of special characteristics. For example, regulatory guidance on breach notification issued by the European Data Protection Board's predecessor, the Article 29 Working Party,[3] which the EDPB has endorsed, draws attention to the need to understand these aspects when assessing the risks to rights and freedoms that may be caused by a personal data breach. Extracts from the guidance are shown in the box below.

> **The importance of special characteristics recognised by law**
>
> Special characteristics of the individual – A breach may affect personal data concerning children or other vulnerable individuals, who may be placed at greater risk of danger as a result. There may be other factors about the individual that may affect the level of impact of the breach on them.
>
> Special characteristics of the data controller – The nature and role of the controller and its activities may affect the level of risk to individuals as a result of a breach. For example, a medical organisation will process special categories of personal data, meaning that there is a greater threat to individuals if their personal data is breached, compared with a mailing list of a newspaper.

---

[3] WP250 rev.01.

Examples of some of the kinds of special characteristics that are relevant to the causation, size and impact of challenge and scrutiny risks are shown in Table 14.4.

**Table 14.4 Special characteristics of the controller and processor**

| | |
|---|---|
| Economic/public sector | • Some sectors of the economy have multiple regulators, often with overlapping duties for data protection, meaning that organisations in these sectors will have a greater risk of regulator challenge and scrutiny than in organisations with a lower regulatory burden. |
| | • For example, a telecommunications company will be regulated by Ofcom as well as ICO and if they are providing financial services (e.g. insurance for handsets) they might also be regulated by the Financial Conduct Authority. |
| | • In contrast, many retailers will have a lower regulatory burden. |
| Geographical location | • Following the judgment of the CJEU in the *Schrems II* (2020) case, there was a spike in adverse scrutiny by privacy activists concerning data transfers to the US and other countries outside Europe. |
| | • Geographical location is a key factor within the material scope rules of the GDPR and the rules on the one-stop shop. |
| | • Some data protection regulators are perceived to be more interventionalist and aggressive than others. Italy has this long-held reputation. In contrast, Ireland has been criticised as being weak on US businesses with European headquarters in Dublin. |
| | • The UK is perceived to be the group litigation epicentre of Europe. |
| Processing activities | • Some processing activities are more controversial than others. Cutting-edge, large-scale surveillance technologies spike the interests of leading civil society organisations, which are well resourced and highly effective operators in the court environment. |
| | • In the UK, website cookies are quickly becoming a source of 'micro claims' by savvy individuals who understand the value of making nuisance claims for compensation. |
| Business plan | • A business plan might involve mergers and acquisitions, which unintentionally lead to an organisation absorbing legacy problems that were not discovered during due diligence. |
| | • Some very high-profile personal data breach cases relate to these acquired risks, making the acquirer subject to multiple forms of adverse scrutiny. |

Other special characteristics of the organisation that are relevant to the modelling of challenge and scrutiny risk include: legal and organisational structures; regulatory track record; culture and ethics, resources and risk appetite; and its processing operations.

### The special characteristics of the challenger and scrutineer – motivations and motives

Some of the special characteristics of the challenger and scrutineer have already been touched on. For example, the leading civil society organisations are well resourced, highly skilled and expert in mounting legal challenges. The regulator is also well resourced and has awesome statutory powers (albeit we are still yet to see them being exercised to their limit). Claims management companies have access to all the litigation funding and lawyers they need to drive group litigation.

This points to the motivation and motive of the challenger and scrutineer as being essential parts of their special characteristics. Understanding motivation and motive can help with understanding the situations when challenge and scrutiny can arise, as well as levels of adversity applied, which in turn help with assessing impacts. There are no hard-and-fast rules that apply to the categorisation of motivation and motive, but some categories are set out in Table 14.5.

**Table 14.5 Motives and motivations of challengers and scrutineers**

| | |
|---|---|
| Neutral | • This encompasses a group of challengers and scrutineers who should have no axe to grind. |
| | • Regulators and the judiciary fall into this category, due to the functions they hold and the laws that apply to them. |
| | • Professionals, such as lawyers and auditors, have professional duties that place them naturally within this group. |
| | • Data protection officers, chief information security officers and similar officers are other examples. |
| | • The news media is more complex. Legal rules around balanced journalism are consistent with a benign motivation, but political alignments, the need to drive sales and the changing nature of journalism may place some of the news media in the self-interest category or cause it to straddle both camps. The phone-hacking scandal illustrates what can happen when the press take on a malign spirit. |
| Self-interest | • The range of self-interests that data subjects may protect and advance through their use of their rights, such as the right of access, can extend beyond the parameters of data protection itself, hence the earlier reference to weaponisation of rights. |
| | • However, there are some statutory boundaries to how far that can go. For example, GDPR Article 12.5 says that a controller can refuse to act on rights requests that are 'manifestly unfounded or excessive'. |

*(Continued)*

**Table 14.5 (Continued)**

| | |
|---|---|
| Public-spirited | • This would cover the classic whistle-blower situation. |
| Malign | • Rogue internal and external actors fall within this category. |
| | • Cybersecurity threats can be placed within this category. |

### *Opportunity and persistence*

Thinking about how to categorise challengers and scrutineers by reference to their motivation and motive can help with assessing impacts, because it can bring into focus important questions about the opportunity and persistence of challenge and scrutiny.

For example, while many rogue events might seem to be purely opportunistic, such as bot-controlled cybersecurity threats that scan the web for vulnerabilities (such as open ports to cloud instances), many involve considerable feats of ingenuity, planning and persistence. Therefore, in an impacts sense, rogue challenge and scrutiny may need considerable investment in skills, resources and apparatus to deter, detect, deflect or otherwise deal with them. This is also key to understanding the nature of the technical and organisational measures that are needed to deal appropriately with risks of challenge and scrutiny.

### *Ransomware compared to litigation*

The scourge of ransomware may help to understand some of the connections that the motive and motivation of the adverse scrutineer have to the impacts they cause and how to deal with them. The basic modus operandi of ransomware is as follows:

- data are encrypted and often exfiltrated;
- the attacker sets a financial demand and a time to pay;
- if they are not paid an agreed amount by the deadline, they will publish information about the attack online with the data they have exfiltrated.

In this situation the victim has no leverage other than money. Even if they have backups, which renders the need for decryptors otiose, they will not avoid a public naming and shaming without paying the ransom. The threat actor does not care about the collateral damage they will cause, nor do they care about trying to preserve an asset value, by holding on for payment after the deadline has expired. Once the deadline has expired, the asset value of the data they have encrypted and exfiltrated is gone and they will leave the victim to their suffering and move on to the next one.

In contrast, if the adverse scrutineer is a claimant law firm that is pursuing group litigation on behalf of people whose data have been impacted by the ransomware attack against the attacked organisation, the defendant will still have leverage despite being operationally non-compliant and, therefore, legally exposed. This is because litigation is a costly and time-consuming endeavour for claimants even when they are on very strong ground. Therefore, the claimant law firm will be exposed to the risk of not recovering its investments for lengthy periods, which might create cash-flow risk. In the UK, if they lose their case (or lose on discrete issues) they will also be exposed to adverse costs orders against them. This gives the defendant leverage over the claimant law firm, which they might be able to use to put a halt to the adverse scrutiny of litigation.

## Modelling – challenge and scrutiny as reactive events

Perhaps the standout feature of the examples of internal and external challengers and scrutineers given above is how varied and diverse they are. They do not seem to have much in common. However, a search for common denominators is illuminating, because it points to a critical one: challengers and scrutineers are usually reactive to things that they see, or things that they experience, as the illustrations in Table 14.6 seek to show.

**Table 14.6 Adverse scrutiny as a reactive event**

| | |
|---|---|
| Data subjects | • Usually something happens to them, or about things they care about, which causes them to act. |
| | • For example, they might be exposed to a personal data breach, or to disciplinary action in the workplace, or the receipt of spam emails. |
| Regulators | • Regulators publish action plans that can lead them to proactive engagement with controllers, but their most challenging interactions are usually responsive to events. |
| | • These might be a complaint received from a data subject, or to a breach notification given by a controller under GDPR A.34, or to a negative news story. |
| Claims management companies | • These companies operate in a similar way, being reactive to a problem. |
| | • Usually this is an operational failure event that affects a large enough group of people to trigger bulk compensation claims. |
| Criminals and other malign actors | • Although malign actors can display their own subsets of common denominators (one of which is a desire to stay personally hidden, unlike a data subject exercising a rights request, whose identity is visible) they also share the common denominator of the other actors, which is that they are reactive to things. |
| | • Most typically, the criminal/malign actor is reactive to weaknesses and vulnerability in the controller. |
| | • This is also true for automated threats, such as malware that takes advantage of a security gap. |

Understanding the generally reactive nature of challenge and scrutiny is actually empowering for controllers and processors, because they may, or should, have it within their power to make operational changes to remove, or alter, those elements of their special characteristics that trigger challenge and scrutiny. In other words, if they can address the catalysts of challenge and scrutiny, they will reduce their exposure to these risks.

## Tiers of visibility – catalysts of challenge and scrutiny

If challengers and scrutineers are generally reactive to what they see, this points to a useful test that controllers can incorporate into their risk assessment procedures, called the tiers of visibility test.

The tiers of visibility test says that size and speed of the risk of scrutiny and challenge is causally connected to the degree of visibility of the issue that catalyses risk and challenge. Thus, the test requires an organisation to:

1. identify the range of challengers and scrutineers that it is exposed to;
2. stand in the shoes of those actors;
3. look at itself through the eyes of those actors;
4. assess the catalyst potential of what it sees.

This can quickly point to scenarios of challenge and scrutiny, which can then be worked through, for the purposes of probability and impact analysis. Figure 14.2 illustrates how different aspects within a risk scenario are visible to different challengers and scrutineers.

**Figure 14.2 Tiers of visibility**

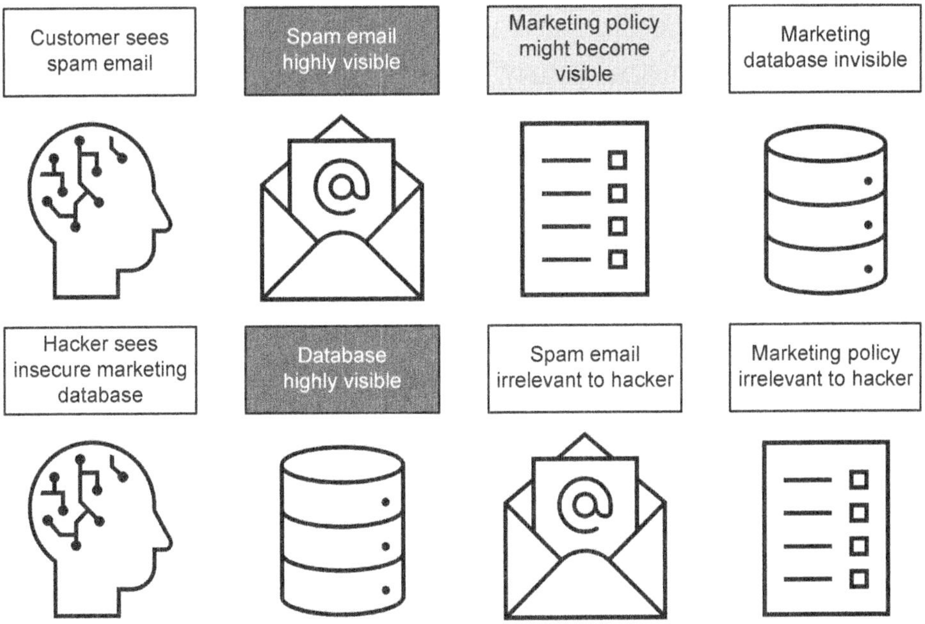

| Customer sees spam email | Spam email highly visible | Marketing policy might become visible | Marketing database invisible |
|---|---|---|---|
| Hacker sees insecure marketing database | Database highly visible | Spam email irrelevant to hacker | Marketing policy irrelevant to hacker |

### *Hot scenarios within challenge and scrutiny*
Reflecting recent events in the data protection and cybersecurity field, it is possible to identify hot scenarios areas that regularly attract challenge and scrutiny. Examples include:

- Direct marketing communications. Due to their purpose, intent and design, these are highly visible to challengers and scrutineers, with potentially very large classes of people being involved, often running into many millions of people being caught by routine marketing campaigns in big business. The class of people affected is such that complaints, rights requests, compensation claims and referrals to the regulator are highly foreseeable.
- Personal data breaches. The inbuilt legislative transparency mechanisms that require personal data breach notifications put the controller on the regulator's map and, like direct marketing communications, can involve huge classes of affected people. It is no surprise then that they lead to regulatory investigations, enforcement actions and financial penalties, and individual compensation claims, group litigation and regulatory action.
- International transfers. The transfer of personal data has been an open sore in the data protection world for many years, and is of particular interest to privacy activists. Following the *Schrems II* (2020) judgment, many activists were inspired to challenge organisations with whom they had relationships. The lesson for controllers is that whenever the topic of international transfers becomes newsworthy, there will be spikes in challenge and scrutiny by people who are especially concerned about privacy issues abroad, most notably in the United States.
- Redundancy and other dismissals. These cases are a sure-fire trigger for data subject access requests. Controllers need to work on the basis that this is now an inevitable part of the HR process.
- Surveillance technology. There are many examples of how new technologies can unite various types of challengers and scrutineers. This effect is most notable when there is a surveillance angle to the technologies. Google Glass is an example from a few years back. AFR is more modern.
- Cybersecurity. This must be on the first page of every organisation's risk register, due to the size of the threat landscape. In data protection terms, there must be an impact on personal data for a cybersecurity problem to fall within the regulatory scheme (subject to the rules within the Privacy and Electronic Communications framework), but that is not a high bar to cross in most situations. The list of cybersecurity issues that have bothered challengers and scrutineers in the data protection field is simply too long to set out here, but for illustration of the extent of the risks, recent cases have involved acquired risks (in a mergers and acquisition sense) and threat vectors such as Magecart, affecting ecommerce payments. Often the cases reveal significant weaknesses in the supply chain.

### *Transparency as a deliberate catalyst*

The correlation between the visibility of issues and the happening of reactions is at the heart of the transparency mechanisms within the GDPR.

The rules in Articles 13 and 14, which are about the provision of information about data processing to the data subject at the point of data collection, or shortly thereafter, are intended to catalyse reactions, in the sense of instilling understanding of processing activities, through to enabling the exercise of choices and personal autonomies about the use of personal data. Therefore, it can be said that once information about processing is visible, things will happen in the data subject's mind and then through the choices that they make. The visibility of information leads to outcomes: cause and effect.

### Breach notification as a deliberate catalyst

Breach notification provides another example of the connection between the tiers of visibility of issues and the reactions that are generated. Where Article 34 applies, requiring the communication of personal data breaches to the individuals affected, if the breach 'is likely to result in a high risk to the rights and freedoms of natural persons', the law is intending to generate a reaction to a visible issue, which is the taking of steps by the individual to mitigate their risks (see Recital 86, for more discussion of the mitigation goal).

## Modelling the domino effect of challenge and scrutiny

As mentioned above, challenge and scrutiny can have a domino effect, with one form leading to another. The example given in Table 14.7 is extreme but not uncommon.

**Table 14.7 Personal data breach – the domino effect of adverse scrutiny and tiers of visibility**

| | |
|---|---|
| 1. Hacker searches for a vulnerability | • A hacker looks for and discovers a security vulnerability in a controller's IT system. |
| | • The hacker then commits unauthorised access to the controller's IT system and exfiltrates personal data, putting them for sale on the Dark Web. |
| 2. Security researcher discovers the vulnerability | • A security researcher discovers the vulnerability in the controller's system. |
| | • They alert the controller, seeking a reward. |
| 3. Controller triggers scrutiny through transparency | • Due to this being a personal data breach, the controller is advised to notify the incident to its regulator under GDPR A.33 and to its contracting partners. |
| | • It also notifies its insurer, to make a claim on a cybersecurity policy. |
| 4. Regulator commences investigation | • The regulator commences an investigation. |
| | • They recommend that the controller communicates the incident to people affected, under GDPR A.34, which it does. |
| 5. Press reporting | • After making these communications, someone contacts the press. |
| | • The press publishes news reports. |

*(Continued)*

## Table 14.7 (Continued)

| | |
|---|---|
| 6. Claims management companies spring into action | • The news reports come to the attention of claims management companies.<br>• They put together an online marketing campaign, calling for people affected to join a compensation claim. |
| 7. Regulator concludes investigation | • The regulator concludes their investigation.<br>• They find the controller in breach of A.5.1.f and A.32 of the GDPR (the rules on preventative security).<br>• The outcome is published on the regulator's website. |
| 8. Solicitors instructed | • Having compiled a group of claimants, the claim management companies instruct solicitors to represent the claimants.<br>• The solicitors serve data subject access requests on the claimants' behalf.<br>• Due to being unprepared, the controller cannot answer the DSARs on time.<br>• The solicitors make complaints to the regulator. The regulator reopens its investigation. |
| 9. Security researcher becomes a witness | • Due to not being paid a reward, the security researcher joins forces with the claimants, acting as a paid expert witness.<br>• The claimants issue proceedings, relying upon the regulator's findings under the preventative security rules. |
| 10. Insurers decline cover | • The controller's insurance company declines cover, due to material non-disclosures when the policy was taken out, because the controller had misrepresented the quality of its security.<br>• This becomes disclosable in the litigation, piling up the case against the controller. |

## Other interests to be considered when modelling challenge and scrutiny risks

When modelling these risks, controllers and processors need to think holistically, because steps taken in isolation can have wider consequences.

### *Police investigations and impact for regulatory investigations*

If a rogue employee commits a crime against a controller, the controller might report the crime to the law enforcement agencies. If the police launch an investigation, it is foreseeable that they will examine the quality of security in the organisation, to understand the degree of criminality involved. If there was a parallel regulatory investigation by the Information Commissioner, it would be of interest to them to understand whether the police have formed a view on the quality of the controller's security, which in turn would be relevant to the decisions taken by the Commissioner about regulatory action against the controller.

### *Insurance cover and the material of historical challenge and scrutiny*
In the field of insurance, the law requires the insured to make material disclosures to the insurance company concerning the matters that are being insured against. Where the insured events are related to data protection, the controller's history of challenge and scrutiny may be relevant to the issue of insurance cover and the materiality of the disclosures made. The challenge and scrutiny that the insurance company provides concerning the historical challenge and scrutiny of others might result in cover being refused, premiums being increased, or coverage being declined altogether.

### *Audits as smoking gun evidence*
Audit reports provide another example. While the internal auditor might be categorised as a neutral challenger or scrutineer, their reports might have different impacts in the hands of others. In regulatory investigations, for example, the Information Commissioner will regularly seek the disclosure of audit evidence and where audit reports show operational deficits that have not been resolved, the audit report can act as smoking gun evidence within the investigation. The same is true within civil litigation, where parties have to give disclosure of documents that are relevant to the facts in issue in the case. Unclosed audit reports are gold dust for compensation claimants, claims farms and their lawyers.

### *Regulatory cooperation*
Controllers in regulated areas also need to bear in mind the risks of cooperation between their regulators. The Information Commissioner's Office and the Financial Conduct Authority have a long-standing memorandum of understanding for regulatory cooperation, meaning that challenge and scrutiny arising in one zone of regulation can move to another. The ICO cooperates with many regulators in the UK and abroad.

The one-stop shop idea within the GDPR provides a fine example of the point. The idea behind the one-stop shop is that controllers involved in cross-border processing activities will have a lead regulator who will have jurisdiction over those activities. The lead regulator will liaise with the regulators for the other countries affected by the cross-border processing, which gives the practical effect of the controller being subjected to challenge and scrutiny from all the countries involved.

## THE RELATIVE IMPACTS OF CHALLENGERS AND SCRUTINEERS

In a relative sense it is difficult to weight the impacts of different forms of challengers and scrutineers, but that is not to say that the impacts cannot be compared.

### The impacts of data subject challenge and scrutiny

If we begin with data subjects and the exercise of their rights, some controllers report having to deal with high volumes of cases, yet they feel the impacts only in a resources sense, in having to put in place systems and operations to handle the requests, rather than in having the requests escalate into more serious legal problems, or causing a domino effect of new and additional forms of scrutiny and challenge. On the other hand, some controllers are deeply challenged by rights requests, with considerable disruption caused to their organisations, considerable time and costs expended and with considerable added legal risk.

### Data subject as an employee versus data subject as a customer
When these cases are broken down, interesting evidence emerges. Often the more challenging rights requests to deal with are those that are received from the data subject as an employee, in contrast to the data subject as a consumer.

The differences may be attributed to the tiers of visibility and the degree of motivation and motive.

For example, when the data subject is an employee, the event that catalyses the use of their rights is likely to be connected to the health of their career, with potentially a huge amount riding on the outcome, such as dismissal or other disciplinary impacts, with possibly immediate and long-term financial consequences. In such a case, the controller may be facing a highly motivated individual who has inside knowledge of how the organisation operates and who might know where the skeletons are buried.

Furthermore, if the issue really does have career connotations, the likelihood of the personal data being held in a distributed and unstructured form, such as email and other free text communications systems, may be high. Sorting this out can be difficult and time-consuming, involving issues such as:

- finding and retrieving the data;
- weeding out irrelevant data;
- reviewing the data;
- considering and applying the exemptions to the right of access;
- treating the data, in preparation for the actually delivery of information to the employee.

### Data subject as a customer, versus data subject as an employee
Compare the above with the situation of the data subject as a customer.

A high volume of consumer data protection problems are concerned with direct marketing and customer service-type issues and while there might be significant impacts, they might not be as acute as those faced by an employee who could be losing their job. Also, the consumer will have less knowledge about the situation on the inside, while there will be a higher chance of their data being held in structured environments, such as in databases. In a relative sense, it is not hard to see why handling a consumer data subject is less challenging for a controller in an impacts sense than handling an employee data subject.

However, in contrast with dealing with business as usual data subject events, such as interventions about direct marketing, dealing with exceptional personal data breaches can involve untold pressures and complications. Due to the nature of transparency after a personal data breach and the presence of the compensation claims industry, these events often involve a pile on of challenge and scrutiny of a kind that makes all other forms seem timid in comparison.

## Privacy activists

There are different kinds of privacy activists. Some of them are formally constituted as civil society organisations, with sophisticated business operations and sources of funding. Others are single individuals with relatively meagre resources compared to the organisations and the issues that they are challenging and scrutinising.

Whatever their kind, when comparisons are drawn between the activities of privacy activists with regulators at the sharp end of the law (i.e. at the point of enforcement of the law), the privacy activists seem to be the ones that are driving the most spectacular forms of interventions in the markets and in behavioural change. Indeed, they are changing not just the landscape for controllers and processors, but also the landscape for the regulators.

### Schrems and international transfers

Some examples of the successes of privacy activists have been mentioned above, but the best example must be that of Max Schrems, who led a seven-year campaign about data transfers to the United States, which culminated twice in proceedings before the Court of Justice of the EU and two spectacular victories against European Commission data transfer adequacy decisions. The genus to these cases was Edward Snowden's disclosures in 2013 of mass surveillance in the United States, the UK and elsewhere. Schrems took the view that the disclosures and the insights that they gave into US law rendered the European Commission's Safe Harbor decision unlawful, on the basis that it could not create an environment for data processing in the US that was essentially equivalent to that in the EU. In 2015 the CJEU found in Schrems' favour and declared the Safe Harbor decision invalid. In response, the European Commission immediately went about standing up a replacement, called Privacy Shield, which was adopted in a decision in 2016. Schrems challenged the Privacy Shield decision and the Commission's standard contractual clauses decisions in fresh litigation, on which the CJEU gave judgment in July 2020. In that judgment the CJEU declared the Privacy Shield decision invalid, while maintaining the lawfulness of the standard contractual clauses decision. In doing so, the CJEU changed the operating environment for the EU data protection authorities.

The data protection authorities will now have to rule on the lawfulness of data transfers from Europe based on the standard contractual clauses on a case-by-case basis if they receive a complaint. Through his actions, Schrems has led to a situation whereby the regulators cannot hide from making very tough decisions on matters of critical importance to the global economy and the EU's place within it. The first complaints were received by the regulators within a matter of days of the CJEU giving judgment.

### Schrems – a repeatable methodology for challenge and scrutiny

Every controller operating on the world stage needs to understand the magnitude of the challenge and scrutiny risks that flow directly out of the Schrems judgments. These extend much further than risks about the subject matter of the cases, that is, international transfers: Schrems provides a template methodology for creating utmost challenge and scrutiny domino effects, involving a marshalling of regulator, judicial, other privacy activists to the cause, alongside the claims management industry, the press and media, and data subjects themselves. The methodology for challenge that Schrems utilised is extendable to every area of data protection. Controllers who are operating in perceived high-risk areas, such as AdTech, profiling and automated facial recognition, will need to factor in the risks of the methodology being used against them.

### Hacked Off
The Hacked Off campaign against the phone-hacking scandal provides another example of the impact of challenge and scrutiny and how the approach of an adverse scrutineer can provide a template methodology for others to follow.

In this case, the methodology consisted of garnering the profile of affected celebrities, then combining it with wider political concerns, press concerns and regulator concerns. This created an unstoppable momentum for litigation, a judicial inquiry (the Leveson Inquiry), criminal prosecutions and reform of press supervision. The impacts included the closure of the *News of the World* newspaper, vast amounts of compensation and custodial sentences.

### The impacts of data protection regulators

The GDPR has granted the Information Commissioner exceptional fining powers and has vastly improved the quality of the regulatory toolkit that the ICO can employ in regulatory investigations and inquiries, when compared to the regime prior to the GDPR coming into effect. It is also clear from the annual reports to Parliament that the Commissioner is required to publish by virtue of section 139 of the Data Protection Act 2018 that the regulator deals with a very large case load and high volumes of requests for advice, help and assistance. Despite this, the volume of formal enforcement actions and monetary penalties is very low, both in absolute terms and relative to the size of the case load. The conclusion, therefore, is obvious: most controllers who experience operational failure that leads to a referral to the regulator will not experience sanction and will not be forced to change their business practices.

Does this mean that controllers can discount the risks of regulatory challenge and scrutiny? It would be an act of huge folly for a controller to adopt such a mindset, because the regulatory powers are perpetual and so they can be used at any time and it will always be open to the regulator to adopt a different regulatory action policy, which could prioritise hard regulatory action over the softer measures that have been deployed in recent years.

Moreover, after three years of the GDPR being in force, there is a sense that the regulators are starting to get into their stride in some countries. The picture is still somewhat patchy, but the overall trajectory for the use of regulator powers and penalties is likely to involve increased use of fines, of increasing size, both in absolute terms and as a percentage of turnover where companies are the ones being penalised.

### Impact of privacy activists on regulators
Furthermore, other challengers and scrutineers can change the circumstances within which the regulators operate. The *Schrems I* (2015) case commenced with a challenge

to the exercise of powers by the Irish Data Protection Commissioner, through judicial review proceedings. That began the legal journey that led to the CJEU. No doubt, the data protection regulators have appreciated their vulnerability to challenge and scrutiny by motivated individuals. This reality, in conjunction with the legal powers to challenge regulators contained within GDPR A.78, means that there is potential for motivated individuals to have the regulatory system do their bidding, albeit this is a situation that regulators would be unlikely to acknowledge in public.

## OUTCOMES VERSUS STRUCTURES AND ARTEFACTS

There are many ways to approach the design of systems and operations for data protection. In recent years, there has been a real effort around the economy to meet the requirements of the GDPR, with countless numbers of organisations undergoing GDPR readiness programmes. Yet, it can be guaranteed that there are significant levels of operational inadequacy and legal non-compliance within organisations still unaddressed. Therefore, efforts to deliver on the GDPR's requirements should continue.

### Examples of structures and artefacts

The focus on scenarios of challenge and scrutiny correlate to a need to focus on data protection outcomes, in distinction to focusing only on the creation of structures and artefacts for operations and compliance. Examples of structures include the governance structures and management systems that are put in place for data protection. A data protection officer appointed under Article 37 of the GDPR can be considered to be such a structure. So would executive sponsors, steering committees and Programme Offices. Examples of artefacts are policies, procedures, notices, registers, contracts, controls libraries and similar materials. One outcome would be good complaints handling, for example. Figure 14.3 shows how structures and artefacts should knit together to create the desired outcome.

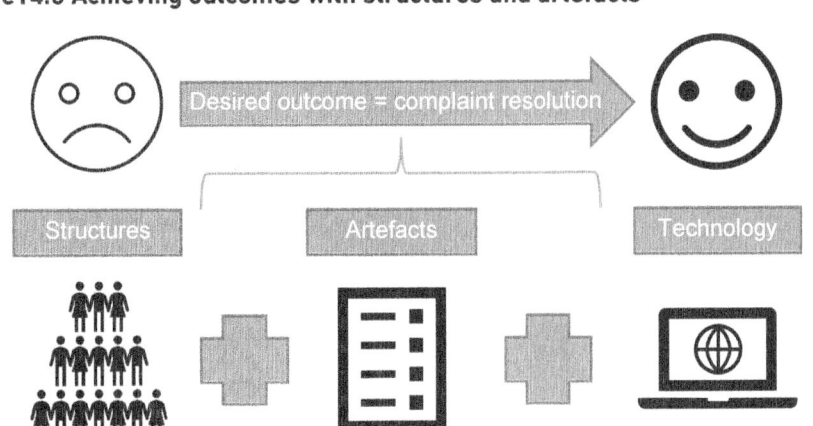

**Figure 14.3 Achieving outcomes with structures and artefacts**

## Root cause analysis for operational failure

The controller's goal should not be the delivery of structures and artefacts by themselves. Instead, the goal should be defined data protection outcomes, the achievement of which are facilitated by the creation of the structures and artefacts. When root cause analysis of operational failure takes place, it is often discovered that the controller failed to understand the true goal. Simply put, the presence of structures and artefacts by themselves are no guarantee of data protection success.

The difference between outcomes and the creation of structures and artefacts is essentially the same as the difference between outcomes and outputs. Whenever a data controller commences a data protection project, the project will deliver outputs, which will be a variety of structures and artefacts, such as policies, procedures and lists of roles and responsibilities for various persons. However, the creation of outputs is not the goal of the project; instead, the data controller will be looking for specific outcomes. So, for example, if the project concerns a CRM, the desired outcomes might include an increase in data accuracy levels within the CRM, to support a more efficient direct marketing programme. The outputs of the project need to knit together, to deliver the desired outcomes of accuracy and efficiency.

Therefore, organisations should consider performing outcomes analysis, to understand the goals that will be achieved through the creation of structures and artefacts. Fitting these ideas into the framework of the GDPR, it will then be clear that outcomes analysis will form part of the various compliance ideas specifically set out in the legislation, such as DPIAs, DPbDD and, of course, the functions of the DPO. By doing this, the organisation will be more resilient to challenge and scrutiny risk.

## Confidence testing and sentiment analysis

Scenario planning points the organisation in the right direction of travel for data protection outcomes. The achievement of the outcomes has to be measured, of course, and there are a variety of techniques that can be deployed. For example:

- In cyberspace, the achievement of a security outcome might be tested through penetration testing, which is sometimes called ethical hacking.
- The functioning of controls might be tested through audit processes.

These forms of testing can be complemented by confidence testing and sentiment analysis. Confidence testing and sentiment analysis looks at the extent to which a person is confident about how their organisation has achieved its desired outcomes. Focusing on how people feel about outcomes, rather than spot checking performance of controls (as in audit) will give the organisation a more holistic understanding of its risks, as well as enabling decisions to be taken rapidly about areas for more detailed testing, such as security testing and controls testing (including by audit).

Moreover, confidence testing and sentiment analysis has the potential to provide a much richer body of evidence on the quality of the outcomes that the controller has achieved, because it can cover more ground than the testing of controls.

For example, utilising the right design principles, the entire employee base of an organisation could take part in confidence testing and sentiment analysis (perhaps alongside annual data protection training). This is because every employee can express a view on the quality of data protection in their organisation. If their points of view are captured, it would provide the controller with a range of insights that are often simply ignored due to the limitations of conventional approaches to testing, such as audit. Table 14.8 illustrates some of the differences between forms of data protection testing.

**Table 14.8 Differences between confidence testing/sentiment analysis and audit**

| Issues | Confidence testing | Audit |
| --- | --- | --- |
| Focus of examination: outcome versus artefact | 'How confident are you that our system for identify and access management is delivering the outcomes that we desire?' | 'Do you have a policy for identity and access management?' 'Is there any evidence of the policy being operationalised?' |
| People evidence acquired | Can be unlimited. | Usually directed to a limited class of persons, often technical in nature. |
| Frequency of testing | Can be done at any time. | Usually done at fixed points in time, often in cycles. |
| Ease of set-up | Once testing methodology is designed and built, very low set-up impacts. | After testing methodology is designed and built, there is usually a significant organisational load. |
| Utility of evidence | Very broad utility, as everyone's opinion counts in data protection. Provides a different lens for the identification of priority areas for treatment/re-examination. | Narrower utility but can also be used to identify priority areas for treatment/re-examination. |

## SUMMARY

In conclusion, this chapter gives readers a better understanding of:

- why challenge and scrutiny of data processing activities is inevitable and why it needs to be dealt with operationally;
- the range of stakeholders who challenge and scrutinise data processing, their motives and modus operandi;
- the significance of understanding the special characteristics of challengers and scrutineers;
- how to model and cope with challenge and scrutiny risks;
- the relative impacts of difference types of challenge and scrutiny.

# 15 COMPLAINTS, RIGHTS REQUESTS, REGULATORY INVESTIGATIONS AND LITIGATION

Jamie Taylor

This chapter examines the mechanisms in the GDPR and the UK Data Protection Act that can be used by data subjects, regulators and litigators to further challenge and scrutinize data processing activities performed by controllers and processors.

## AWARENESS LEVELS DRIVING SCRUTINY AND CHALLENGE

Public awareness of data protection rights and remedies has risen significantly. This can be attributed to many different factors, including the introduction of the GDPR, the rise of the privacy activist and consumer champions and the fact that in our increasingly digital society, significant data protection failures and disputes are often played out publicly across social and mainstream media (for example, the Cambridge Analytica scandal). Arguably one of the greatest impacts of the GDPR, so far, has been to provide some of the fuel that has helped to propel data protection into the mainstream conversation. This elevation in the perceived importance of data protection and privacy rights, in the social conscience, can exert a powerful influence on public opinion, a fact that is not lost in commerce or even in politics. Against this backdrop of heightened awareness of individual rights and a more powerful privacy voice, the GDPR provides supervisory authorities with the legal powers to impose significant financial and reputational consequences on data controllers and processors who fail to ensure adequate data protection compliance.

This combination of increased enforcement powers, in the hands of well-funded and higher-profile supervisory authorities, and increased public awareness of data protection rights, including the availability of compensation, are all drivers that can contribute to increased scrutiny of compliance. In turn, that increased scrutiny may contribute to and manifest in more frequent complaints, rights requests, and incidences of regulatory investigations, enforcement or even litigation.

The ability, therefore, of controllers and processors to prevent, identify and respond effectively to these challenges is a critically important part of their role and will often be fundamental in determining not only the likelihood and scale of any regulatory action, but, more broadly, whether they are perceived by the wider public as being responsible, trusted custodians of personal data or inherently risky organisations.

## ACCOUNTABILITY

One of the most significant changes that the GDPR introduced to data protection law is the addition of the accountability principle in Article 5.2. This overarching principle requires a controller to demonstrate compliance with the other six data protection principles in Article 5.1. The accountability principle therefore provides data subjects and supervisory authorities with an additional gateway through which compliance can be monitored, challenged and remedies sought.

### Accounting for readiness to deal with challenge and scrutiny

Within the context of managing complaints, rights requests and other remedies, the accountability principle requires controllers to evidence what steps they take, so that if something does go wrong, they can demonstrate that risks were actively considered and suitable controls and measures were put in place to deal with those risks. In practical terms, in addition to having appropriately documented policies and procedures, this might also include having centralised complaint logs, appropriate staff training materials and records, breach response plans, records of breaches, audit controls, documented procedures for assessing risk with appropriate internal escalation and responsible reporting structures. In determining the level of evidence required to satisfy the accountability principle, factors such as the size of the data controller's organisation, their processing activities and the volume and type of data will be key.

## DEALING WITH COMPLAINTS

Individuals have a range of different remedies available to address data protection concerns or perceived non-compliance with data protection legislation. Data protection rights are often a source of complaint (46% of complaints to the ICO in 2019/2020 related to access requests), but they can also in themselves, when fulfilled, amount to both a remedy and a mechanism for enforcement.

For example, a rectification request may appropriately remedy inaccurate data, and a request for erasure of data may satisfactorily address retention issues. Within the range of available remedies, rights requests might be put at one end of the scale and litigation or regulatory enforcement action at the opposing end, with complaints perhaps representing a notional mid-point. There is in fact no mandated sequence in which remedies must be pursued, however. For example, there is no rule preventing an individual from seeking compensation without first having lodged a complaint, but complaints will usually be the most sensible and cost-effective starting point to address an individual's concerns about data protection. In fact, in most cases, supervisory authorities will not intervene unless the individual has already complained to the controller.

Article 77 of the GDPR makes express provision that the right to lodge a complaint with a supervisory authority is without prejudice to any other remedy that an individual may choose. The corresponding provision within the UK DPA is Section 165, which extends the scope of the right to complain, beyond GDPR to apply also to law enforcement processing (Part 3, UK DPA) and processing by the intelligence services (Part 4, UK DPA).

## Point of contact

One of the first steps that a controller will need to consider is who will be their point of contact for data protection complaints. In practice, this may be the same point of contact that a controller is required to provide for other purposes, for example:

- A controller is required to provide contact details to the supervisory authority for regulatory enquiries, when paying annual fees.[1]
- Information provided to individuals when personal data are collected must include contact details of the controller.[2]

If an organisation is required to appoint a DPO, they will be the organisation's key point of contact with the supervisory authority, both generally and specifically in relation to complaints. Indeed, acting as such a point of contact and cooperating with the supervisory authority are some of the principal tasks of a DPO, mandated by Article 39 of the GDPR. Controllers who are not legally obligated to appoint a DPO may nevertheless decide to do so, to assist compliance. If a DPO is not appointed then an alternative suitable point of contact for data protection complaints will need to be visibly identified.

For the purposes of the GDPR, a point of contact is required within an EU or EEA State. Therefore, where the controller is established outside the EEA and meets the criteria set out in Article 3.2 to be regulated in relation to the processing of personal data of EU citizens, it is likely to be required to appoint a designated representative located within an EU or EEA State. The tasks of such a representative may include receiving complaints and requests and ensuring their safe transmission to the data controller.

## Managing complaints and concerns received direct from data subjects

Although there is no legal obligation to do so, individuals wishing to complain about the way an organisation is processing their personal data should, in the first instance, and as a matter of practicality, raise those concerns with the relevant data controller before lodging a complaint with a supervisory authority. This is in keeping with regulatory guidance. For example, the Information Commissioner provides the following guidance to individuals:[3]

> You have the right to be confident that organisations handle your personal information responsibly and in line with good practice.
>
> If you have a concern about the way an organisation is handling your information; if it:

---

[1] The Data Protection (Charges and Information) Regulations 2018.

[2] Article 13.1 (a) and Article 14.1 (a).

[3] Information Commissioner's Office. 2020. Raising a concern with an organisation. https://ico.org.uk/your-data-matters/raising-concerns/

- is not keeping your information secure;
- holds inaccurate information about you;
- has disclosed information about you;
- is keeping information about you for longer than is necessary; or
- has collected information for one reason and is using it for something else, we believe that the organisation responsible should deal with it. We expect them to take your concern seriously and work with you to try to resolve it.

This guidance also includes a template letter for individuals to use when first raising concerns, which stipulates that a full response is required from the relevant controller, within one calendar month.

The stance of the Information Commissioner is clear. Controllers are expected to:

- Take responsibility for resolving concerns raised by data subjects.
- Treat concerns seriously and engage with the data subject in a helpful manner.
- Respond without undue delay. This usually means within one month of receipt of a complaint.
- Have in place a documented complaints procedure.
- Acknowledge complaints promptly.
- Provide the data subject with a time estimate and an explanation of what will happen next. For example, if a period of investigation is likely, prior to a substantive response being provided.
- Ensure, where possible, that responses include a reasoned explanation for any decision and also set out what steps the data subject can take next, if they remain dissatisfied, such as contacting the relevant supervisory authority.

Complaints are generally escalated to supervisory authorities when individuals do not have confidence in how a data controller has handled their data and when there is a failure to explain decision making, or a lack of transparency.

## Managing complaints escalated to a supervisory authority

It is important for controllers to have measures in place that enable them quickly and accurately to identify communications from the supervisory authority that constitute complaints (that have been lodged with them in accordance with Article 77 of the GDPR and section 165 UK DPA). This may seem obvious, but not all communications from the regulator will be notifications of a complaint. A controller might receive an Information Notice (section 142 UK DPA); an Assessment Notice (section 146 UK DPA); a written determination of special purposes processing (section 174 UK DPA); or they might be conducting an examination of an issue of broader concern or public interest at the time. However, it is fair to say that complaints are more prevalent and according to its

Whatever the method or nature of the investigation, there are some basic principles of best practice that should be observed by controllers and processors, to ensure that they respond to regulatory investigations appropriately.

First, in the same vein as handling complaints, approaches from the supervisory authority should be treated seriously and professionally. Any communications from the supervisory authority should be responded to promptly and adopting a helpful and conciliatory tone from the outset is likely to pay dividends. An obstructive or aggressive stance will almost certainly prove counterproductive. It may be appropriate for a controller or processor to seek legal advice or representation, for example if criminal proceedings are envisaged or if advice is required in relation to whether material is covered by legal privilege and therefore protected from disclosure under an Information Notice or Assessment Notice.

## Information Notices

Information Notices are the mechanism (conferred by A.58) by which supervisory authorities can formally seek 'any information' from controllers, processors, or their representatives. The type of information that might be demanded is elaborated on in section 142 of the UK DPA and includes information that the Commissioner reasonably requires in order to:

- carry out its functions under data protection legislation;
- investigate a suspected failure of GDPR (as defined by section 149 (2) of the UK DPA);
- determine whether the processing of personal data falls within the 'purely personal or household' activity exemption.

It is important that controllers or processors receiving an Information Notice, fully understand what information is being sought and why; the legal rights and obligations that are engaged; together with the potential consequences for non-compliance. Such consequences include committing a criminal offence if an Information Notice is not complied with, or if a false statement is made in response.

The Information Commissioner's Regulatory Action Policy[5] provides organisations with some insight into what factors might influence their decision to issue an Information Notice, which include:

- the risk of harm to individuals or the level of intrusion into their privacy potentially posed by the events or data processing under investigation;
- the utility of requiring a formal response within a defined time period;
- the utility of testing responses, by the fact that it is an offence to deliberately or recklessly make a false statement in a material respect in response;
- the public interest in the response.

---

[5] Information Commissioner's Regulatory Action Policy. ICO, 2018.

An Information Notice will specify the period for compliance, which will usually be 28 days. However, compliance strategies need to also make provision for much shorter response timescales as urgent information notices can be issued (section 142 (7) of the UK DPA) where appropriate, requiring compliance, providing at least 24 hours' notice is given.

## Assessment Notices

Article 58 of the GDPR provides supervisory authorities with both the power to carry out audits and the power to access all necessary personal data, including special category data and information. These provisions constitute the power of assessment and are amplified in sections 146–147 of the UK DPA. A controller or processor may be served with an Assessment Notice under section 146 (1) of the UK DPA, enabling the Commissioner to investigate whether their processing is in compliance with data protection legislation.

The ICO's Regulatory Action Policy provides the following examples of circumstances that may cause them to issue such a notice:

- where they have conducted a risk assessment or other regulatory action, there is a probability that personal data are not being processed in compliance with the data protection legislation, together with a likelihood of damage or distress to individuals;
- it is necessary to verify compliance with an Enforcement Notice;
- communications with or information (e.g. news reports, statutory reporting or publications) about the controller or processor suggest that they are not processing personal data in compliance with the data protection legislation;
- the controller or processor has failed to respond to an Information Notice within an appropriate time.

The Regulatory Action Policy also includes a helpful (non-exhaustive) list of the types of documentation that the ICO might expect to see after serving an Assessment Notice, which should define and explain how the controller's data protection obligations have been met:

- strategies;
- policies;
- procedures;
- guidance;
- codes of practice;
- training material;
- protocols;
- frameworks;
- memoranda of understanding;

- contracts;
- privacy statements;
- privacy impact assessments;
- control data;
- job descriptions.

Controllers should also be prepared to have ready and available additional relevant documentation, such as logs of complaints or breaches, records of processing activity, special category data handling policies, legitimate or public interests assessments, post-incident reviews and documented key decision making.

The expanded Assessment Notice powers under the GDPR and UK DPA mean that all organisations can now be subject to a compulsory inspection. Furthermore, section 146(9) of the UK DPA operates so as to enable the ICO to conduct an assessment without notice, akin to a dawn raid. However unlikely this scenario might be in practice, controllers and processors should be prepared for such an eventuality, by building it into incident response plans and related testing.

## Investigations and prosecutions of criminal offences

One of the more serious consequences of failure to comply with data protection legislation is that a supervisory authority may commence an investigation in contemplation of initiating criminal proceedings. Such proceedings may, for example, be brought in connection with obtaining or disclosing personal data unlawfully (section 170 of the UK DPA) or for enforced subject access (section 184 of the UK DPA). However, it should also be noted that the ICO also has the power to prosecute beyond data protection legislation. For example, in 2018 it brought a successful prosecution under s.1 Computer Misuse Act 1990 resulting in a six-month custodial sentence.[6]

### Search warrants
Where the ICO has reasonable grounds that an offence has been committed, it may apply for a warrant to enter premises, conduct a search and seize evidence. The relevant powers of entry and inspection are contained within Schedule 15 of the UK DPA and controllers and processors need to be aware of their obligations and their rights, in the event that they receive either a surprise visit, or a visit on notice, under the authority of a warrant. The key points to be aware of are:

- The ICO will ordinarily be required to provide 7 days' notice in writing to the occupier of the premises (unless a judge is satisfied that the ICO requires access urgently and prior notice would defeat the object).
- Reasonable force may be used when executing a warrant.
- A copy of the warrant must be provided to the occupier (or, if they are not present, a copy left in a prominent place).

---

6  https://ico.org.uk/about-the-ico/news-and-events/news-and-blogs/2018/11/six-month-prison-sentence-for-motor-industry-employee-in-first-ico-computer-misuse-act-prosecution/

- A receipt must be provided to the occupier for any documents or other evidence seized.
- Obstructing, failing to assist, or making a false statement to a person executing a warrant, is an offence.
- Documents protected by legal professional privilege cannot be inspected or seized.
- Controllers and processors are entitled to request legal advice before answering questions about their processing activities and as the ICO does not have the power of arrest, interviews may only take place by consent.
- If the controller or processor does consent to be interviewed, this must take place under caution and also be recorded. Everything that a controller or processor says under caution is admissible in evidence.

## *Cautions*

The ICO's prosecution policy[7] states that when a decision is made to commence a criminal prosecution, they will usually first notify defendants in writing and may offer them an opportunity to make representations at that stage. However, where an interview has either been previously refused, or already conducted in accordance with the Police and Criminal Evidence Act, they are likely to proceed to a prosecution without seeking representations. The policy also states that where a reliable admission of an offence is received, they may decide to issue a caution rather than to prosecute in the following (example) circumstances:

- offending is low-level in terms of seriousness;
- there are no particular aggravating factors;
- it is a first-time offence;
- the accused has or is willing to provide assistance to an investigation/prosecution.

In contrast, the following examples are provided to illustrate circumstances where a caution will not be offered:

- the accused is breaching the law for financial gain;
- has abused a position of trust;
- has engaged in a systematic approach to obtaining or attempting to obtain personal data;
- there has been damage or distress caused to data subjects;
- the accused has a relevant previous conviction(s) or caution(s) for a similar offence or has breached an undertaking;
- has ignored prior warnings or advice regarding compliance;
- there are grounds for believing the offending will be repeated or continued.

---

7   Information Commissioner's Prosecution Policy. ICO, 2018.

If a prosecution is commenced then specialist legal advice should be sought, if this is not already in place (for example, it is anticipated that legal advice will be sought in connection with any interview under caution). The ICO will carry the legal burden of proving offences, to the criminal standard, of beyond all reasonable doubt. However, as was discussed in *Shepherd v. Information Commissioner* (2019),[8] defendants may bear the legal burden of proving certain defences. For example, under section 170 of the UK DPA the ICO would carry the legal burden of proving the offence of unlawfully obtaining or disclosing personal data, but if a defendant wished to raise the defence under section 170(2) that their actions were necessary for the purposes of preventing crime, then the legal burden (on the balance of probabilities) would rest with the defendant.

There are several steps that controllers or processors faced with a criminal prosecution can take to assist their own lawyers. In particular:

- Copies of all relevant documentation and evidence will need to be collated. This will include any communications with the ICO, including copies of any evidence provided voluntarily; copies of documents relating to the data processing activities; a copy of any warrant; a copy of any receipts for evidence seized; and copies of any court documentation, such as a summons, if received.
- Contact details for any relevant witnesses will need to be provided.
- A written account of everything that has happened so far, in chronological order, including details of any conversations with the ICO's investigators.

## EXERCISE OF DATA SUBJECT RIGHTS

One of the primary aims of the GDPR is to provide individuals with greater control over their own personal data. This goal is substantially advanced by giving individuals the tools to assess a data controller's compliance and by providing them with direct remedies. Data subjects rights deliver these tools and certain remedies and their central importance to data protection legislation demands special attention from data controllers.

### Escalation of problems – rights requests leading to adversity

The fact that the vast majority of complaints received by supervisory authorities relate directly to the handling of rights requests, and in particular subject access requests, illustrates the risks that the mishandling of rights requests involves. Data subject rights can quickly lead to complaints, regulatory investigations and enforcement actions, if mishandled, and so compliance strategies need to facilitate and ensure the effective delivery of all subject rights at all times. Strategies and procedures for dealing with data subject rights need to be embedded within the data controller's organisation, embracing the principles of Data Protection by Design and Default, and woven into the fabric of the controller's public interactions.

---

[8] (2019) EWCA Crim2.

As part of a compliance strategy, a controller should ensure that the following requirements are met:

- Information about individuals rights and how they can exercise those rights should be made easily accessible and understood.
- When an individual exercises their rights, the controller should be able to easily identify the request and react, not just in respect of written requests but also requests made verbally or via corporate social media channels. This will require relevant staff to be appropriately trained and systems and procedures to be appropriately configured.
- Requests should be logged and promptly acknowledged.
- The controller needs to be able to identify that data subjects are who they say they are, before substantive responses are provided. Failing to do so may result in a breach of data security obligations. There may be occasions where the identity of the person making the request is obvious and further verification may not be required. However, if a controller has reasonable doubts, then additional proof of identity should always be requested.
- Requests need to be responded to within one calendar month from the date of receipt. This requires planning and resources. Roles and responsibilities need to be defined and understood. Staff training will be required in relation to not only recognising but also taking appropriate action in response to requests. Communications channels and technology that will be used to assist the search for and collation of relevant information will need to be identified and made operational. Controllers are permitted a degree of flexibility in the format and mode of response (save that responses have to be both in writing and clear) and so will need to be decide how responses will be provided.
- Reassurances (beyond purely contractual provisions) will also need to be gained from processors who may be acting on the controller's behalf, in relation to their ability to identify requests and provide assistance with the response, within the time limit. The details of how all of this will work, operationally, both within the controller's organisation and between organisations, need to be clearly defined. If the controller is working with another organisation acting as a joint data controller, they will need to clearly document agreed responsibilities in relation to how data subject rights requests will be managed.
- If a request is refused, controllers are required to respond to the data subject within one month of receipt of the request, informing them of the reasons why the request has not been actioned and of their rights to complain to the supervisory authority.
- Accountability. Controllers need to be able to demonstrate that they have taken responsibility for facilitating data subject rights. This will look different depending upon the size of the organisation, but proportionate, documented policies and controls need to be in place and be operationalised.

## Timing

Responses to rights requests need to be provided without undue delay and in any event within one calendar month. When calculating the time limit, the clock starts with the day that the request is received and runs until the corresponding date in the next calendar month. For example, a request received on 20 July requires a response by no later than 20 August. However, if the corresponding date falls on a weekend or on a public holiday, then responses can be provided on the next working day.

## Extensions

For requests that are complex or numerous, Article 12.3 of the GDPR permits the one calendar month response timeframe to be extended by up to two further months, where necessary. Where a controller wishes to take advantage of this provision, they are required to inform the data subject within one month of receipt of the request, explaining the reasons for the delay.

## Manifestly unfounded or excessive requests

Article 12.5 of the GDPR enables controllers to either charge a fee or refuse to comply with a request from a data subject if it is manifestly unfounded or excessive. The burden of proof is on the controller. The ICO has defined manifestly unfounded as including situations where it is obvious or clear that the request is malicious and designed to harass an organisation. Excessive has been defined as a request that essentially repeats the substance of a previous request, where a reasonable interval (not defined) has not elapsed. Controllers who refuse requests on these grounds still need to respond to data subjects to explain their reasoning (and also be prepared to explain those reasons to the ICO). In relation to the charging of a fee, no regulatory guidance has yet been produced in relation to what the appropriate feel level might be, but the GDPR states that any fee charged must be reasonable, taking into account the administrative cost of providing the information.

## Compliance orders

Another remedy available to individuals, in relation to data subject rights specifically, in addition to the right to complain, is the right to seek a judicial remedy. Individuals have a right to apply to either to the County Court or the High Court for a compliance order, requiring (at the court's discretion) a controller to take certain steps, or refrain from taking steps. Such an order may, for example, require a controller to erase or rectify data, or restrain unlawful processing. The basis for this remedy is Article 79 of the GDPR and section 167 of the UK DPA.

# LITIGATION

There are numerous gateways through which a controller or a processor might be faced with civil proceedings in connection with their data processing. This is a further illustration of the choice individuals have when it comes to seeking a remedy for contraventions of the law.

Court proceedings demand urgent attention and will usually need to be promptly acknowledged, to prevent the defendant's position from being prejudiced. It is important that controllers and processors are able to quickly identify when court proceedings have been received, and to help ensure this, it will be necessary to communicate to staff, processors, joint controllers and third parties, where and to whom such proceedings are required to be served and directed. Specialist legal advice will usually be required to help with any response and defence.

### Subject access and litigation

Often, the true motive behind a subject access request will be to obtain documents for the purposes of anticipated (or ongoing) litigation. The law now permits such requests, and even if there is a collateral purpose of assisting litigation, that will not render the request invalid; see *Dawson Damer v. Taylor Wessing* (2017).[9] However, controllers dealing with such requests will need to be mindful that they are not a substitute for disclosure in litigation and a subject access request only entitles an individual to their personal data, not to copies of documents.

### Data protection and litigation

The Civil Procedure Rules 1998 (CPR) are the procedural rules that govern civil proceedings in England and Wales. They include specific rules about the disclosure and inspection of documents (see Rule 31). However, there may be occasions when disclosure obligations in connection with litigation appear to be in conflict with data protection legislation. The interplay between these two regimes was considered by the Court of Appeal in *Durham County Council v. Dunn* (2012),[10] where it was held that the CPR rather than data protection legislation was the governing regime for litigation and this was recognised by data protection legislation itself, through the legal proceedings exemption (formerly s.35 of the 1998 Act and now Para 5. Sch 2 of the UK DPA).

### Compensation and liability

Controllers and processors now face a heightened risk of civil claims for compensation for infringements of data protection legislation. Although the right to be able to claim compensation is not new, the circumstances in which a claim can be made has broadened considerably, obligations placed on controllers and processors are now more stringent and the public awareness of the right to claim has skyrocketed.

Individuals are able to claim compensation for material damage, such as financial losses or personal injury, and also for non-material damage, such as distress. It is important that controllers and processors appreciate that the trigger for a claim is an infringement of GDPR or a contravention of the UK DPA that results in loss. This might be viewed as a relatively low threshold. For example, there is no requirement to establish that the GDPR's definition of a personal data breach is met, or to prove that some financial loss has been suffered. Indeed, the concept of what constitutes damage for the purposes of a compensation claim has been extended to include circumstances where there has been a loss of control of personal data, even if no distress has been suffered. However, this will not be appropriate in every case and awards are fact-specific. Specialist legal advice should be sought in order to fully understand the potential risk and liabilities.

---

9 (2017) EWCA Civ 74.

10 (2012) EWCA Civ 1654.

It is often the case that the data processing that gives rise to a civil claim involves multiple organisations, potentially more than one data controller and potentially a joint controller or various processors or sub-processors. The GDPR provides that any data controller involved in processing is liable for any damage it causes. Processors, on the other hand, will only be liable if the damage was caused by an infringement of a part of the GDPR for which processors have direct liability, for example a breach of security obligations. Where there is more than one controller or more than one processor involved, then there is in effect joint and several liability imposed on each of them. However, a controller or a processor who pays compensation to a data subject has the right to claim an indemnity or a contribution from other controllers or processors, corresponding to their responsibility for the damage.

The procedural management of data protection claims is governed by the Civil Procedure Rules 1998. In particular, prior to any proceedings being issued, claims need to follow the Pre Action Protocol for Media and Communication Claims. This specifies the conduct that is expected of all parties to a claim. It stipulates the amount of detail that a claimant must provide in a letter of claim. Of particular significance is that controllers and processors are required to respond to a letter of claim within just 14 days and their response is expected to include details such as whether they accept responsibility, whether further information is required, or if the claim is rejected (then the reasons why need to be explained). In practice, controllers and processors receiving a letter of claim may require a longer period of time to respond, to enable them, for example, to seek legal advice and conduct their own investigation. In these circumstances the letter of claim should be promptly acknowledged and an extension of time requested, explaining why this is needed.

Once proceedings are commenced, data protection claims will usually fall within the scope of Part 53 of the Civil Procedure Rules. This provides that data protection claims should fall within the court's specialist media and communications list, which should ensure that any judge dealing with the matter has expertise in this area.

## Mass claims

A single data protection breach can potentially result in a very large number of claims being made against a single controller or processor. Within the US, class action style litigation following a data breach is commonplace. For example, following a data breach suffered by Equifax in 2017 a class action law suit alleged that the data of 147 million people was exposed, resulting in a settlement of US$425 million in 2020.

While the UK legal system does not have the same class action mechanism, there are a number of ways in which large numbers of claimants seeking compensation for a data breach can effectively band together in a single set of civil proceedings. The first method is by asking the court to make what is known as a Group Litigation Order. This enables the court to manage large numbers of individual claims together. A recent example of this is *WM Morrison Supermarkets Plc v. Various Claimants* (2020),[11] where 9263 claimants brought compensation claims after their payroll data was disclosed online by a rogue employee. Unlike a Group Litigation Order where each individual

---

[11] (2020) UKSC 12.

claimant is an active participant, a representative action involves just one claimant commencing proceedings, as a representative of a much larger group who are said to have all suffered the same loss. A recent example of this is *Lloyd v. Google LLC* (2019), in which a single claimant issued proceedings on behalf of four million other iPhone users who had allegedly lost control of their personal data. One of the fundamental differences between these two different methods of bringing mass claims is that whereas a Group Litigation Order requires active participation of the individual claimants involved, a representative action is an opt-out procedure where claimants are automatically and unwittingly included within the cohort of claimants. Having an understanding of these potential litigation scenarios will help controllers and processors to understand their risks and liabilities.

## SUMMARY

In conclusion, this chapter gives readers a better understanding of:

- the risks of adverse scrutiny arising from the data subject rights and regulators' powers;
- how to handle complaints from data subjects and the exercise of their rights;
- how to handle the regulators, when they use their investigatory and enforcement powers;
- the litigation risks that may arise.

# 16 REGULATORY ACTION

**Richard Hall**

This chapter considers the different investigative, enforcement and punitive powers available to the supervisory authorities under the GDPR. It also touches on some of the practical considerations to be taken into account by organisations if they want to prepare for these risks, noting the potential reputational impacts that regulatory actions can involve.

## THE IMPACTS OF NATIONAL LAWS AND OTHER CONTINGENCIES ON GDPR ENFORCEMENT POWERS

The data protection regulators, such as the Information Commissioner in the UK, are the supervisory authorities tasked by the GDPR with the enforcement of the law.

The regulators' powers under the GDPR and associated national legislation are complex and wide-ranging. They allow the regulators to investigate compliance with the law, to enforce compliance and to punish infringements.

There are many factors in play that may impact or influence the regulators' effectiveness, such as the funding or other resources available to them. Therefore, to fully understand the true nature of regulatory risk, particularly the risk of the use of regulatory powers, the circumstances when they are likely to be used and the impacts of their use need to be considered. This involves understanding any restrictions, limitations or controls on those powers operating at a national level, because the rules differ from country to country.

Put simply, reading what is written within the text of the GDPR without an understanding of the wider context within which regulatory powers operates will leave controllers and processors unprepared and incapable of properly understanding:

- the steps that they can take to reduce both the risk of regulatory action and the severity of it;
- whether regulatory powers are being used properly and lawfully;
- the action that they need to take in response to regulatory action;
- the options for challenging regulatory action;
- when information can be protected from the regulators, such as through the assertion of privilege.

## WHEN CAN REGULATORY POWERS BE USED?

If a regulator perceives that there is a risk of non-compliance with the GDPR, or finds evidence of non-compliance, whether through an investigation or by other means, they have the discretion to use their regulatory powers, to investigate the situation and take enforcement action if needed. The use of regulatory powers is subject to the rules that regulate the regulators, such as public law rules concerning proportionality, due process and the avoidance of bias and undue influence.

If a regulatory intervention is appropriate, it can include the taking of steps to investigate the suspected contravention, such as by the issuance of an Information Notice or an Assessment Notice; or advisory actions to steer the organisation under investigation toward compliance (i.e. the issuing of words of advice); or formal enforcement action that demands the taking of specific steps to achieve compliance, such as through the imposition of an Enforcement Notice; or the imposition of penalties, such as the imposition of fines. Criminal prosecutions are also envisaged by the GDPR for the most serious cases.

### The investigatory phase of regulatory action

A regulator's general approach to enforcement will usually follow an initial investigatory phase, whether that is an investigation of their own making, or an investigation prompted by a complaint or some other external factor, such as a news report. This can be followed by advisory, corrective and/or punitive powers, as outlined above.

In most situations the regulator will seek to engage without using its formal investigatory powers. Instead, in most cases the regulator will rely upon an understanding that the organisation being investigated recognises its duty of cooperation (see GDPR A.31) and the requirements of the accountability principle and that it will be wise enough not to inflame the situation unnecessarily. In other words, most regulatory investigations proceed by way of a consensual agreement, albeit that agreement flows simply from the disposition of the organisation under investigation rather than being documented as an agreement as such.

However, not all investigations will continue along a consensual path forever. Sometimes it will be necessary for the regulators to use their formal investigatory powers, which in the UK are represented by the Information and Assessment Notice powers set out in the UK DPA. In very serious cases, again dealt with in the UK DPA, the regulator might also obtain a search warrant that results in a dawn raid.

## POWERS IN ARTICLE 58

Article 58 of the GDPR provides the basis of the regulatory powers, which can be broken down into the following categories:

- investigatory powers;
- corrective and punitive powers;

- authorisation and advisory powers;
- referral powers.

The investigatory powers are used to gather information, to enable the regulator to take decisions on compliance and, if need be, to support the use of corrective and punitive powers. All of the powers in A.58 are geared towards achieving compliance, but their use can extend beyond achieving compliance in the organisation under investigation. Due to the principle of regulatory transparency and the supervisory authorities' duty to 'promote public awareness and understanding of the risks, rules, safeguards and rights in relation to processing',[1] corrective and punitive powers may also be published, to act as a deterrent to others.

## Warnings of potential infringements – action to prevent things going wrong

Article 58.2(a) provides regulators with the power to issue warnings to a controller or processor that intended processing operations are likely to infringe provisions of the GDPR. This power can be used where a planned processing activity has come to the attention of a supervisory authority through a complaint, engagement with a controller in relation to a DPIA, or through use of an investigatory power and the regulator assesses that the planned activity is likely to constitute a breach the law.

Where such a warning is provided, the receiving organisation will need to take care in assessing whether any mitigations can be put in place to remedy the problem before moving ahead with the processing. Simply carrying on regardless is not a safe option, as it will invite further scrutiny from the regulator and potential enforcement action based on aggravating features.

## Reprimands

The power to issue reprimands comes from Article 58.2(b). Reprimands should be used where more punitive measures (i.e. financial penalties or other sanctions) are not appropriate in the circumstances. Whether or not a reprimand is issued instead of a more punitive measure, will be dependent on several factors, including the nature and extent of the infringement, the aggravating and mitigating factors present, and any harm suffered by data subjects.

Reprimands may be considered as an aggravating factor when dealing with any future infringements by the same organisation, in the same way as warnings of potential infringements. As such, the clever use of reprimands by the regulator can act as an effective deterrent against future infringements by that organisation.

## Enforcement Notices

Enforcement Notices are served to compel action, or stop action, for the purposes of bringing about compliance. Supervisory authorities will usually serve Enforcement Notices following a period of investigation, meaning that controllers and processors will have warning of the risk. However, where a genuine urgency exists, they can be

---

[1] Art. 57(1)(b), GDPR.

issued on an urgent basis, with reduced timescales for compliance (see section 150(8) of the UK DPA).

A number of the powers in A.58 can be crystallised in the form of an Enforcement Notice. They include powers to:

- order the controller or the processor to comply with a data subject's request to exercise their rights;[2]
- order the controller or processor to bring processing operations into compliance, in a specified manner and within a specified period;[3]
- order the controller to communicate a personal data breach to effected data subjects;[4]
- impose a limitation on processing, including a permanent ban;[5]
- order the rectification or erasure of personal data or restriction of processing (pursuant to Articles 16, 17 and 18) and the notification of such actions to recipients to whom the personal data have been disclosed (pursuant to A.17(2) and 19);[6]
- order the suspension of data flows to a recipient in a third country or to an international organisation.[7]

An Enforcement Notice can be extremely costly to deal with and very damaging to the receiving organisation's reputation, especially where conditions are imposed that seek to limit or prevent processing activities. For most organisations, personal data processing is a fundamental requirement within successful business operations, so although Enforcement Notices are not ordinarily designed to be punitive in nature, a ban or restriction on processing could have an equal, if not a greater, impact than a financial penalty. Therefore, organisations would be unwise to treat Enforcement Notices as being somehow inferior to fines in an impact sense. In fact, many regulators consider Enforcement Notices to be the most powerful tool in their regulatory action toolkit.

An example of Enforcement Notices powers being used by the ICO to great effect is provided by their investigation into the direct marketing and data brokering sector between 2018 and 2020, which culminated in both preliminary and final Enforcement Notices being issued to a number of credit reference agencies and data brokers, requiring them to make changes to processing activities and associated policies and procedures. This led to some of those organisations withdrawing certain services from the market, to stop the preliminary Enforcement Notices being issued in their final form.[8]

---

2  Art. 58(2)(c), GDPR.
3  Art. 58(2)(d), GDPR.
4  Art. 58(2)(e), GDPR.
5  Art. 58(2)(f), GDPR.
6  Art. 58(2)(g), GDPR.
7  Art. 58(2)(j), GDPR.
8  Information Commissioner's Office, Investigation into data protection compliance in the direct marketing data broking sector, October 2020.

Clearly, Enforcement Notices are to be treated with the utmost seriousness. They demand priority attention. Organisations will have a limited amount of time to respond to them, including commencing appeals. If they fail to comply, a supervisory authority can impose a fine, or refer the matter to the national courts for enforcement by way of a court order. These are situations that controllers and processors must be keen to avoid.

## Withdrawal of certification

Article 58.2(h) of the GDPR provides the regulators with the power to withdraw a certification or to order a certification body to withdraw a certification issued pursuant to Articles 42 and 43, or to order a certification body not to issue certification if the requirements for the certification are not met.

This is a fringe issue in data protection at the moment, due to the fact that we have not yet entered an era of meaningful certification systems for data protection, but as time passes and certifications become adopted and widely utilised by organisations to demonstrate compliance, the regulators will be bound to use these powers as part of their ordinary course of business.

## Financial penalties

Arguably, the risk of financial penalties remains one of the primary reasons why many organisations take compliance with the GDPR seriously. During the GDPR readiness era of 2016 to 2018, when organisations were putting in place new systems and operations to get ready for the law coming into effect, it was the fear of fines that provided the loudest and most compelling drivers for action.

The power to impose financial penalties (referred to as administrative fines in the GDPR) is contained in Article 58.2(i). When considering whether to issue a financial penalty, a regulator must also consider Article 83, which establishes the criteria for when and how a financial penalty can be imposed and the relevant fine ranges that apply to different types of infringement.

In deciding whether a financial penalty is appropriate and the size of it, regulators must consider:

- the obligations that have been infringed by the organisation;
- the extent to which those obligations have been infringed;
- the associated fine ranges that apply based on the infringements;
- any aggravating or mitigating factors that may apply.

Table 16.1 shows the financial penalty limits under the GDPR depending on the type of violation.

**Table 16.1 GDPR fines**

Lower limit – an organisation can be fined up to €10m/£8.7m, or in the case of an undertaking, up to 2% of the total worldwide annual turnover of the preceding financial year, whichever is higher for breaches of the following:

- The obligations of the controller and the processor pursuant to Articles 8, 11, 25 to 39 and 42 and 43.
- The obligations of the certification body pursuant to Articles 42 and 43.
- The obligations of the monitoring body pursuant to Article 41(4).

Higher limit – an organisation can be fined up to €20m/£17.5m, or in the case of an undertaking, up to 4% of the total worldwide annual turnover of the preceding financial year, whichever is higher for breaches of the following:

- The basic principles for processing, including conditions for consent, pursuant to Articles 5, 6, 7 and 9.
- The data subjects' rights pursuant to Articles 12 to 22.
- The transfers of personal data to a recipient in a third country or an international organisation pursuant to Articles 44 to 49.
- Any obligations pursuant to Member State law adopted under Chapter IX of the GDPR.
- An order or a temporary or definitive limitation on processing or the suspension of data flows by the Supervisory Authority pursuant to Article 58(2) or failure to provide access in violation of Article 58(1).
- An order by the Supervisory Authority as referred to in Article 58(2).

## DETERMINATION OF PENALTIES

When determining whether a penalty should be applied, and the extent of it, a regulator must take account of the relevant mitigating and aggravating factors present. Article 83 of the GDPR provides a list of these factors:

- the nature, gravity and duration of the infringement, the number of data subjects affected and the level of damage suffered by them;
- the intentional or negligent character of the infringement;
- any action taken by the controller or processor to mitigate the damage suffered by data subjects;
- the degree of responsibility of the controller or processor, taking into account the technical and organisational measures implemented by them for compliance;
- any relevant previous infringements by the controller or processor;
- the degree of cooperation with the supervisory authority, to remedy the infringement and mitigate the possible adverse effects of it;

- the categories of personal data affected by the infringement;
- the manner in which the infringement became known to the supervisory authority, including whether the controller or processor notified the infringement;
- where enforcement action has previously been ordered against the controller or processor with regard to the same subject matter and, if so, the degree of compliance;
- adherence to approved codes of conduct pursuant or approved certification mechanisms, within the meaning of Articles 40 and 42;
- any other aggravating or mitigating factor applicable to the case, such as financial benefits gained, or losses avoided, directly or indirectly, from the infringement.

In addition to the factors highlighted in A.83, each supervisory authority will have their own non-exhaustive list of factors that they will use on a case-by-case basis to assess the presence and absence of any aggravating and mitigating factors. These can be found in the ICO's Regulatory Action Policy, for example.

## Mitigating factors

Where an organisation feels that there are relevant mitigating factors that should be considered, they should bring them to the attention of the regulator. This would also include highlighting the absence of any aggravating factors. However, an organisation should fully consider its position before rushing to provide mitigating factors, because there is a potential risk that they could create new lines of inquiry for the regulator.

Furthermore, information that turns out to be factually incorrect or potentially misleading may be treated as an aggravating factor. In some circumstances, the provision of mitigation may also be interpreted as an acceptance of the prior finding of non-compliance, which could have wider ramifications outside the process in which it is presented (e.g. within civil litigation brought by data subjects for compensation). It is therefore a fine balancing exercise for organisations to ensure that the mitigating factors they present are factually correct, provide true mitigation and are presented at the correct time.

## REPUTATIONAL IMPACT

The fact that regulatory actions are published or reported on by the regulators as part of their duty to act transparently[9] and to deter others from also infringing the law can have a long-lasting effect on the offending organisation's reputation. This is just one reason why it is important for organisations to properly consider and, if necessary, challenge regulatory findings if they do not accept them. Where those findings cannot be challenged, an organisation may need to carry out damage limitation exercises, which will likely revolve around its public relations strategies.

Reputational harm can occur at any time during a regulatory investigation whether that is through confirmation that an investigation is under way, or at its conclusion, when

---

[9] Art. 57(1)(b), GDPR.

wrongdoing has been found. Organisations will often have to try and deal with this reputational harm at the same time as responding to, or challenging, the enforcement action or decision. This can create heightened pressure for organisations and cause strain on resources.

With the rise in individuals choosing to pursue their data protection rights through direct and group litigation organisations must also be wary of how publication of regulatory action can influence individuals and any future proceedings. Claims management companies routinely rely on the outcomes of regulatory actions to support the bringing of compensation claims. The publication of an adverse outcome by a regulator against a high-profile organisation can be expected to result in a flurry of letters of claim being received shortly afterwards.

## APPEALS AGAINST REGULATORY ACTION

Where a regulator issues an enforcement decision or finding against an organisation, they will generally issue a preliminary notice, giving the organisation an opportunity to challenge it before it is finalised. If after exhausting this process the regulator and the organisation are still in dispute, the organisation will need to consider the merits of an appeal. This may include assessing potential challenges to the decision as a whole or the severity of the decision (e.g. whether any financial penalty is excessive).

Appeals can be pursued where the decision is potentially wrong in fact or law, or where the decision itself is deemed to be disproportionate or potentially unfair due to the circumstances in which it was made.

The ability to seek a judicial remedy is captured in Article 78 of the GDPR, which provides that 'each natural or legal person shall have the right to an effective judicial remedy against a legally binding decision of a supervisory authority concerning them' and that 'proceedings against a supervisory authority shall be brought before the courts of the Member State where the supervisory authority is established'. This right may take different forms across different Member States, however.

The relevant timeframes and method of appeal will be communicated in the notice provided by the regulator to the organisation. It is important that organisations comply with these timescales because failing to do so may affect their ability to appeal the decision. If further time is required, a request for an extension of time should be made to the regulator explaining the reasons why.

If an organisation fails to submit an appeal within the given timeframes, it does not mean that they are then automatically barred from appealing, because they can ask the court to allow the appeal out of time. When requesting an appeal out of time, an organisation will need to request an extension and provide justification for their failure to submit the appeal within the given time limits.

The methods of redress and judicial remedy will differ from country to country. However, these will generally involve an appeals or judicial review process, which would allow an organisation to bring matters in dispute before the relevant national court. Using England and Wales as an example, where an organisation wishes to appeal a decision of the ICO, they would appeal that decision to the First Tier Tribunal. If unsuccessful in that appeal, they have a further opportunity to appeal.

## PREPARING FOR THE RISK OF REGULATORY ACTION

To give itself the best chances of preparing for and dealing with regulatory investigations and enforcement actions, an organisation should take account of:

- the mechanisms under which the regulators use their powers;
- its own special characteristics;
- jurisdictional considerations;
- the regulator's enforcement profile.

Table 16.2 provides examples of the information that should be considered.

**Table 16.2 Preparing for the risk of regulatory action**

| Category | Considerations |
| --- | --- |
| Special characteristics of the organisation that is at risk of enforcement action | Economic sector; geographical location; legal and organisational structures; business plan and processing operations; prior regulatory track record; risk appetite; culture, values and purpose; and so on. |
| Jurisdictional considerations | Lead supervisory authority; national legislation (including common law versus civil law considerations); disclosure rules (including application of privilege); rules in relation to redress and appeals; and so on. |
| Regulator enforcement profile | Propensity for enforcement; types of enforcement powers most regularly utilised; actions taken for different infringements; regulatory action policy (e.g. any industry focuses); public profile; political and public interest motivations; and so on. |

Once an organisation has collected and brought together the information outlined in Table 16.2, in should be able to measure its enforcement risk profile and prepare effectively for the potential risks of regulatory action. This can include scenario planning and war-gaming, drafting guidance for people to follow, putting in place an enforcement response team and creating required artefacts that could be used in an emergency, such as press releases. Playbooks might consist of:

- overviews of the powers of the regulators and how those powers can be used;
- guidance on how to respond to and challenge enforcement powers;
- descriptions of roles and responsibilities;
- rules on internal communication flows, the maintenance of confidentiality and the application of legal privilege;

- procedures for internal investigations;
- protocols for instruction of external third parties;
- lists of pre-agreed actions to stand up necessary functions (e.g. strategy and board meetings);
- boilerplate documents, such as response letters, international communications scripts and press packs.

It is those organisations that are better prepared for adverse scrutiny that fare the best during regulatory investigations and when defending their interests in respect of any subsequent enforcement action.

## Preparation through understanding the true extent of regulator powers – privilege example

A crucial part of that preparation is understanding the true extent of the regulator's powers.

For example, Article 58(1)(a) of the GDPR provides a regulator with the power to 'order the controller and the processor, and, where applicable, the controller's or the processor's representative to provide any information it requires for the performance of its tasks'. On the face of it, this appears to be a very expansive power that could, in the absence of expert advice, lead to an organisation handing over any information that a regulator asks for. In practice, however, there are a number of other laws that can and should be applied, to protect certain information from disclosure. An important example of this would include where the doctrine of legal privilege applies. Organisations often unwittingly share information with regulators during investigations that could otherwise have been considered privileged information and therefore withheld.

## Disposition – the stance and style to adopt when faced with regulatory action

The disposition that an organisation adopts when faced with regulatory action can have a significant bearing on its risks and the outcomes. In other words, it is not just the law that dictates the outcomes of regulatory investigations and action – the stance and style of the organisation being investigated can also be a factor in these outcomes. Of course, a rude and aggressive stance is not going to get an organisation anywhere, but on the other hand, taking a clear and firm stance, albeit politely, is likely to be an appropriate strategy in most cases.

There is plenty of anecdotal evidence to suggest that the regulators often prefer to take on low hanging fruit rather than organisations that seem to provide a harder challenge. This may help to explain why in the UK regulatory action has disproportionately focused on public authorities and small to medium-sized enterprises, which lack many of the characteristics of large businesses, especially as they concern the resources needed to mount successful legal defences to regulatory action. If an organisation can show that it is disposed to standing its ground, it might be one that achieves greater success in regulatory action than one that conveys the impression that it will quickly yield to the regulator without mounting a defence. Clearly, an economically strong controller or processor will have financial resources and access to skills and support that might not be open to economically weaker organisations, and regulators, will need to weigh up whether they can actually afford to take on difficult cases.

## SUMMARY

In conclusion, this chapter gives readers a better understanding of:

- the end-to-end processes of regulatory supervision and action;
- the different stages of regulatory supervision and action;
- how to prepare for the risks of regulatory action;
- steps that can be taken to challenge regulatory action.

# 17 HANDLING PERSONAL DATA BREACHES

## Stewart Room and Ben Johnson

This chapter examines the legal and operational requirements for security within the GDPR and the duties of transparency that apply to personal data breaches, which trigger obligations to notify regulators and to issue communications to impacted individuals.

### THE LEGAL OBLIGATION TO BE SECURE

The security regime within the GDPR consists of the following parts:

- The sixth data protection principle in A.5.1.f says that personal data shall be processed in a manner that ensures appropriate security of the personal data. It also sets out a non-exhaustive list of the protections that need to be achieved for personal data undergoing processing. The sixth data protection principle is named 'integrity and confidentiality', but is usually called the 'security principle'.

- A.32 requires controllers and processors to implement appropriate technical and organisational measures for the security of processing, utilising a risk-based approach. It also provides a non-exhaustive list of the protections and outcomes that need to be achieved through the implementation of these measures. A.32 indirectly applies to processors, due to A.28.3.c, which requires controllers to engage processors through contracts or other binding legal acts that require processors to take all the measures required by A.32.

- A.33 requires controllers to notify the regulators of personal data breaches that are likely to result in risks to the rights and freedoms of individuals. It also requires processors to notify controllers of personal data breaches. A.33 also applies indirectly to processors, due to A.28.3.f.

- A.34 requires controllers to communicate personal data breaches to impacted individuals, where these breaches are likely to result in a high risk to their rights and freedoms. A.34 indirectly applies to processors, again due to A.28.3.f.

#### Relationship to ePrivacy

The ePrivacy regime with PEC (and the UK equivalent, PECR) contains an equivalent security framework for the providers of electronic communications services. Due to Article 95 of the GDPR, communications services providers need only address the breach notification regime in PEC, rather than both regimes.

## Relationship to cybersecurity

Likewise, there is an equivalent regime for the purposes of network and information security, rather than the protection of personal data, within the EU NIS Directive[1] (sometimes called the 'Cyber Security Directive'). This applies to the operators of essential services, which covers undertakings operating in the energy, transport, banking, finance, health and digital infrastructure services, and to digital services providers, which covers online marketplaces, online search engines and cloud computing services. The NIS Directive has been implemented in the UK by the NIS Regulations 2018.[2] The NIS Directive and UK Regulations are undergoing review at the time of writing and are likely to be amended in due course.

## The protections to be achieved under GDPR A.5.1.f

The non-exhaustive list of protections for the security of personal data undergoing processing within the sixth data protection principle are:

- protections against unauthorised or unlawful processing;
- protections against accidental loss, destruction or damage to personal data undergoing processing.

These protections have to be achieved through the implementation of appropriate technical and organisational measures.

## Protections to be achieved under GDPR A.32

A.32.1 requires controllers and processors to take a risk-based approach to security, through the implementation of appropriate technical and organisational measures, so that the measures ensure a level of security that is appropriate to the risk. When determining what is appropriate, they need to take account of:

- the state of the art;
- the costs of implementation;
- the context and purposes of processing;
- the risks of varying likelihood and severity for the rights and freedoms of individuals.

The non-exhaustive list of factors that they need to consider when deciding upon the nature of the technical and organisational measures include:

- Pseudonymisation and the encryption of personal data (A.32.1.a).
- The ability to ensure the ongoing integrity, availability and resilience of processing systems and services (A.32.1.b).

---

1 Directive (EU) 2016/1148 of the European Parliament and of the Council of 6 July 2016 concerning measures for a high common level of security of network and information systems across the Union.

2 The Network and Information Systems Regulations 2018, SI 2018/506.

- The ability to restore the availability and access to personal data in a timely manner in the event of a physical or technical incident (A.32.1.c).
- A process for regularly testing, assessing and evaluating the effectiveness of technical and organisational measures for ensuring the security of the processing (A.32.1.d).
- The risks that are presented by the processing, which include a set of considerations that are broadly the same as those listed in A.5.1.f, for example, accidental and unlawful destruction of personal data (A.32.2). Recital 83 expands upon this, pointing out the risks of physical, material or non-material damage that can result from security breaches affecting personal data. Recital 75 points to risks such as identity theft, fraud, financial loss, damage to reputation and loss of confidentiality.

The phrase 'appropriate technical and organisational measures' is sometimes paraphrased as 'security controls' and this chapter uses these phrases interchangeably. Security controls need to be present across the three layers of the organisation, namely the people layer, the paper layer and the technology and data layer. People controls will cover roles and responsibilities. Paper controls will cover policies, notices, contracts, and so on. Technology and data controls will include IT software, CCTV and purely physical controls having a technical effect, such as a door lock and key.

### Security of the full data processing environment

A.32.4 requires controllers and processors to take steps to ensure that any people acting under their authority who have access to personal data do not process them except on the controller's instructions. Reading this alongside A.5.1.f and A.32, it is clear that the GDPR provides full legal coverage for security within the processing environment, including within supply chains and within the workplace, which is achieved through direct legislative duties and indirect contractual duties:

- A.5.1.f places a direct legislative duty on controllers for security.
- A.32.1 places direct legislative duties on controllers and processors for security.
- A.28.3.c places a direct legislative duty on controllers to apply security requirements equivalent to A.32 on processors, through contracts/other legally binding mechanisms and supported by other technical and organisational measures.
- A.32.4 places legislative duties on controllers and processors to apply processing restrictions on workers with access rights (workers are employees and contractors). These will be applied through contracts/other legally binding mechanisms and supported by other technical and organisational controls.

### Processing data for security purposes as a legitimate interest

The GDPR recognises that personal data can be processed for security purposes, under the legitimate interests basis for lawful processing contained in A.6.1.f, provided that the processing is limited to the extent that is strictly necessary and proportionate for the security objective. Recital 49 providers a non-exhaustive list of situations where this can apply:

- for the purposes of ensuring network and information security;
- for the security of related services offered by, or accessible via, those networks and systems;
- by public authorities;
- by computer emergency response teams (CERTs) and cybersecurity incident response teams (CSIRTs);
- by providers of electronic communications networks and services;
- by providers of security technologies and services.

This security goals envisioned by R.49 include:

- preventing unauthorised access to electronic communications networks;
- preventing malicious code distribution;
- stopping denial of service attacks;
- preventing damage to computer and electronic communication systems.

R.71 expands on this, saying that automated decision making, including profiling, can be allowed 'to ensure the security and reliability of a service provided by the controller', which, if so, would also fall within the legitimate interests basis of lawfulness.

## Accountability for security

The accountability principle in GDPR A.5.2 requires controllers to be able to demonstrate their compliance with the security principle. A.24 amplifies this duty, by requiring controllers to be able to demonstrate that their processing is conducted in accordance with the regulation.

Other elements of accountability for security include:

- A.28, which cascades the requirements of A.32 via contracts or other legally binding mechanisms into the processor relationship, requires controllers to use only processors 'providing sufficient guarantees' about the technical and organisational measures required by the regulation (A.28.1). This language contains inherent requirements for accountability, in the sense that a guarantee cannot be satisfied without proof of compliance with its terms.
- A.28.3.h is explicit about accountability, as it requires the processor to make available to the controller 'all information necessary to demonstrate compliance', which includes contributing to audits and inspections conducted by the controller or its nominated auditor.
- A.32.3 says that adherence to an approved code of conduct or certification measure (which can be approved under A.40 and 42 respectively) may be used as an element by which to demonstrate compliance. As discussed elsewhere in this book, these mechanisms have not yet taken off for the purposes of the GDPR. However, in the wider world there are many security codes and certifications for organisations to choose from, so it seems almost inevitable that some of these will receive formal endorsement for the purposes of A.40 and 42 in due course.

## OPERATIONAL SECURITY

The legal duties discussed above need to be operationalised by controllers and processors. All of the GDPR's compliance mechanisms apply to achieve this, such as Data Protection by Design and Default, which can be paraphrased as Security by Design.

### Expanded requirements for security found outside the GDPR

While the GDPR's legal obligations provide for the security of the full data processing environment, apart from the specified compliance obligations (appropriate technical and organisational measures, personal data breach notifications, etc.) and compliance mechanisms (DPbDD, DPIAs, DPOs, ROPAs, etc.), it provides very little by way of detail on how operational security is to be achieved, save for specifying a limited number of techniques such as encryption and pseudonymisation. This is true for all of the other data protection principles (and a notable feature of EU law more generally), so controllers and processors need to supplement their knowledge and understanding from other sources. These other sources include:

- case law;
- regulatory guidance and enforcement decisions;
- industry and professional standards for best practice;
- alerts and advisories, such as those issued by cybersecurity authorities (e.g. National Cyber Security Centre in the UK), IT security companies and professional services firms.

Currently, case law on security obligations is thin and patchy, so there is little to be found there to provide meaningful instruction on the day-to-day operational requirements for security. The picture is likely to change over the coming years, due to the growth in security-related compensation claims that is being driven by the introduction of the personal data breach notification rules in the GDPR.

Regulatory guidance and enforcement decisions provide much more fertile ground for understanding the detail of the operational requirements, however. In contrast to case law, the regulators see a greater number of cases than the judiciary, again driven by the personal data breach notification rules, plus their legislative duty to issue advice to aid compliance means that they have to address security risks on a proactive, not just reactive, basis, resulting in more materials for controllers and processors to consider.

Taking the Information Commissioner's Office as an example, they have published accessible and comprehensive guidance that covers many bases, such as:

- Guidance on discrete security issues, such as asset disposal, security of online services, bring your own device (BYOD), cloud computing and encryption.
- They have endorsed, by reference, standards published by other bodies, such as the Payment Card Industry Data Security Standard (PCI-DSS), which covers security in the cardholder data environment.

- They have partnered with the National Cyber Security Centre to create guidance on required security outcomes. This stands alongside NCSC guidance and initiatives such as Cyber Essentials.
- They refer to the work of the EU Agency for Cyber Security.

Further granularity about obligations is found in the ICO's enforcement decisions, which provide context-specific insights into the regulator's views. These documents can be very helpful, because they take abstract and high-level concepts and apply them to real-life situations. Recent Monetary Penalty Notices issued by the ICO are must-read publications for persons responsible for delivering operational security and for those responsible for related governance, advisory and assurance functions. The EDPB publishes regular updates on enforcement action taken by the regulators in the EU Member States, which, again, is essential reading.

## The state of the art

Part of the reason why the GDPR does not provide exhaustive details about the nature of the technical and organisational measures needed for security is because enshrining such matters in legislation at a particular moment in time would quickly lead to the law's obsolescence. Instead, by using phrases such as the state of the art within the context of the law's goals, the law is future-proofed.

### *The consensus of professional opinion*
The state of the art is generally accepted to mean the level of development that has been achieved in a particular area. It can cover matters that are seemingly absolute in nature, such as the state of invention of technology, but other areas are less certain, such as processes, methods and ideas. Therefore, the state of the art on many matters might be a matter of debate and dispute, rather than undisputed fact, particularly where there is a range of options available for dealing with issues that require expert input.

In those cases, a solution is needed to chart a way through ambiguities. That solution is found within the consensus of professional opinion. This is a lodestar for identifying the correct, or acceptable, course of action in complex and challenging areas such as security where there are a range of reasonable, or appropriate, responses that can be adopted in given situations.

The GDPR is designed to embrace the consensus of professional opinion on security. A critical consequence, which can be liberating for controllers and processors to understand, is that the law will not and should not supplant reasonable managerial decision making on security, if those decisions can be justified by reference to the consensus of professional opinion on the matter in hand. In those cases, it should not matter if the controller or processor could have made a different decision.

The consensus of professional opinion is found within the expert community of security professionals. This is a large and diverse community, consisting of, for example:

- security professionals working in operational functions, such as a chief information security officer;

- those working in advisory and oversight functions (such as consultants and auditors);
- those working in security technology companies;
- those working in academia;
- those working in official agencies, such as law enforcement and CERTs.

The breadth and complexity of the subject matter is such that it would be a highly challenging, if not impossible, task for most organisations to keep on top of the consensus of professional opinion for security, were it not for the fact that the consensus has been reduced into smaller subject matter areas, with corresponding operational aims and objectives defined – that is, within standards for best practice.

Therefore, controllers and processors that adhere to recognised standards of best practice, such as management systems and controls frameworks published by organisations like the International Organization for Standardization, will likely be treated by the data protection regulators as having operated in accordance with the consensus of professional opinion as a matter of law. The fact that many of the standards are subject to accreditation, including through processes of independent assurance, bolsters that likelihood even further.

### *The state of technological development*
The legal obligation to take appropriate technical measures for security embraces technology, which includes information technology in its broadest sense. The state-of-the-art requirements within A.32 therefore mean that controllers and processors need to have an understanding of the state of technological development (this was actually written into the Data Protection Act 1998, the UK legislation that was repealed and replaced by the UK DPA). In turn, this means that they need to keep abreast of changes in technology. This covers not only the invention and commercial offering of new forms of security technology, but also enhancements to current technologies. Examples of how this works in real life are easy to find, including the need to download and install the latest versions of computer operating systems, anti-virus updates and the implementation of software patches.

The state of technological development can also cover advisories issued by CERTs, such as NCSC, and agencies such as ENISA, but there is another, darker universe within the state of technological development, which consists of the developments of threats and threat actors. Obviously, legitimate vendors of IT security and security services will react to developments in threats, such as through the release of software patches and updates, but the nature of the threats that controllers and processors face depend ultimately on their special characteristics. As the ICO says in its security guidance, 'there is no "one size fits all" solution to information security', so they will have to ensure that they design and implement security solutions that correspond appropriately to the state of technological development in the threat landscape that they actually face. Again, to cite ICO's security guidance, 'you must ensure that you are aware of the state of technological development in this area and that your processes and technologies are robust against evolving threats'.

The EDPB has considered the meaning of the state of the art as it relates to the state of technological development in its guidance[3] on the Data Protection by Design and Default rules in A.25. Due to the mirroring of the language of A.25 in A.32, it is safe to assume that this represents the EDPB's point of view for security:

> In the context of Article 25, the reference to 'state of the art' imposes an obligation on controllers, when determining the appropriate technical and organisational measures, to take account of the current progress in technology that is available in the market. The requirement is for controllers to have knowledge of, and stay up to date on technological advances; how technology can present data protection risks or opportunities to the processing operation; and how to implement and update the measures and safeguards that secure effective implementation of the principles and rights of data subjects taking into account the evolving technological landscape.

> The 'state of the art' is a dynamic concept that cannot be statically defined at a fixed point in time, but should be assessed continuously in the context of technological progress. In the face of technological advancements, a controller could find that a measure that once provided an adequate level of protection no longer does. Neglecting to keep up to date with technological changes could therefore result in a lack of compliance with Article 25.

## Costs of implementation

Controllers and processors are required to have regard to costs when implementing their technical and organisational measures. This requirement does not mean that they will be absolved from their responsibilities to implement appropriate measures simply due to them being too expensive. Rather, expense is a factor within the assessment of risks and controllers and processors need to quickly understand if their processing operations will expose personal data to risk due to safeguards being too expensive to implement. They also need to have regard to costs so that they do not overrun on budgets, or leave themselves short. However, the idea of costs within the GDPR is not simply a financial one. It covers costs in all senses of the word, such as the expenditure of time, effort and resources. Some of these ideas are encompassed with the EDPB guidance on DPbDD:

> The controller may take the cost of implementation into account when choosing and applying appropriate technical and organisational measures and necessary safeguards that effectively implement the principles in order to protect the rights of data subjects. The cost refers to resources in general, including time and human resources.

> The cost element does not require the controller to spend a disproportionate amount of resources when alternative, less resource demanding, yet effective measures exist. However, the cost of implementation is a factor to be considered to implement data protection by design rather than a ground to not implement it.

> Thus, the chosen measures shall ensure that the processing activity foreseen by the controller does not process personal data in violation of the principles, independent

---

[3] Guidelines 4/2019 on Article 25 Data Protection by Design and by Default Version 2.0, adopted on 20 October 2020.

of cost. Controllers should be able to manage the overall costs to be able to effectively implement all of the principles and, consequentially, protect the rights.

The baseline philosophy of the GDPR is that if the risks of processing are too costly to appropriately manage in an operational sense, the processing activities must cease.

## The nature, scope, context and purpose of processing

The formula for the calculation of a risk-based approach to the security of personal data undergoing processing needs to take a holistic view of all the circumstances of the processing, hence why A.32 refers to the nature, scope, context and purposes of processing. Security risks are scenario-specific, differing from one scenario to another, and the special characteristics of the controller and processor include the scenarios of risk that they face. Again, referring to the EDPB guidelines on DPbDD, these issues are summarised as follows:

> In short, the concept of nature can be understood as the inherent characteristics of the processing. The scope refers to the size and range of the processing. The context relates to the circumstances of the processing, which may influence the expectations of the data subject, while the purpose pertains to the aims of the processing.

The guidance indirectly points to three key questions:

- What processing is being done?
- How is it being done?
- Why is it being done?

These questions are central to all elements of the GDPR, not just security. They are implicit in the initial transparency requirements in A.13 and 14; the information access rules in A.15; the general obligations of controllers in A.24 and 25; the records of processing rules in A.30; and the risk management rules in A.35. Together they require controllers and processors to understand their scenarios of risk, which provide the foundation stone upon which a risk-based approach to security can be built. Once the scenarios are identified, controllers and processors are then able to answer the next key question within A.32:

- What are the risks of varying likelihood and severity for the rights and freedoms of individuals?

## The risks of varying likelihood and severity

The rights and freedoms that A.32 is intended to protect are those within the EU Charter of Fundamental Rights and, for the UK post-Brexit, those protected through the Human Rights Act 1998. As clarified by Recital 75, where these rights and freedoms are infringed, they can cause individuals to suffer physical, material and non-material damage. A loss of control over data, whether permanent or transient, is an inherent harm within the idea of a personal data breach, and R.75 confirms that this falls within the risks of varying likelihood and severity that A.32 is concerned with. Therefore, it follows that any unlawful or unauthorised processing event that falls within the ambit of A.32.2 and A.5.1.f constitutes a risk to rights and freedoms.

In other words, a personal data breach always involves a risk to rights and freedoms. This point is returned to later, within the discussion about breach notification.

The ICO guidance on security provides a succinct list of examples of the kinds of harm that can flow from a security breach and, by implication, involve risks to the rights and freedoms of individuals:

- identity fraud;
- fake credit card transactions;
- targeting of individuals by fraudsters, potentially made more convincing by compromised personal data;
- witnesses put at risk of physical harm or intimidation;
- offenders at risk from vigilantes;
- exposure of the addresses of service personnel, police and prison officers, and those at risk of domestic violence;
- fake applications for tax credits;
- mortgage fraud;
- causing embarrassment and inconvenience.

It should also be remembered that the law is concerned with the prevention of risks to rights and freedoms, not just the occurrence of actual infringement of rights and freedoms. Therefore, controllers and processors can be held to be in contravention of the law even if it subsequently transpires that a security breach did not cause harm to individuals and, therefore, no infringement of their rights and freedoms. Risk prevention is the first goal of security law – albeit it is an adage in the security community, which is recognised and appreciated by the regulatory community, that it is impossible to eliminate completely all security risks.

## Required outcomes

In summary, the security rules in the GDPR require these outcomes to be achieved:

- Controllers and processors need to fully understand their scenarios of security risk. Their understanding needs to be holistic.
- Within each of these scenarios they need to understand the nature of the risks to rights and freedoms that they may involve and the harms that might result if a breach were to occur.
- They need to identify and implement appropriate technical and organisational measures, or controls, to address those risks.
- When identifying and implementing those controls, they must have regard to the state of the art, which includes the consensus of professional opinion on security threats, risks and controls and the state of technological development.

- They must also understand and address their ability to deliver the controls that are required, having regard to all relevant factors, including costs in the broadest sense.

The Information Commissioner's Office and the National Cyber Security Centre have collaborated to identify a set of outcomes that are required to deliver on A.32 and A.5.1.f of the GDPR, which are based on four aims, namely managing security risk; protecting personal data against cyberattack; detecting security events; and minimising the impact. Table 17.1 summarises the outcomes.

**Table 17.1 Security outcomes defined by ICO and NSCS**

| | |
|---|---|
| Manage your security risk | • Governance – including policies, processes, records of processing and appointment of DPOs. |
| | • Risk management – taking appropriate steps to identify, assess and understand security risks to personal data and processing systems. |
| | • Asset management – including understanding and cataloguing personal data processed and the purpose of processing. |
| | • Processors and supply chain – understanding and managing security risks arising from third parties such as processors. |
| Protection against cyberattack | • Service protection policies and processes – including defining, implementing, communicating and enforcing appropriate policies and procedures that direct the overall approach to securing data processing systems. |
| | • Identity and access control – including understanding, documenting and managing access to personal data and processing systems. |
| | • Data security – implementing technical controls to prevent unauthorised or unlawful processing. |
| | • System security – implementing measures to protect systems, technologies and digital services that process personal data from cyberattack. |
| | • Staff awareness and training – including giving them appropriate support to help them manage personal data securely, including the technology they use. |
| Detect security events | • Detecting events that affect data processing systems – including monitoring authorised user access. |
| Minimise the impact | • Response and recovery planning – including defined and tested incident management processes. |
| | • Improvements – including understanding root cause, breach notification and other communications to third parties, and taking remediating action. |

Security professionals will recognise that all of the elements of the security outcomes listed in Table 17.1 fall within the consensus of professional opinion on operational good practice, but that they are not exhaustive. The principal lesson taught by the outcomes and the approach adopted by the ICO in their development, that is, partnering with NCSC, is that controllers and processors will rarely go wrong if they adhere to the consensus of professional opinion, such as within industry and professional standards, to provide a skeleton framework for their security responses. Of course, they need to flesh out those frameworks by taking full account of their security risk scenarios and the state of the art on the threat landscape, the responses those threats require and the state of technological development.

### Appropriateness – what risks will the law tolerate?

The risk-based approach within A.32 and the appropriateness qualifier to the obligation to implement technical and organisational security measures might suggest that the GDPR is willing to tolerate some kinds of security breaches. In other words, not all security breaches will constitute a breach of security law.

However, there is another way to read the GDPR: aside from zero-day security threats (i.e. those that are entirely novel), perhaps all breaches of security will be a breach of security law. In other words, the risk-based approach and the idea of appropriateness does not set a floor for the operation of the law, below which breaches will not be regulated. Instead, what the law is saying is that controllers and processors need to identify and understand their risks, then act appropriately to achieve the prescribed outcomes, namely preventing unauthorised and unlawful acts harming data processing systems, personal data and data subjects. On balance, it seems unlikely that the law will be interpreted this expansively. The courts have already shown great sympathy for organisations that have fallen victim to cybercrime.

These points are yet to be fully resolved. Adding to the ambiguity, the law has not yet developed (whether through court cases or regulatory intervention) a bright line test that enables controllers and processors to understand with certainty whether their security operations are fully in accordance with the law, nor is it ever likely to do so. The problem is compounded further by the disparities in regulatory approaches across the EU and the UK and the opacity that clouds decision making by the regulators in most cases; only a very small percentage of their cases result in the publication of materials, such as Enforcement Notices and Monetary Penalty Notices that enable the public to understand what is really going on in the regulatory system. Controllers and processors can mitigate against this problem somewhat by tracking legal developments, such as court decisions, regulatory enforcement decisions and guidance, which will give them good insights into the prevailing regulatory priorities for security.

## PERSONAL DATA BREACHES, BREACH NOTIFICATION AND COMMUNICATIONS

There are two distinct, but connected, security regimes in the GDPR and PEC. The first, discussed above, is the legal regime for operational security, which in the GDPR is represented by A.5.1.f, 32 and 28. In effect, it requires controllers and processors to take a risk-based approach to the implementation of appropriate security measures

– in other words, to protect data processing systems and personal data; detect and respond to threats and risks; and remediate security problems as they are discovered. All of these outcomes will protect controllers and processors themselves, due to the added resilience that is achieved, but the ultimate concern of the law is to protect data subjects from harm.

The second security regime is personal data breach notification and communications. This picks up the baton of protecting data subjects, by injecting transparency into operational failure situations, that is, personal data breaches.

## Philosophies within breach notification and communications – transparency and its effects

Breach notification is a US concept, which first emerged in legislation in California in 2003. The EU borrowed the concept in 2009, through amendments to PEC,[4] then expanded it through the NIS Directive, GDPR and Law Enforcement Directive, all adopted in 2016. The rules are contained in A.33, which concerns the notification of personal data breaches to the regulators, and A.34, which requires communication of them to people affected.

### *Transparency aids mitigation of harm*
The philosophical heart of breach notification is that controllers and processors need to be transparent following personal data breaches, so that any risks of harm to individuals can be mitigated and so that the lessons of failure can be learned, to help avoid recurrences. Upon being informed of a breach, the regulators have the power to intervene, which includes the power to require controllers and processors to put a stop to risky processing and to remediate underlying problems. Impacted individuals might be able to take practical steps to protect themselves, such as changing passwords to accounts, being on alert to possible scams and frauds and monitoring their bank accounts.

### *Power shift – moving from being in credit to being in debt*
Controllers and processors who dig a little deeper into the philosophies will understand that transparency in these situations is intended to shift power from themselves. Controllers and processors do not own personal data, in the sense of data being tangible or intangible property; instead, they have rights in data. These rights exist as a form of licence, which the law grants, but on conditions. Until such time as the conditions are breached, controllers and processors are relatively free to go about their business. However, once a breach occurs, the freedoms are immediately curtailed in the sense that power shifts to the regulators and to people affected, through transparency, as they gain new legal and operational controls. Another way to look at things is that until a breach occurs, the controllers and processors are in credit with the regulatory system, but when a breach occurs, the credit runs dry, leaving the controllers and processors in debt to the system.

### *Transparency creates a production line for the industrialisation of adverse scrutiny*
The effects of transparency go much further than the goals of immediate risk mitigation and preventing recurrences. As a matter of course they trigger regulatory investigations

---

[4] In 2009 the EU also adopted breach notification for cybersecurity purposes, for the providers of publicly available communications services. This was the forerunner to the NIS Directive.

and inquiries, by acting as a catalysts for regulatory action that, in the most serious cases, can result in the imposition of enforcement orders and fines. They also trigger action by data subjects, claims management companies and litigation lawyers, whose reactions can range from making access requests under GDPR A.15, through to advertising for claimants to joint group litigation, through to the commencement of representative court cases by privacy activists. All these things are happening in the UK at the moment due to transparency after personal data breaches. In other words, personal data breach notifications and communications provide the raw ingredients for an adverse scrutiny production line on an industrial scale.

### *Reputation damage, trust, confidence and stigma*

Personal data breaches can become national and international news stories, although the volume and frequency of breach notification and communications being pumped out means that individual cases can easily be hidden in the torrent. Moreover, breach fatigue is a problem, which lessens the newsworthiness of most cases. However, news stories are not the only contributors to reputation damage, loss of trust and confidence and ongoing stigma. Having to tell regulators means that there will be a black mark against the controller or processor concerned. Having to tell business partners means that they might be more cautious in their dealings going forward. Having to tell impacted people means that they might consider their options for the future, or be less cooperative and forthcoming. Personal data breaches always have negative results, often transient or hard to quantify, but the possibility of more lasting and consequential impacts can never be discounted.

## Personal data breach definition

The meaning of personal data breach is defined in GDPR A.4.12 as a 'breach of security leading to the accidental or unlawful destruction, loss, alteration, unauthorised disclosure of, or access to, personal data transmitted, stored or otherwise processed', which conforms to the concepts within A.5.1.f and 32. There are two ideas within this definition:

- there has to be a breach of security;
- the breach has to lead to one of the prohibited outcomes, such as accidental loss of data.

## Breach of security

In most situations, once the facts are established, there is very little ambiguity about whether a breach of security has occurred, but occasionally questions arise about the meaning of the phrase 'a breach of security' within A.4.12.

These questions are easy to resolve:

- The security principle in A.5.1.f requires appropriate security of personal data undergoing processing, then provides examples of what security should achieve, such as protection against accidental loss of data.
- Therefore, if there is (for example) accidental loss of data, that should create a presumption that a breach of security has occurred.

- However, A.32 requires appropriate measures to be taken for security. This firmly suggests that a breach of security means that security measures either have been circumvented, or are simply not in place. Construing the law in this way closes a loophole, whereby a controller or processor could otherwise avoid the application of the breach notification rules by choosing not to implement security measures. That is an outcome that the law cannot tolerate. This construction also conforms the GDPR to the approach taken in other security legislation, such as in the Computer Misuse Act 1990 (as amended), which has not made the commission of computer misuse offences conditional on the circumvention or overcoming of security controls.
- Additional clarity is provided by the title of the security principle, 'integrity and confidentiality', and regulatory guidance, such of the ICO, which says that security is concerned with integrity, availability and confidentiality of personal data.
- Finally, the long-standing approach to the interpretation of data protection legislation, called the purposive approach, requires the law to be interpreted in an expansive fashion, for its goals to be achieved, namely protecting the integrity and confidentiality of personal data (including its availability) and data subjects.

Therefore, apart from a zero-day attack, any event that leads to, for example, accidental loss of data (or any of the other prohibited acts) will constitute a breach of security for the purpose of the definition in GDPR A.4.12. The presence, absence or nature of security controls (technical and organisational measures) is immaterial to the issues in A.33 and 34. They are only material to the questions of compliance within A.5.1.f and 32.

## Incident detection and response

The technical and organisational measures that controllers and processors adopt for security must include ones for detection and responding to incidents. This capability must support not just the operational security needs of security breaches, but the transparency needs of breach notifications and communications. Again, controllers and processors cannot avoid the operation of the law by failing to implement measures that enable them to achieve compliance with GDPR A.33 and 34.

Recital 87 supports this view:

> It should be ascertained whether all appropriate technological protection and organisational measures have been implemented to establish immediately whether a personal data breach has taken place and to inform promptly the supervisory authority and the data subject. The fact that the notification was made without undue delay should be established taking into account in particular the nature and gravity of the personal data breach and its consequences and adverse effects for the data subject. Such notification may result in an intervention of the supervisory authority in accordance with its tasks and powers laid down in this Regulation.

## Types of personal data breaches – risks to rights and freedoms

All personal data breaches need to be notified to regulators under A.33, unless they are unlikely to result in a risk to the rights and freedoms of individuals. In contrast, communications to individuals are required only where personal data breaches are likely to result in a high risk to rights and freedoms:

- **A.33 notifications.** Notifications of personal data breaches must be made to regulators, unless they are unlikely to cause a risk to rights and freedoms.
- **A.34 communications.** Communications of personal data breaches to individuals are only required if they are likely to cause a high risk to rights and freedoms.

## Timetables for notification and communications

The time period for giving notifications to regulators under A.33 and communications to data subjects under A.34 begins with the controller becoming aware of the personal data breach, but in the case of A.34, awareness requires the controller to be aware that the breach involves a likely high risk to rights and freedoms.

Once fixed with the necessary awareness, these notifications and communications should be made without undue delay, although in the case of notifications this is subject to a 72-hour longstop, where feasible, beginning from the point of awareness.

Processors are required to notify controllers of personal data breaches without undue delay. This is not qualified by whether or not the breach constitutes a risk to the rights and freedoms of individuals. That is immaterial to the fulfilment of the processor duty in A.33.2.

According to regulatory guidance[5] published by the EDPB's predecessor, the Article 29 Working Party, ('the WP guidance'), 'a controller should be regarded as having become "aware" when that controller has a reasonable degree of certainty that a security incident has occurred that has led to personal data being compromised'. The guidance goes on to say:

> When, exactly, a controller can be considered to be 'aware' of a particular breach will depend on the circumstances of the specific breach. In some cases, it will be relatively clear from the outset that there has been a breach, whereas in others, it may take some time to establish if personal data have been compromised. However, the emphasis should be on prompt action to investigate an incident to determine whether personal data have indeed been breached, and if so, to take remedial action and notify if required.

### *Investigation period*

If a suspected security breach is discovered, the law allows the controller a reasonable period to investigate it, to help it understand whether the breach constitutes a personal data breach within the meaning of A.4.12. An investigation period is helpful, because the nature of breaches is not always immediately apparent. However, as mentioned above, the consensus of professional opinion requires controllers and processors to have appropriate technical and organisational measures in place to quickly detect and respond to suspected security breaches, which is reflected in R.87 and regulatory

---

[5] Guidelines on personal data breach notification under Regulation 2016/679, adopted on 3 October 2017, as last revised and adopted on 6 February 2018, WP 250 Rev.01.

guidance, so they cannot hide behind absence or weakness of necessary controls to justify delayed notification.

The WP guidance puts things in this way:

> After first being informed of a potential breach by an individual, a media organisation, or another source, or when it has itself detected a security incident, the controller may undertake a short period of investigation in order to establish whether or not a breach has in fact occurred. During this period of investigation the controller may not be regarded as being 'aware'. However, it is expected that the initial investigation should begin as soon as possible and establish with a reasonable degree of certainty whether a breach has taken place; a more detailed investigation can then follow.

### *Phased notifications*

Controllers should try not to delay notification under A.33 until they have acquired the full facts of the breach, nor should they delay notification under A.33 pending the assessment of whether the breach involves a high risk to rights and freedoms within the meaning of A.34.

A.33.4 points to the possibility of interim and subsequent notifications, saying that 'where, and in so far as, it is not possible to provide [the information required to be notified to regulators by A.33] at the same time, the information may be provided in phases without undue further delay'.

### Risks to rights and freedoms and the carve-out for encrypted data

The carve-out from having to notify under A.33 that applies to personal data breaches that are unlikely to result in a risk to the rights of freedoms of individuals has very narrow application, due to the very expansive meaning of risk and rights and freedoms, so it will not be an effective cloak against transparency in most personal data breach situations.

Dealing with the expansive nature of rights and freedoms, as mentioned earlier they cover the rights and freedoms in the EU Charter and the UK human rights regime. The Charter includes a right to data protection, with the result that any event that contravenes the data protection principles will constitute an interference with rights and freedoms. UK law can be construed in the same manner. What this means is that all personal data breaches will constitute either a risk to, or actual interference with, rights and freedoms, due to them constituting a loss of control over data in the broadest sense of the word, even if that loss is just momentary.

This construction needs to be squared with the carve-out in A.33, which has been done by the WP guidance and revolves around the use of encryption. In summary, the carve-out will only apply to encrypted data that have been backed up, provided that the encryption key itself is not compromised by the breach. In effect, through the data remaining unintelligible there will not be a risk to rights and freedoms. The guidance puts it in this way:

> Consequently, if personal data have been made essentially unintelligible to unauthorised parties and where the data are a copy or a backup exists, a confidentiality breach

involving properly encrypted personal data may not need to be notified to the supervisory authority. This is because such a breach is unlikely to pose a risk to individuals' rights and freedoms. This of course means that the individual would not need to be informed either as there is likely no high risk. However, it should be borne in mind that while notification may initially not be required if there is no likely risk to the rights and freedoms of individuals, this may change over time and the risk would have to be re-evaluated. For example, if the key is subsequently found to be compromised, or a vulnerability in the encryption software is exposed, then notification may still be required.

Therefore, if personal data are not properly protected by encryption, A.33 will always apply, so controllers will have to move to assessing whether the breach constitutes a likely high risk to rights and freedoms for the purposes of A.34. A.34.3.a explicitly refers to encryption as a measure that means that the communications to impacted individuals under A.34 are not required.

### *Likely high risks to rights and freedoms*
There are many considerations within the idea of risks to rights and freedoms, which need to be factored into the assessments that controllers make when addressing their notification and communications requirements.

**Action taken after a breach**   A.34.3.b refers to the taking of 'subsequent measures' by a controller, that is, after a personal data breach has occurred, that 'ensure that the high risk to the rights and freedoms ... is no longer likely to materialise' as ones that mean that communications to impacted individuals will not be required. These measures can include steps to recover data and all copies of them and to prevent further unauthorised use, such as asking an unintended recipient of data in a trusted relationship to provide confirmation and assurance of these steps being taken. Where the personal data breach relates to a threat actor, discovery of them and their activities accompanied by remedial actions, for example to block access to networks, might immediately eliminate the risks.

**A.34 requires something more than A.33**   It is self-evident that A.34 is concerned with more serious situations than A.33, otherwise there would be no sense having separate notification and communications obligations. To give sense to the distinction, it should follow that a mere loss of control over data does not by itself constitute a likely high risk to rights and freedom. A.34 has to be pointing to risks that are subsequent to a loss of control.

For example, a threat actor focusing on a business fraud might incidentally acquire data. If they do, undoubtedly A.33 will apply in the absence of encryption, due to the loss of control that is involved. However, A.34 cannot apply simply because of that loss of control, as that would remove the distinction between it and A.33. Instead, A.34 must require a likelihood of other, additional risks to rights and freedoms, which in themselves must be high risks. Such other, additional risks might include a risk that the threat actor will utilise the incidentally acquired personal data to target or harm the impacted people, such as by using the data for a phishing campaign, or for harassment, or for identity theft, or to sell to other threat actors such as on the Dark Web or in other rogue fora, or to cause harm by publishing the data. In this situation, the assessment will turn to whether the other, additional risks are likely to arise, which must mean something more than possible, or conceivable. It cannot be right that guesses are made about likelihoods because that would deprive A.34 of any meaning, data subjects of effective protections and controllers of legal and operational certainty.

Unfortunately, the GDPR and the supporting regulatory guidance does not get to grips with these issues. The WP guidance merely points to the issues that may be relevant to an assessment of the risks, but it does not help with understanding likelihoods or the levels of risks. The guidance on these points is very thin and the logic to justify erring on the side of caution is not explained:

> Therefore, when assessing the risk that is likely to result from a breach, the controller should consider a combination of the severity of the potential impact on the rights and freedoms of individuals and the likelihood of these occurring. Clearly, where the consequences of a breach are more severe, the risk is higher and similarly where the likelihood of these occurring is greater, the risk is also heightened. If in doubt, the controller should err on the side of caution and notify.

The ICO guidance does not take things any further:

> A 'high risk' means the requirement to inform individuals is higher than for notifying the ICO. Again, you will need to assess both the severity of the potential or actual impact on individuals as a result of a breach and the likelihood of this occurring. If the impact of the breach is more severe, the risk is higher; if the likelihood of the consequences is greater, then again the risk is higher. In such cases, you will need to promptly inform those affected, particularly if there is a need to mitigate an immediate risk of damage to them.

**The special characteristics**  Elsewhere in this book, attention has been drawn to the need for controllers and processors to understand their special characteristics and those of data subjects and possible adverse scrutineers. This is baked into the WP guidance, in the context of assessing the rights to rights and freedoms:

> Special characteristics of the individual
>
> A breach may affect personal data concerning children or other vulnerable individuals, who may be placed at greater risk of danger as a result. There may be other factors about the individual that may affect the level of impact of the breach on them.
>
> Special characteristics of the data controller
>
> The nature and role of the controller and its activities may affect the level of risk to individuals as a result of a breach. For example, a medical organisation will process special categories of personal data, meaning that there is a greater threat to individuals if their personal data is breached, compared with a mailing list of a newspaper.

**Other regulatory guidance on likelihood and size of risks**  The WP guidance refers to guidance published by ENISA[6] for measuring the severity of personal breaches. This

---

6  Recommendations for a methodology of the assessment of severity of personal data breaches, Working Document, v1.0, December 2013.

is a useful document, insofar as it helps with understanding what some of the risks might be and because it provides a repeatable formula for assessing severity, but, again, it does not get to grips with the question of likelihoods.

The WP guidance contains some examples of situations where A.33 and 34 may or may not apply. The EDPB has also published guidance[7], which contains 18 case studies, but like the WP guidance it suffers from failing to get to grips with idea of likelihood.

These problems do not erode the guidance of all value, however. While being of questionable utility on the issue of likelihood, they provide insights into the regulatory mindset, giving controllers and processors benchmarks to begin understanding the likely disposition of the regulators in given cases.

**Interests of law enforcement**

An obvious effect of making communications under A.34 is that the personal data breach is put into the public domain, which might lead to wider publicity.

A potential downside of transparency is that it might impede the interests of law enforcement, by tipping off criminals and other people of interest, with an obvious risk of destruction of evidence and interference with witnesses. Recital 88 of the GDPR recognises this and requires the interest of law enforcement to be taken into account during the development of rules and processes for breach communications. The development of rules and processes lies with the European Commission and national regulators, but R.88 also suggests that controllers should take these interests into account during the development of their incident response procedures:

> In setting detailed rules concerning the format and procedures applicable to the notification of personal data breaches, due consideration should be given to the circumstances of that breach, including whether or not personal data had been protected by appropriate technical protection measures, effectively limiting the likelihood of identity fraud or other forms of misuse. Moreover, such rules and procedures should take into account the legitimate interests of law-enforcement authorities where early disclosure could unnecessarily hamper the investigation of the circumstances of a personal data breach.

**A.34 communications and disproportionate effort**

A.34 anticipates that communications to individuals will be made directly to them, such as by sending them letters, emails and other personal communications. As an exception to this rule, A.34.3.c allows substitute notice, through public communications or similar measures, where making personal communications will involve disproportionate effort. A.34.3.c says:

> 3. The communication to the data subject referred to in paragraph 1 shall not be required if any of the following conditions are met:

---

[7] Guidelines 01/2021 on Examples regarding Data Breach Notification, adopted on 14 January 2021, Version 1.0.

(c) it would involve disproportionate effort. In such a case, there shall instead be a public communication or similar measure whereby the data subjects are informed in an equally effective manner.

The disproportionate effort exception operates where the controller has already assessed that the personal data breach will likely result in a high risk to the rights and freedoms of individuals. Therefore, the law envisages that there are situations where despite the risks being high, it will be appropriate for individuals not to benefit from personal communications. In those situations, the effort will be just too much.

The regulatory guidance on what is meant by disproportionate effort is thin. The WP guidance says:

> It would involve disproportionate effort to contact individuals, perhaps where their contact details have been lost as a result of the breach or are not known in the first place. For example, the warehouse of a statistical office has flooded and the documents containing personal data were stored only in paper form. Instead, the controller must make a public communication or take a similar measure, whereby the individuals are informed in an equally effective manner. In the case of disproportionate effort, technical arrangements could also be envisaged to make information about the breach available on demand, which could prove useful to those individuals who may be affected by a breach, but the controller cannot otherwise contact.

### *Effort expended versus gains achieved*
The meaning of disproportionate effort is not defined in the GDPR. However, giving these words their ordinary meaning, disproportionate effort is likely to mean that the energy and resources expended on personal communications are too large in comparison to the gain that will be achieved through the effort that is applied.

The idea of disproportionate effort is contained in other parts of the GDPR, that is, in the rules on transparency notices (A.14) and the rules on rectification, erasure and restriction (A.19). Recital 62, which expands on A.19, indicates that disproportionate effort may encompass issues such as the number of data subjects, the age of data and the safeguards adopted.

In a Court of Appeal case in 2017, *Dawson-Damer*, under the Data Protection Act 1998 (now repealed), the idea of disproportionate effort was examined as it applied to subject access requests, including the effort of searching for data. The Court of Appeal confirmed that the issue of (dis)proportionality applied to the full process of complying with subject access requests:

> The passage which Mr Swift cites from the Code of Practice suggests that the IC reads section 8(2) as applying only to the process of supply. I do not consider that the difficulties that can be taken into account in determining whether the supply of information in permanent form would be disproportionate for a data controller are limited to those which arise in the process of producing a copy of a document, but include difficulties which occur in the process of complying with the request which might result in the supply of the document involving disproportionate effort. This is

consistent with EU law, which would apply proportionality to all stages of the process of compliance.

The Court of Appeal said that the test to apply is not simply a cost and time test, however:

> So it is not open to a data controller to avoid substantive compliance by arguing that work would be expensive or time-consuming. The cost of compliance is the price data controllers pay for processing data.

Instead, the Court of Appeal defined the test as follows:

> In my judgment, the word 'supply' is used so that what is weighed up in the proportionality exercise is the end object of the search, namely the potential benefit that the supply of the information might bring to the data subject, as against the means by which that information is obtained. It will be a question for evaluation in each particular case whether disproportionate effort will be involved in finding and supplying the information as against the benefits it might bring to the data subject.

### *The disproportionality*
Taking account of the scenario of the personal data breach, the end-to-end processes involved in making personal communications, the efforts that they involve, of which cost and time are factors, and the nature of the risks to rights and freedoms that a case involves, some of the disproportionality issues might include:

- The effort expended in the end-to-end process might be a material distraction from taking other, more meaningful steps in mitigation.
- The process might be an exercise in futility, in that it might not be able to deliver personal communications at its conclusion, for example because the controller lacks up-to-date contact details.
- The process might be so long and convoluted that it fails to deliver outcomes (whether gainful or not) without undue delay. If a process cannot overcome this problem, it might be argued that this is the essence of disproportionality, because the proportional goal of A.34 is speedy communications. Recital 86 points to this, at least implicitly, where it says that 'the need to mitigate an immediate risk of damage would call for prompt communication with data subjects whereas the need to implement appropriate measures against continuing or similar personal data breaches may justify more time for communication'.

### *Substitute notice by way of public communications*
The phrase 'in an equally effective manner' within A.34.3.c is very interesting, but it is not likely to require public communications to be as effective as personal communications. This is because there must be an inherent quality gap between personal communications and indirect communications and for the disproportionate effort exception to make a sense, it must permit this gap.

The words are more likely to mean that there must be similarity of effect between a public communication and a different type of communication. If a public communication is a website statement or a press release, a different type of communication might be a reactive message that is played when people call a contact centre. Construing A.34.3.c. in this way overcomes the problem of having to construe the words 'in an equally effective manner' as requiring equivalency between personal communications and indirect communications.

## Contents of notifications and communications

Communications and notifications under A.33 and 34 both require this information to be supplied:

- The nature of the personal data breach. This includes, where possible, the categories and approximate numbers of data subjects and records impacted.
- The name and contact details of the DPO, or other contact person.
- A description of the likely consequences of the breach.
- A description of the measures taken, or proposed to be taken, by the controller to address the breach and, where appropriate, to mitigate possible adverse effects.

Article 34.2 expands upon these requirements by saying that communications should be written in clear and plain language.

### *Additional information*

The requirements of notifications and communications identified above is the minimum amount of information that must be provided. Of course, controllers can elect to provide more information and regulators and data subjects can seek to elicit more. The stance that the controller takes to deal with follow-up questions will need to take account of its legal obligations (e.g. accountability, the duty of regulatory cooperation and whether any other legal powers have been triggered); commercial, brand and reputational interests; litigation strategy, if it is facing serious enforcement action or compensation claims; and the need to protect interests such as legal privilege.

## Ordering A.34 communications

A.34.4 gives the regulators the power to order controllers to make communications to impacted individuals. It can order personal communications, or public communications if the disproportionate effort carve-out from personal communications is satisfied. Recital 86 sets an expectation that controllers with work with regulators to deal properly with these matters.

## Breach logs

Controllers could seek to bypass these rules on transparency to bury bad news. A.33.5 addresses this by requiring them to 'document any personal data breaches', with the record to comprise the facts of the breach, its effects and the remedial action taken. The purpose of the record is to 'enable the supervisory authority to verify compliance with this Article'.

Failure to keep breach logs is an enforceable contravention of the GDPR, which can result in the imposition of fines.

## SUMMARY

In conclusion, this chapter gives readers a better understanding of:

- the legal obligations for security;
- how the law helps to define the requirements of operational security;
- when personal data breaches must be notified to the regulators;
- when personal data breaches must be communicated to impacted individuals;
- the contents of personal data breach notifications and communications.

# GLOSSARY

**Accountability principle:** A principle of data protection that requires controllers of personal data to be able to prove their compliance with the law. See GDPR A.5.2.

**Adequacy:** For the purposes of transfers of personal data from the GDPR land mass to third countries, the GDPR permits these transfers without restriction if an adequacy decision has been adopted in respect of the country to which the data are transferred. See GDPR A.45.

**Adverse scrutiny:** A concept developed by the editor of this book, which is used in client engagements to help them understand, prepare for and manage the risks of challenge and scrutiny that data processing activities can attract.

**Anonymisation:** The permanent and irreversible removal of personal identifiers so that information no longer identifies a living individual. Information that is anonymised does not fall within the scope of data protection regulation.

**Appropriate technical and organisational measures (ATOM):** The measures, or 'controls', that are adopted for the purposes of compliance with data protection law. See GDPR A.24, 28 and 32.

**Article 29 Working Party:** The predecessor to the European Data Protection Board. An independent body with advisory status that was constituted under Article 29 of the Data Protection Directive 1995, composed of representatives of the national supervisory authorities for data protection and European Union officials.

**Binding corporate rules (BCRs):** A mechanism for international transfers of personal data from the GDPR land mass to other countries, which can be used by groups of undertakings and groups of enterprises to overcome the prohibition against transfers to non-adequate third countries (i.e. to countries that do not benefit from an adequacy decision). See GDPR A.47.

**Controller:** A person or body that determines the purposes and means of data processing. A controller can determine the purpose and means of processing by itself or jointly with another controller (a 'joint controller'). The controller is the person or body that carries most of the obligations under data protection law. See GDPR A.4.7.

**Controls:** A term in general use in the data protection community to describe the technical and organisational measures that are implemented by controllers and processors to ensure that their processing activities are legally compliant. The controls should be appropriate, having regard to the overall context of the processing and the risks to rights and freedoms that are involved.

**Council of Europe:** An intergovernmental human rights organisation founded after the Second World War. The European Court of Human Rights (ECtHR) is the court for the Council. The Council adopted the Data Protection Convention in 1981 (sometimes referred to as 'Treaty 108'). The UK is a member of the Council and a signatory to the Convention.

**Data Protection Act 2018 (UK DPA):** The UK's primary legislation for data protection. Repealing and replacing the Data Protection Act 1998, the 2018 Act should be read alongside the UK GDPR, as it fills the gaps in the law that the GDPR left for Member States to deal with, as well as applying it to areas of data processing not covered by the GDPR, such as processing by the intelligence services.

**Data Protection by Design and Default (DPbDD):** The legal obligations placed on controllers to implement appropriate technical and organisational measures for data protection before the processing activities begin and to minimise processing. Sometimes referred to as 'Privacy by Design'. See GDPR A.25.

**Data protection impact assessment (DPIA):** A risk management technique that is compulsory for the controller to perform where its processing activities are likely to result in a high risk to the rights and freedoms of individuals. In certain circumstances the controller is required to consult with the regulator before commencing high-risk processing. See GDPR A.35.

**Data protection officer (DPO):** An independent person who is appointed by a controller or processor to perform various advisory, monitoring and other compliance tasks, including cooperation with the regulator. The GDPR sets out the situations where the appointment of a DPO is compulsory, but controllers and processors can also make voluntary appointments. See GDPR A.37.

**Data protection principles (or 'principles of data protection'):** The foundational compliance obligations of data protection law, which the controller is responsible for. The principles are: lawfulness, fairness and transparency; purpose limitation; data minimisation; accuracy; storage limitation; integrity and confidentiality; and accountability. See GDPR A.5.

**Data subject:** A living individual who is the subject of personal data that are undergoing processing. The data subject is the protected party under the law, who enjoys various rights and entitlements, including a right of transparency; right to information; right to intervene in processing; and right to various remedies.

**Data subject access request (DSAR):** Sometimes referred to as a 'SAR'. See GDPR A.15.

**ePrivacy:** The data protection and privacy legal framework represented by the EU Directive on Privacy and Electronic Communications 2002 (as amended) and the UK Privacy and Electronic Communications Regulations 2003 (as amended), which relates to the provision and use of electronic communications services. The protected parties under these laws are subscribers and users of electronic communications services.

**Establishment:** The concept of establishment is central to the territorial scope of the GDPR. Controllers and processors that are established in the GDPR land mass are subject to the GDPR for all processing activities that are conducted in the context of their establishment. An establishment implies the effective and real exercise of activities through stable arrangements, such as by having a physical presence in a particular country. Where a controller or processor is established in more than one EU Member State, it will be regulated by the national supervisory authority for its main establishment. The GDPR also regulates controllers and processors that are established outside the GDPR land mass, if they offer goods and services to people within the EU or the UK, or if they monitor the activities of people that take place in the EU or the UK. See GDPR A.3.

**European Data Protection Board (EDPB):** The successor body to the Article 29 Working Party, the EDPB is a body of the European Union, with legal personality. The EDPB's purpose is to ensure the consistent application of the EU GDPR. See GDPR A.70.

**Filing system:** A filing system relates to manual data, that is, data that are not being processed wholly or partly by automated means. Data will form part of a filing system when the data are accessible according to specific criteria, which implies an index or another form that enables manual data to be searched for and retrieved. See GDPR A.4.6.

**General Data Protection Regulation (GDPR):** The primary legal framework for data protection, adopted by the EU in 2016, replacing the Data Protection Directive 1995. The UK was subject to the GDPR at the point of its adoption, but now that Brexit has been implemented, the UK is subject to the 'UK GDPR', which mirrors the original EU version. At the date of publication of this book, the UK GDPR and EU GDPR are identical in all material respects.

**General Data Protection Regulation (GDPR) land mass:** A phrase used in this book to identify the countries in Europe where the GDPR applies as the principal data protection law, namely the EU, the EEA States, the UK and Switzerland, to help contrast those countries from 'third countries' where the GDPR's rules on international transfers apply.

**Information Commissioner:** The UK's national supervisory authority for data protection, that is, the data protection regulator.

**Legitimate interests assessment (LIA):** The processing of personal data can be lawful where it takes place for the purposes of the legitimate interests of the controller, except where those interests are overridden by the interests or fundamental rights and freedoms of the data subject. A legitimate interests assessment is a risk management technique that helps the controller to understand whether it can justify processing on the basis of its interests.

**Life cycle:** As in 'data life cycle', or 'information life cycle', the continuum of activities and period of time starting with the initial collection or obtaining of personal data and concluding with the final deletion, destruction or anonymisation of data.

**National supervisory authority:** The GDPR requires the EU Member States to appoint independent national supervisory authorities to monitor, supervise and enforce the law. See GDPR A.51.

**Necessity test:** A precondition for reliance upon many of the grounds for the lawful processing of personal data and special category data. See GDPR A.6 and 9.

**Operational adequacy schemes:** A concept developed by the editor of this book, which is used in client engagements to help them understand, prepare for and manage the need to deliver operationally adequate outcomes for data protection, particularly where personal data are transferred to non-adequate third countries.

**Personal data:** Any information that relates to an identified or identifiable living individual. Personal data that are undergoing processing is the protected subject matter under data protection law. See GDPR A.4.1.

**Personal data breach:** A breach of security that involves risks to the rights and freedoms of individuals, to which the GDPR's rules on breach reporting apply. See GDPR A.4.12.

**Processing:** Any operation, or set of operations, which is performed on personal data, or sets of personal data, whether or not this is done by automated means. Processing is the activity that is regulated by data protection law and it covers the end-to-end life cycle of data use, from initial collection through to deletion and destruction. The GDPR regulates processing that is performed wholly or partly by automated means and non-automated processing that forms part of a filing system. See GDPR A.4.2.

**Processor:** A person or organisation that processes personal data on behalf of a controller. A processor has to be appointed by a contract, or similar legal instrument, that guarantees its compliance with the requirements of the GDPR. A processor must always act on the controller's instructions. It if acts independently or in breach of the controller's instructions, it risks becoming a controller in its own right, with all of the compliance and liability obligations that are involved. See GDPR A.4.8.

**Profiling:** Any form of automated processing of personal data, whereby the data are used to evaluate certain personal aspects and behaviours of people. See GDPR A4.4.

**Pseudonymisation:** A treatment that is applied to personal data, to mask or obfuscate personal identifiers so that the data cannot be attributed to a specific person without the use of additional information. That additional information must be kept separate from the other information and protected by technical and organisational measures to ensure that it is not attributed to an identified or identifiable person. Pseudonymisation is treated by the GDPR as a measure that supports the minimisation and security of personal data. Unlike anonymised data, pseudonymised data can be reverse engineered to identify specific individuals. See GDPR A.4.5.

**Recipient:** Any person to whom personal data are disclosed in the course of processing done by, or on behalf of, the data controller, apart from persons who receive personal data as a result of a particular inquiry made in the exercise of legal powers, such as the Information Commissioner or the police. See GDPR A.4.9.

**Records of processing activities (ROPA):** A core compliance obligation of the GDPR, which requires the controller to maintain records of processing activities under its responsibility. Containing prescribed information, the ROPA is a foundational requirement for operational data protection and a core record that enables controllers to prove their compliance with the law in accordance with the accountability principle. Sometimes referred to as 'data maps'. GDPR A.30.

**Regulatory bear market:** A concept developed by the editor of this book, which is used in client engagements to help them understand, prepare for and manage the risks of multiple and concurrent forms of adverse scrutiny of their data processing activities by people with actual or quasi-regulatory powers.

**Rights request:** The exercise of the data subject rights. See GDPR A.15–22.

**Special category data:** Sensitive types of personal data, the processing of which involves heightened risks for the rights and freedoms of the individuals to whom they relate. The processing of special category data is prohibited, unless one of the grounds in the GDPR is satisfied. See GDPR A.9.

**Special characteristics:** A concept developed by the editor of this book, which is used in client engagements to help them understand, prepare for and manage the need to take account of their unique operating and environment features to deliver operationally adequate outcomes for data protection.

**Standard data protection clauses:** Sometimes referred to as 'standard contractual clauses' or 'model clauses', these are approved mechanisms that can be used by controllers and processors to overcome the prohibition on the transfer of personal data from the GDPR land mass to non-adequate third countries. See GDPR A.46.

**Subscriber:** In the context of ePrivacy law, a person or organisation that subscribes to a publicly available electronic communications service.

**'The Journey to Code':** A concept developed by the editor of this book, which is used in client engagements to help them understand, prepare for and manage the need to deliver operationally adequate outcomes for data protection within technology and data themselves. This concept is inspired by Prof. Lawrence Lessig's seminal work *Code and Other Laws of Cyberspace* (1999, Basic Books).

**Third countries:** Countries outside the GDPR land mass, to which the GDPR rules on international transfers apply. See GDPR A.44.

**Third party:** Anyone other than the controller, the data subject or the processor. A third party can be a natural person or legal persons, such as companies.

**Transborder data flows:** The movement of personal data across national boundaries.

**Transfer assessment:** A term commonly used in the data protection community to describe an assessment of the data protection risks that may arise in a country outside the GDPR land mass to which personal data are transferred.

**Transparency:** The provision of information about the controller and processing operations that is provided to data subjects at the point of collection of their personal data, or shortly afterwards, or in response to the exercise of the data subject rights, or as a result of personal data breach. See GDPR A.13, 14, 15 and 34.

**User:** In the context of ePrivacy law, a person who uses an electronic communications service.

**Weaponisation:** A term used in the data protection community to describe the use of the data subject rights for a collateral purpose unrelated to data protection, such as to further a grievance or litigation.

**White list:** A term commonly used in the data protection community that refers to the countries situated outside the GDPR land mass whose laws, according to adequacy decisions, ensure an adequate level of protection for personal data that are undergoing processing.

# INDEX

Page numbers in italic refer to figures.

4-Ts 272–3

accountability 44, 46–8, 101, 126, 187, 228, 256, 257–77
   4-Ts 272–3
   accumulation of evidence 276–7
   adverse scrutiny 276
   ATOM 270–1
   continuum *258*
   data protection principle 72, 76, 89, 108–11, 116, 123, 126, 134, 146, 254, 257–9, 269, 321
   demonstrating 258
   documentation 223
   DPbDD 254–5, 265–7
   DPIA 235, 236
   end-to-end 258
   GDPR 258
   in practice 259–67
   legitimate interests 267–70
   risk management 270–6
   ROPAs 231–3, 261, 265–7
   security 350
   'the accountability rule' 33, 40
accuracy 36, 89, 102, 106–7, 138–9, 142, 179, 216, 263, 276, 286, 288, 291, 318, 372
adequacy
   assessing 179
   decisions 21, 56–7, 71, 79, 94, 113, 121, *178*, 179, 180–2, 187, 190, 195–6, 199, 205, 315, 317
   international transfers 56, 93, 94, 179, 182
   operational 72, *200*, 201–2
   regulations 94, 187
   status 205, 206
   test 91, 275
   UK 94, 181
adequate protection 180, 191, 194
AdTech 12, 13, 17, 64, 92, 149, 162, 302, 316
'adverse scrutineers' 200, 201
AI (Artificial Intelligence) 14, 17, 22, 87–8, 148, 292
anonymisation and pseudonymisation 42, 44, 80, 83, 131, 291, 371, 373
APEC (Asia-Pacific Economic Cooperation) Privacy Framework 205
appropriate safeguards 37, 43, 93, 94, 105, 113, 123, 124, 128, 176, 178, 179, 182–3, 187, 190, 196–7
Article 28 167, 170, 184, 241–3
Article 29 Working Party 62, 304, 362
assessments
   impact *see also* DPIA 43, 47, 77, 97, 166, 223, 227, 229, 235, 239, 242, 266, 304, 328
   legitimate interests 66, 77, 109, 257, 266, 284
   risk 77, 80, 90, 109, 188, 228, 229, 262, 266, 271, 282, 284, 285, 303
   threat and vulnerability 91
   transfer 77–8, 93
assurance 43, 76, 83–5, 109, 125, 187, 201, 252, 255, 274–6, 301, 331, 352–3, 364
ATOM (appropriate technical and organisational measures) 42, 73, 269, 270–4, 371
attestations 43, 85

audit/auditing 21, 48, 52, 73, 75, 83–4, 85, 185, 190, 267, 223, 274–6, 294, 301, 313, 318, 319, 321
automated decision making 14, 17, 45, 78, 82, 113, 122, 128, 138, 148, 217, 236, 350

Binding Corporate Rules (BCR) 47, 56, 57, 79, 84, 94, 166, 167, 170, *178*, 182, 183, 188–90, 201, 275, 371
breach notification 48, 67–9, 80, 81, 86, 98, 205, 242, 244, 253, 261, 303–4, 308, 310–11, 347, 351, 356, 358–69
Brexit 16, 18, 19, 20, 26–7, 61, 71, 164, 171, 181, 355
   European Union (Withdrawal) Act 2018 55
   GDPR 26, 55–6
   international transfers of data 56–7
   IP Day 20, 27, 55
   UK GDPR 55, 373

CCPA (California Consumer Privacy Act, 2018) 206, 209, 210, 211
CCTV 31, 50, 349
CDPA (Consumer Data Protection Act, US, 2021) 206, 211, 212
certifications 43, 85, 167, 168, 170, 185, 228, 274, 275, 325, 340, 350
Charter of Fundamental Rights of the European Union 5, 7–9, 59
Children's Online Privacy Protection Act (COPPA) (US, 1998) 208
Citizens' Rights Directive 36, 61, 62

377

codes of conduct 96, 166, 167, 170, 228, 273, 293, 342
collection transparency 45, 46
communications
   confidential 297
   data 21, 36, 68, 80, 370
   direct marketing 60, 65, 80, 268, 269, 310
   electronic 16, 17, 19, 42, 58, 60, 61, 67, 68, 70, 347, 350, 372, 375
   personal 366-9
   services 16, 36, 58, 60, 67, 70, 347, 372
   technology 204, 292
compatibility 105, 270
compensation 35, 48, 185, 243, 298, 300, 316, 320, 321, 333-5, 342
   claims 12, 15-17, 23, 24, 49, 65, 80-1, 92, 126, 138, 151, 302, 305, 308, 310, 312, 315, 334-5, 343, 351, 369
   right to 152-3, 189, 211, 215, 293
compliance
   duty of 101
   framework 32, 35-44
   operational 83, 119, 227-44, 279
confidential references 53, 133
confidentiality of communications 16, 60-5, 70
consent
   AdTech 12
   conditions and quality 40-1, 62
   cookie 18, 41, 63-5, 164
   derogation 191-2
   EDPB guidance 191-2
   explicit 37, 39, 64, 94, 117, 150, 190, 215, 268
   for processing 39-42, 45, 79, 122, 140, 143, 144, 211, 213
   freely given 41, 79, 112
   GDPR-level 164, 190, 269, 341
   informed 40, 112-13
   lawful basis 111-13, 141, 215, 217, 253
   management 253, 290
   parental 14, 41, 86
   prior 65, 66, 67, 219
   proof of 40
   specific 112
   storage 61-2

tools 87
transparency 45, 63
UK DPA 131
unambiguous 113
withdrawal of 40, 45, 122, 192, 217, 299
contracts 42, 47, 60, 72, 73, 78-9, 95, 111, 183, 210, 227, 241-4, 287, 317, 328, 347, 349, 350
   controller 243, 244
   processor 241, 242, 243
contractual clauses 16, 47, 56, 166, 167, 170, *178*, 183-8, 193, 315, 375
contractual lawful basis 113
controls 47-8
   accountability 44
   anonymisation and pseudonymisation 44
   assessing 44-5
   code-based 279
   compliance framework 42-4
   outcomes 45-7
   prescribed 43
   requirements 42-3
convergence 207, 209, 211, 212, 214, 220
cookies 20, 60, 61, 62, 151, 152, 164, 305
   AdTech 12
   behavioural advertising 64
   consent 18, 41, 63-5, 164
   direct marketing 65-7
   legal risk 65
   legislation 70
   monitoring people 31
   types 63
   walls 62
corporate finance 53, 133
Council of Europe 4, 19, 20, 35, 36, 204, 372
Council of Europe Resolution (1973) 22, explanatory report 4
COVID-19 6, 13, 17, 88, 91, 248, 292, 297
criminal offences 9, 19, 38, 61, 132, 328-30
criminal proceedings 9, 324, 326, 328
criminal prosecutions 316, 337

data
   analytics 247
   biometric 11, 38, 117, 213, 215

brokers 247, 339
communications 21, 36, 68, 80, 370
controller 30, 33, 46, 47, 51, 82, 88, 124-6, 150, 184, 188, 195, 204, 207, 219, 236, 237, 257, 263, 269, 270, 274, 276, 283, 304, 318, 320-3, 330, 331, 334, 365, 367, 368, 374
discovery 259, 262, 263, 264, 265, 267, 286, 288
electronic 135
encrypted 363
exporter 16, 77, 183-6, 191, 194, 195, 198, 199, 201, 202
flows 9, 56, 284, 288, 339, 341, 375
governance 233, 237, 255
intelligence technology 89, 278, 282, 284, 286-91, 293
international transfers 13, 21, 56, 84, 95, 151, 176-202, 302
localisation 216, 217, 218, 219, 220, 224
location 10, 14, 16, 67, 69 145
minimization 36, 44, 75, 105-6, 179, 189, 204, 246, 279, 294, 372
obtaining 121, 122, 328, 329, 330, 373
porting 145-6
privacy 89
processor 43, 76, 79, 81, 184, 188, 216, 217, 223, 241-3, 272, 283
quality 45, 187, 189, 204, 233, 319
recipient 34, 264
sensitive 17, 117, 180, 186, 211, 214, 215, 236
sharing 9, 21, 48, 79, 80, 244, 279
structured 145
third-party 131, 272, 286, 289, 291
traffic 61, 67
transfers 176, 177, 183, 186, 188, 190, 192, 194, 196, 201, 202, 250, 315
data processing 3, 21, 24, 32-4, 76, 96, 104, 106, 109, 114, 126, 198, 216, 218, 223, 224, 227
   activities 28, 34, 41, 48, 72, 74-5, 83, 171, 175, 247, 249, 253, 261, 266, 273, 282, 330
   environment 72, 259, 264, 266, 274, 275, 276, 349, 351

foreign 20
impacts of 16
law enforcement 19
lawful bases of 36–8, 46–7, 77
life cycle 32, 246, 258
operations 45, 162, 213, 258, 263, 264, 270, 276
personal 31, 49, 105, 111, 219, 258, 273, 339
regulation 78
rights over 120, 138–48
scrutiny of activities 276, 319, 320, 371
security 349
systems 91, 292–3
techniques 13, 31, 278
data protection
Brazil 212–14
Brexit 26
China 216–17
definitions 3, 4
DPbDD 43, 76, 86, 233–5, 240, 245–56, 265, 282, 294, 318, 354, 355, 372
ePrivacy 59, 60
goals of 3
impact assessments see DPIA
implementing 72, 74–98
India 214–16
introduction to 3–24
law 9, 5, 18–19, 21, 24, 48, 59, 60, 62, 72, 101, 102, 109, 120, 205–20, 278–9, 298, 304, 321, 371
operational 72–98, 282, 375
penalties and litigation 23, 24, 333
policy 80, 227, 229–30, 231, 233, 239
principles see data protection principles
protection officer see DPO
regulators 12, 16, 23, 34, 84, 85, 125, 253, 276, 301, 305, 316, 317, 336, 353, 373
risk 7, 13, 14, 74, 201, 223, 239, 261, 266, 270, 271, 273, 284, 286, 300, 354, 375
United States 208–12
weak 48
Data Protection Act (DPA, 1984) 19
Data Protection Act (DPA, 1998) 19, 49, 76, 124, 127, 138, 353, 367

Data Protection Convention (1981, 2018) 19, 36, 203, 204, 217, 372
Data Protection Directive (1995) 19, 29, 44, 51, 59, 62, 115, 371, 373
data protection principles 50, 52–4, 89, 97, 101–19 141, 189, 229, 246, 265–6, 278, 298, 324, 363, 372
    accountability 44, 254, 258, 259, 269, 321
    compliance 258, 259, 279
    Council of Europe Resolution (1973) 4, 19
    development of 13
    implementation design 234
    operational delivery of 282, 290
    quality standards 33
    six principles, the 35–6
data subject rights 15, 45, 47, 50, 51, 103, 106, 122, 125, 126, 129, 134, 141, 144, 207, 232, 240
    enforceable 178, 179, 180, 182, 183
    exercise of 330–2
    legitimate interests and 270
    requests 80, 227, 243, 253, 259, 282, 286, 287, 332
derogations 56, 93, 94–5, 178, 190–3, 196, 201, 202
direct marketing 65–7, 92, 115, 123, 268, 314, 318
    accountability 270
    breach of requirements 221
    communications 60, 65, 80, 268, 269, 310
    ePrivacy 16, 17, 60
    preference setting 80
    right to object to 46, 82, 111, 141, 147, 249, 269
Directive on Privacy and Electronic Communications (DPEC) 2002 372
directories 69
disclosures 54, 131, 133, 136, 312, 313
disproportionate effort 123–5, 140, 366–9
DP Exit Regulations 2020 55
DPbDD (Data Protection by Design and Default) 43, 76, 86, 233–5, 240, 245–56, 265, 282, 294, 318, 354, 355, 372
DPIA (data protection impact assessment) 43, 53, 86, 97, 117,

124, 215, 216, 229, 235–7, 271, 318, 338, 372
DPO (data protection officer) 43, 73, 74, 79, 84, 121, 189, 212, 213, 215, 227, 231, 237–41

EDPB (European Data Protection Board) guidelines 180, 191, 192, 235, 237, 355
EHCR (European Convention on Human Rights) 5, 6, 7, 20, 203
electronic communications 16–17, 19, 42, 58–61, 67–8, 70, 71, 347, 350, 372, 375, 376
employees 73–6, 80, 82, 85, 106, 112, 114, 186, 189, 192, 201, 241, 272, 275, 349
enforcement action 12, 88, 109, 166, 199, 221, 230, 231, 298, 310, 316, 330, 337–8, 343–5, 352, 369
    data subject's powers 49
    decisions 163, 165, 171, 173, 220, 343, 351, 352, 358
    GDPR powers 336–46
    information commissioner's powers 48–9
    law 6, 13, 19, 50, 79, 90, 118, 119, 148, 312, 321, 353, 366
    notices 17, 49, 247, 299, 327, 337, 338–40, 358
    regulator's powers 48
ePrivacy 16, 17, 58–71, 347, 372, 375, 376
EU Directive on Privacy and Electronic Communications 2002 372
European Convention for the Protection of Human Rights and Fundamental Freedoms (ECHR) 5, 7, 20, 203
exceptions 66, 120–1, 122, 123–4, 129, 134, 135, 137–40, 143, 150, 170, 219
    confidentiality, to 61
    cookie consent, to 41, 42
    GDPR 49–54
    right of portability, to the 146
    right of privacy, to the 5
    right to be forgotten, to the 141
    right to erasure 210
    right to object, to the 147
exemptions 50, 51, 81, 124, 191, 219, 230, 267
    Data Protection Act 2018, in 52–4
    domestic purposes 51, 326

379

..., to 314

...essing 102, 204
..ness 36, 102, 179, 279,
290, 372
firewall 42
free movement 3, 9, 18, 19,
59, 218
freedom of expression 5–6, 7, 50,
132, 140, 141

GDPR (General Data Protection
Regulation, EU, 2016)
breach notification rules 69
Brexit 55–6
building blocks of 32–6, 57
comparisons with
international laws 208–17
compliance framework 35–44
compliance mechanisms 227,
229, 237, 244, 351
consent 39
controls 42–4
DPbDD within 245–6
enforcement powers 336–46
European Union (Withdrawal)
Act 2018 55
exceptions and restrictions
49–54
frozen GDPR 26, 55, 56
international processing
157–8
introduction to 26–58
jurisdiction 27–31
land mass 72, 163, 176, 203,
205, 371, 373, 375, 376
obligations 229, 239, 240, 242
personal data 10, 11
processing 10, 12, 14
protections 5, 6, 7, 9, 10, 57,
348–9
recitals 3, 27, 51, 59–60, 63,
85, 105, 111, 114, 115, 124,
143, 145, 173, 231, 235–6, 238,
241, 267, 349, 361, 366–9
requirements 76, 77, 84, 85–6,
96, 137, 158, 176, 210, 238–9,
249, 288–9, 293, 317, 356, 374
risk assessments within
303–4
scope 32, 57

specific obligations 229
standards 27, 93, 180
transparency 16, 120–6
UK Data Protection Act 18
UK GDPR 26, 55, 56
governance 42, 73, 88, 107, 160,
233, 253, 271, 276, 279, 283, 285,
357
data 233, 237, 255
frameworks 245, 254–5
information 263
practices 261
reporting 274, 275
structures 74, 76–7, 267, 317

Health Insurance Portability and
Accountability Act (HIPPA) (US,
1996) 208
Human Rights Act (UK, 1998) 355

ICO (Information Commissioner's
Office) 14, 15, 21, 83, 84, 87, 313,
324, 351, 357
information
notices 48, 298, 325, 326, 327
technology 353
Information Commissioner 12,
15, 17, 20, 34, 46, 48, 49, 67, 79,
247, 316, 323, 324, 336, 373
enforcement powers 48–9
guidance 38, 39, 123, 322
office 14, 15, 21, 83, 84, 87,
313, 324, 351, 357
Information Commissioner's
Technology Strategy 2018–2021 13
Information Tribunal 324
interception of communications 21
international transfers 12, 16,
45, 47, 56, 72, 79, 91, 93, 121,
176–202, 204, 207, 253, 279, 288,
310, 315
interpretation of legislation 21,
164, 165, 166, 173, 241, 361
investigations 46, 76, 118, 168,
172, 173, 230, 261, 286, 288, 328,
337, 345
ICO 83, 84, 316
legal 288
police 312–13
regulatory 17, 75, 81, 261, 277,
298, 302, 310, 312–13, 320–5,
337, 344, 345, 359
technical 264

joint controllers 33, 79, 80,
231–2, 243–4, 260, 262, 269, 333,
334, 371
journalism 306

lawful basis
consent 111–13
contractual 113
legal obligation 114
legitimate interests 115–16
processing 38, 46–7, 53, 78,
102, 109, 110–11, 141, 144,
253, 262, 267–70, 282
public task 115
vital interests 114, 115
lawful processing 36, 45, 66, 102,
208, 267, 349, 374
LED (Law Enforcement Directive)
12, 18, 19, 38, 50, 79, 119,
181, 359
legal advice 324, 326, 329, 330,
333, 334
legal proceedings 52, 88, 133,
137, 141, 143, 146, 148, 151, 152,
182, 227, 298, 333
legal professional privilege 53,
93, 133, 137, 230, 297, 329
legal rights 84, 120, 142, 149, 326
legitimacy 66, 127
LGPD (Lei Geral de Proteção de
Dados) (Brazil, 2018) 206, 212–14
Lindqvist case 51
litigation
data protection and 23, 333
enforcement and 16, 109, 137,
221, 321
investigations and 320–35
penalties and 23
subject access and 333
localisation laws 218, 219
location data 10, 14, 16, 67,
69 145

management forecasts 53, 133
manual data discovery 262–4,
265, 267, 373
monitoring 31, 58, 75–6, 80, 84,
94, 162, 163–4, 166–7, 174, 181,
189, 196, 202, 220, 222, 223,
236–8, 274–6, 341, 372

national security 5, 6, 21, 50, 61,
132, 179, 180, 193

380

necessity
  contractual 111, 112, 113, 114, 192, 217
  DPIA 235, 236
  legal 217
  meaning 38
  objective 113, 114
  PIPL 216
  test 38, 116, 374
  third country guarantee 78
negotiations 53, 133, 235
non-adequate country 56, 94, 202, 371, 374, 375
non-compliance 57, 129, 137, 152, 175, 185, 233, 237, 271, 321, 342
  addressing 12, 33, 180
  consequences of 25, 212, 214, 326
  enforcement 208
  evidence of 15, 84, 275, 337
  legal 317
  remedying 48–9, 76
non-disclosure provisions 79, 312
not-for-profit organizations 35, 37, 43, 118, 152, 211, 302
notices
  assessment 48, 84, 298, 325, 327
  cookie 63
  enforcement 49, 299, 338–40, 358
  information 48, 298, 325, 326, 327
  penalty 49, 352, 358
  privacy 78, 113, 125, 229, 233, 249
  transparency 78, 367

obtaining
  access 325
  consent 41, 62, 105, 113, 211
  data 121, 122, 328, 329, 330, 373
  transparency 121
offences 9, 12, 19, 38, 43, 61, 96, 116, 118, 132, 328, 330, 361
opt-in 63, 65, 66, 113
opt-out 65, 66, 335
Organisation for Economic Cooperation and Development (OECD) 35

parliamentary privilege 52
PDPB (Personal Data Protection Bill) (India, 2019) 207, 214–6
personal data
  breaches 67–9, 137, 347–70
  lawful processing 109–15
  special category 116–18
  transborder flows 204
PIPL (Personal Information Protection Law) (China) 207, 216–17
political parties, processing by 247
prescribed information 375
privacy
  activists 12, 13, 16, 24, 65, 151, 201, 247, 272, 278, 293, 302, 305, 310, 315–16, 320, 360
  definitions 4, 5
  electronic communications see ePrivacy
  freedom of expression, versus 5–6
  law 4, 209
  management technology 89, 282–6, 289, 290
  OECD Guidelines 35, 101, 203, 204–5
  Privacy Shield 16, 65, 72, 77, 151, 181, 193, 194, 201, 315
  protection of 24, 35, 101, 203, 204–5
  public health, versus 6
  right to 3, 5, 6, 7, 59, 70, 90, 113, 194, 245, 320
  security and law enforcement, versus 6
  statements 103, 125, 328
  technology 87, 282
Privacy and Electronic Communications Directive (PEC) 16, 18, 36, 41, 55, 59, 60–3, 65–70, 298, 347, 358, 359
Privacy and Electronic Communications Regulations (PECR) 2002 16, 41, 58 66, 67, 269, 347, 372
private sector 4, 181, 209
public sector 4, 22, 181, 305
publicly available electronic communications services 16, 60, 61, 67, 68, 375
publicly available information 123, 124, 125, 211
purpose limitation 36, 104, 105, 198, 141, 179, 189, 289, 372

quality of data 45, 187, 189, 204, 233, 319

recipient of data 34, 364
regulatory gap 292
reputational damage 23, 24, 69, 339, 349, 360
reputational impact 270, 336, 342–3
research 21, 42, 53, 133, 143, 146, 148, 213, 281, 294
  historical 38, 51, 104, 108, 118, 123, 124, 132, 141, 147
right
  access, of 8, 45, 46, 52–4, 78, 124, 126–8, 129–31, 133, 210, 211, 213, 215, 306, 314
  compensation, to 152–3, 189, 211, 215, 293
  complain, to 45, 122, 128, 134, 151, 321, 332
  data portability, to 144, 210, 212, 213, 217, 270
  data protection, to 37, 38, 363
  erasure, to 47, 106, 140, 141, 210, 212, 215
  forgotten, to be 29, 86, 89, 97, 140, 141, 247, 302
  freedom of expression, to 5, 140
  human rights 4, 5, 7–9, 14, 20, 23, 149, 179, 203, 355, 363
  information, to 8, 373
  object, to 46, 53, 82, 111, 138, 141, 146, 147, 148, 213, 215, 217, 249, 269, 299
  privacy, to 3, 5, 6, 7, 59, 70, 90, 113, 194, 245
  rectification, to 53, 106, 138, 141
  redress, of 120, 150–3
  restriction of processing, to 46, 139, 142–3
  withdraw consent, to 40, 45, 111, 112, 122, 217
ROPA (records of processing activities) 77, 96, 104, 109, 110, 231–3, 259–67, 351, 375

Schedule 2 52, 53, 131, 133
Schedule 3 53, 54
schools 54, 287
*Schrems I* 13, 20, 93, 193–4, 315, 316
*Schrems II* 13, 16, 20, 93, 94, 95, 184, 188, 193, 194–5, 199–202, 247, 305, 310

381

...5, 151, 193, 194,
..., 133, 280, 345
...ation 133
...personal data 11, 213,
special purposes 53, 133, 142, 143, 146, 148, 323
staff training 228, 321, 331
state-of-the-art 86, 89, 233, 274, 281
storage limitation 35, 42, 89, 107–8, 179, 217, 282, 289, 291, 372
structured data 145
structures and artefacts 317–19
subject access
   enforced 328
   and litigation 333
   request 15, 16, 49, 82, 126, 145, 228–30, 233, 310, 312, 330, 367, 372
subscriber 58, 60, 61, 62, 63, 66, 67, 68, 69, 372, 375
supervisory authority 34, 122, 128, 151, 157–75, 182–3, 185, 188–9, 193–5, 231, 239, 241–3, 261, 272–3, 275, 298, 321–6, 340–4, 369

surveillance 4, 15, 17, 21, 61, 92, 144, 148, 149, 193–4, 221
   advanced 13
   government 15
   laws 61, 194, 201
   mass 13, 92, 180, 193, 301, 315
   system 13, 92, 148, 149
   techniques 4, 13
   technology 305, 310

technological
   change 22, 248, 354
   developments 3, 4, 85, 86, 278, 292, 353–4, 356, 358
   measures 108, 228
   threats 281
third-party data 131, 272, 286, 289, 291
traffic data 61, 67
transborder data flows 375
transparency 45–6
   breach 46, 359
   collection 45–6
   consent 63
   data protection principle 102
   framework 46

   general obligation 120
   information 14, 45, 46, 47, 103, 122, 125, 126, 229, 253
   notices 78, 367
   obtaining 121
   rights 46, 52, 120–37, 372

UK GDPR 26, 27, 39, 50, 55, 56, 71, 74, 119, 147, 187, 188, 269, 373
Universal Declaration of Human Rights 7, 203
unlawful acts 127, 358
unlawful destruction 67, 68, 349, 360
unlawful disclosure 131, 136
unlawful processing 97, 108, 141, 332, 348, 357
unsolicited communications 269

value added service 67

websites 46, 49, 63, 64, 90, 208, 268
white list 376

'zone of precedent' 200, 201